Frida Kahlo

Beneath the Mirror

Text: Gerry Souter

Layout: Baseline Co. Ltd

19-25 Nguyen Hue Blvd, District 1, Ho Chi Minh City, Vietnam

ISBN 1-85995-930-X

Printed in South Korea

Frida Kahlo

Beneath the Mirror

Gerry Souter

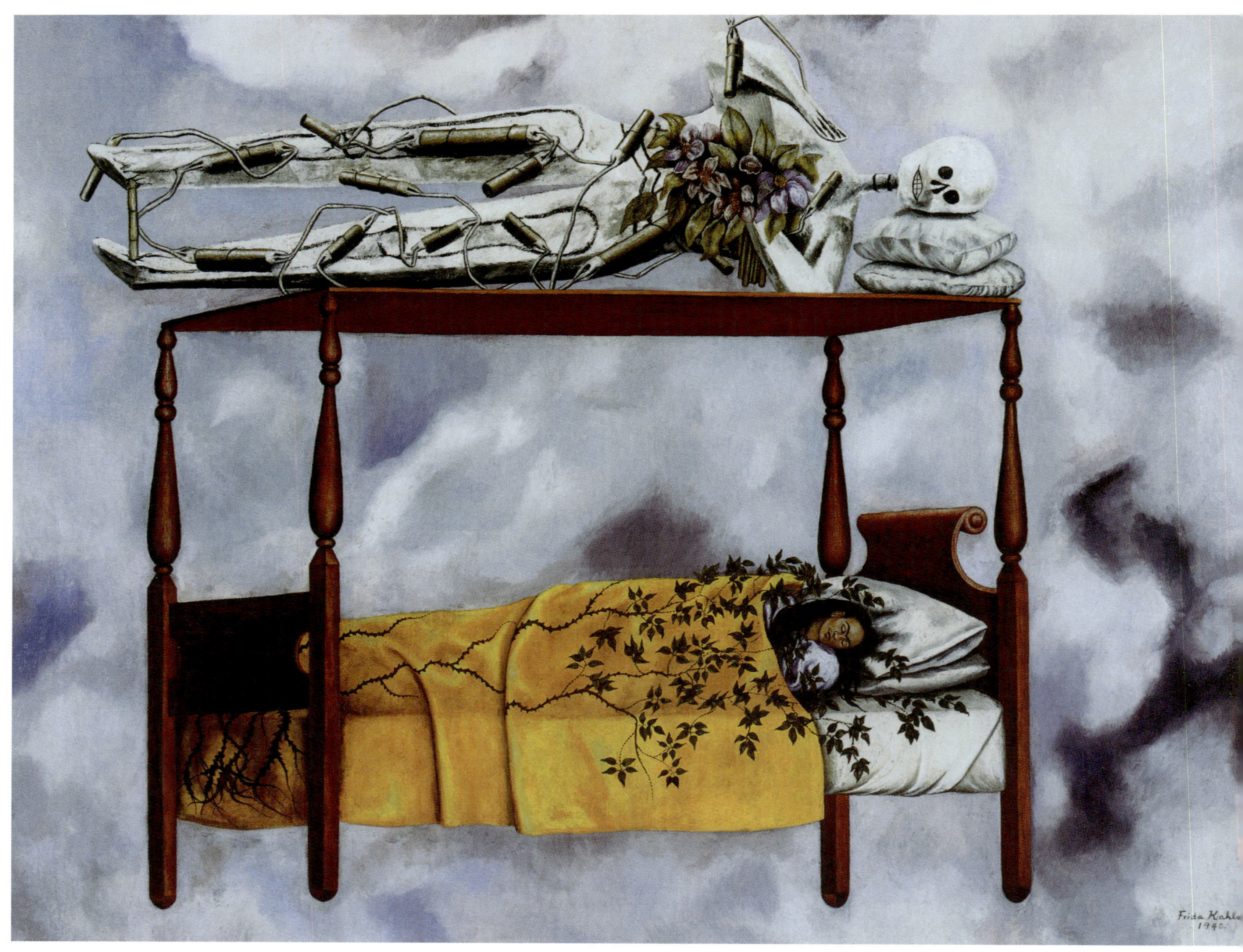
Frida Kahlo
1940

Summary

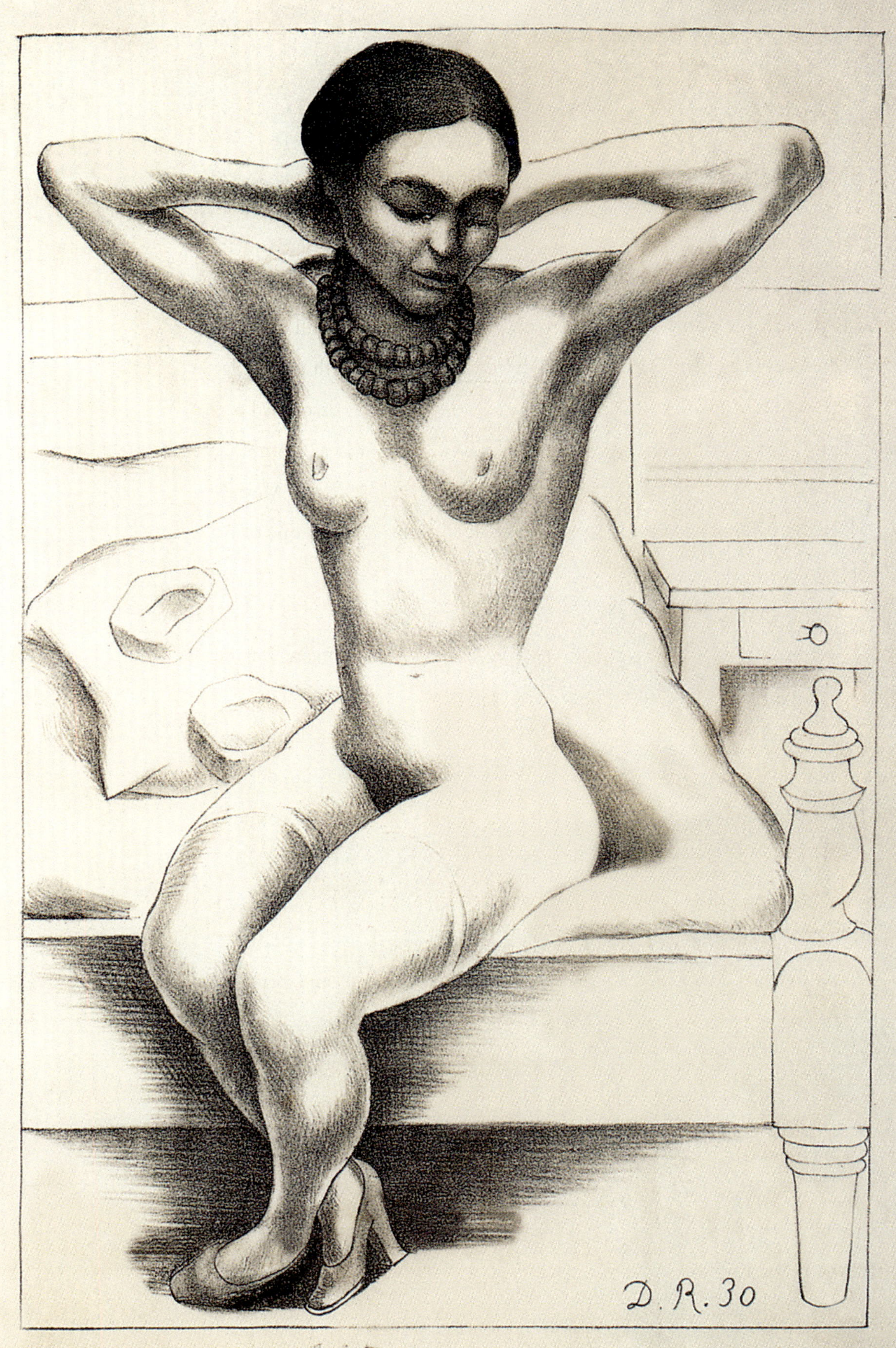
D.R.30

Introduction

Her serene face encircled in a wreath of flaming hair, the broken, pinned, stitched, cleft, and withered husk that once contained Frida Kahlo surrendered to the crematory's flames. The blaze heating the iron slab that had become her final bed replaced dead flesh with the purity of powdered ash and put a period - full stop - to the Judas body that had contained her spirit. Her incandescent image in death was no less real than her portraits in life. As the ashes smoldered and cooled, a darkness descended over her name, her paintings and her brief flirtation with fame. She became a footnote, a "promising talent" forever languishing in the shadow of her husband, the famed Mexican muralist Diego Rivera, or as a *New York Times* art critic stated with a yawn over one of her works: "...painted by one of Rivera's ex-wives."

Frida Kahlo should have died 30 years earlier in a horrendous bus accident, but her pierced, wrecked body held together long enough to create a legend and a collection of work that resurfaced 30 years after her death. Her paintings struck sparks in a new world prepared to recognize and embrace her gifts. Her paintings formed a visual diary, an outward manifestation of her inward dialog that was, all too often, a scream of pain. Her paintings gave shape to memories, to landscapes of the imagination, to scenes glimpsed and faces studied. Her paintings, with their symbolic palettes, kept madness (yellow) and the claustrophobic prison of plaster and steel corsets at arm's length. Her personal vocabulary of iconic imagery reveals clues as to how she devoured life, loved, hated, and perceived beauty. Her paintings, seasoned with words and diary pages and recollections of her contemporaries, reward us with a life lived at a fractured gallop, ended - possibly - at her own will, and left behind a courageous collective self portrait, a sum of all its parts.

The painter and the person are one and inseparable and yet she wore many masks. With intimates, Frida dominated any room with her witty, brash commentary, her singular identification with the peasants of Mexico and yet her distance from them, her taunting of the Europeans and their posturing beneath banners: Impressionists, Post-Impressionists, Expressionists, Surrealists, Social Realists, etc. in search of money and rich patrons, or a seat

Page 4

The Dream or *The Bed,* 1940.

Oil on canvas, 74 x 98.5 cm,

Collection Isidore Ducasse, France.

Page 6

Diego Rivera, *Nude of Frida Kahlo*, 1930.

Lithography, 44 x 30 cm,

Signed and dated on bottom, right hand corner: D.R. 30.

Museo Dolores Olmedo Patiño, Mexico City.

in the academies. And yet, as her work matured, she desired recognition for herself and those paintings once given away as keepsakes. What had begun as a pastime quickly usurped her life. Frida's conversations were peppered with street slang and vulgarisms that belied her petit stature, Catholic upbringing and conservative love of traditional Mexican customs. While strolling a New York street wearing her red-trimmed *Tehuantepec* dress, jewelry studded with thousand-year-old jade and with a scarlet *reboso* shawl across her shoulders, a small boy approached and asked, "Is the circus in town?" She was a one-person show in any company, a Dadaist collection of contradictions.

Her internal life caromed between exuberance and despair as she battled almost constant pain from injuries to her spine, back, right foot, right leg, fungal diseases, many abortions viruses and the continuing experimental ministrations of her doctors. The singular consistent joy in her life was Diego Rivera, her husband, her frog prince, a fat Communist with bulging eyes, wild hair and a reputation as a lady killer. She endured his infidelities and countered with affairs of her own on three continents consorting with both strong men and desirable women. But in the end, Diego and Frida always came back to each other like two wounded animals, ripped apart with their art and politics and volcanic temperaments and held together with the tenuous red ribbon of their love.

Her paintings on metal, board and canvas with their flat muralist perspectives, hard edges and unrepentant sweeps of local color reflected his influence. But where Diego painted what he saw on the surface, she eviscerated herself and became her subjects. As Frida's facility with the medium and mature grasp of her expression sharpened in the 1940s, that Judas body betrayed her and took away her ability to realize all the images pouring from her exhausted psyche. Soon there was nothing left but narcotics and a quart of brandy a day.

Diego stood by her at the end as did a Mexico slow to realize the value of its treasure. Denied singular recognition by her native land until the last years of her life, Frida Kahlo's only one-person show in Mexico opened where her life began and acted out its brief 47-year arc. When she was gone, the eyes of that life remained behind, observing us from the frame with a direct and challenging gaze.

Page 9
Diego Rivera, *Self-Portrait*, 1906.
Oil on canvas, 55 x 54 cm,
Collection Gobierno del Estado de Sinaloa,
Mexico.

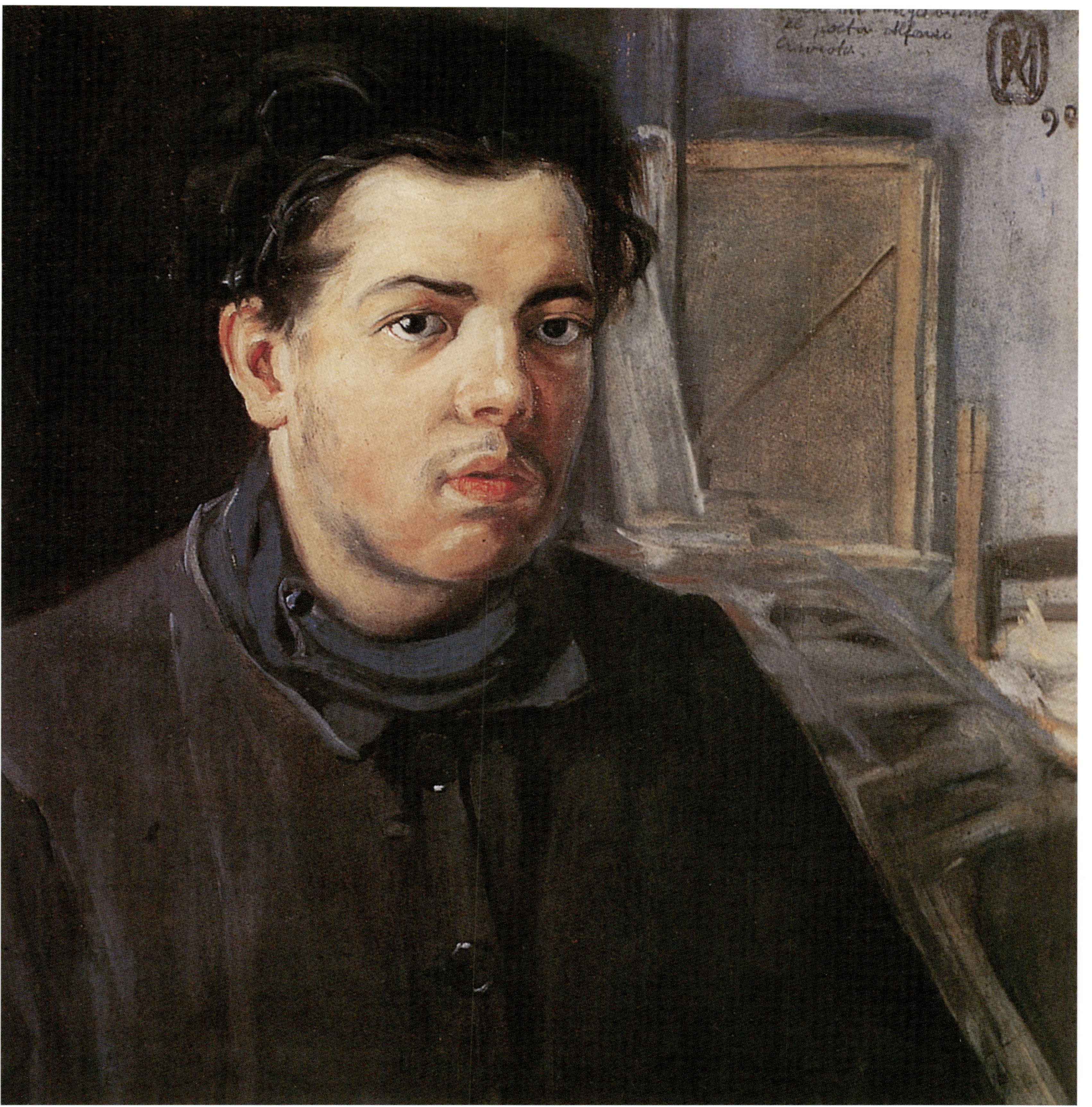

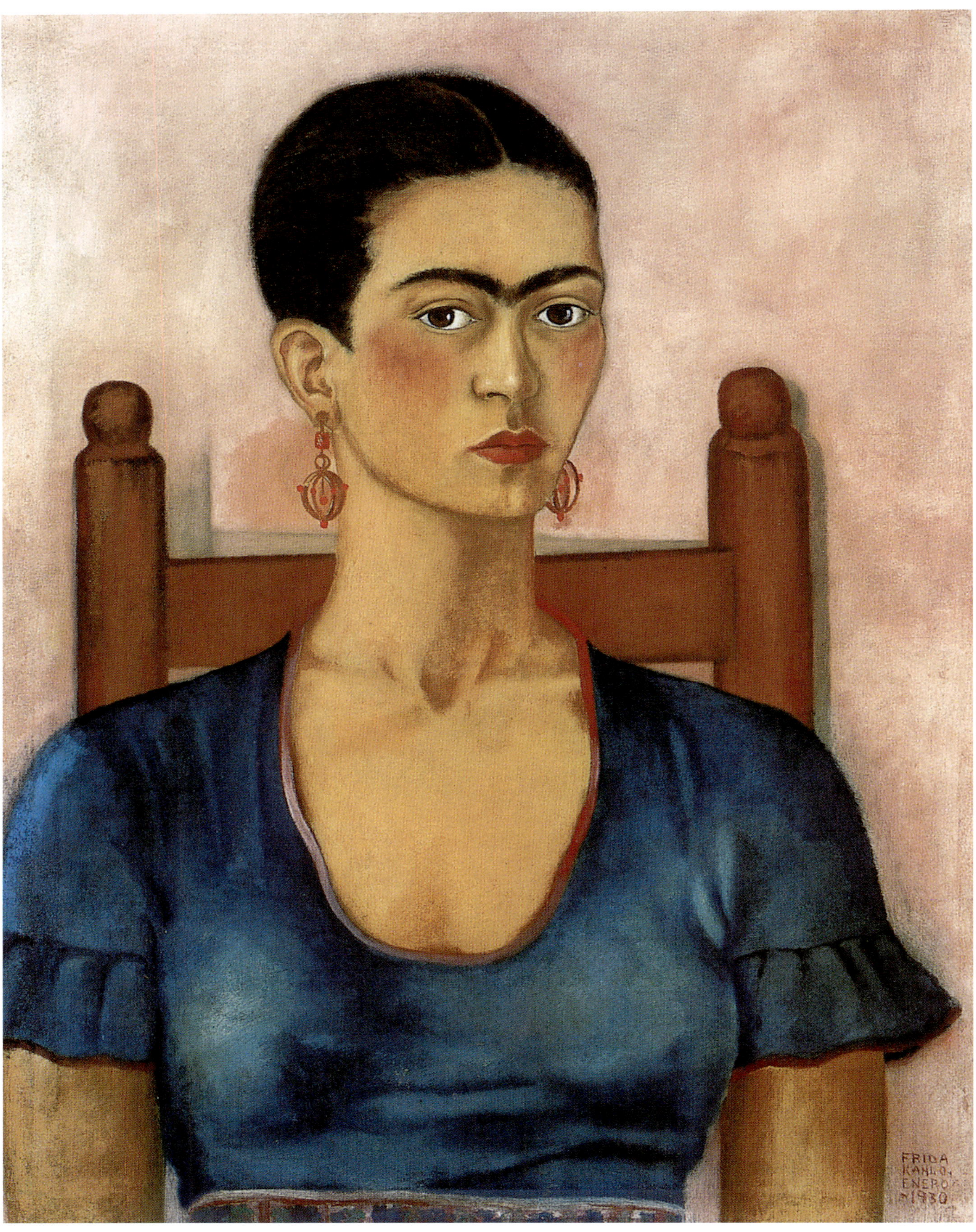
FRIDA
KAHLO,
ENERO
1930

The Wild Thing

As a young girl, wherever she went she seemed to run as if there was so little time left to her and so much to be done. Magdalena Carmen Frida Kahlo y Calderon was born on July 6, 1907 in Coyoacan, Mexico. By that time running, hiding, and learning to quickly identify which army was approaching the village were everyday survival skills for Mexican civilians. Frida eventually dropped the German spelling of her name, inherited from her father, Wilhelm (changed to Guillermo), a Hungarian raised in Nuremberg. Her mother, the former Matilde Calderon, a devout Catholic and a *mestiza* of mixed Indian and European lineage, held deeply conservative and religious views of a woman's place in the world. On the other hand, Frida's father was an artist, a photographer of some note who pushed her to think for herself. Guillermo was surrounded by daughters in *La Casa Azul* (the Blue House) at the corner of Londres and Allende Streets in Coyoacan. Amidst all the traditional domesticity, he fastened onto Frida as a surrogate son who would follow his steps into the creative arts. He became her very first mentor that set her aside from traditional roles accepted by the majority of Mexican women. She became his photographic assistant and began to learn the trade, though with little enthusiasm for the photographic medium. She traveled with him to be there if he suffered one of his epileptic seizures.

Guillermo Kahlo was a proud, fastidious man of regular habits and many intellectual pursuits from the enjoyment of fine classical music - he played almost daily on a small German piano - to his own painting and appreciation of art. His work in oil and watercolor was undistinguished, but it fascinated Frida to watch him use the small brush strokes of a photo retoucher to create scenes on a bare canvas instead of just removing double chins from vain portrait customers.

He rigidly maintained his own duality: outwardly active, but trapped with his epilepsy as he regained consciousness lying in the street, felled by a grand mal seizure with Frida kneeling

Page 10
Self-Portrait, 1930.
Oil on canvas, 65 x 55 cm,
Museum of Fine Arts, Boston.

at his side holding the ether bottle near his nose, making sure his camera was not stolen. He played his music and read from his large library, but inside was constantly in turmoil about money to support his family. He wore what Frida described as a "tranquil" mask. She adopted that self-control, or at least the appearance of it, in the darkest moments of her life, never willing to display any public face that revealed what lay behind the stoic image.

Frida Kahlo was spoiled, indulged and impressionable. Her father's success landed him a job with the government of Porfirio Diaz, photographing Mexican architecture as a sort of advertisement to lure foreign investment. Since 1876 Diaz had enjoyed some 30 years as president of Mexico and adopted a Darwinian philosophy toward governing the Mexican people. This "survival of the fittest" concept meant virtually all government money and programs went to building up the rich and successful while ignoring less productive peasants. Mexico became the economic darling of international trade as countries took advantage of its mineral wealth and cheap labor. European customs and culture ruled while native Mexican and Indian traditions languished. Diaz personally selected Guillermo Kahlo to show the best side of Mexico to foreign investors, vaulting the photographer from an itinerant portraitist into the coveted middle class.

Kahlo wasted no time in buying a lot in the nearby suburb of Coyoacan on the outskirts of Mexico City and building *La Casa Azul,* a traditional Mexican wrap-around home – painted a deep blue with red trim – with its rooms opening onto a central courtyard. In 1922, to assure her a better than average education, he also entered Frida into the free National Preparatory School in San Ildefonso. She became one of 35 girls admitted to the school's enrollment of 2,000 students and rose to become a class character alongside other male pupils who became some of Mexico's leading intellectuals and government leaders. She devoured her new freedom from mind-numbing domestic chores and hung out with a number of cliques within the school's social structure. She found a real sense of belonging with the *Cachuchas* gang of intellectual bohemians – named after the type of hat they wore. Leading this motley elitist mob was Alejandro Gomez Arias, who reiterated in countless speeches that a new enlightenment for Mexico required "optimism, sacrifice, love, joy" and bold leadership. His good looks, confident manner and impressive intellect drew Frida to him.

Page 13

Pancho Villa and Adelita, c.1927.

Oil on canvas, 65 x 45 cm.

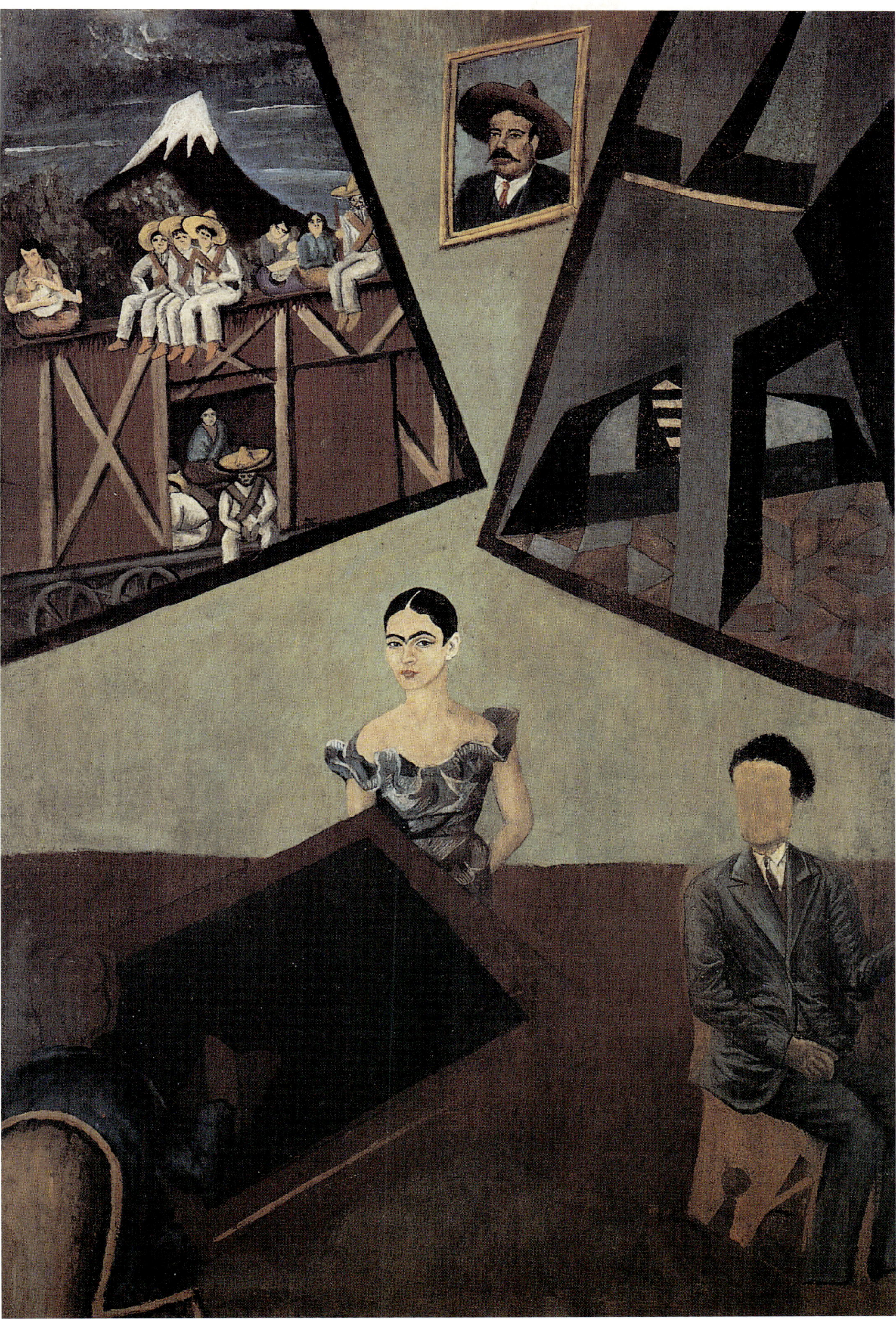

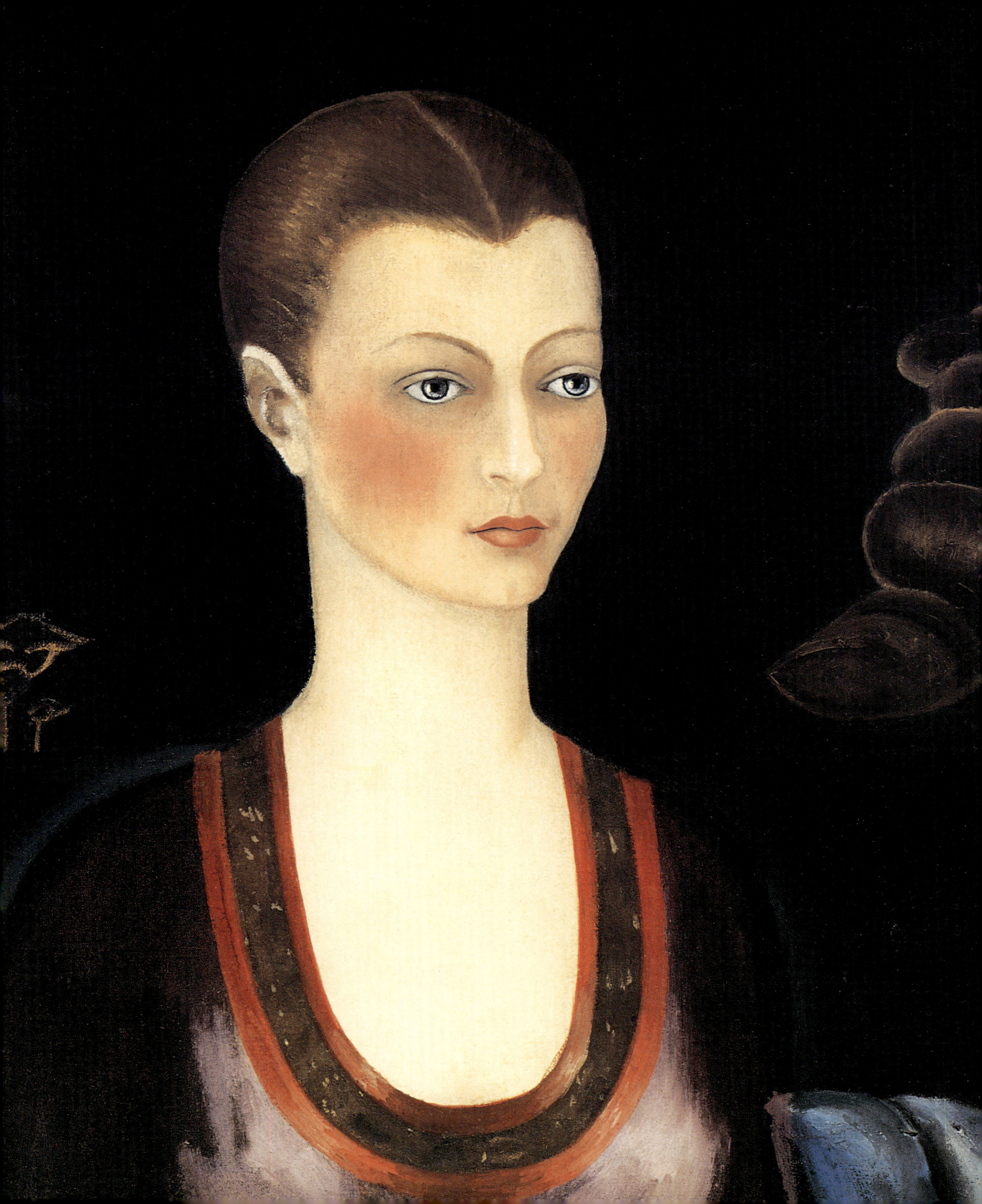

All her life, Frida attracted men of this stripe and, once conquered, each became enmeshed in her passionate, possessive web. But each conquest also puzzled the country girl as she pondered what these strong decisive men saw in her.

She was short, dark, slender and a cripple. At age 13, Frida had been felled by a bout of polio that withered her right leg leaving it shorter than her left. Neighborhood children taunted her with shouts of, "*pata de palo*" or "*peg leg*". To conceal her affliction, she wore layers of stockings on her thin leg and had a half-inch added to the heel of her shoe. Considering the state of medicine in Mexico of the 1920s - hot walnut oil baths and calcium doses - she was lucky to be alive. To further compensate for her limp, she plunged into sports: running, boxing, swimming and wrestling, every strenuous activity available to girls. But her greatest sport was intellectual debate, and with Arias she found a true soul-mate.

By 1923 they were lovers and sharing hours at the Ibero American Library, absorbing Gogol, Tolstoy, Spengler, Hegel, Kant and other great European minds. From these sessions and her own reading, she gradually developed a deep-seated affinity for socialism and the uplifting of the masses. To her in that circle of social climbing students, these two concepts were abstractions for lip service, but she remained a committed and vocal Communist for the rest of her life. She even substituted the 1910 date of the start of the Mexican Revolution for her actual birth year, 1907, as an affirmation of her commitment to revolutionary ideals.

The atmosphere in Mexico City was alive with political debate and danger as volatile speakers stepped forward to challenge whatever regime claimed power only to be gunned down in the street, or absorbed into the corruption. Diaz fell to Madero who lasted 13 months until he stopped a lethal load of bullets from his general Victoriano Huerta. Populist heroes Francisco "Pancho" Villa and Emiliano Zapata split the country's peasant population between them, hunting down anyone who disagreed with their land reform manifestos, but neither managed to build a majority and neither was equipped by temperament or education to govern.

Page 14
Portrait of Alicia Galant, 1927.
Oil on canvas, 107 x 93.5 cm,
Museo Dolores Olmedo Patiño, Mexico City.

Venustiano Carranza assumed power as Huerta fled Mexico, and was no better than the lot who had preceded him. All of these politicians were products of Diaz' Eurocentric economic policies that nurtured the rich and ignored the poor. Into this vacuum were thrust the proletariat ideals of the Communist revolution that had swept Russia following the assassination of the Czar and his family in 1917. The socialist theories of Marx and Engels looked promising after the slaughter of the seemingly endless Mexican revolution.

And yet, for all this progressive political dialectic and debate, Frida retained some of her mother's Catholic teachings and – after a satiric flirtation with European dress and attitudes including cross-dressing as a man in a tailored suit – developed a passionate love of all things traditionally Mexican. During this time, her father gave her a set of water colors and brushes. He often took his paints along with his camera on expeditions and assignments. She began this habit as she accompanied him.

Ten years of revolution had wiped out Mexico's economy and cost Guillermo Kahlo his job with the government. Matilde sent her servants packing and the quality of life in the Blue House dropped a peg or two as the daughters took over all household chores and Guillermo shouldered his Graflex camera in search of portrait commissions.

With the general population breathing easier under the government of a pair of generals, Alvaro Obregon and Plutarco Calles, some local intellectuals and artists drifted into favor among the government ministries. "Revolutionary" land reforms were pledged. But the same old story prevailed, keeping a fire lit beneath the political debates and burgeoning movements that left the Mexican capitol in constant ferment.

Frida became a casual student at the Preparatory School, enjoying the stimulation of her intellectual friends rather than the formal studies. At age 15, her intellect was sharp and she tested political and philosophical doctrines with her pals in innocent debate where telling points were not measured in death and destruction. During this period, she learned the minister of education had commissioned a large mural to be painted in the Preperatory School courtyard. It was titled *Creation* and covered 150 square meters of wall. The muralist was the

Page 17

Portrait of a Lady in white, c.1929.

Oil on canvas, 119 x 81 cm,

Private collection, Germany.

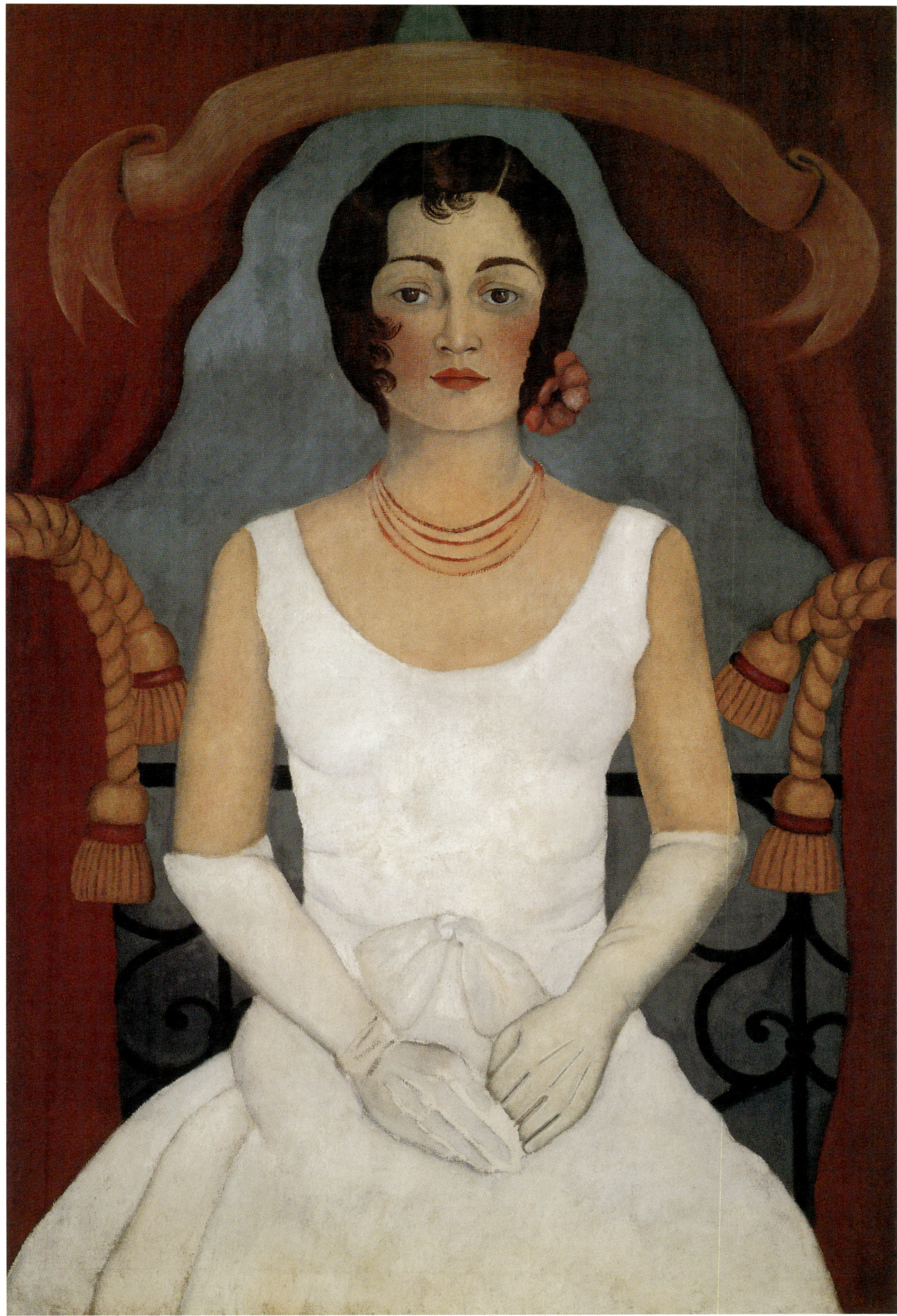

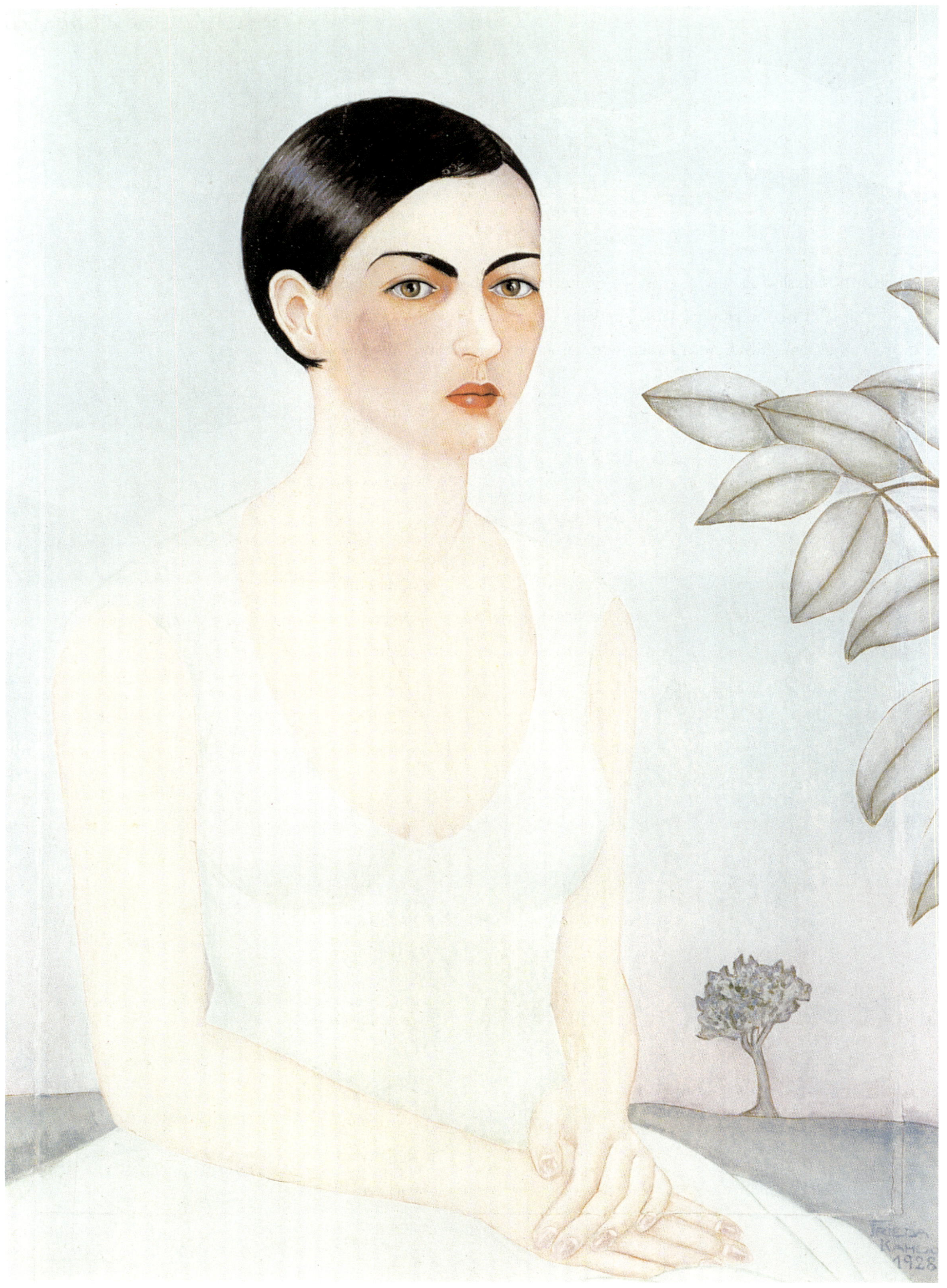
FRIEDA
KAHLO
1928

Mexican artist, Diego Rivera who had been working in Europe for the past 14 years. Assisted by his wife, Guadalupe (Lupe) Marin, and a team of artisans, he assembled scaffolding and the colored wax that required blow torch heat to fuse to a resin base spread on the charcoal-sketched wall grid. This slow encaustic process was eventually abandoned for plaster fresco, but to Frida the creation of the growing scene spreading its way across the blank wall was fascinating. She and some friends often sneaked into the auditorium to watch Rivera work.

His image was far from that of a starving artist. The scaffolding creaked under his weight as he paced back and forth across the wall. Everything about him was oversized from his unruly mop of black hair to the wide belt that held up his pants which sagged in the seat and bagged at the knees. The students nicknamed him, *Panzon* (fat belly).

Eventually these intrusions ended when another group of students, representing the views of their elite ultra-conservative parents, began damaging other murals in progress by the artists David Siquieros and Jose Clemente Orozco, claiming the murals promoted atheism and socialist ideology. Rivera's assistants armed themselves and acted as guards when they were not mixing colors or transferring sketches to the wall. Rivera himself cultivated the image of a revolver-packing defender of creative freedom and often turned up at parties with a big Colt pistol stuffed in his belt or in his jacket pocket.

From a very early age, Frida had been taught by her father to appreciate the art of painting. As part of her education he encouraged her to copy popular prints and drawings of other artists. To ease the financial situation at home, she apprenticed with the engraver, Fernando Fernandez, a friend of her father's. Fernandez praised her work and gave her time to copy prints and drawings with pen and ink. But she painted with the same enthusiasm as she collected hand-made toys, dolls, and colorfully embroidered costumes - as a hobby, a means of personal expression, not as "art" because she had no thought of becoming a professional artist. She considered the skills of artists such as Diego Rivera far beyond her capabilities. Her earliest works were studies in colors and shapes of buildings such as *Have Another One*, painted in 1925. It is an aerial view of a town square and has a child's naïve approach to its flat perspective and the donkey cart

Page 18
Portrait of My Sister Cristina, 1928.
Oil on wood, 99 x 81.5 cm,
Collection Otto Atencio Troconis, Caracas.

making its way across a foreground avenue. Another work, *Paisaje Urbano (Urban Landscape)*, is a composition of architectural planes and linear smokestacks that indicates a more sophisticated structure and an appreciation of the work accomplished by subtle use of shadow and control of values. This application hints at the knowledge gained from her line art copies under Fernandez' tutelage. It also reflects an eye for composition not unlike the photographs of Edward Weston who had spent a year in Mexico and was in the process of creating a new way of seeing shapes, textures and their interrelationships. Though she did not consider her painting to be anything but a pleasant pastime, that didn't stop her from conniving her way into a seat in the auditorium where she watched Rivera work – even under the jealous eye and insults of Lupe Marin. His wife regularly brought Diego his lunch in a basket. It was one way she managed to keep an eye on him, especially when he was painting from a particularly beautiful model. Lupe was his second wife and knew him very well.

And then everything changed forever. In Kahlo's words to author, Raquel Tibol:

> *The buses in those days were absolutely flimsy; they had started to run and were very successful, but the streetcars were empty. I boarded the bus with Alejandro Gomez Arias and was sitting next to him on the end next to the handrail. Moments later the bus crashed into a streetcar of the Xochimilco Line and the streetcar crushed the bus against the street corner. It was a strange crash, not violent, but dull and slow, and it injured everyone, me much more seriously… I was eighteen then but looked much younger, even younger than (my sister) Cristi who was 11 months younger than I… I was an intelligent young girl but not very practical, in spite of the freedom I'd won. Maybe for that reason I didn't size up the situation, nor did I have any inkling of the injuries I had… The collision had thrown us forward and the handrail went through me like a sword through a bull. A man saw I was having a tremendous hemorrhage and carried me to a nearby pool hall table until the Red Cross picked me up…*
>
> *As soon as I saw my mother I said to her: "I'm still alive and besides I have something to live for and that something is painting." Because I had to be lying down with a plaster*

Page 21

Portrait of Miguel N. Lira, 1927.

Oil on canvas, 99.2 x 67.5 cm,

Instituto Tlaxcala de Cultura, Tlaxcala.

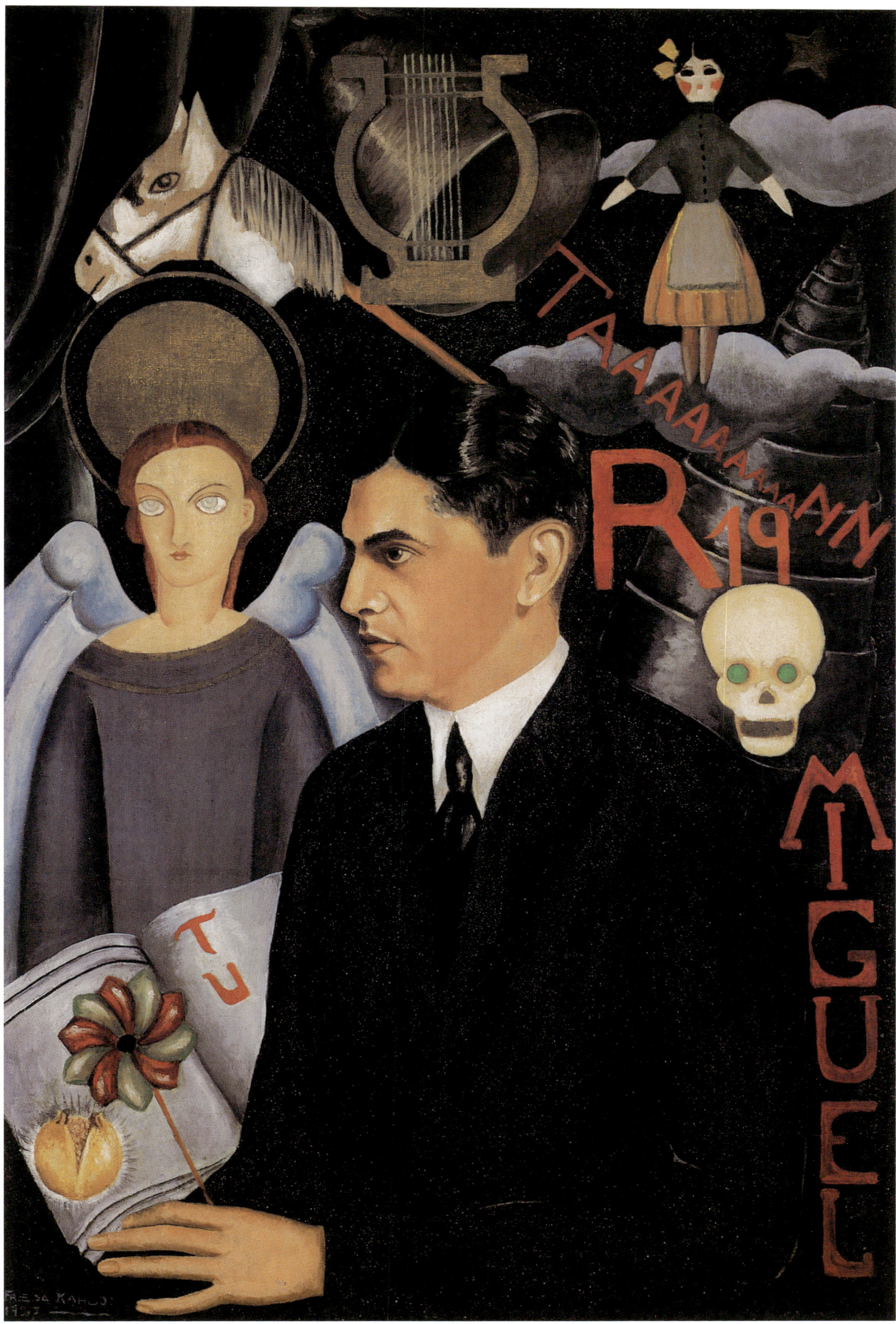
R 19
MIGUEL
TU

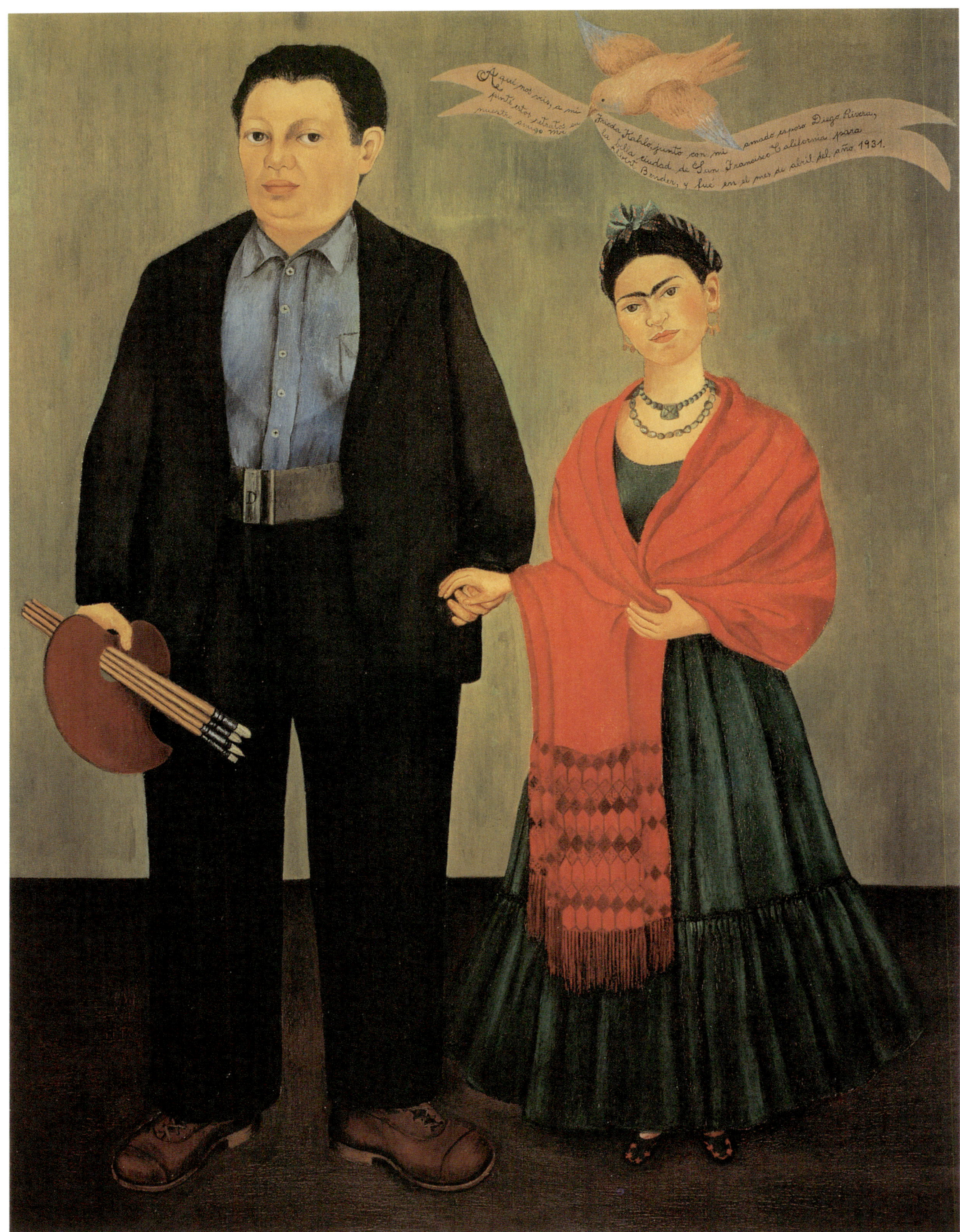
Aqui nos veis, a mi Frieda Kahlo, junto con mi amado esposo Diego Rivera,
pinté estos retratos en la bella ciudad de San Francisco California para
nuestro amigo mr. Albert Bender, y fué en el mes de abril del año 1931.

corset that went from the clavicle to the pelvis, my mother made a very funny contrivance that supported the easel I used to hold the sheets of paper. She was the one who thought of making a top to my bed in the Renaissance style, a canopy with a mirror I could look in to use my image as a model.[1]

The scene of the accident was gruesome. Somehow, the collision tore off Frida's clothes, dumping her nude onto the shattered floor of the bus. Seated near Frida had been a painter or artisan carrying a paper packet of gold gilt powder. It burst, showering her naked body. The iron handrail had stabbed through her hip and emerged through her vagina. A gout of blood hemorrhaged from her wound, mixing with the gold gilt. In the chaos, bystanders, seeing her bizarre pierced, gilded and blood splashed body began screaming, "La Balarina! La Balarina!" One bystander insisted the hand rail be removed from her. He reached down and tore it from the wound. She screamed so loud the approaching ambulance siren could not be heard.

In 1946, a German physician, Henriette Begun, composed a clinical history of Frida Kahlo. Its entry for September 17, 1925 reads:

Accident causes fractures of third and fourth lumbar vertebrae, three fractures of pelvis (11) fractures of the right foot, dislocation of the left elbow, penetrating abdominal wound caused by an iron hand rail entering the left hip, exiting through the vagina and tearing left lip. Acute peritonitis. Cystitis with catheterization for many days. Three months bed rest in hospital. Spinal fracture not recognized by doctors until Dr. Ortiz Tirado ordered immobilization with plaster corset for nine months... From then on has had sensation of constant fatigue and at times pain in her backbone and right leg, which now never leaves her.[2]

Page 22
Frida and Diego Rivera or *Frida Kahlo and Diego Rivera,* 1931.
Oil on canvas, 100 x 79 cm,
San Francisco Museum of Modern Art,
Albert M. Bender Collection, bequest of
Albert M. Bender, San Francisco.

---

[1] Tibol, Raquel, *Frida Kahlo An Open Life*, Translated by Elinor Randall, University of New Mexico Press, 1993

[2] Ibid, page 13, Tibol, Raquel

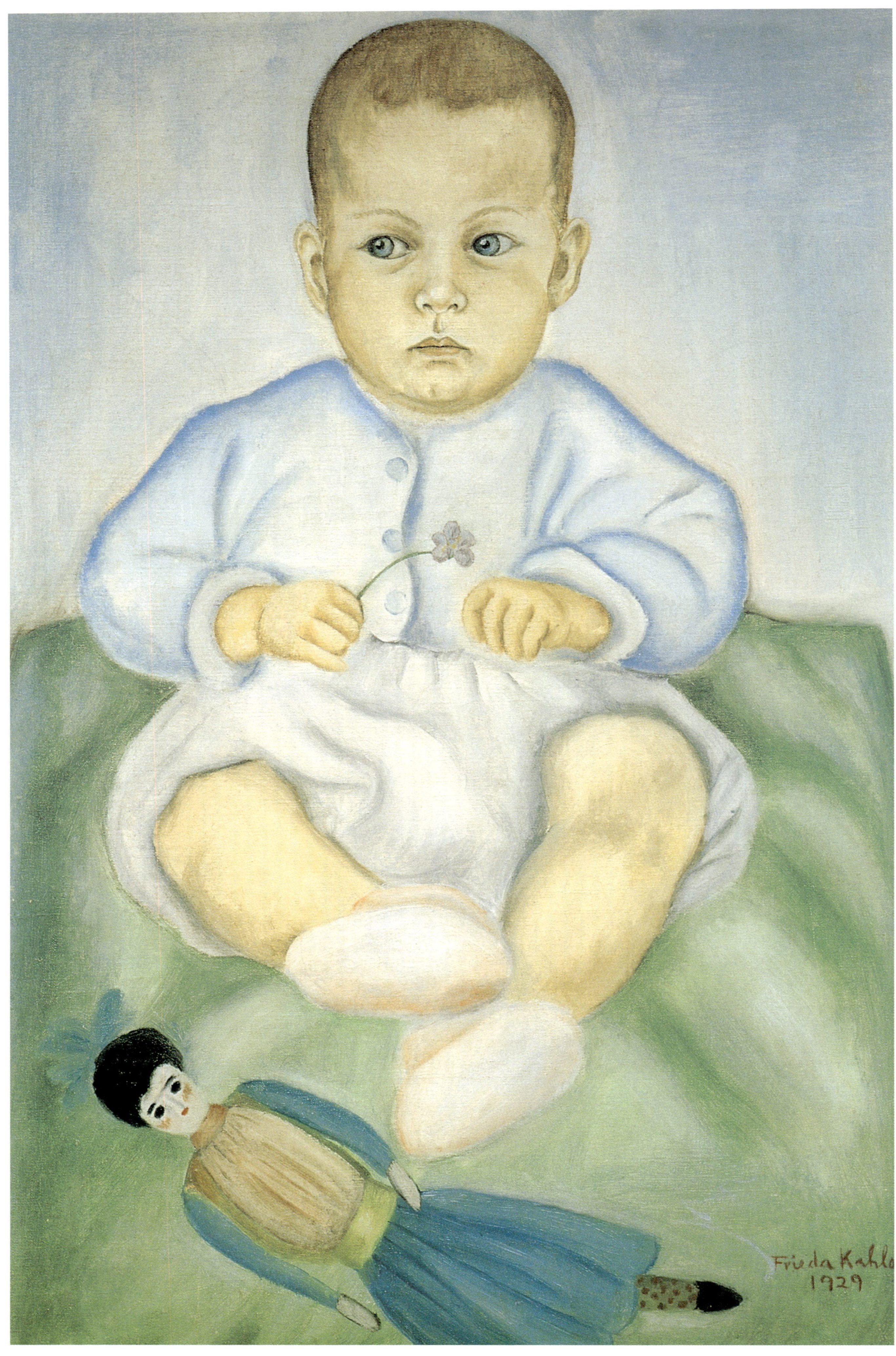
Frieda Kahlo
1929

Death of Innocence

The devastation to Frida Kahlo's body can only be imagined, but its implications were far worse once she realized she would survive. This vital vivacious young girl on the brink of any number of career possibilities had been reduced to a bed-bound invalid. Only her youth and vitality saved her life, but what kind of life did she face? Her father's ability to earn enough money to feed his family and pay Frida's medical bills had diminished with the Mexican economy. This necessitated lengthening her stay in the overburdened, undermanned Red Cross hospital for a month.

> *The (Red Cross Hospital) was very poor. We were kept in a kind of tremendous slave quarters, and the meals were so vile they could hardly be eaten. One lone nurse took care of 25 patients.*[3]

After being pinned to her bed, swathed in plaster and bandages, she was eventually allowed to go home to *La Casa Azul*. Being away from her friends in Mexico City, she penned a voluminous correspondence to them and especially to Alejandro Arias. Their sexual relationship ended prior to the accident and they had agreed each could see other people. When they met as "friends" however, Frida shrugged off Alejandro's boasts of female conquests. But he became sullen when she ticked off the young men she had bedded. They were too much alike.

While she was recuperating from the accident, Alejandro's parents sent him to Europe and to study in Berlin. The long separation and worldly adventure considerably cooled what ardor remained in him for the small town Mexican girl he left behind. Frida, conversely, kept up a flurry of letters filled with pitiful longing to see him as she lay in her plaster prison.

> *"When you come I won't be able to offer you anything you'd want. Instead of having short hair and being a flirt, I'll only have short hair and be useless, which is worse. All these things are a constant torment. All of life is in you, but I can't have it… I'm very*

Page 24
Girl in Diaper, 1929.
Oil on canvas, 65.5 x 44 cm,
(Portrait of Isolda Pinedo Kahlo).

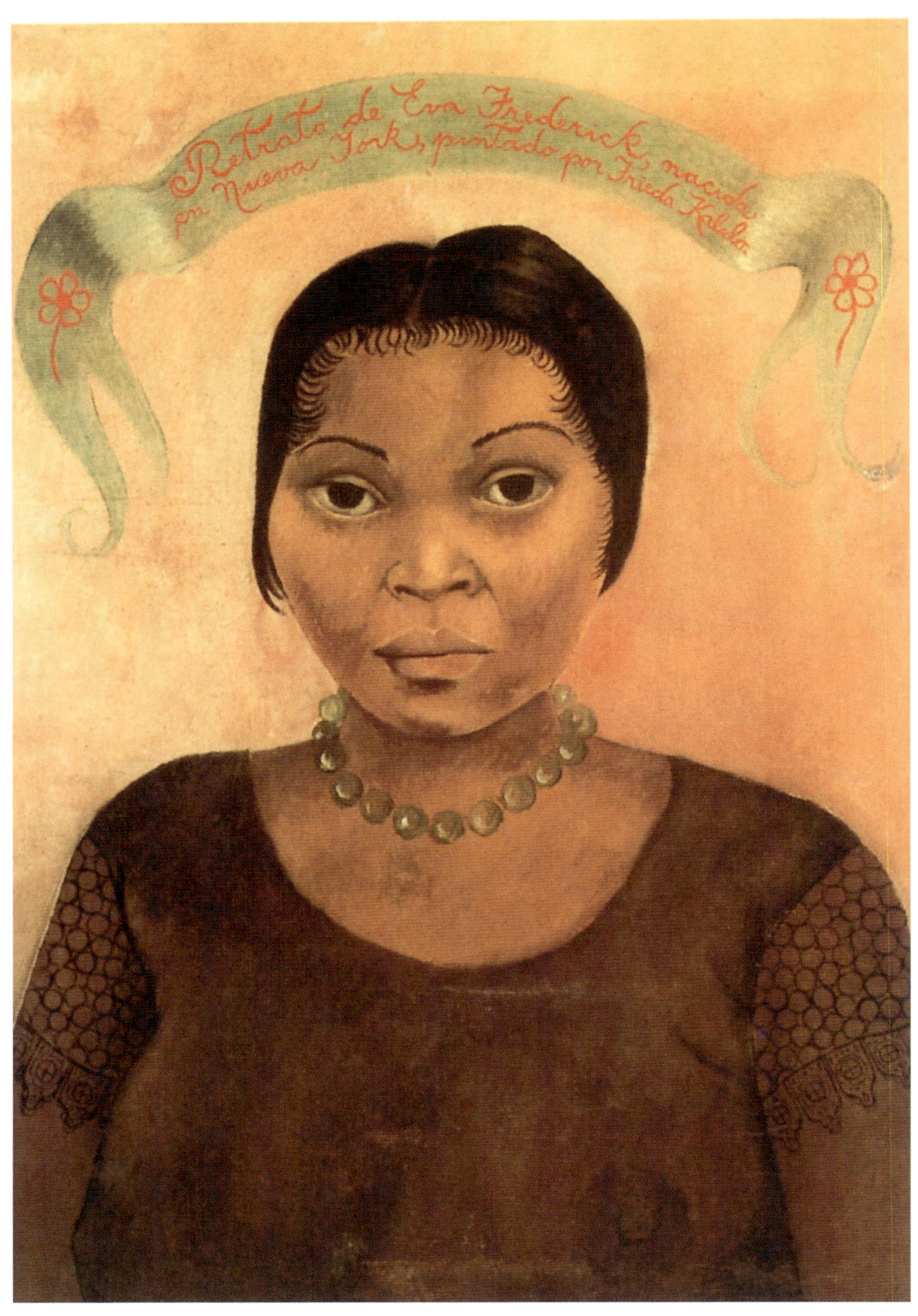

Page 26

Portrait of Eva Frederick, 1931.

Oil on canvas, 63 x 46 cm,

Museo Dolores Olmedo Patiño, Mexico City.

Page 27

Portrait of Alejandro Gómez Arias, 1928.

Oil on canvas, Bequest of Alejandro Gómez Arias, Mexico City.

foolish and suffering much more than I should. I'm quite young and it is possible for me to be healed, only I can't believe it; I shouldn't believe it, should I? You'll surely come in November."[4]

Gradually, her indomitable will asserted itself and she began to make decisions within the narrow view she commanded. By December, 1925, she regained the use of her legs. One of her first painful journeys was to Mexico City and the home of Alejandro Arias just before

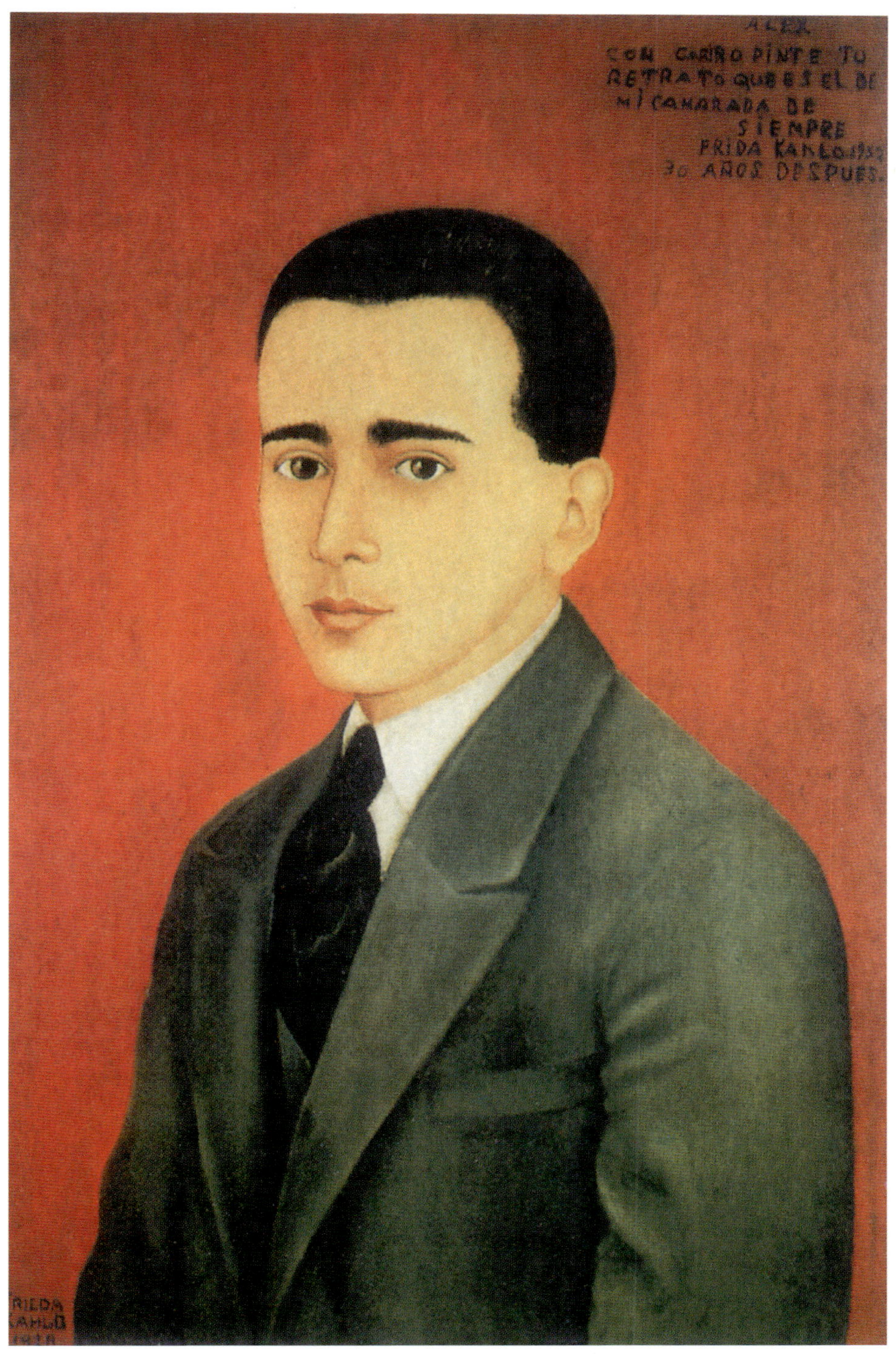

Christmas. She waited outside his door, but he never came out to meet her. Shortly thereafter, she was felled by shooting pains in her back and more doctors trooped into her life. Her three undiagnosed spinal fractures were discovered and she was immediately encased in plaster once again.

Trapped and immobilized after those brief days of freedom, she began realistically narrowing her options. At the Preparatory School she had begun studies that would lead to

Page 28-29
The Bus, 1929.
Oil on canvas, 25.8 x 55.5 cm,
Museo Dolores Olmedo Patiño, Mexico City.

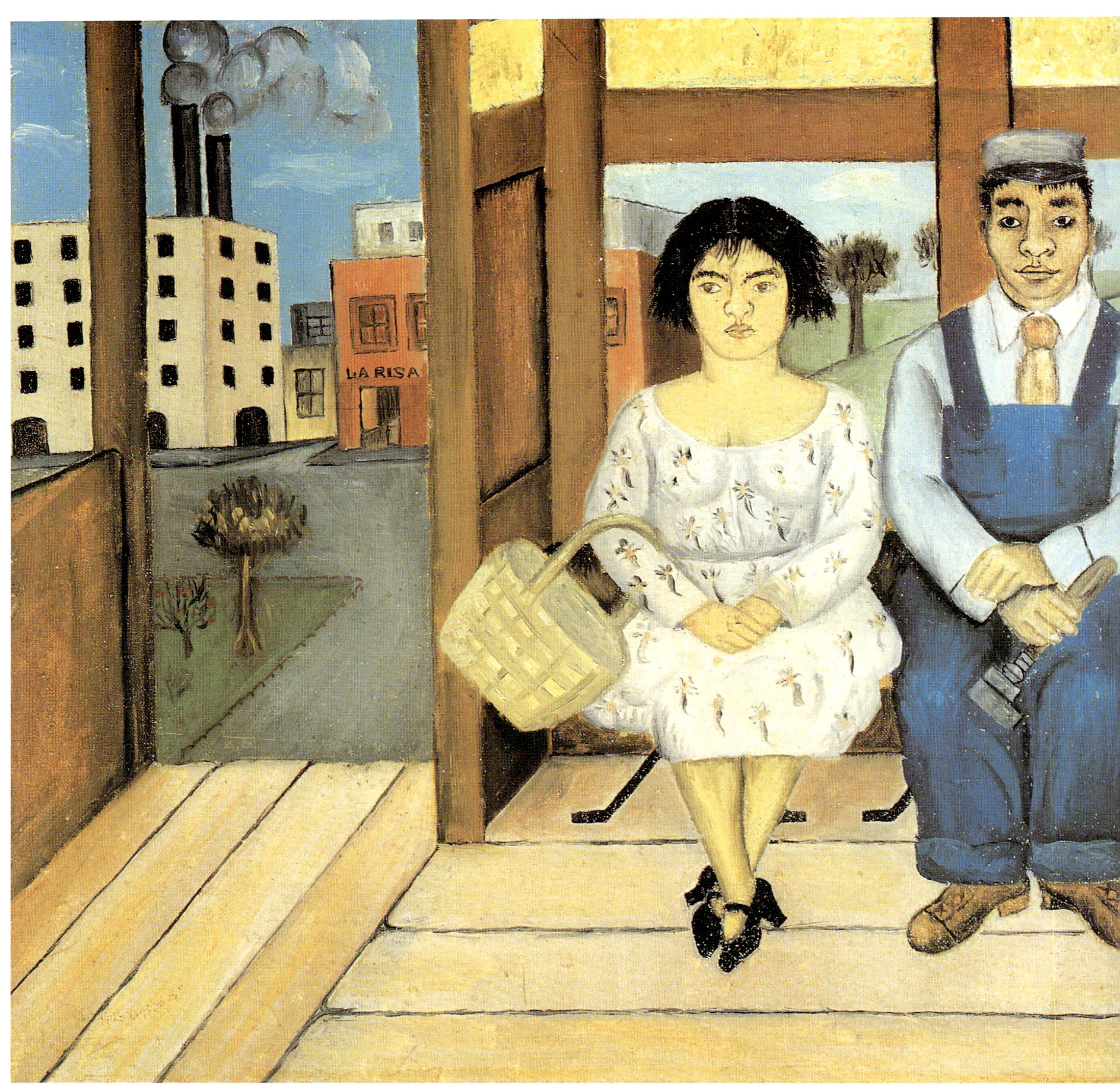
LA RISA

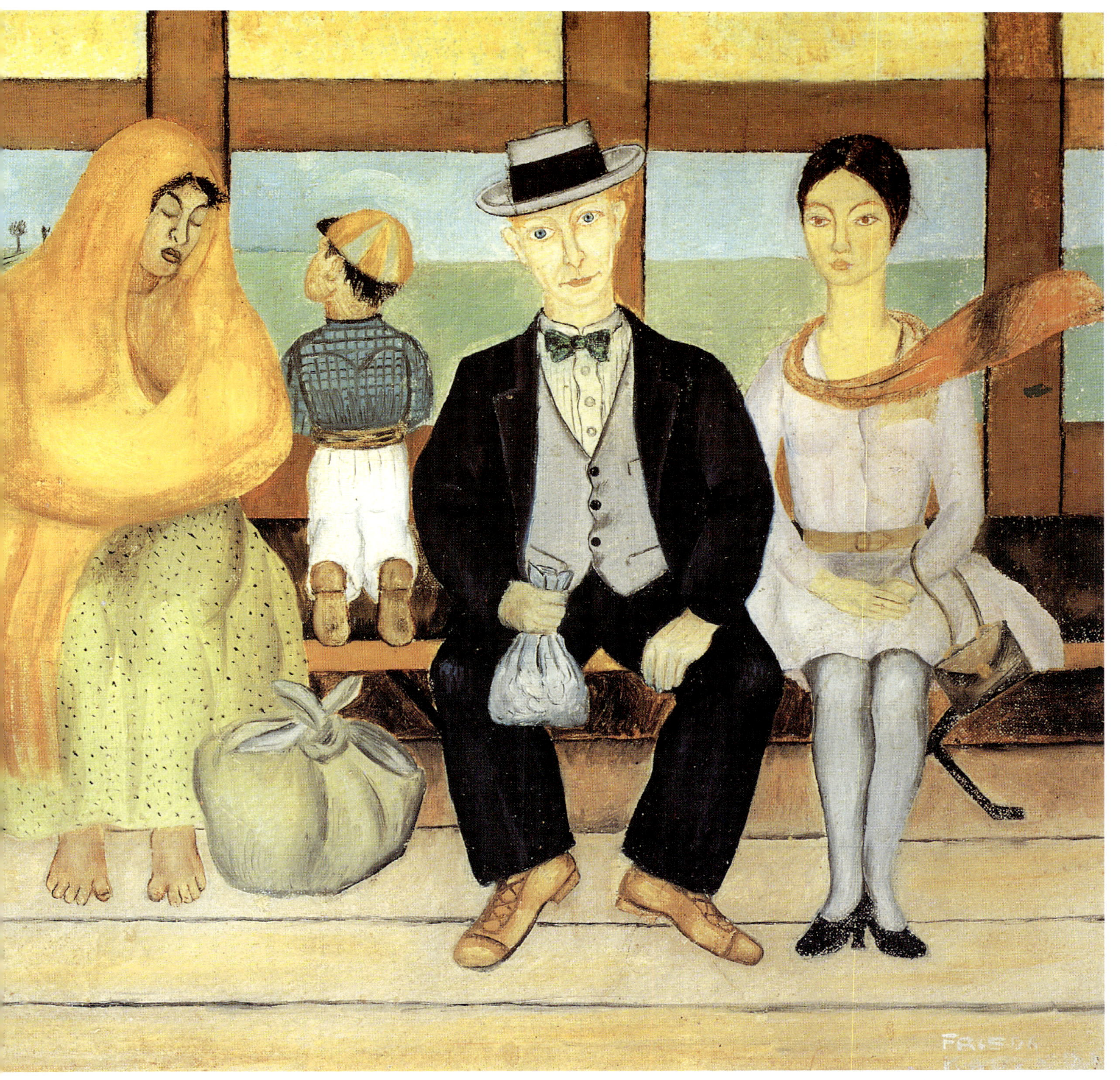

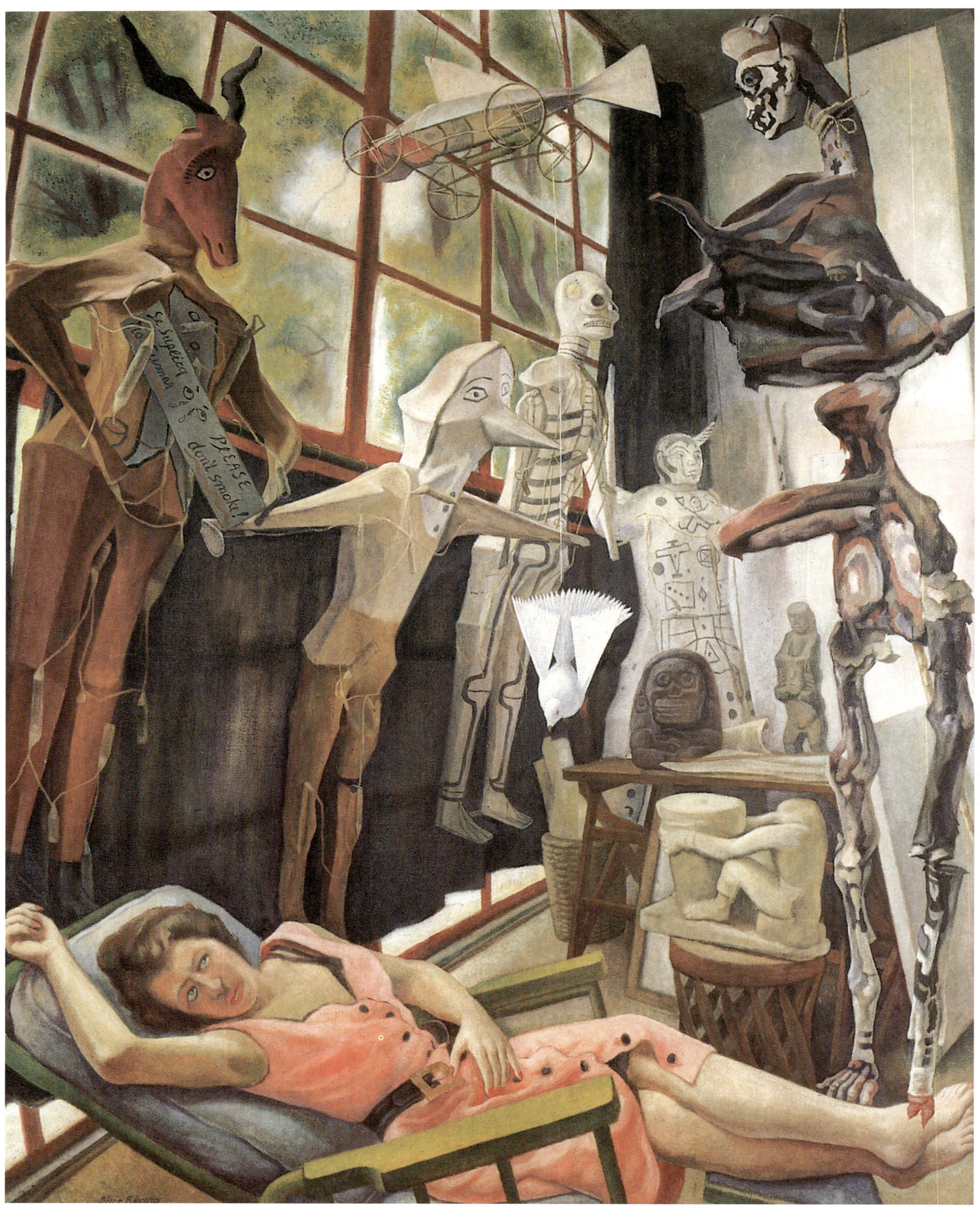
Se suplica no fumar
PLEASE don't smoke!

a career in medicine. That dream faded when she accepted her physical limitations. As days of soul searching continued, she passed the time painting scenes from Coyoacan, and portraits of relatives and her friends who came to visit. As an artist, she only visited the scene of her accident once in a pencil drawing that showed her bandaged body with the small bus and the trolley car crushed together against the corner of the market building. It was a cathartic drawing, pulled from her imagination and the testimony of others. How many times in her dreams and day dreams had she stood apart from that terrible scene before she drew it - and then left it unfinished?

The praise her paintings elicited surprised her and she began deciding who would receive the painting before she started it - often writing the name of the recipient on the canvas. She gave them away as keepsakes, assigning them no value except as tokens of her feelings. Of these early efforts, her best portraits succeeded in reaching beneath the skin of the sitter and stood alone and original without technical tricks, or imposed sentiment. Her most successful work was a self-portrait, painted specifically for Alejandro Arias in yet another vain attempt to win him back. With this painting, she began a remarkable lifetime series of fully realized Frida Kahlo reflections, both introspective and revealing, that examined her world from behind her own eyes and from within that crumbling patchwork of a body. Officially titled *Self-Portrait with Velvet Dress* (p. 40), her 1926 gift to Alejandro was named, "Your Botticelli" (sic).

While on his tour of Europe, Arias had mentioned that Italian girls were "so exquisite, they look like they were painted by Botticelli." Frida added some of the elegant mannerisms of the sixteenth century painter, Bronzino (1503-1572), a favorite of hers. In the portrait she holds her hand open to Arias, a possible desire for reconciliation. Her skin glows with an ivory cast and the blush of health in her cheeks, not the pasty face of a surrendering invalid. Her gaze is direct and challenging beneath her exaggerated single eyebrow. What she gives away with her open Bronzino hand, she takes back with the defiance of a survivor. This stoic, examining and unsmiling gaze is the pose that she adopted in real life. As if to add a period to her message, across the bottom of the canvas she wrote:

> *"For Alex, Frida Kahlo, at the age of 17, September 1926 – Coyoacan – Heute Ist immer noch (Today is like always)."*

Page 30
Diego Rivera, *Artist's Studio*, 1954.
Oil on canvas, 179 x 150 cm,
Collection Acervo Patrimonial de la Secretaría de Hacienda y Crédito Público, Mexico.

In other words, she is saying "If you ever did love me, then today is like always and that love is still there." Frida Kahlo consistently maintained her own demanding reality that no one, not even Diego Rivera, ever succeeded in penetrating to its steel core.

Through 1927 and 1928, Frida painted portraits of those close to her. She captured the glacial beauty of her friend, Alicia Galant. Frida's younger sister, Cristina, is rendered in shimmering pastel tints that surround a sharply executed and resolute face. Frida painted her toddler niece, Isolda Pinedo Kahlo as cotton soft with the child's favorite doll lying ignored at her feet, but with roaming eyes looking for escape from the boredom of sitting. With each painting, Frida's confidence grew along with her technical facility. The diminished state of her relationship with Alejandro Gomez Arias is obvious in her 1928 portrait of him. He looks like a school boy in his first grown-up suit. His expression is haunted and unsure. The boy in the painting has either missed a great opportunity and is completely unaware – or, more likely, he has dodged a passionate, all-consuming bullet and is relieved. As with almost all the men in her life, he remained a close friend, held in her orbit by the mutual fascination that first drew them together.

Page 33
Self-Portrait with Monkey, 1940.
Oil on masonite, 55.2 x 43.5 cm,
Private collection, USA.

Page 34
Thinking about Death, 1943.
Oil on canvas, mounted on masonite,
44.5 x 36.3 cm, Museo Dolores Olmedo
Patiño, Mexico City.

Page 35
Self-Portrait with Monkey, 1938.
Oil on masonite, 40.6 x 30.5 cm,
Albright-Knox Art Gallery, Buffalo.

By 1928, Frida had recovered enough to set aside her orthopedic corsets and escape the narrow world of her bed to walk out of *La Casa Azul* once again into the social and political stew that was Mexico City. She began re-exploring the heady world of Mexican art and politics. She wasted no time in hooking up with her old comrades from the various cliques at the Preparatory School. Soon, as she drifted from one circle to another, she fell in with a collection of aspiring politicians, anarchists and Communists who gravitated around the American expatriate, Tina Modotti. Tina was a beautiful woman who came to Mexico in 1923 to study photography with her lover, the artistically ascetic American photographer Edward Weston. When he returned to California in 1924, she remained behind to begin a short storied life as an excellent photographer in her own right and companion to an assortment of revolutionaries. During the First World War and the early 1920s, many American intellectuals, artists, poets and writers fled the United States to Mexico and later to France in search of cheap living and political idealism. They banded together to praise or condemn each other's works and drafted windy manifestos

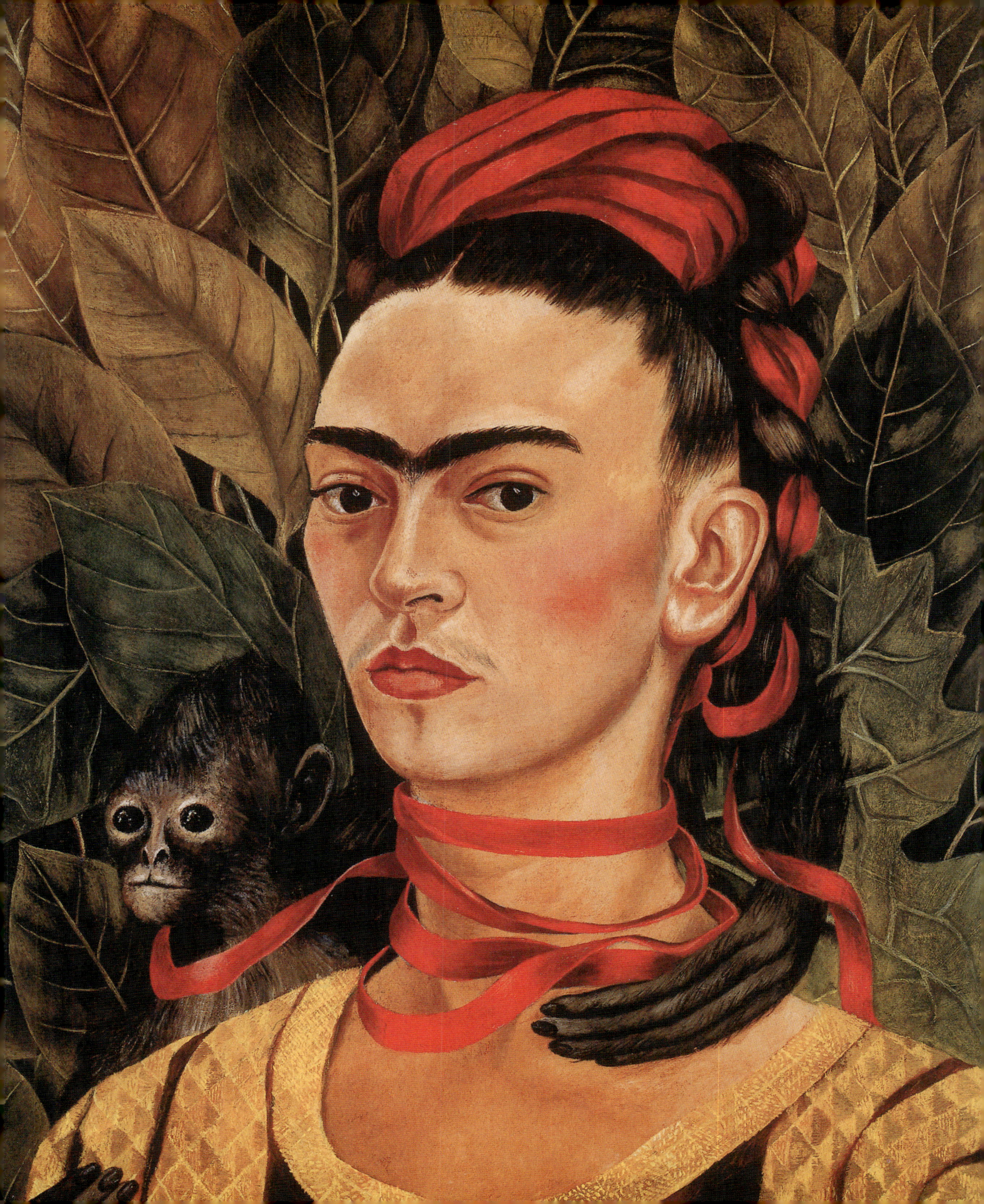

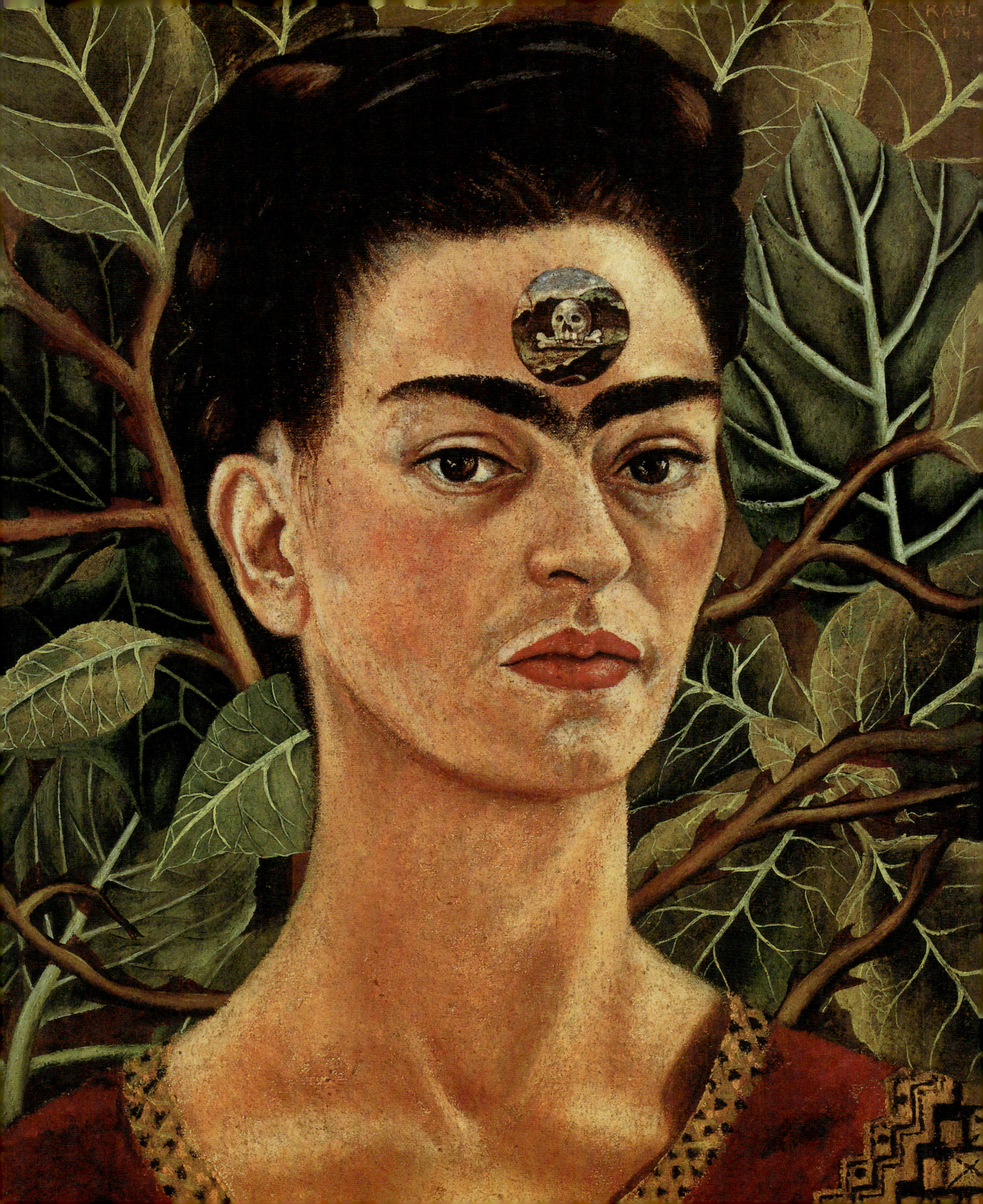

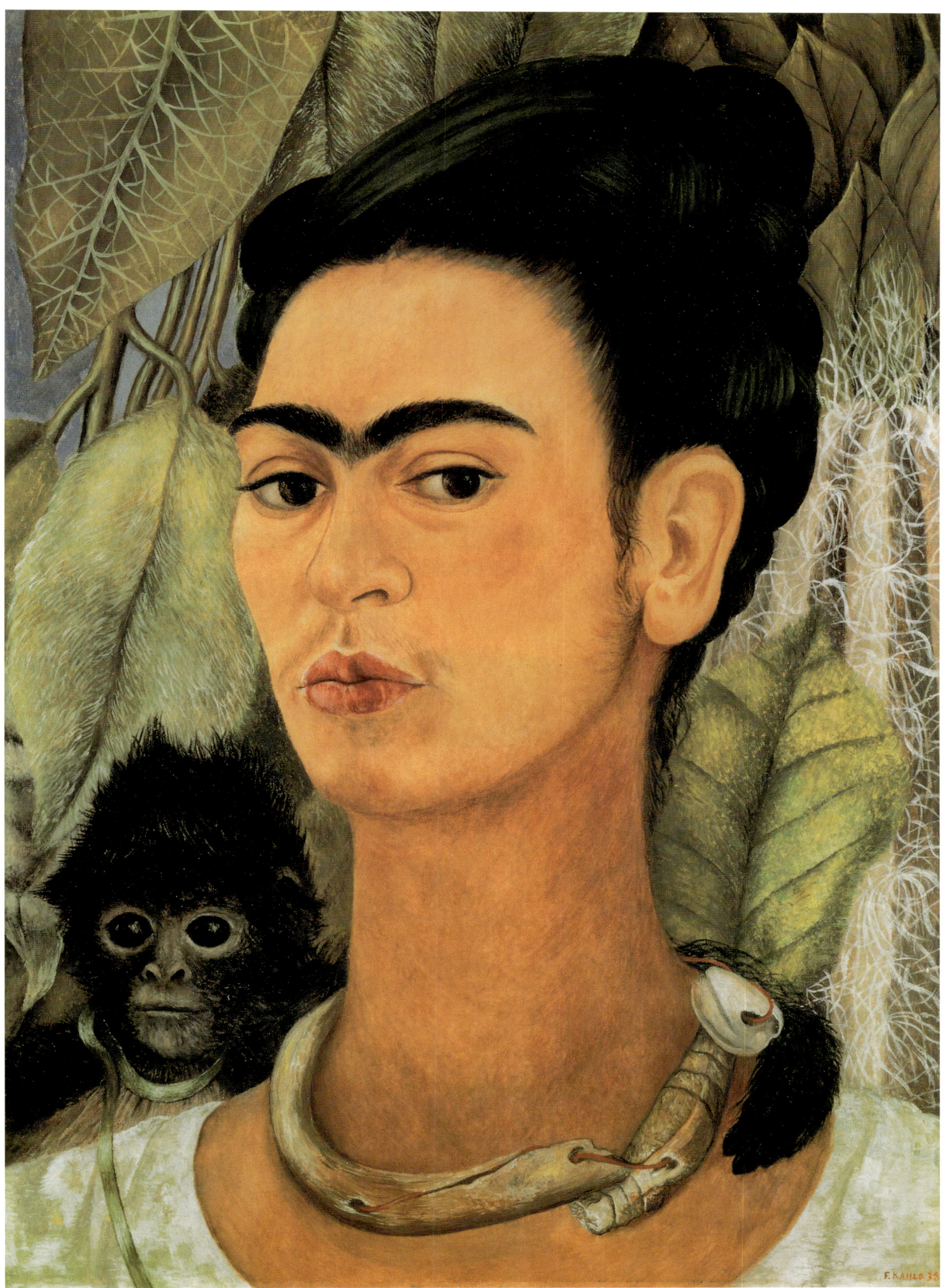
F. KAHLO. 3

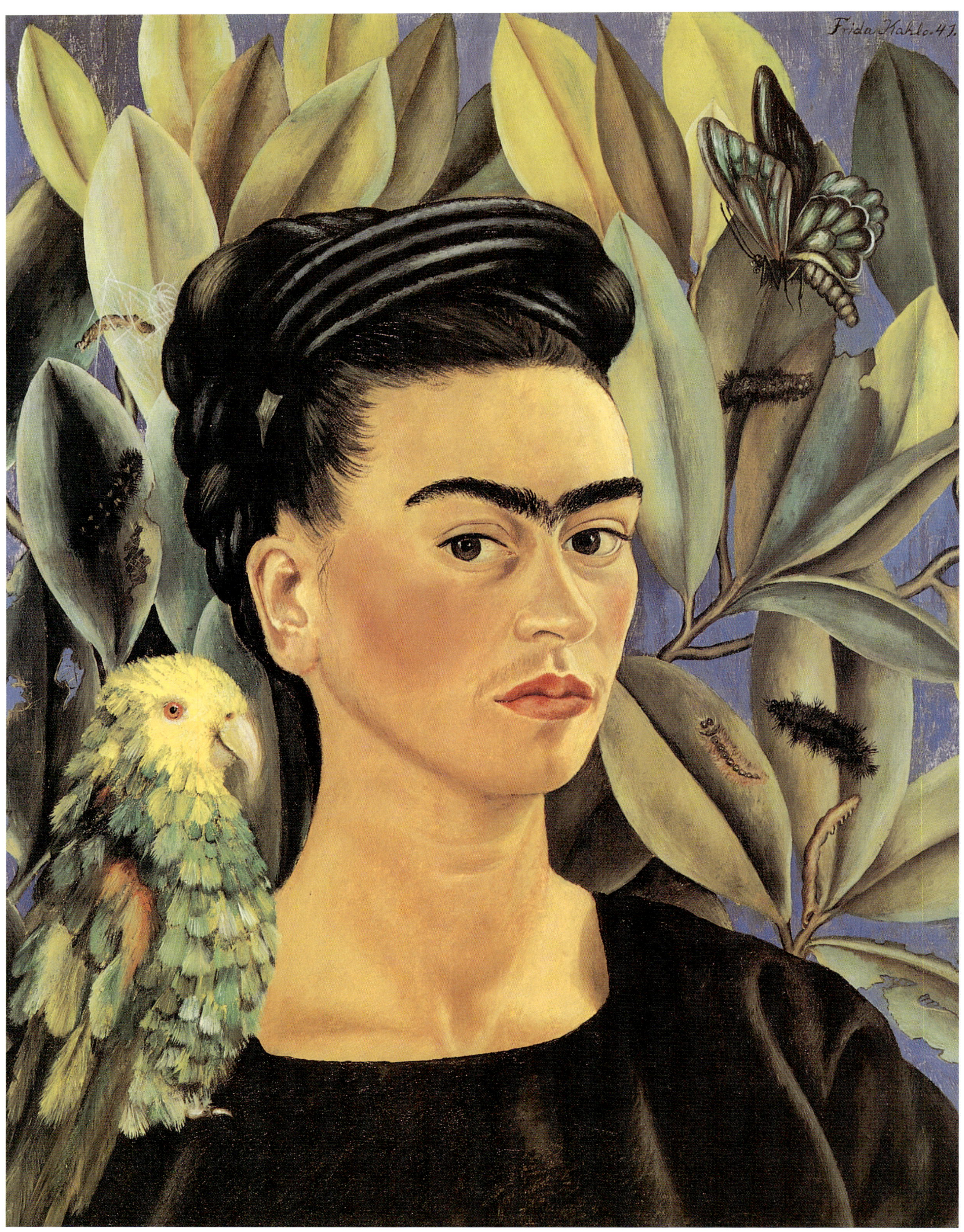
Frida Kahlo. 41.

while participating in one long inebriated party that lasted several years, lurching from apartment to salon to saloon and back. While most were a motley collection of exiles who skipped across the border just ahead of bankruptcy and bad debts, some genuine talents added their luster to Mexican society. John Dos Passos lived for some periods in Mexico City as did Katherine Anne Porter and poet Hart Crane.[5] These expatriates fashioned a sentimental vision of the noble peasant toiling in the fields and promoted the Mexican view of life as *fiestas y siestas* interrupted by the occasional bloody peasant revolt and a scattering of political assassinations.

Into this tequila-fueled debating society stepped the formidable presence of Diego Rivera, the prodigal returned home from 14 years abroad and having been kicked out of Moscow. Despite his rude treatment at the hands of Stalinist art critics and the Russian government's unveiled threats of harm if he did not leave, Diego embraced Communism as the world's salvation. Soon after his arrival in 1921, he sought out pro-Mexican art movements, Mexican muralists and easel painters, photographers, and writers. Within this deeply Mexicanistic society, Tina Modotti's circle of expatriates and fellow travelers fit right in to the party circuit. Diego also went to work on another series of murals for the government ministry of education.

Frida drifted into this stimulating circle. She and Tina Modotti became friends. Possessing similar incendiary personalities and sensual vitality, they drank and danced deep into the hot Mexican nights at the moveable salons. In the sweltering rooms, crowded with drunken eccentrics and oblivious hangers-on, political rhetoric or denunciations of artistic merit often took on an edge. Challenges sometimes required redress by gunplay. Gulping down a quart of tequila did not enhance marksmanship and usually, when the smoke cleared, the only casualties were the furniture, walls, streetlamps and at one particular salon, a record player. As Frida recalled her first meeting with her future husband:

> *We got to know each other at a time when everybody was packing pistols; when they felt like it, they simply shot up the street lamps in Avenida Madero. "Diego once shot a gramophone at one of Tina's parties. That was when I began to be interested in him although I was also afraid of him."*[6]

Page 36

Self-Portrait with "Bonito", 1942.

Oil on canvas, 55 x 43.5 cm.

So the small and still physically frail Frida Kahlo had a chance to see old soft *Panzon* in a different light, gripping a smoking Colt revolver in a crowded room suddenly fallen silent. The chubby muralist had hidden layers to him as well as a manly set of *cojones.* And Diego saw the same flash in the school girl who had stood eye to eye with his now ex-wife, Lupe Marin, and held her ground. This was more than a spoiled child of the bourgeoisie who smiled back at him through the cigar smoke, punctuating her intelligent vocabulary with vulgar street slang for effect. She challenged him and Diego Rivera, ever the swordsman, never refused a challenge. The actual point of their first meeting is difficult to discover since they were both elaborate story tellers who often bent the truth to fit the moment. There's a charming tale that has Frida rising from her bed, tucking some of her work under her arm and hobbling with a cane to where Diego worked on the ministry of education murals. She calls to him high on the scaffolding:

"Diego, come down!"

He peers into the courtyard at this young girl wearing a blue and white European school costume, long braids and leaning on a cane. It was his curse to be easily distracted from his work so he lumbers down the rickety stairs.

"But I haven't come here to flirt," she says, "even though you're a notorious ladies' man. I just want to show you my pictures. If you find them interesting, tell me; if not, tell me anyway because then I'll find something else to do to support my family."

The big man with the shaggy head of hair and paint-smeared apron wrapped around his girth looks at each painting. He separates one from the other three and looks at it for a longer time.

"First of all, I like the self portrait. That is original. The other three pictures seem to have been influenced by things you must have seen somewhere. Now, go home and paint another picture. Next Sunday I'll come and tell you what I think of it."

Page 39

Self-Portrait with Monkey and Parrot, 1942.

Oil on masonite, 54.6 x 43.2 cm.

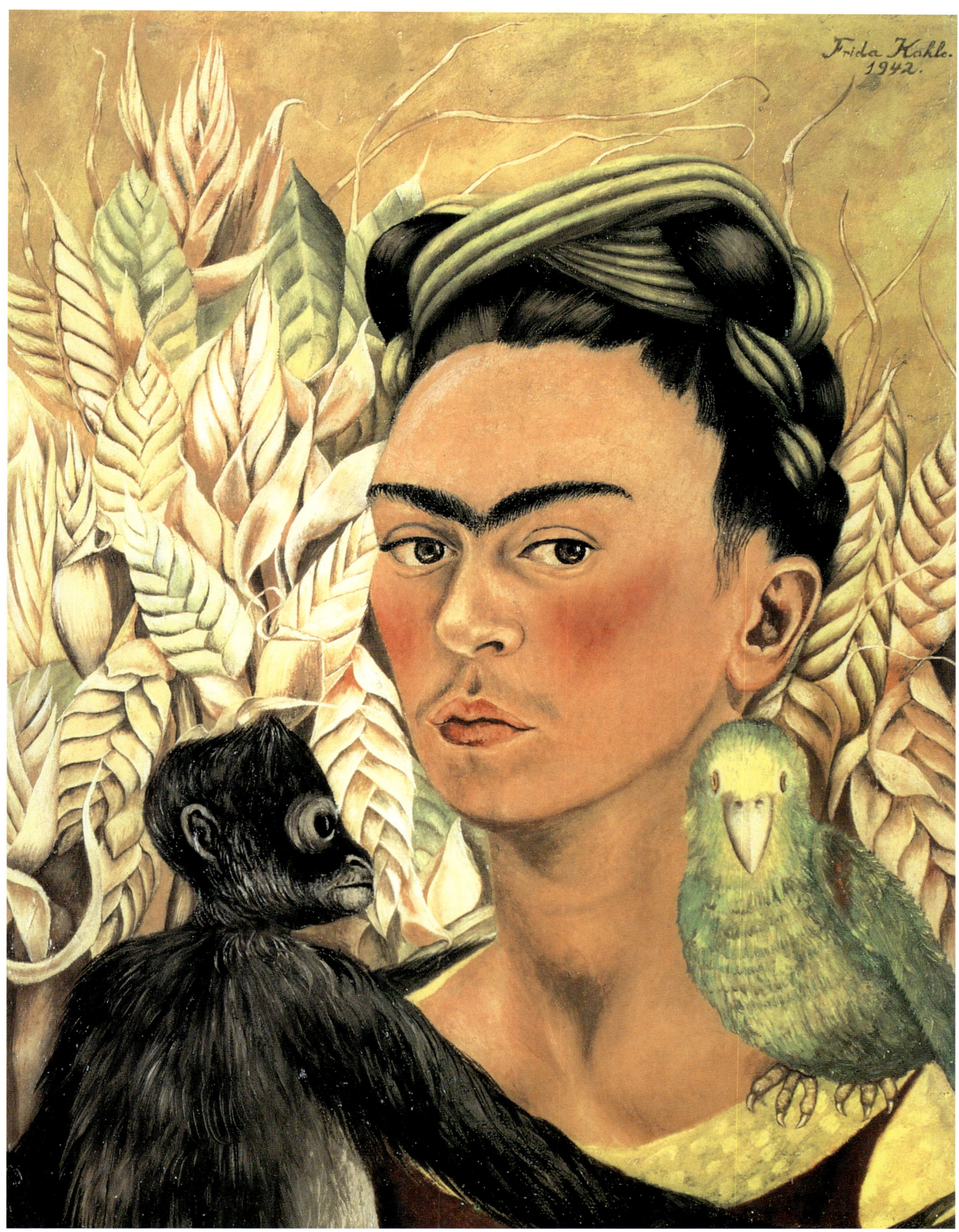
Frida Kahlo.
1942.

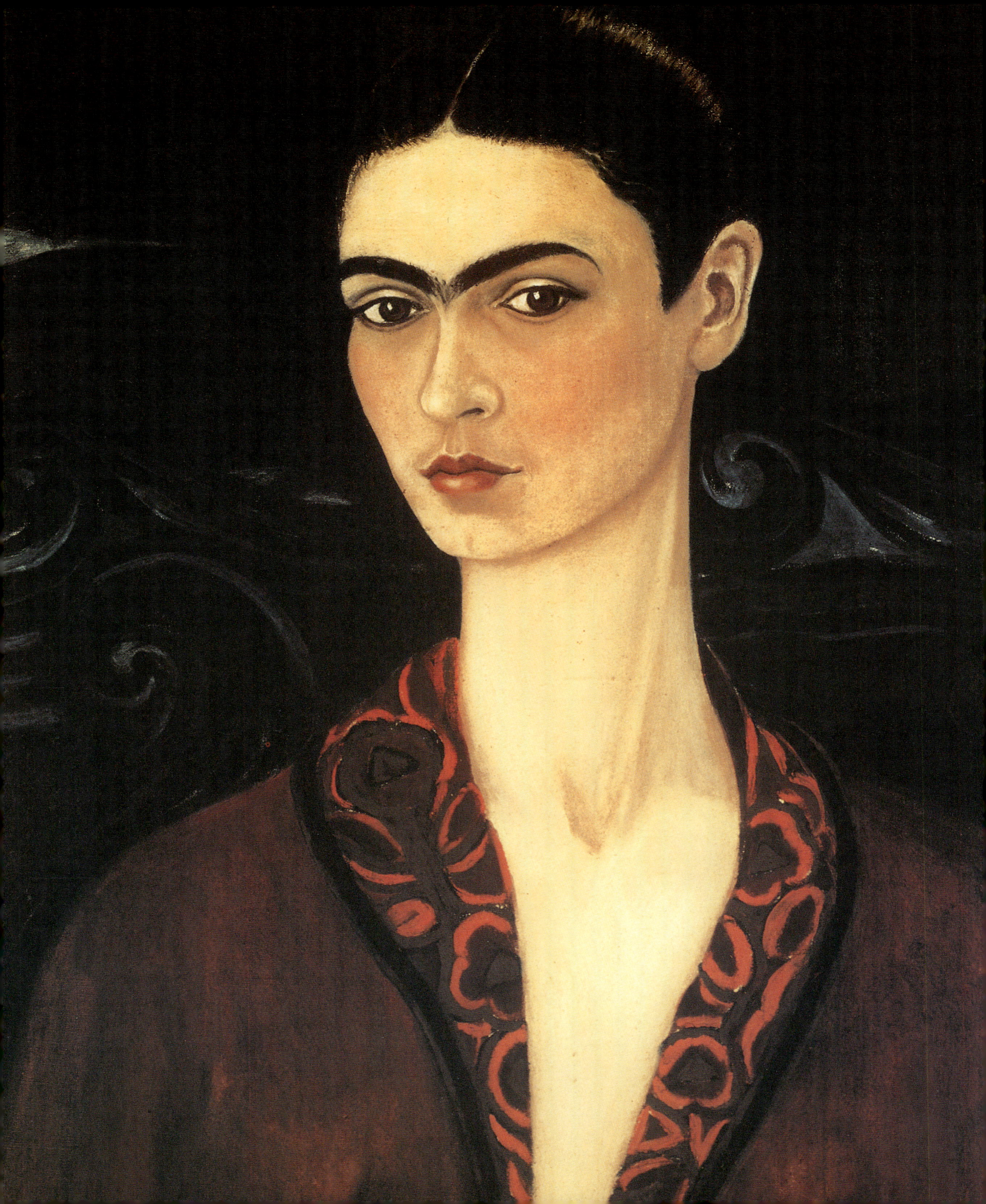

Frida finishes her tale, "He did just that and concluded that I was talented."[7]

If this romantic story is to be believed, Diego Rivera concluded more than the depth of her talent. His original interest in the cheeky young girl, whose feisty attitude had charmed him, turned to a deeper respect, an appreciation of her as a fellow artist to whom he could relate on many different levels. It wasn't long before he dusted off his brown Stetson hat, shook out his sagging jacket, polished the toes of his boots on the backs of his pant legs and began showing up at *La Casa Azul* every Sunday. Diego had become a courting suitor. Frida's mother was against the match. She likened Diego to a big toad standing in the doorway. Guillermo Kahlo took Diego aside, steering him into the central courtyard. Diego may have looked like a fat toad. He may have been twenty years her senior. He was divorced - twice - and an atheist, and a Communist to boot, but he was also a famous painter who had commissions and money and the respect of both the government and the artistic community to which Guillermo Kahlo aspired.

Guillermo leaned close. "Do you realize she's a little devil?"

Diego nodded, "I know."

Guillermo made a final appeal, "She is a sick person and all her life she will be sick. She is intelligent, but not pretty. Think it over if you want, and if you wish to get married, I give you my permission."

Diego nodded again, *"Gracias."*

Guillermo nodded. "All right, you've been warned."[8]

---

[1] Ibid, page 43, Tibol, Raquel

[2] Ibid, page 60, Tibol, Raquel

[3] Rummel, Jack, *Frida Kahlo – A Spiritual Biography*, The Crossroad Publishing Company, New York, 2000

[4] Herrera, Hayden: *Frida – A Biography of Frida Kahlo*, New York, 1983, pp 73-4

[5] Ibid., page 74

[6] Ibid., page 77

Page 40

Self-Portrait with Velvet Dress, 1926.

Oil on canvas, 79.7 x 60 cm,

Bequest of Alejandro Gómez Arias.

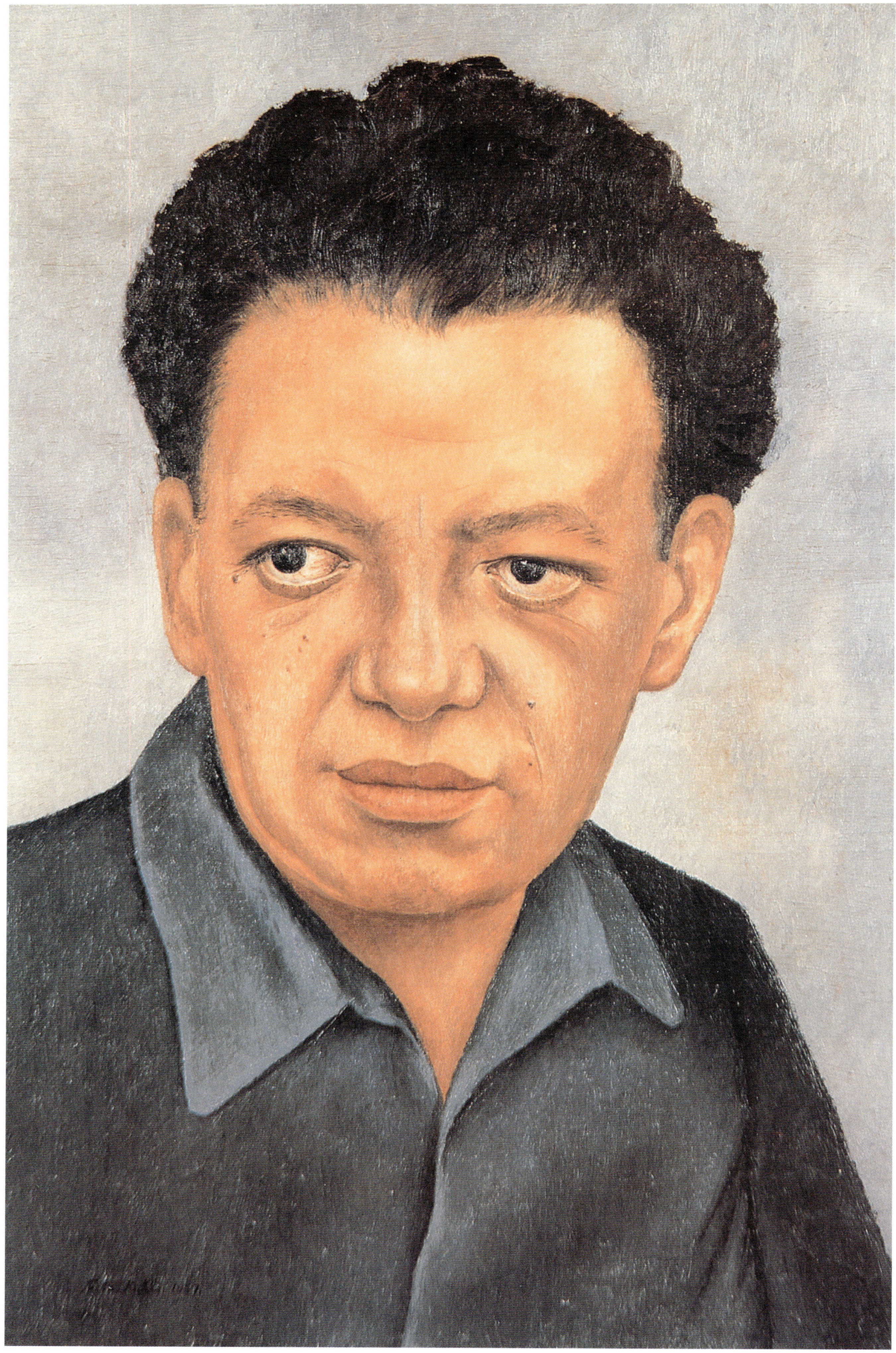

Señora Diego Rivera

On August 21, 1929, Frida Kahlo, age 22, married Diego Rivera, age 42, in a civil ceremony, joined by a few close friends at the Coyoacan City Hall. Looking on as official witnesses were a homeopathic doctor and a wig maker. The Judge was a pal of Rivera's from his student days at the School of Fine Arts. Diego, his hair slicked back, stood up in a plain gray suit, his Stetson hat, wide belt and the Colt revolver in his waistband. Frida had borrowed a long skirt and blouse from her maid and wore a red *reboso* stole over her shoulders. She barely came up to his shoulder, giving the couple the appearance of a small dark china doll next to an immense porcelain pug dog. After the ceremony they posed for a photographer from *La Prensa.* The accompanying story read:

> *Last Wednesday in the nearby village of Coyaocan, the controversial painter Diego Rivera was married to Miss Frida* (sic) *Kahlo, one of his students. The bride was dressed, as can be seen, in simple street garb, and the painter Rivera as an American without a vest. The marriage was not at all pompous, but carried out in an extremely cordial atmosphere with all modesty, without ostentation and minus ceremonious pretentiousness. The newlyweds were extensively congratulated after the marriage by some intimate friends.*

And then the party shifted to *La Casa Azul.* Matilde Kahlo still fumed, muttering that Rivera now looked like a "fat farmer" - an improvement over the "fat toad." Lupe Marin had also been invited and after a liberal sampling of tequila thrust her hands under Frida's dress and hauled it up.

"Do you see those two canes?" Marin screeched. "That's what Diego's going to have to put up with and she used to have my legs!" She hoisted her own skirt, showing off her shapely gams for comparison. Frida made a grab for her. Friends restrained the two women and Frida bolted from the room in a fury.

Page 42
Portrait of Diego Rivera, 1937.
Oil on canvas, 46 x 32 cm,
Jacques and Natasha Gelman Collection,
Mexico City.

Diego, of course, was delighted to see two women he had bedded and wedded fighting over him and to celebrate the occasion headed for the bar. His gay mood continued into the wee hours whereupon he drew his trusty Colt revolver and, aiming through a boozy fog, began blazing away. Guests sought cover until the pistol's hammer clicked empty on spent cartridges.

Frida was smoldering and did not spend the night with him. In fact she didn't move into his house at 104 Paseo de la Reforma for several days.[1]

Though not known at the time, this wedding and its aftermath would be a microcosm of the rest of their lives together.

Señora Rivera began setting up housekeeping in his house as Diego was appointed director of the San Carlos Academy, his youthful alma mater. Within a couple of weeks Diego's reforms of the school's curriculum met with a sour reception and he was summarily requested to leave the campus. At that time, he accepted a commission to create a series of murals in the National Palace forming a visual history of Mexico. The job was huge and he returned to it many times over the following years. It required five years just to complete the stairwell. The palace courtyard mural wasn't begun until 1942.

Continuing in her role as the good wife, Frida reconciled with Lupe Marin who showed her how to prepare Diego's favorite *molé,* rich puddings and other dishes that kept up his energy during ten to twelve hour work days. As Lupe had done, Frida brought Rivera his lunch at the scaffolding each day. With her duties as Rivera's doting wife claiming more of her time, she virtually stopped painting. In 1929, however, she did manage to creatively put her psychological house in order. One canvas seems to mark a step in distancing herself from the cause of her physical turmoil.

She painted *The Bus* (p. 28-29), there is nothing dramatic here, no reenactment, or sentimental rehashing, or even any cursing of the fates. It is an interior view of a bus with six passengers sitting on the side bench in front of the windows: a shopping mother, a plumber

Page 45

Diego Rivera, *Self-portrait*, 1949.

Watercolour on canvas, 31 x 26.5 cm,

Houston, USA.

Page 46

Diego Rivera, *1st May Parade in Moscow*,

1956. Oil on canvas, 133 x 107 cm,

Collection Banco Nacional de México,

Mexico.

Page 47

Diego Rivera, *The Making of a Fresco, Showing the Building of a City*, 1931.

Fresco, 5.68 x 9.91 m,

San Francisco Art Institute, San Francisco.

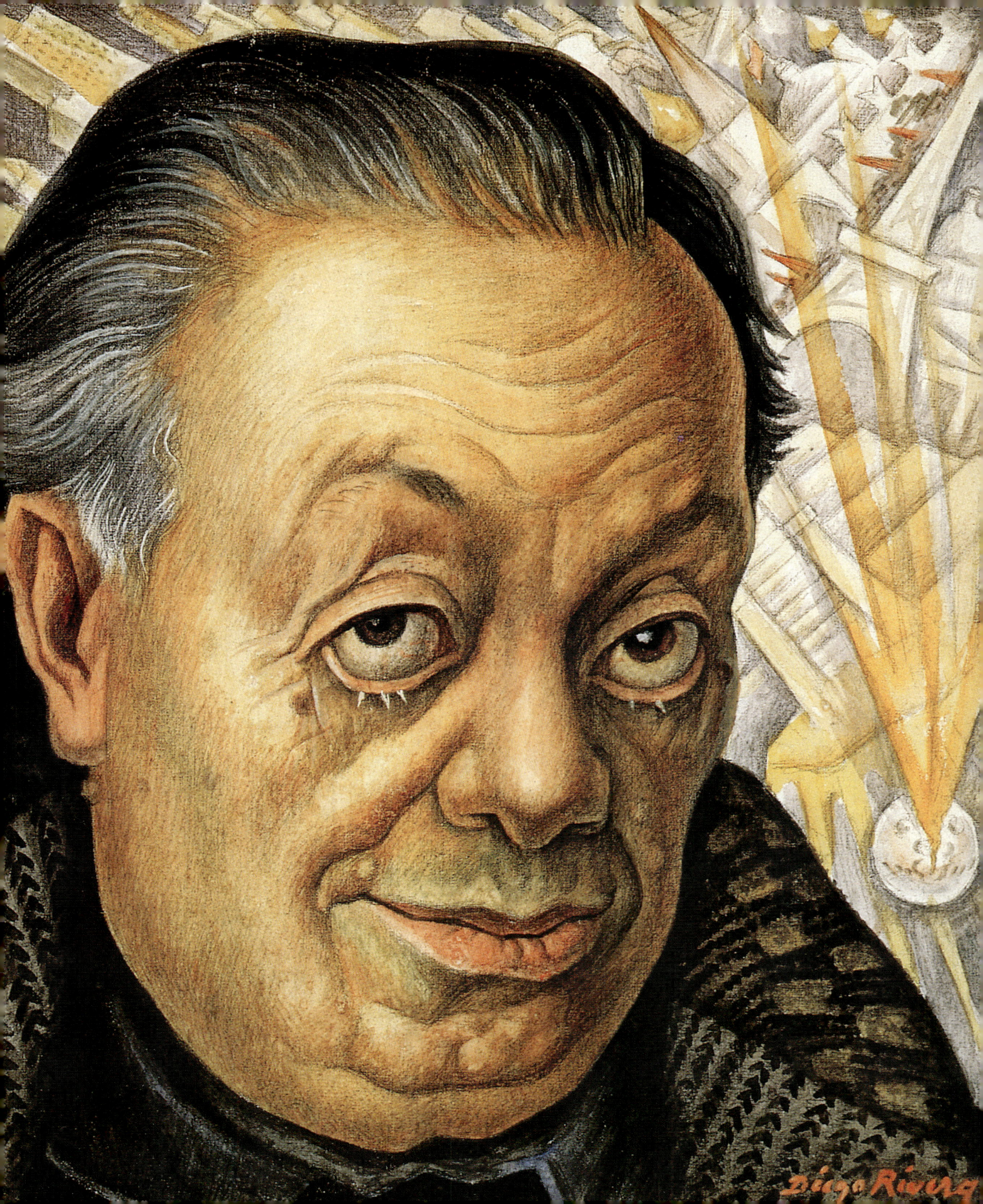
Diego Rivera

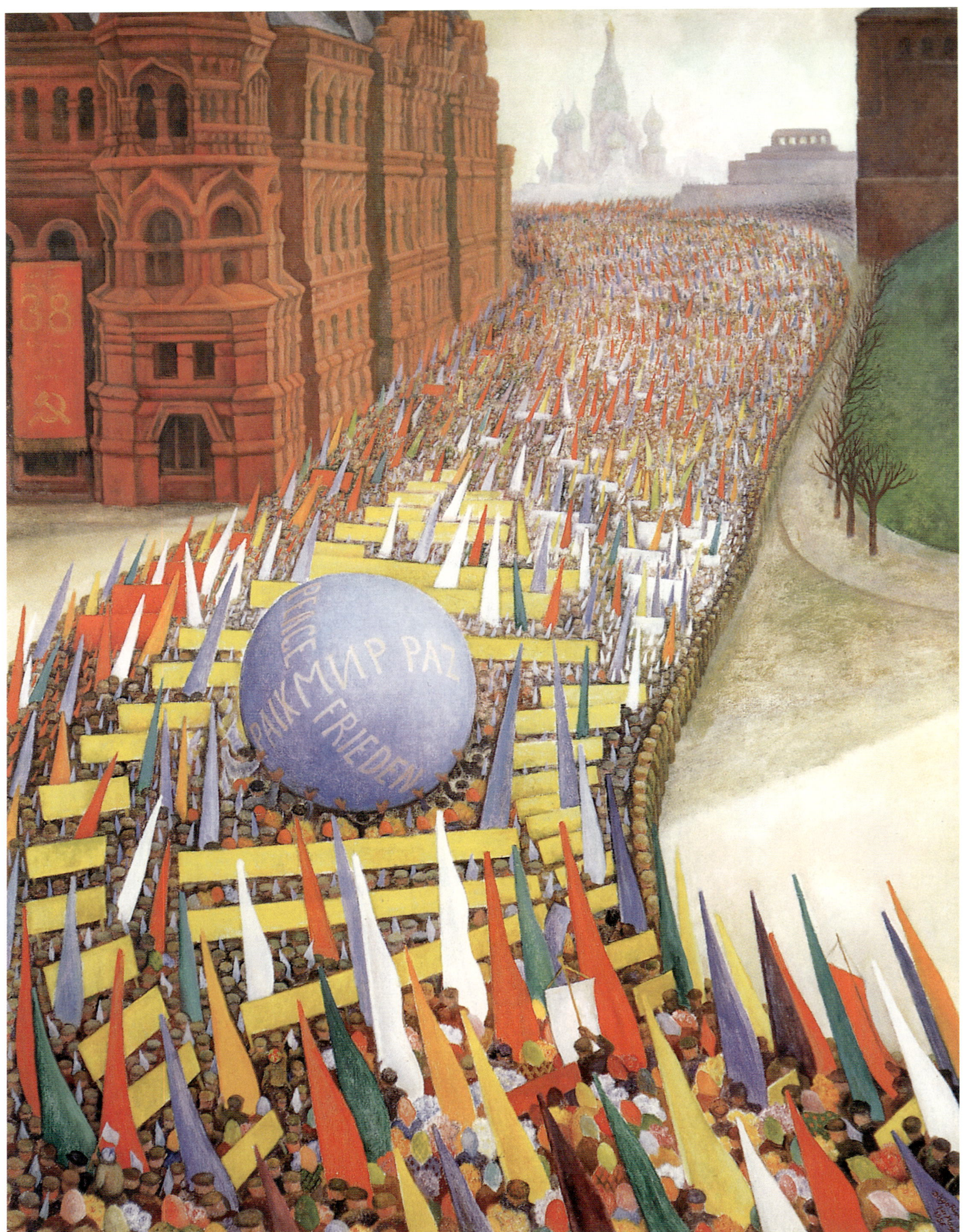
38
PEACE
МИР PAZ
PAIX
FRIEDEN

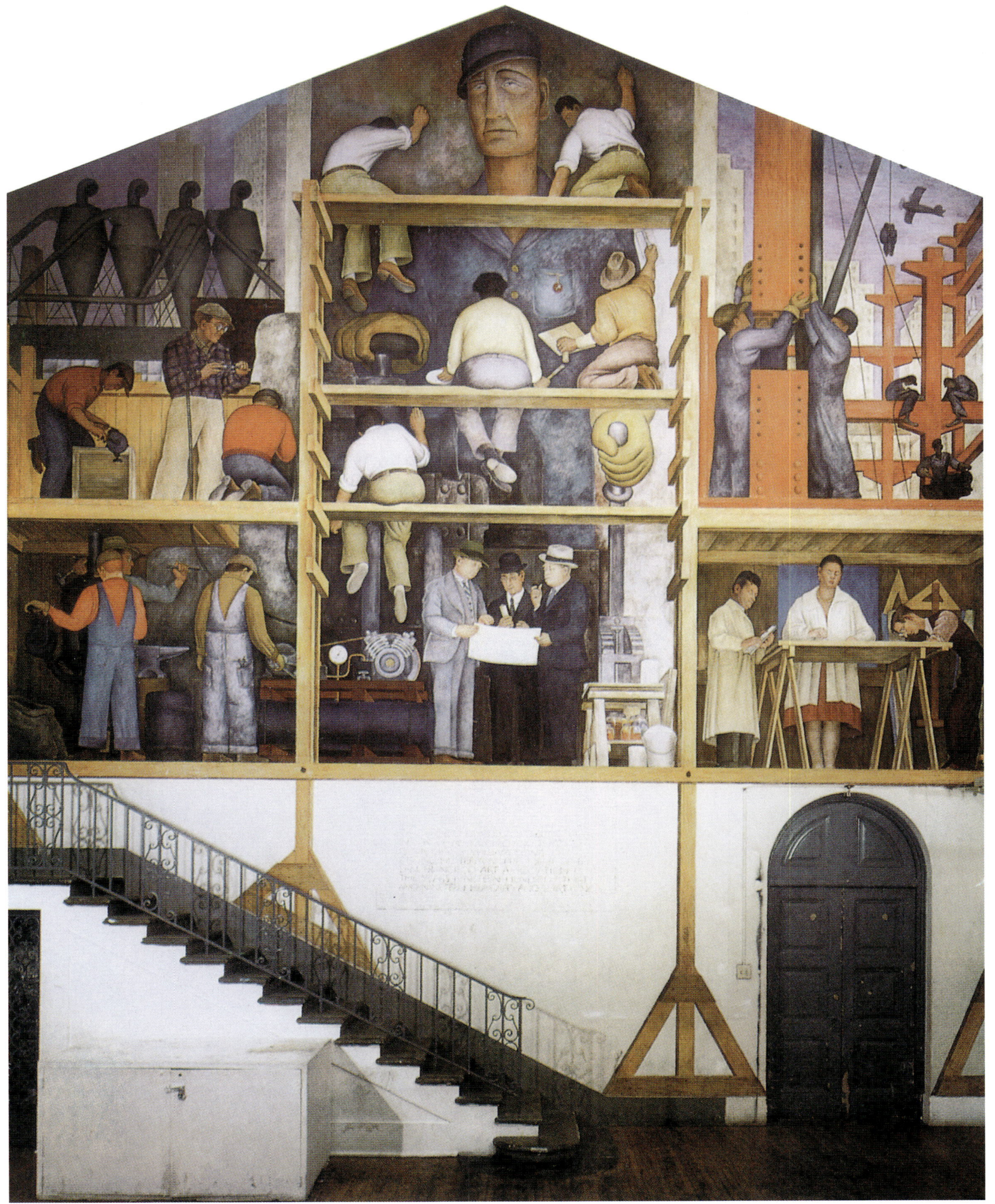

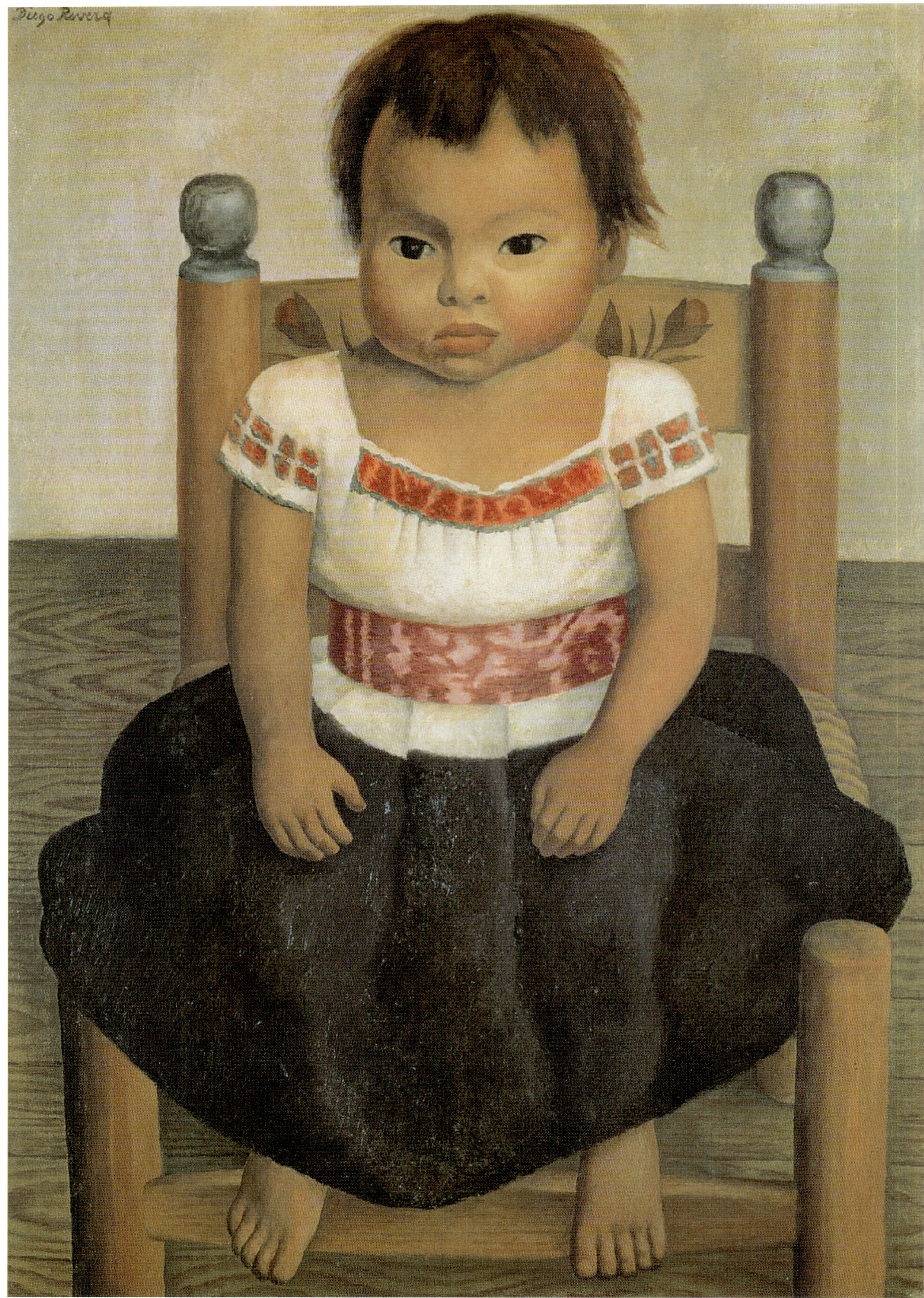
Diego Rivera

in overalls, a barefoot *Indita* with a baby, a young boy, a fair-haired *gringo* in a western suit and porkpie hat, and a young Mexican girl in a western dress. They face us without seeing us, each with their own thoughts. It's as if Frida can ride the bus again without fear; these anonymous sitters are portraits from life and Frida is getting on with her own life as well.

The other painting, on Masonite, is titled *Time Flies*. In this self-portrait, she gazes at us wearing a vulnerable white top trimmed in lace with a heavy Indian jade necklace around her neck. Exceptional antique earrings dangle from each lobe. Her expression is direct, but with a hint of a smile as though waiting for a photographer to click the shutter before dissolving into laughter. A cloud of words have been written interpreting the symbolism of the climbing airplane seen through the black-draped balcony window behind her head, or the significance of the alarm clock on the wooden stand behind her left shoulder. Knowing the place she was in during 1929, the upward turn in her fortunes, a new man in her life, a feeling of confidence in her improving technique and seasoned with her natural ebullience, Frida Kahlo could just as well be enjoying a visual joke, a lightening up: time flies.

In December 1930, Rivera received a commission from the United States Ambassador Dwight Morrow to execute a series of murals – *The History of Cuernavaca and Morelos, Conquest and Revolution* – at the Cortes Palace in Cuernavaca, south of Mexico City. Frida accompanied Diego and established their quarters in Morrow's weekend house. This time, she spent considerable time at the project watching Diego work and offering the occasional question or critique. Instead of being annoyed by this kibitzing, Diego found many of her suggestions to be helpful. Gaining more respect for her artistic eye and intellectual grasp of his work, Diego came to be influenced by her ideas throughout the rest of their relationship.

By this time, the Communist Party had its fill of Diego Rivera. Though he had held office in the party and showed solidarity at their rallies, his casual acceptance of commissions from capitalists went against the grain of the conservative ideologues. In 1929, he was booted from the party and, demonstrating her loyalty to him, Frida quit too. Neither

Page 48
Diego Rivera, *Modesta (Modest)* 1937.

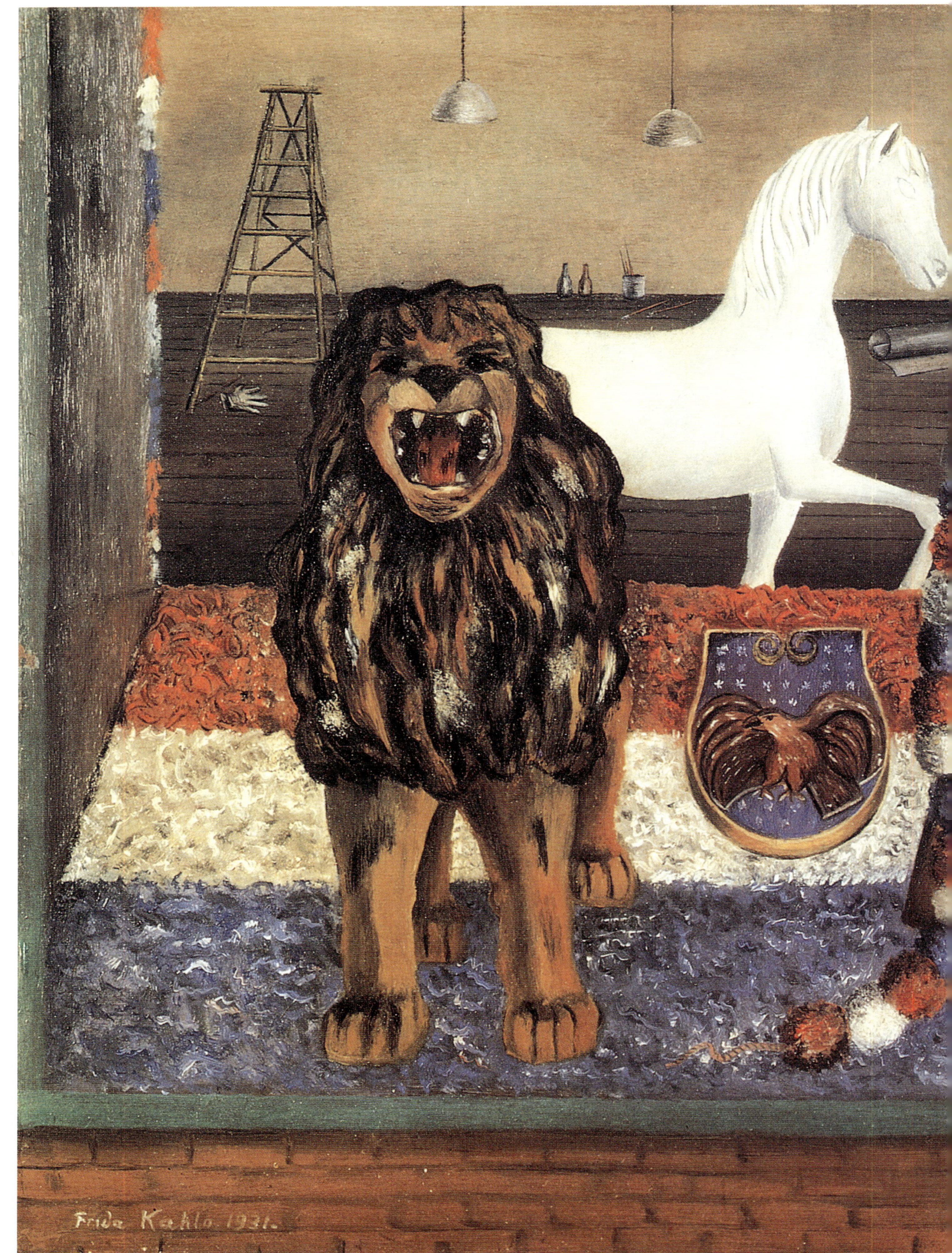
Frida Kahlo 1931.

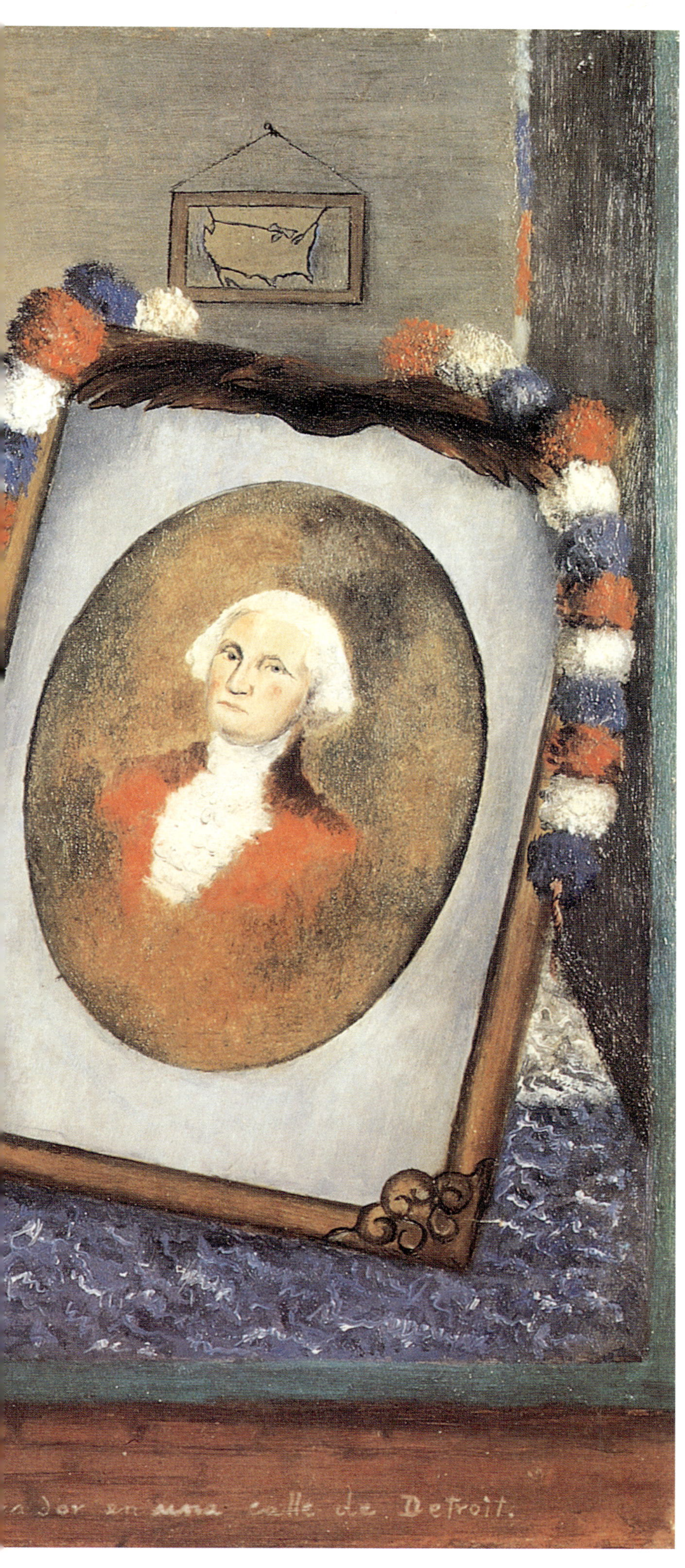

Page 50-51

Window Display in a Street in Detroit, 1931.

Oil on metal plate, 30.3 x 38.2 cm.

abandoned the goals of Communism and continued to espouse its anti-capitalist causes, but their support came from the sidelines.

In Cuernavaca, Frida experienced a miscarriage three months into her first pregnancy. This devastating event was topped shortly thereafter when she discovered Diego had been having an affair with one of his female assistants. At this point, she uttered her most quoted remark to the effect that she had experienced two catastrophes in her life: the first being hit by a tram. The second was Diego.

At the close of the 1920s, Mexico's political climate shifted again and Diego found himself caught in the middle of an ideological battle. Not only was he *persona non grata* at Communist Party Headquarters, but the government had grown tired of seeing socialist themes peering back from "historic" murals popping up all over the country. Feeling the heat on the back of his neck, Rivera accepted some commissions in San Francisco, packed up his brushes and Frida and headed for the United States.

The U.S. had been washing its hands of the Communist backlash following World War I in what came to be known as the "Red Scare". Communists, anarchists and sympathizers had been rooted out all across the country and many deported back to Europe. Two Italians, Sacco and Vanzetti, had been charged with murder during a robbery. Throughout the six-year investigation, both had been linked to the "Reds". The pair were electrocuted in August, 1927. Now one of the world's most famous Communists, Diego Rivera came marching up to the California customs gates for a working visit.

Fortunately, Albert Bender, an internationally famous art collector, prevailed in their behalf and in the name of fine art, the gates swung open.

To express her thanks, Frida dedicated their wedding portrait, *Frida and Diego*, to Bender and added a dove carrying a banderole telling the story of the dedication.[2] He was so pleased he went on to become one of her early patrons. The painting shows Diego, complete with his palette and brushes as the "official" painter in the family and Frida holding his hand, dressed

Page 53
Self-Portrait Sitting on the Bed or *My Doll and I*, 1937.
Oil on metal, 40 x 31 cm,
Jacques and Natasha Gelman Collection, Mexico City.

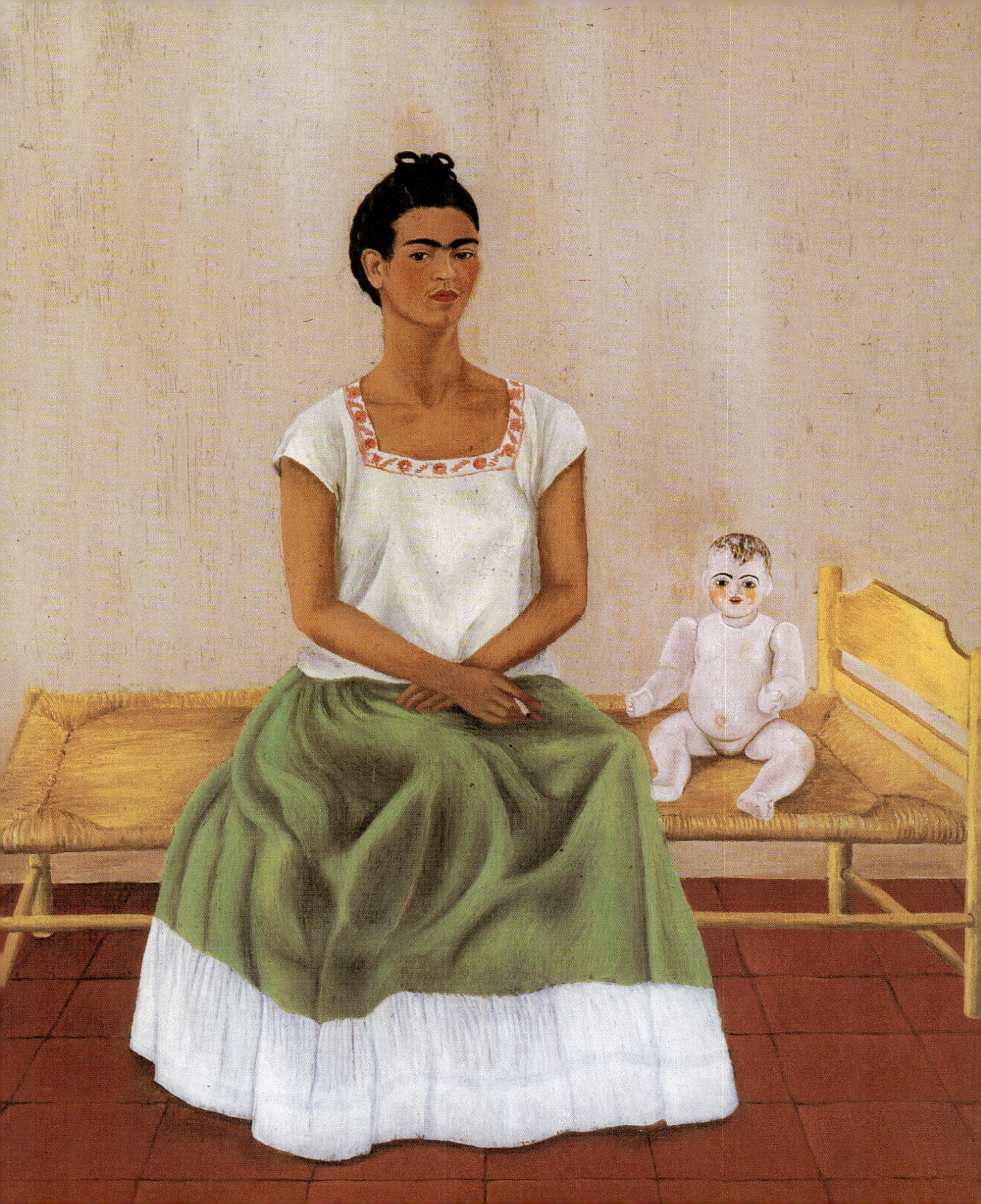

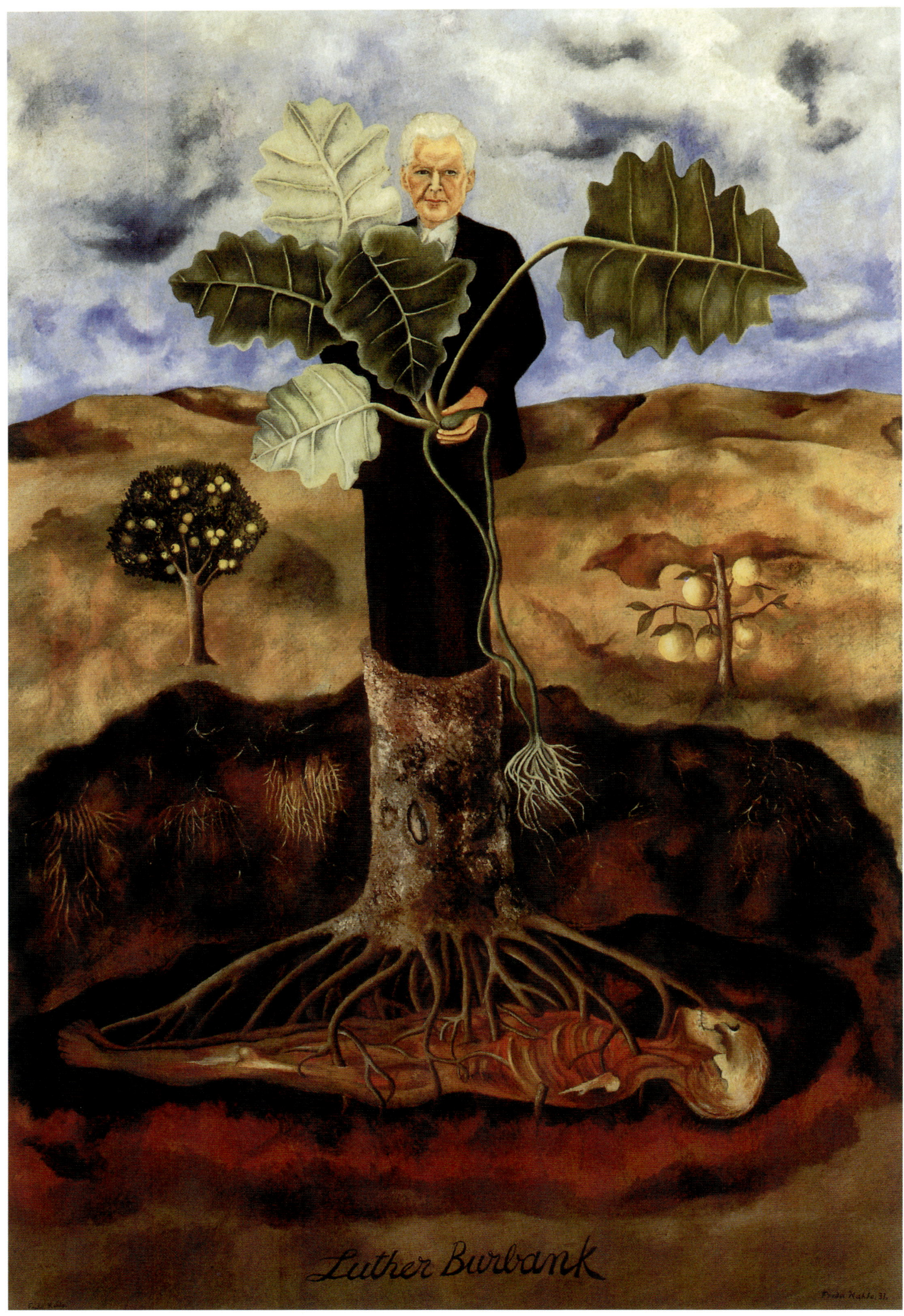
Luther Burbank

as a submissive Mexican wife. If this was the role she had accepted, all that changed during the eight months Diego worked on his mural at the Luncheon Club of the Pacific Stock Exchange. Señora Rivera was undergoing a change of her own.

If the art crowd in San Francisco was ready to spread the red carpet for Diego, nothing had prepared them for Rivera's petite bombshell of a wife. Edward Weston, the photographer, had struck up a friendship with Diego when Weston had spent time creating an extraordinary body of work in Mexico. Now, he photographed Rivera again in California and made Frida's acquaintance. Weston kept scrupulous diaries and wrote of his encounter with Mrs. Rivera:

> *She is in sharp contrast with Lupe* (Marin, Rivera's ex-wife) – *petite, a little doll alongside Diego, but a doll in size only, for she is strong and quite beautiful, shows very little of her father's German blood. Dressed in native costume even to huaraches (leather sandals), she causes much excitement in the streets of San Francisco. People stop in their tracks to look in wonder."*[3]

She arrived in the United States as the Great Depression began settling in, wiping out fortunes, closing banks, and chasing farmers off their land with foreclosures nailed to farmhouse doors. The fun of the Roaring Twenties was a wistful memory. But still, there was money for murals and for welcoming parties among San Francisco's society set where they lionized Diego and scrutinized Frida. She was, for all her philosophical reading and political rhetoric, a provincial girl of 23 on her first trip away from home and her friends. She avoided the people of San Francisco, finding them "boring" and with faces like "unbaked biscuits". She did enjoy shopping trips where she found English a difficult tongue to master and relied on her friend, Lucille Blanch, the artist and wife of one of Diego's American assistants.

Unlike her role as Diego's close partner in Cuernavaca, Frida often found herself with time on her hands in the City by the Bay. Diego had selected Helen Wills Moody, the tennis star, as his model for an "earth mother" in the Pacific Stock Exchange mural, *Allegory of California.* As was his usual practice, he began an affair with Moody. Frida, in turn, took up

Page 54
Portrait of Luther Burbank, 1931.
Oil on masonite, 86.5 x 61.7 cm,
Museo Dolores Olmedo Patiño, Mexico City.

an on-going sexual liaison with Christina Hastings, the wife of one of Rivera's assistants. As Frida's affair proceeded along, her health took another turn for the worse. The tendons in her right foot and ankle became irritated and she found walking difficult. She decided to consult a San Francisco physician and friend of Rivera's, Doctor Leo Eloesser.[4]

The doctor and the artist immediately struck up a friendship. Besides determining that Frida had scoliosis, a congenital spinal deformation, he also discovered what he interpreted to be a connection between the return of her leg and foot problems and the stress of her chaotic emotional life. As small and large crises occurred, such as Diego's latest public dalliance, her physical problems manifested themselves. Eloesser recommended a healthy living regimen to calm both her physical and mental agonies. She kept up their friendship, but, for the most part, ignored his advice.

Instead, she turned to her art and a series of portraits. Meanwhile, Rivera created his humorous mural in the San Francisco Art Institute, *The Making of a Fresco, Showing the Building of a City* (p. 47), depicting himself and his assistants on the scaffolding painting the mural in a trompe l'oeil masterpiece. Frida produced a masterpiece of her own. She painted a portrait of Luther Burbank, the famous horticulturist whose 53 years of cross-breeding plant species had made a huge contribution to California's agriculture. He had recently died, but she memorialized him in a fantasy that wed his body to the soil and the abundance of riches his work had produced. This painting marked a diversion from her standard portrait style as well as a shift to a story-telling narrative that contained an ever-expanding body of symbolism. The *Portrait of Luther Burbank* (p. 54), began the rise of her reputation from competent, dilettante portraitist toiling in the shadow of her famous husband to an emerging talent who may have something important to say.

Her Luther Burbank seems to rise from an ancient hollow tree stump into a desert landscape beneath a vaulted blue sky of swirling cumulus clouds. California sun suffuses the above-ground scene as though coming from all directions. Heavily fruited trees, one rich in greenery and the other, an improbable graft, sink their roots into the soil that glows with a golden luster. The ground beneath the tree stump has been hacked away

Page 57

Diego Rivera, *Paisaje con cactus (Landscape with Cactus)*, 1931.

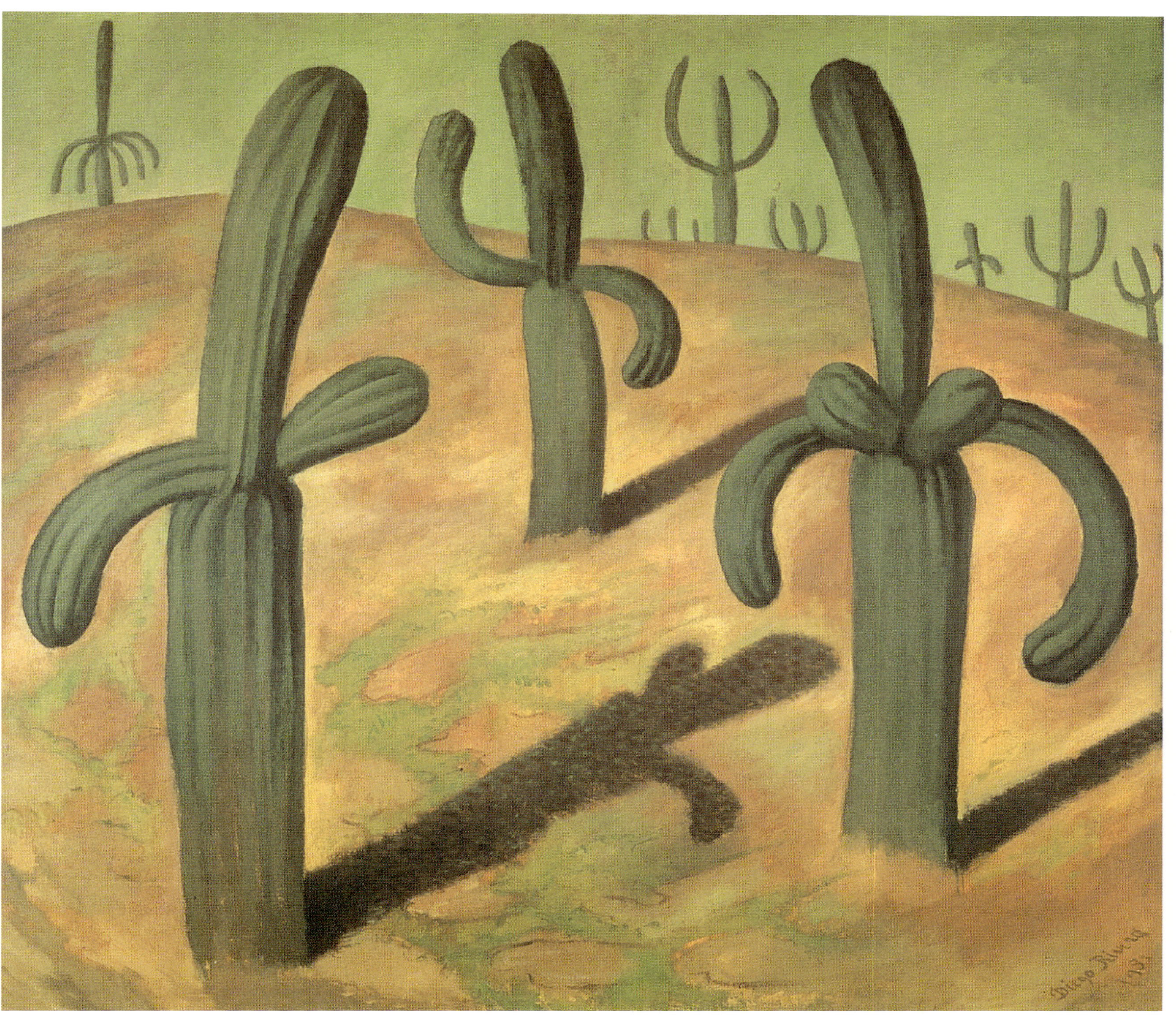
Diego Rivera 1931

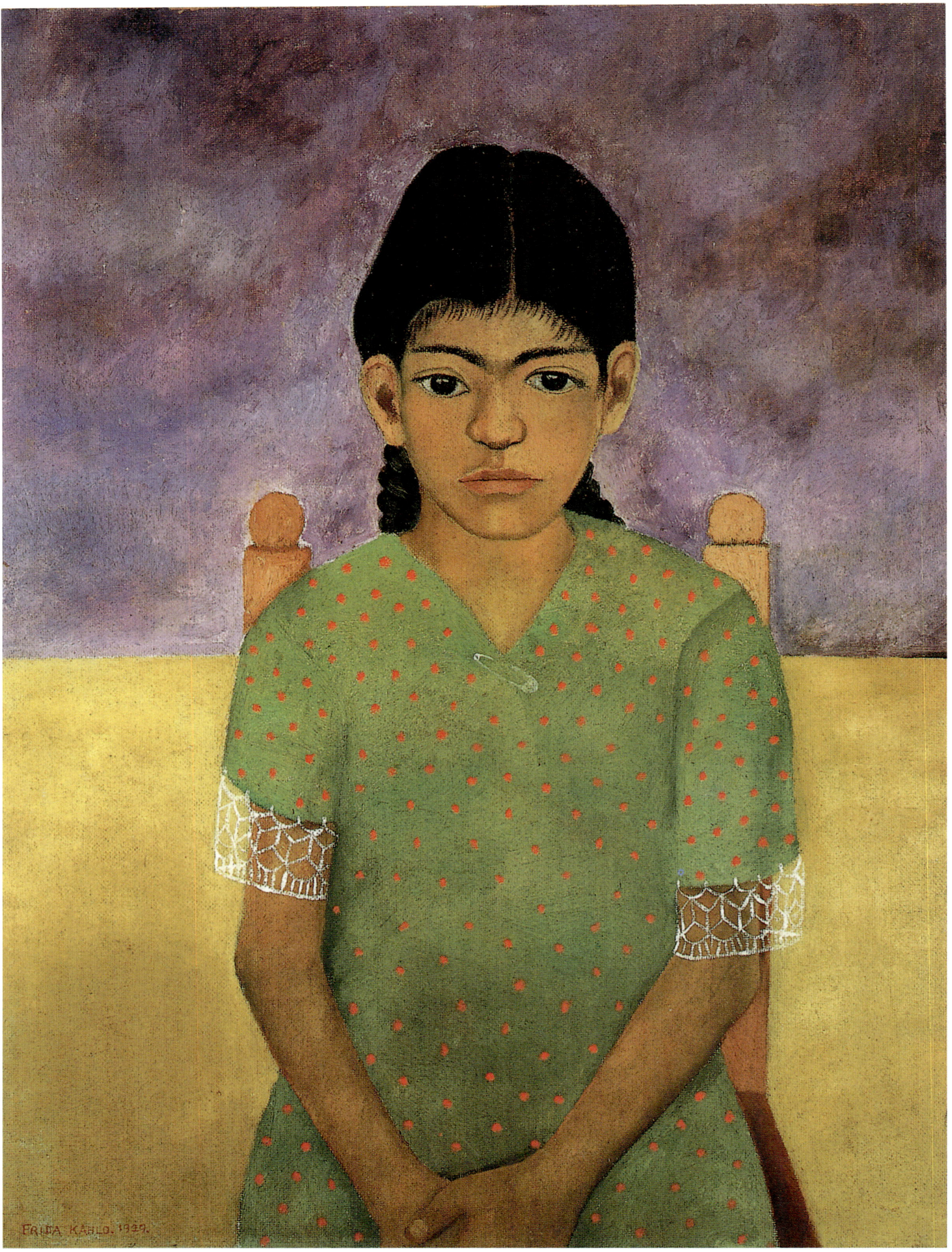
FRIDA KAHLO. 1929.

revealing rich loam, the weathered husk of the ancient tree and its root system greedily drawing sustenance from Burbank's skeletal remains. Even in death he is reborn to fertilize California's agriculture. This simple allegorical tribute marks the start of Frida's fully developed story telling, or *retablo* paintings.

Retablos are small paintings, usually produced on pieces of tin that commemorate a traumatic event. *Retablo* means "behind the altar" and comes from the Christian-Mexican religion. Three components make up a *retablo* painting: a depiction of an event, the vision of the Virgin of Guadalupe, and text that describes the event. The paintings are commissioned from professional *retablo* painters, a 150 year-old tradition that almost died out in the first quarter of the 20th century.

Frida reached back into her own heritage, stripping away the religious context and using only the narrative elements. She also resurrected the Mexican traditional skeleton that represented the celebration of death from her "Day of the Dead" revelries. In Coyoacan, shops and homes were hung with grinning skulls and skeletons. Skulls made of sugar were gobbled up by Mexican children wearing fright masks as families remembered their dead and the continuity of life with gaiety, parades, exploding and fizzing fireworks and candles glowing hot in the night.

Her isolation was put to good use as she completed a pencil portrait of her lover, *Lady Christina Hastings* wearing a tam, painted a full length oil of *Dr. Leo Eloesser* with a schooner-rigged sailboat and an undistinguished portrait of *Mrs. Jean Wright,* the wife of Diego's chief assistant Clifford Wright. The picture reveals Frida's disinterest in her sitter whom she considered to be self-involved and pretentious. Other than her shopping trips to Chinatown where she loved to observe the Chinese children – and they gawked at her Mexican costume – Frida found San Francisco unremarkable. She did not take advantage of its urban sprawl nor its scenic bay for subject matter. Adapting to another culture, thrust into an alien milieu where she was an object of curiosity, separated from her friends and relatives and language, all these influences colored her judgments and priorities.

Page 58
Portrait of Virginia, 1929.
Oil on masonite, 77.3 x 60 cm,
Museo Dolores Olmedo Patiño, Mexico City.

As her loneliness forced her back to her work, she began to consider its value as public art rather than closely held keepsakes for friends. San Francisco's cosmopolitan setting revealed new vistas and possibilities. In a letter to her friend, Isabel Campos, she wrote:

> *I have no women friends... and that's why I spend my life painting. In September, I'll give a show – the first – in New York. I don't have any time and I could only sell a few pictures here, But it was very good for me to come here anyway, because it opened my eyes, and I saw so very many new and good things.*[5]

With the completion of the mural commissions, the Riveras flew back to Mexico on June 8, 1931. With his accumulated wages Diego generously paid off Guillermo Kahlo's mortgage on *La Casa Azul* in Coyoacan and planned to return to the unfinished fresco at the National Palace. He also had an idea for their mutual abode that he proposed to a painter and architect friend, Juan O'Gorman. Diego suggested two houses designed in the Bauhaus International style - minimalist and boxy - be erected in near-by San Angel. They would stand side by side, joined together by a footbridge between the two top stories. Each would have a separate entrance and serve as both living and studio spaces for the two artists, a recognition of Frida's growing independence. Of course, the design also offered Diego privacy for his sexual peccadilloes.

They had been home only a few months when Diego received an invitation from the Museum of Modern Art in New York to help create a retrospective of his work. Though she faced being torn away from her Mexican roots, this news must have brightened Frida's prospects for a show of her own work. For that, she would once again troop back to "Gringolandia", and hob-nob with the rich boring art and society set that fluttered around Diego like so many mouths around a jalapeño. They sailed on the cruise ship *Morro Castle* in mid-November to arrive in Manhattan on December 13, 1931 in time for the December 23 show.

As with San Francisco, upon arrival Diego and Frida were adopted by the rich and famous, by both old and new money and as before, Diego was the center of the maelstrom.

Page 61

Portrait of Dr. Leo Eloesser, 1931.

Oil on masonite, 85.1 x 59.7 cm,

University of California, School of Medicine, San Francisco.

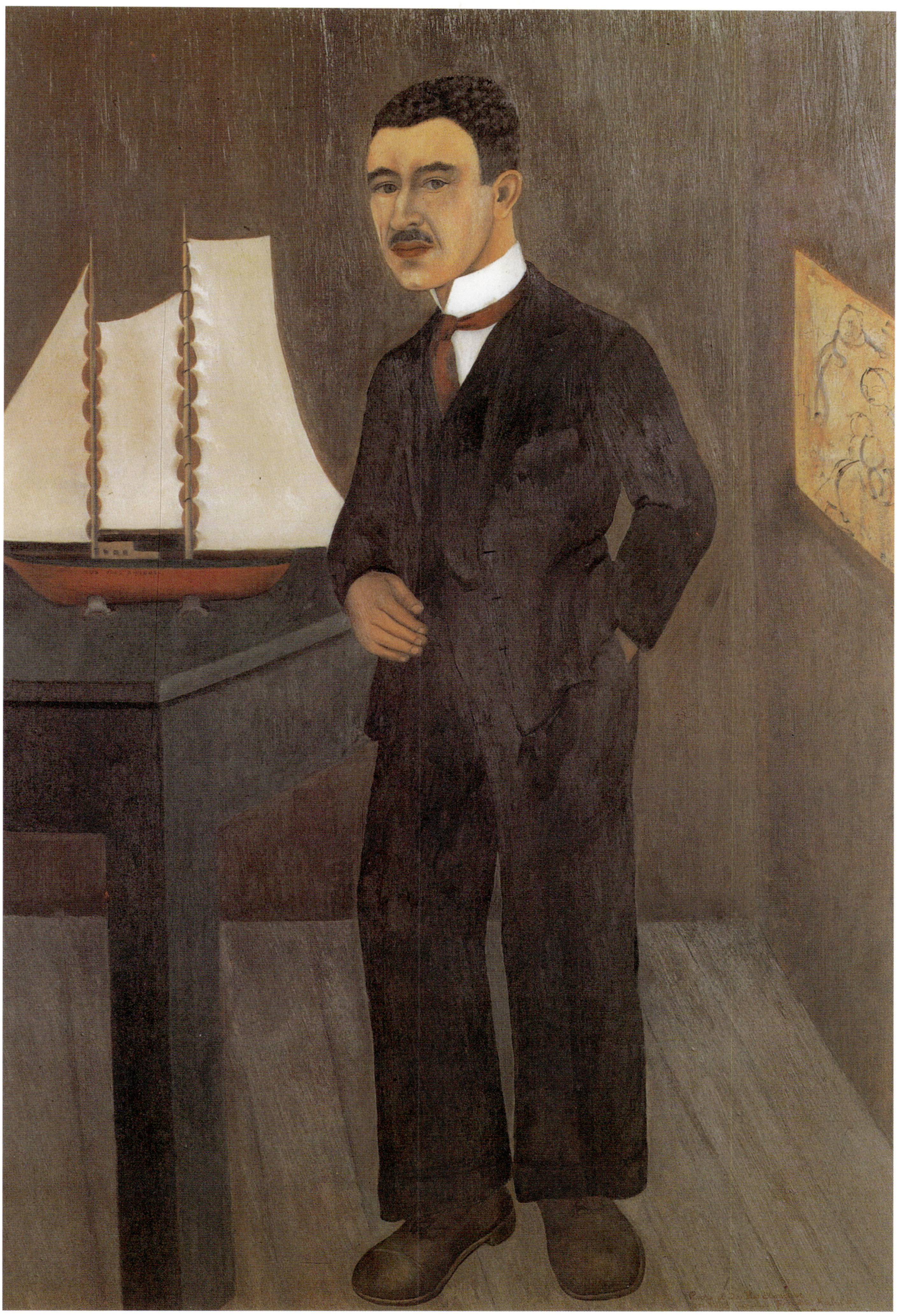

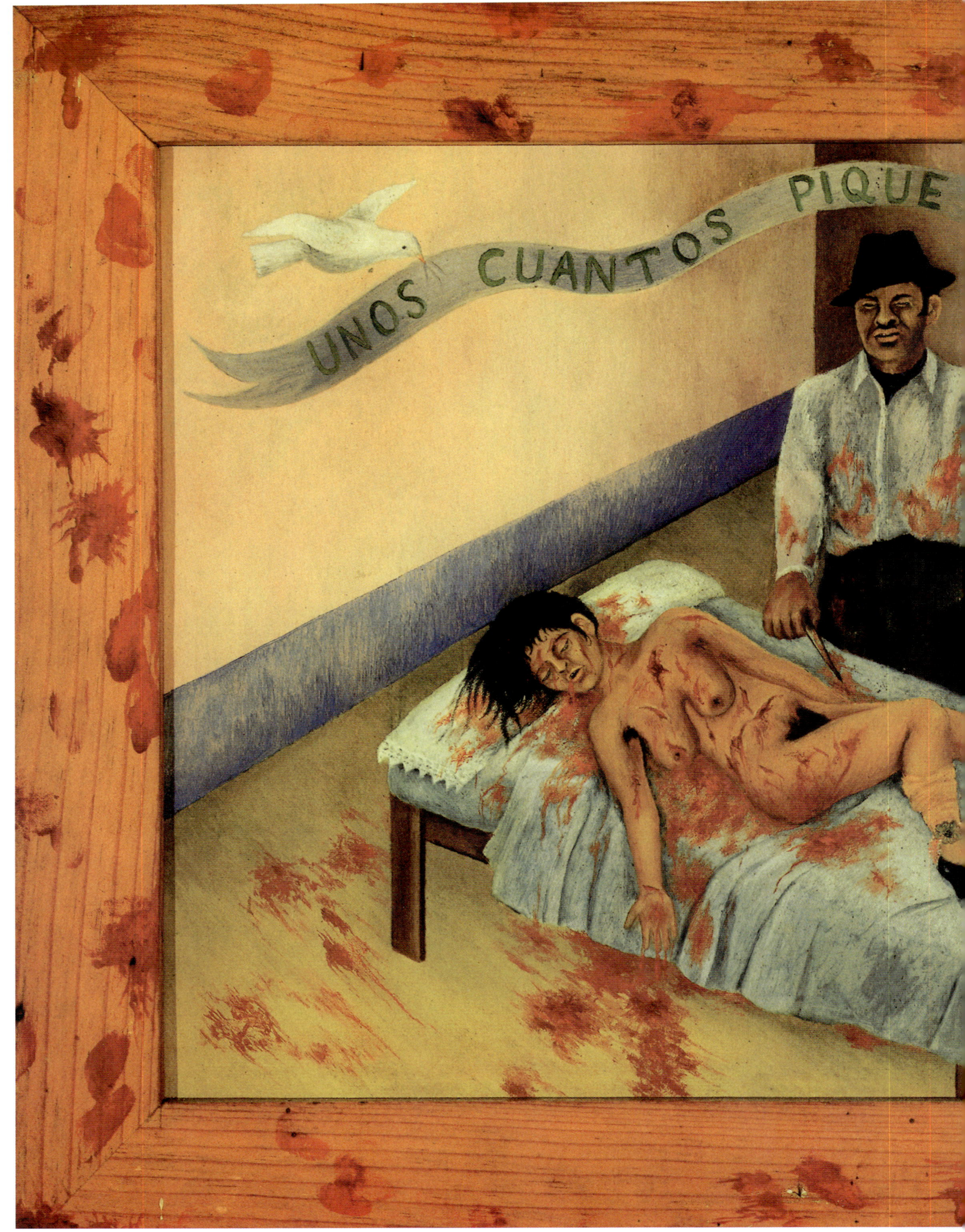
UNOS CUANTOS PIQUE

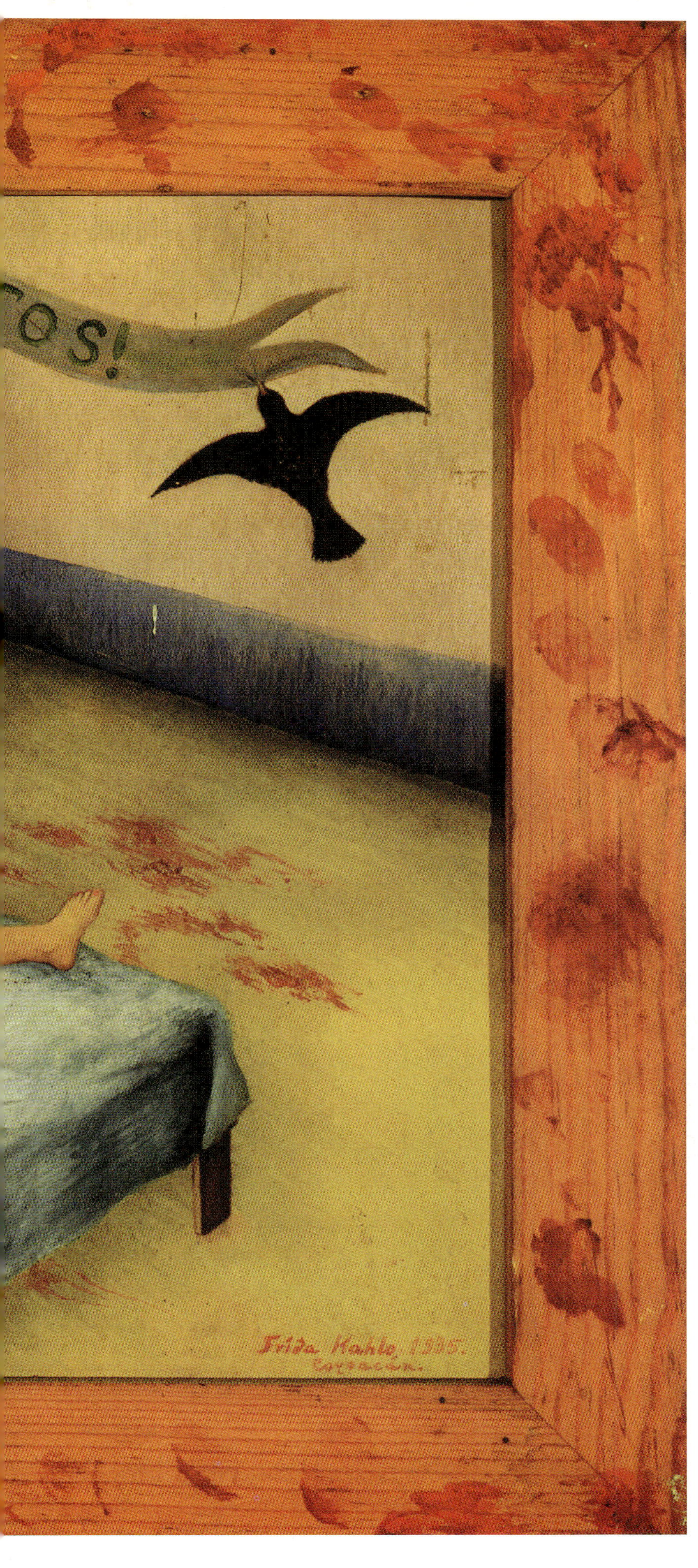

Page 62-63

A Few Small Nips, 1935.

Oil on metal, 38 x 48.5 cm with frame,

29.5 x 39.5 cm without frame,

Museo Dolores Olmedo Patiño, Mexico City.

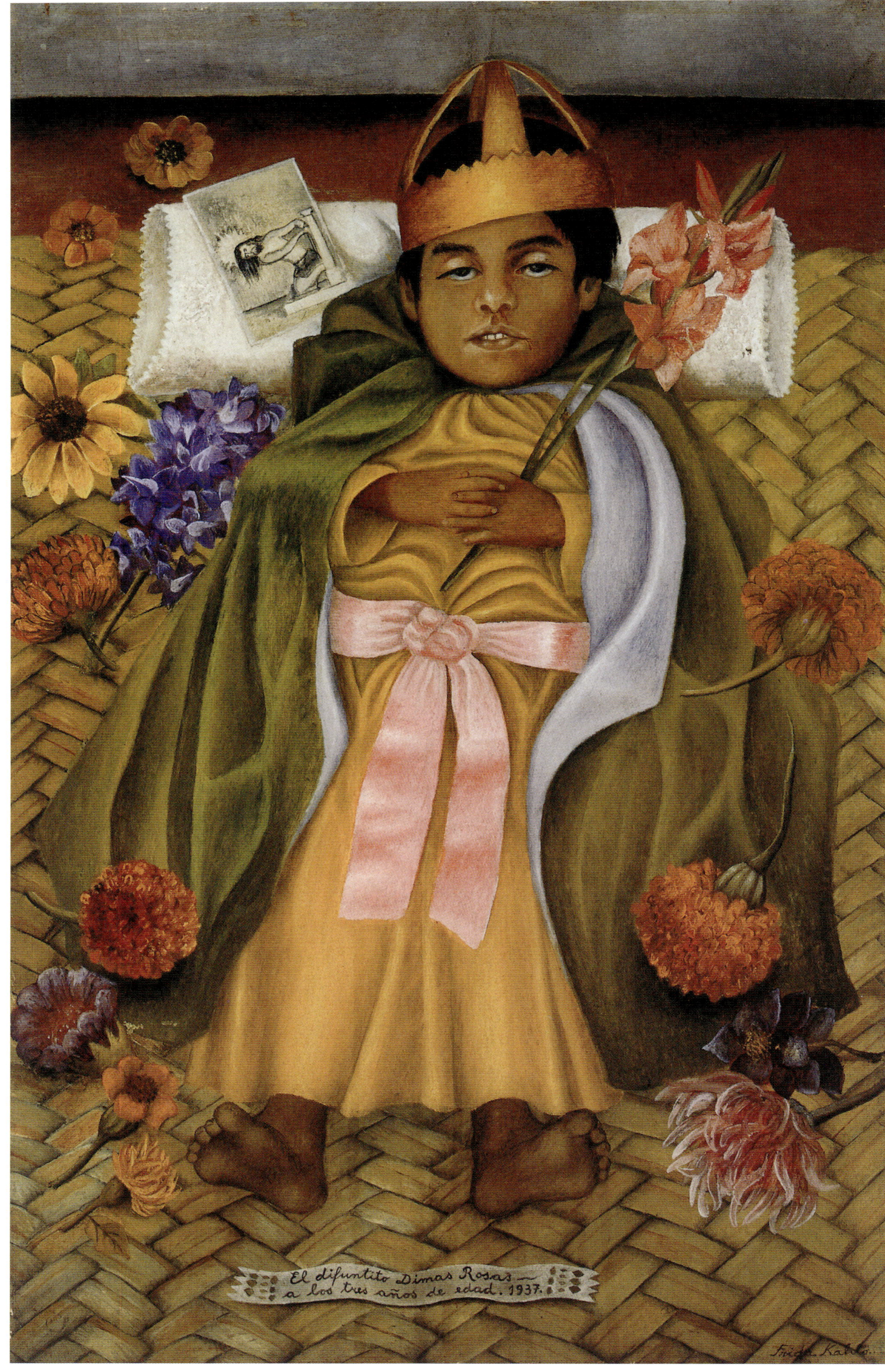
El difuntito Dimas Rosas —
a los tres años de edad. 1937.
Frida Kahlo

The gallery walls held 150 of his works and showed eight mural panels that Diego had prepared for the exhibition. Art critics traveled to New York from around the country to add their two centavos to the pile of newsprint the show generated as 60,000 attendees marched from room to room. The show was a great success.

The petite 24-year-old Mexican girl on Diego Rivera's arm was referred to in the outpouring of prose as "shy" and "retiring" and who, the commentators mentioned in passing, "did a bit of painting herself."

Frida was paraded from one welcoming gala to another, smiled at, toasted and had questions shouted at her slowly as if high volume and low speed made English much more understandable. Back at their hotel, she wrote Doctor Eloesser:

> *This upper class is disgusting and I'm furious at all these rich people here, having seen thousands of people in abject squalor.*[6]

Her quaint rejection of American urban conditions at the start of the Great Depression underscores her own naïve political rhetoric about uplifting the masses when she never really came into contact with her own poverty-stricken Mexican "masses". But in New York, the vast gap between the chauffeured limousines sailing up and down concrete canyons and bread lines shuffling into store-front soup kitchens must have graphically reinforced Frida's socialist sensibilities. Putting down her American hosts might also have been a side effect of being ignored as an artist in her own right yet again. Though Diego praised her painting, no show offers were forthcoming. She continued to be "Mrs. Rivera".

One good outcome to the New York exposure was Frida's opportunity to view original modern works from a variety of contemporary masters. It's not difficult to imagine her wandering from gallery to gallery within the Museum of Modern Art, coming to grips with Surrealists, Expressionists, Picasso, Braque, the dreamscapes of de Chirico and other deeply personal and abstract constructions.

Page 64
The Deceased Dimas Rosas at the Age of Three, 1937.
Oil on masonite, 48 x 31.5 cm,
Museo Dolores Olmedo Patiño, Mexico City.

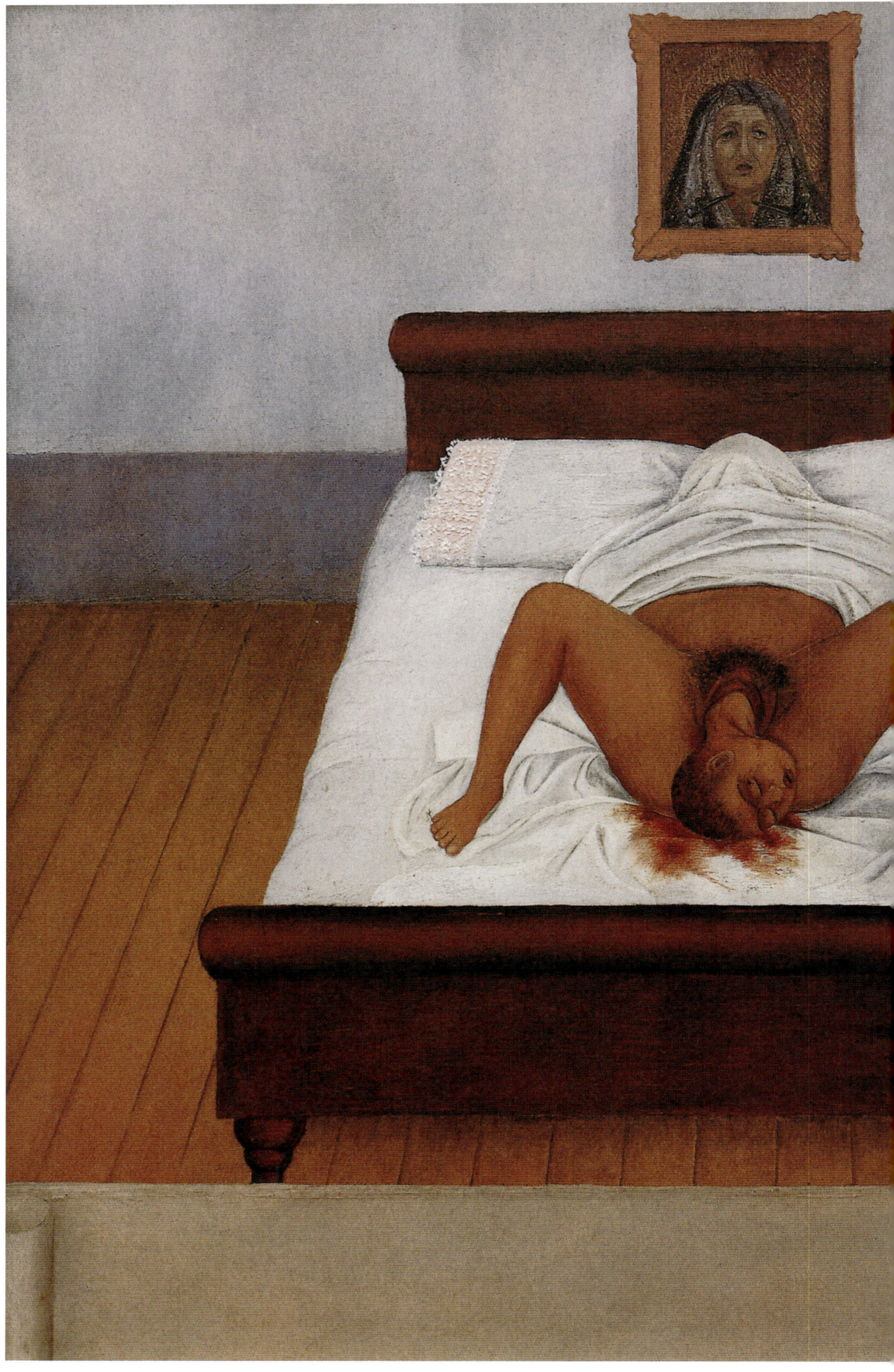

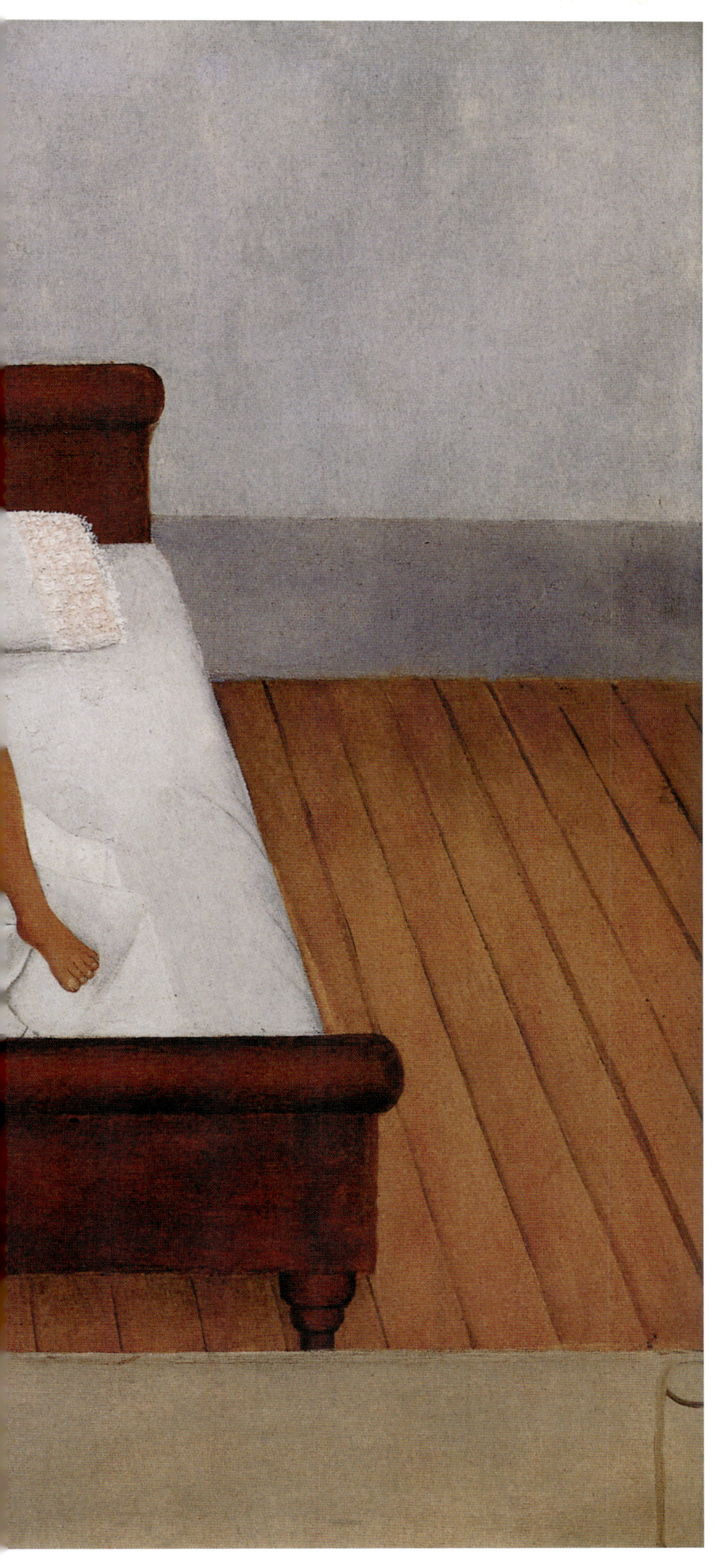

Page 66-67

My Birth, 1932. Oil on metal, 30.5 x 35 cm,

Private collection, USA.

Diego had accepted a commission from Detroit, Michigan in America's industrial heartland to paint a mural in the lobby of the Detroit Institute of Arts. He relished the idea of painting machines and assembly lines that, in his Marxist philosophy, relieved the masses of workers from the drudgery of repetitive toil, leaving them more time to begin the workers' revolution. Detroit represented the quintessential example of American capitalism, where the machine age met the proletariat, the perfect ground zero for the overthrow of the Imperialists who were buying his work. The Rivera entourage arrived by train on April 21, 1932. Frida was far less sanguine about the smoke-shrouded factory town on the Rouge River. She wrote to Doctor Eloesser that Detroit,

> *...seems like a shabby old village. I don't like it at all, but I am happy because Diego is working very happily here, and he has found a lot of material for his frescoes that he will do in the museum. He is enchanted by the factories, the machines, etc. like a child with a new toy.*[7]

Children were on Frida's mind. She had scarcely unpacked when she discovered she was pregnant. The idea both pleased and terrified her. She had always loved children and had a deep maternal instinct that she had lavished on Diego. But she feared her heredity and her ability to carry the pregnancy to term. Frida confided in Eloesser,

> *Do you think it would be more dangerous to abort than to have a child?... You better than anyone know what condition I am in. In the first place with this heredity* (Guillermo's epilepsy) *in my blood, I do not think the child will come out very healthy. In the second place I am not strong and the pregnancy will weaken me more. ...Here, I have no one to take care of me during and after the pregnancy, since poor Diego, no matter how much he wants to take care of me, cannot since he has in addition the problem of work and thousands of things...*[8]

Her conflicts were very real and if she had any idea that sharing a baby would put an end to Diego's affairs, she was probably wrong. He had already abandoned two children from a previous marriage and rarely saw the daughter born by Lupe Marin.

Page 69

Frida and the Cesarean Section, 1932.

Oil on canvas, 73 x 62 cm.

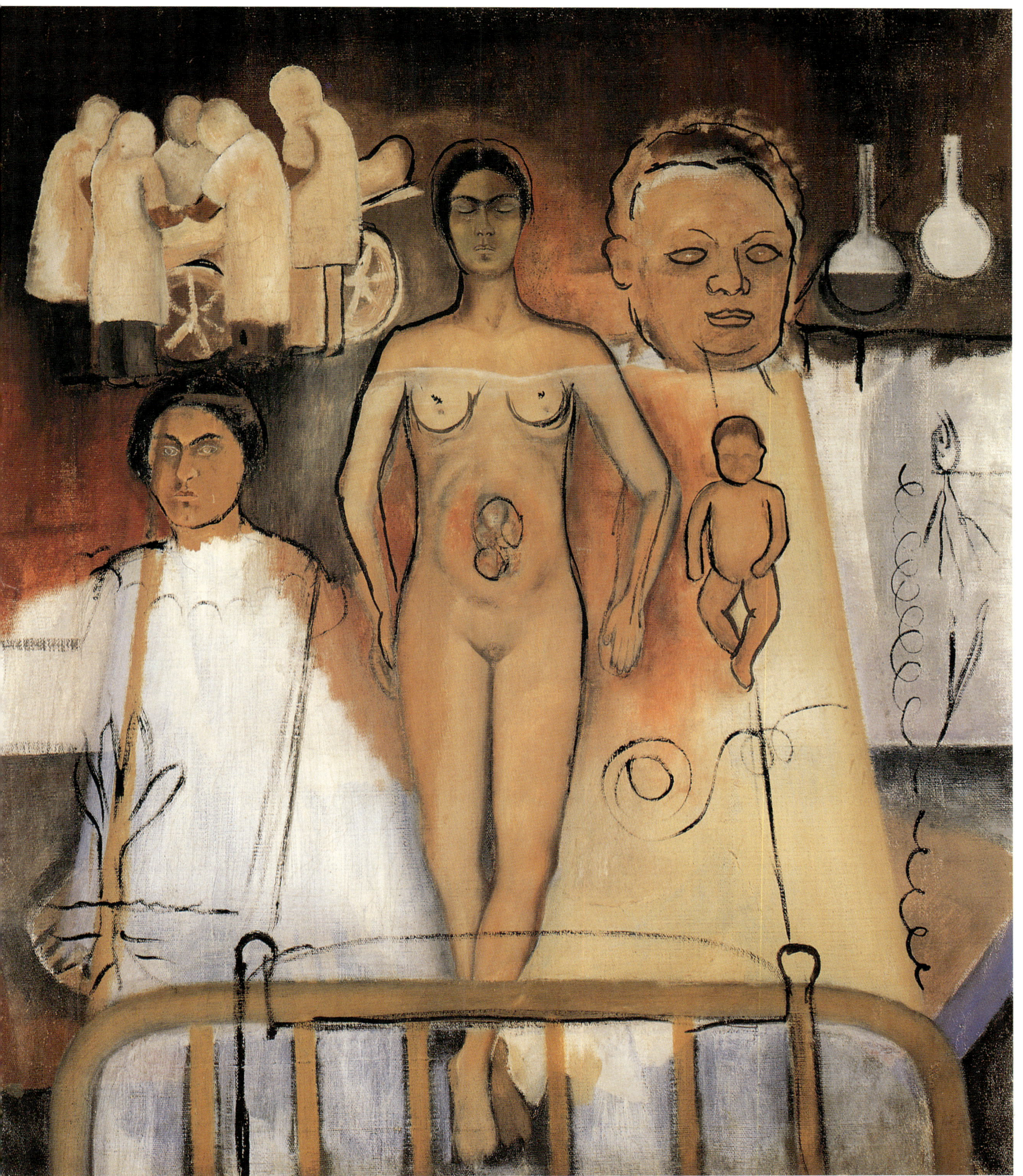

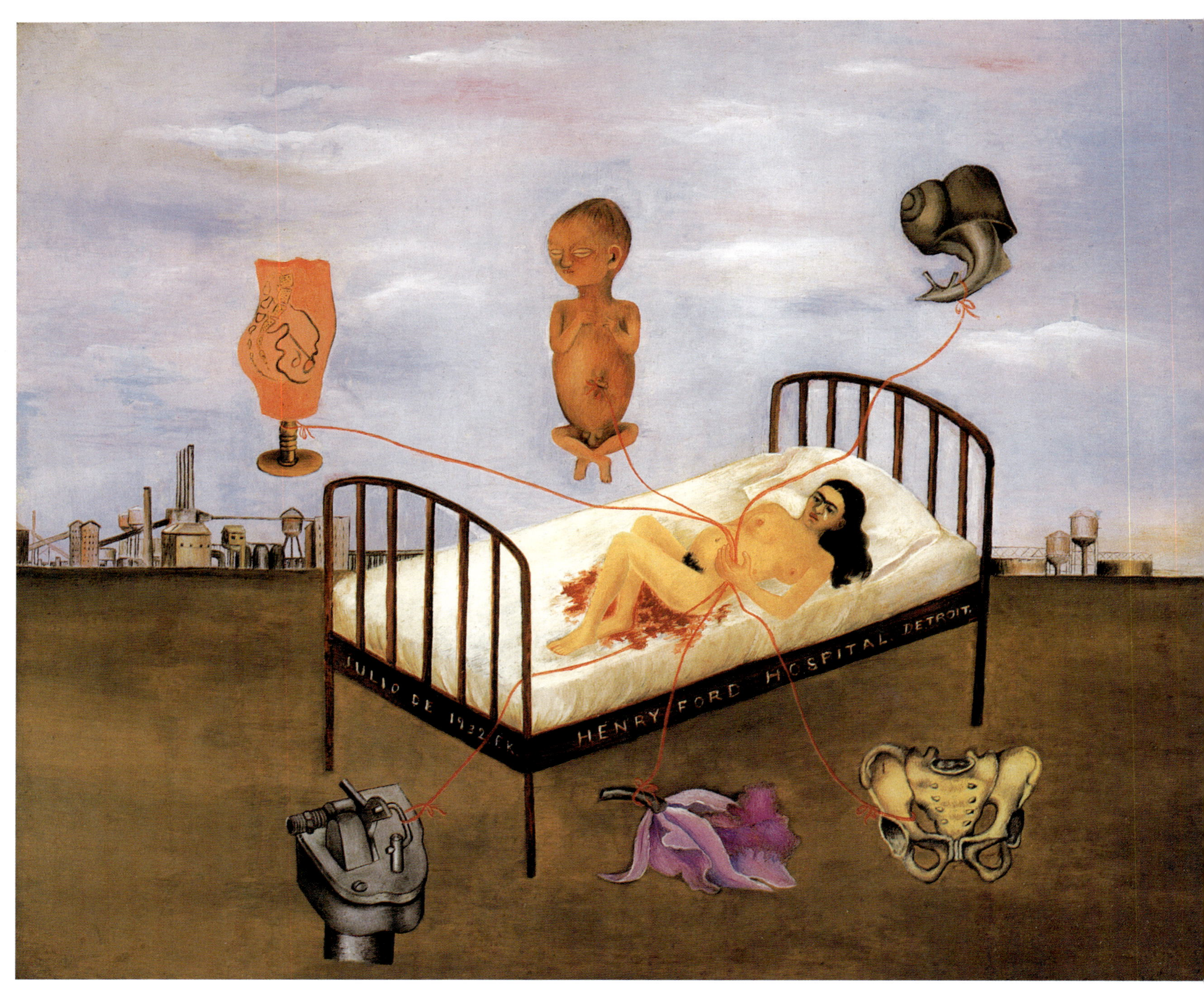
JULIO DE 1932 F.K.
HENRY FORD HOSPITAL. DETROIT.

She also consulted a doctor in Detroit who advised her that the child could be delivered by cesarean section. She decided to have the child. The Detroit doctor ordered bed rest. As usual, Frida ignored him, began driving lessons and made trips to the mural work site. She continued to trail Diego to the homes and parties of the Motor City's smokestack barons wearing her brightly colored *Tehuana* costumes with her arms, neck and fingers layered and looped with antique jewelry. Finding the gringos easily shocked, dull of wit and wrapped up in their pursuit of celebrity, she turned loose her more outrageous personality quirks. On her way into dinner on the arm of Henry Ford - a notorious anti-Semite - more than a few jaws dropped when Frida asked him, "Mr. Ford, are you Jewish?" The Wardell Hotel in which they were staying was restricted against Jews and when Diego told the hotel's management that he and Frida were Jewish, the restriction was immediately dropped.[9]

In the fourth month of her pregnancy, July 4, 1932, Frida miscarried. Lucienne Bloch, one of Diego's assistants and Frida's friend, discovered her early in the morning sitting in a pool of blood and screaming. She continued to hemorrhage on the way to the Henry Ford Hospital and spent much of the day disgorging clots of blood and tissue that had been her child.

"I wish I was dead!" she wailed in despair. "I don't know why I have to go on living like this!"[10]

Emotionally and physically drained, she fell back on her only consolation, her painting. She requested medical books for research pictures of embryos, and anatomy, but the doctors refused. Diego sneaked some books to her and she began to draw. As with the *Portrait of Luther Burbank* (p. 54), she turned her loneliness and depression into creative activity. Only this time, the subjects were far more personal and she scoured her emotions to tell her sad narrative.

Paintings and some lithographs were accomplished during her time in Detroit. When she was well enough to leave the hospital, Diego asked the New Workers School where he was working on a mural to set up a small studio for her that included lithography stones and a

Page 70

Henry Ford Hospital or *The Flying Bed*, 1932.

Oil on metal, 30.5 x 38 cm,

Museo Dolores Olmedo Patiño, Mexico City.

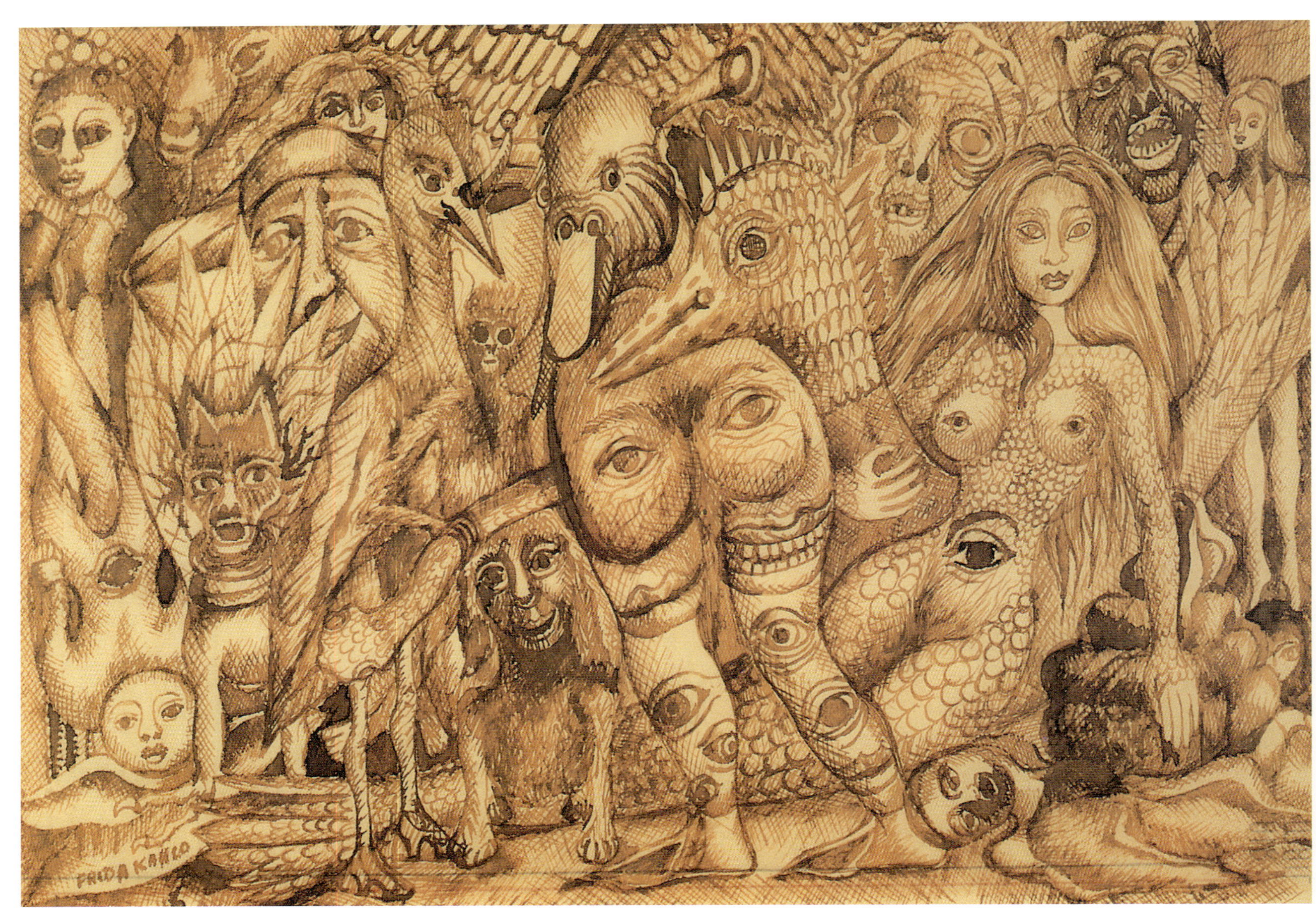

Page 72

Untitled (Drawing with Subject inspired by Eastern Philosophy), 1946.

Sepia ink on paper, 18 x 26.7 cm.

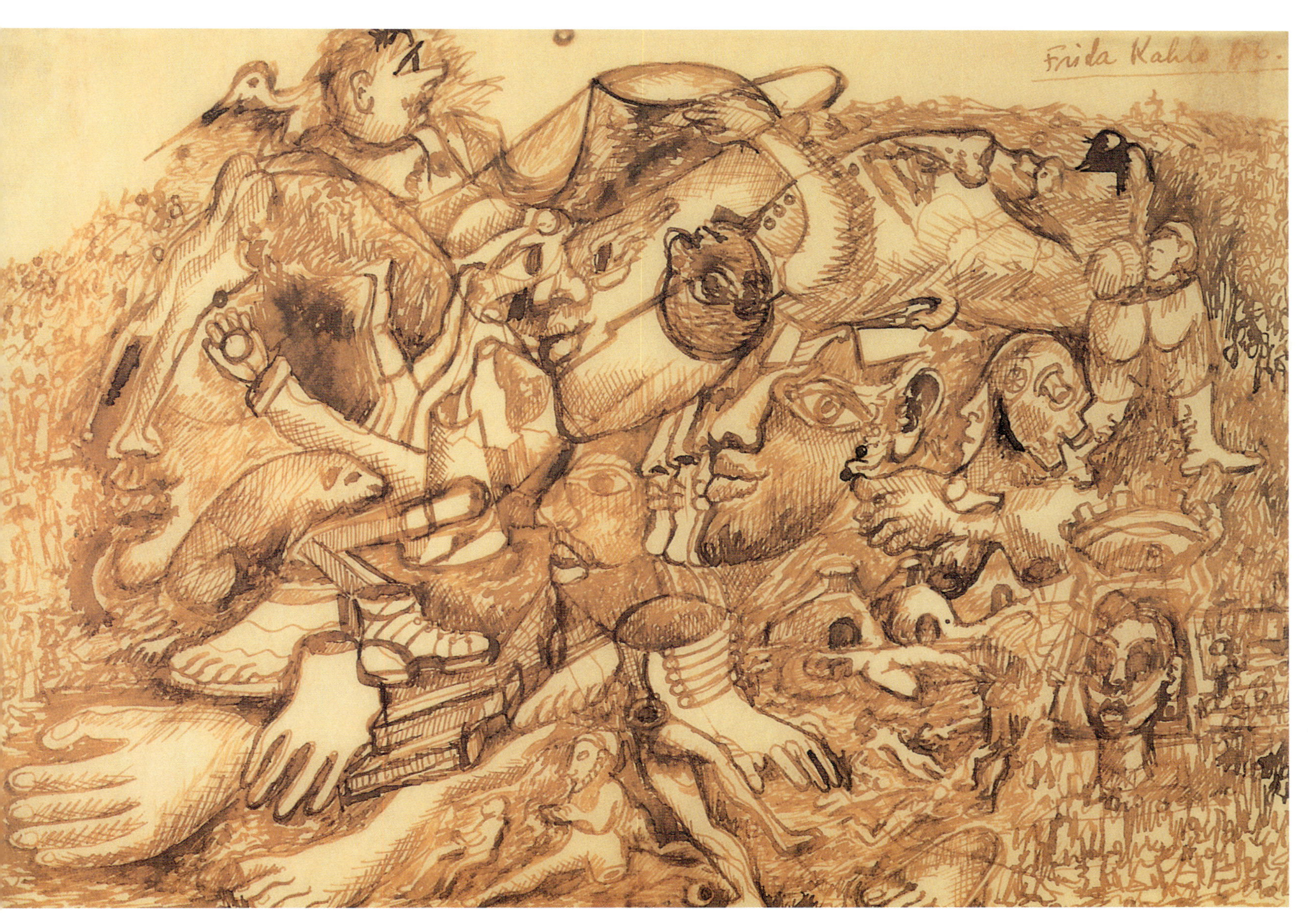

Page 73

Untitled (Drawing with Cataclysmic Theme), 1946.

Sepia ink on paper, 18 x 26.7 cm.

press. Her monochrome lithographs, *Frida and the Miscarriage*, resemble medical illustrations describing the steps that led to the event from sperm and eggs to zygote to fetus tied by its umbilical cord that twines around Frida's leg. Her eyes weep tears as does her vagina ending in a pile of clotted blood at her feet. The blood fertilizes some plants, recalling the Burbank portrait and the cycle of life. It is an analytical collection of images in a flat plane that are antiseptic and sting with their clean incisions. She found lithography unsatisfactory and these prints are the only examples of her work in that medium. The paintings: *Window Display in a Street of Detroit* (p. 50-51), *Henry Ford Hospital* (p. 70), *Self-Portrait on the Borderline Between Mexico and the United States,* and *My Birth* (p. 66-67), are quite something else.

As if the miscarriage was not sufficiently crushing, Frida received news from home that her mother was dying of cancer. Still healing from her trauma, Frida had to return to Coyoacan as soon as possible. There was no flight available and the phones to Mexico were temporarily down. She elected to make the trip by train and bus, an arduous journey for someone in good health. Diego insisted Lucienne Bloch accompany her. She arrived in Mexico on September 8 and her mother died on September 15, 1932. Frida remained with her father and her family and checked on the progress of the twin houses under construction until she became anxious to return to Diego. By October 21, she and Lucienne were back in Detroit and she learned that Diego had been offered another commission, this time to create a mural in the lobby of the RCA building in New York's Rockefeller Center. Following that, the 1933 World's Fair being held in Chicago wanted a mural on the theme of "machinery and industry."[11] More months would be spent in "Gringolandia". Diego worked himself to exhaustion to complete the Detroit project and had little time for her. Frida took up her brushes to restore her spirits.

To combat the silence of the hotel room, Frida endured a local news hen, Florence Davies, whose column *Girls of Yesteryear*, featured "*...visiting homes of interesting people.*" She showed up at Frida's room at the Wardell for a chat. Hayden Herrera, Frida Kahlo's definitive biographer, captured the scene where Frida holstered her acerbic wit and played the cheeky, but adoring wife for the newspaper's scribe. The column is headed: *Wife of Master Mural Painter Gleefully Dabbles in Works of Art.*

Page 75

Diego Rivera, *Retrato de la Señora Natasha Gelman (Portrait of Mrs Natasha Gelman)*, 1943.

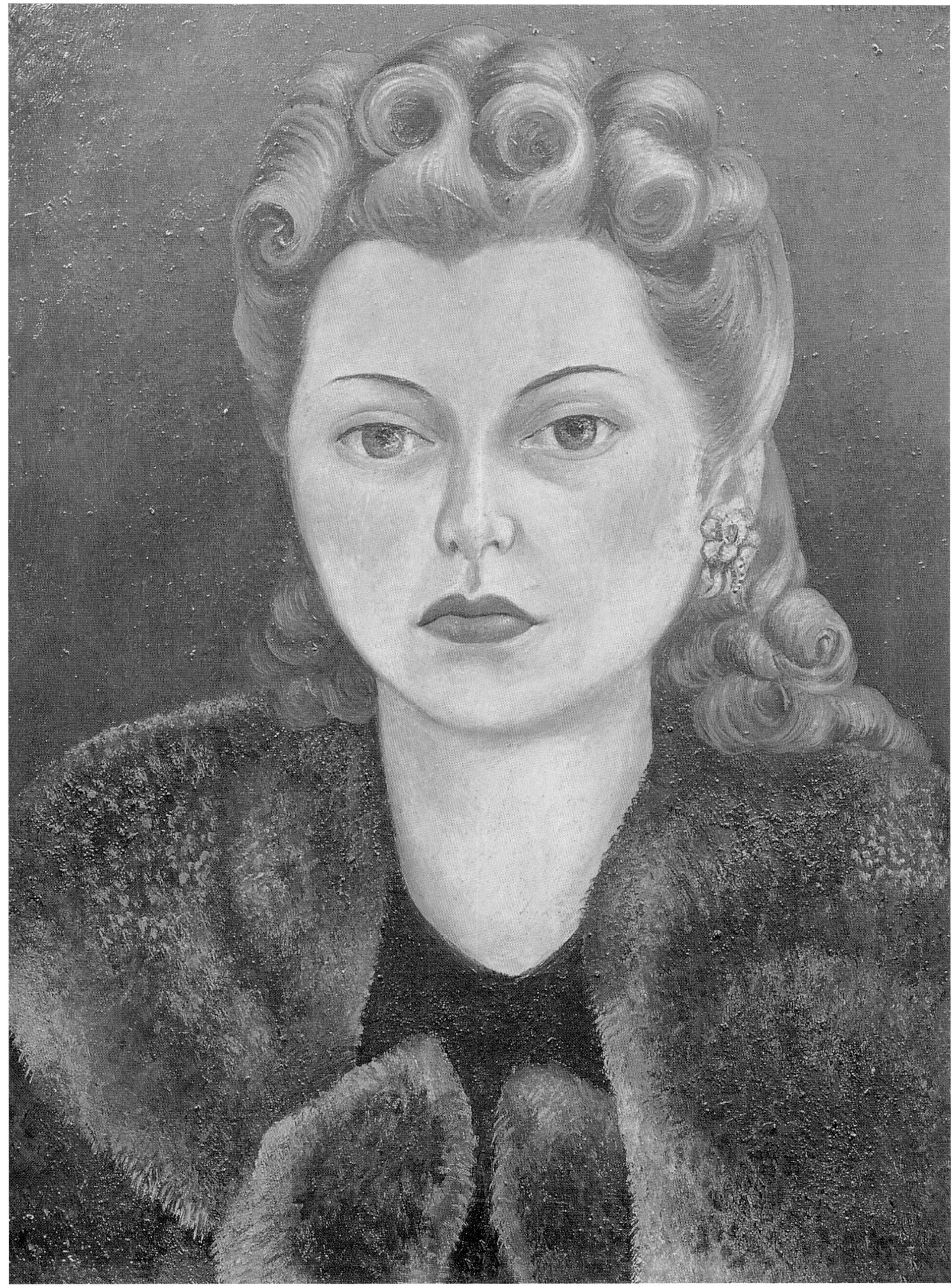

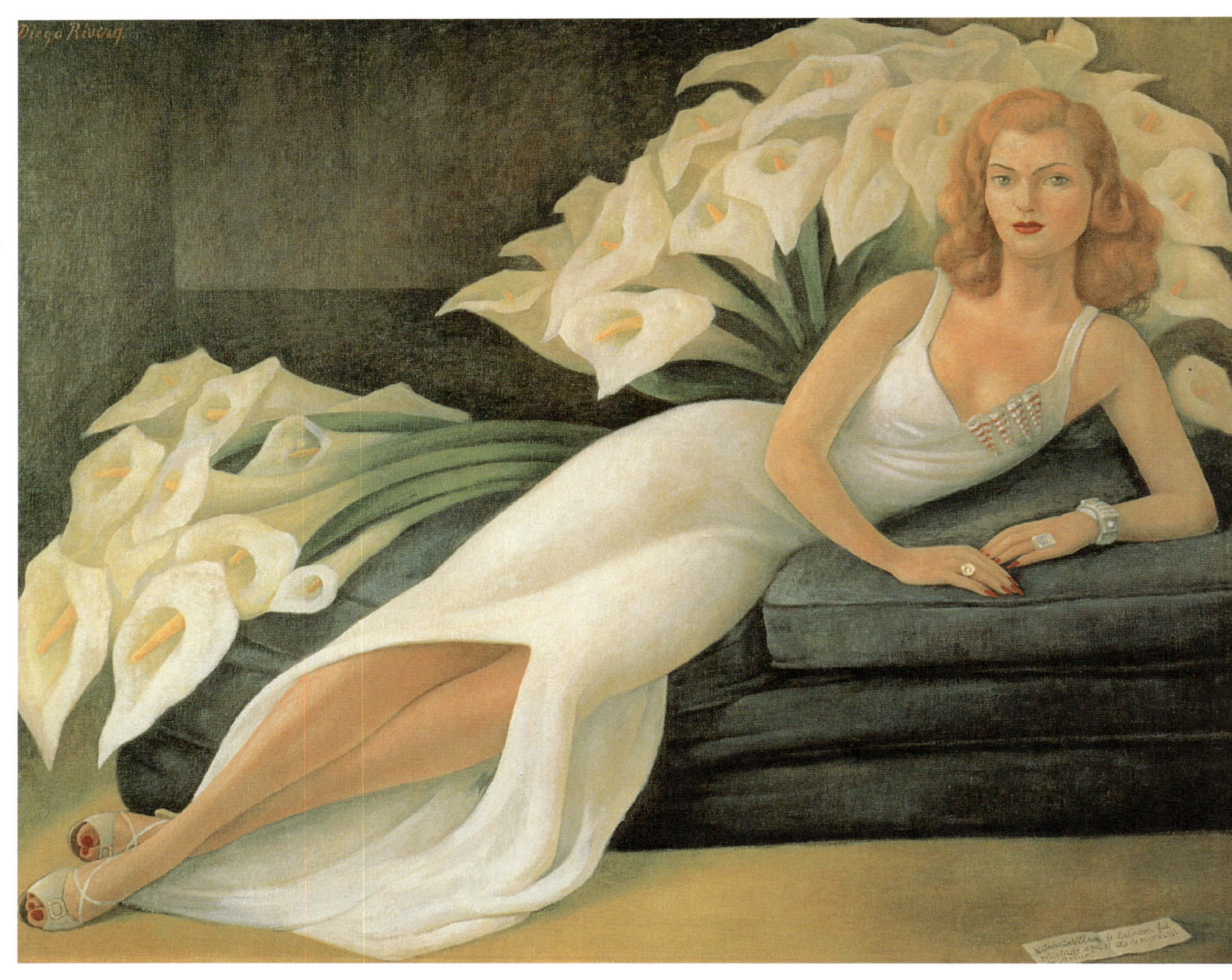
Diego Rivera

Davies wrote:

> *Carmen Frida Kahlo Rivera... is a painter in her own right, though very few people know it. "No," she explains, "I didn't study with Diego. I didn't study with anyone. I just started to paint." Then her eyes begin to twinkle. "Of course," she explains, "he does pretty well for a little boy, but it is I who am the big artist." Then the twinkles in both black eyes fairly explode into a rippling laugh... In Detroit she paints only because time hangs heavily on her hands during the long hours while her husband is at work in the court...*[12]

Even considering the gossipy nature of this "ladies' feature", Frida finally began emerging from "shy and retiring" to feel her wings as these few crumbs of recognition fell her way. While she shopped and had some good times with Lucienne, one by one exceptional paintings surfaced in her wake as reminders of deeper and darker feelings. One in particular, a *retablo* probably begun before she left for Mexico, is titled, *My Birth.* To more faithfully reproduce the *retablo*s that hang in Mexican churches and on which her narrative paintings are based, Diego suggested she paint on metal. And like the metal it is painted upon, *My Birth* is a cold, soulless evocation depicting Frida Kahlo's emergence into the world as her adult head is forced from her own womb, thrust out between splayed legs onto blood-soaked sheets. The mother's face is covered as though wrapped in a burial shroud. There is no one in attendance. It is a joyless birth.

My Birth returns the religious context that had been removed from *Portrait of Luther Burbank*, hanging a picture of the *Mater dolorosa*, a weeping virgin, above the bed in place of the shrouded face. But as one element is returned, another is taken away. Frida places the message banderole across the bottom of the painting that usually describes the event and offers a prayer to the virgin. This time, the scroll is blank. Who's to thank when one is constantly mis-treated by the fates?

In the work, *Henry Ford Hospital*, the city of Detroit clings to a distant horizon, an abstract industrial backdrop as a bed seems to levitate above a brown plain (the alternative name for this work is *The Flying Bed*). On the bed is a naked, weeping Frida with a sick, gray

Page 76

Diego Rivera, *Retrato de la Señora Natasha Gelman (Portrait of Mrs Natasha Gelman)*, 1943.

face, lying in a puddle of blood and tethered by red umbilical cords gathered in her hand at her swollen stomach to floating objects that circle her. A snail uncoils from its shell, her male fetus bobs above her like a grotesque balloon. Beneath the bed is a trodden flower and a misshapen pelvis. Around the edge of the bed is written the title, *Henry Ford Hospital* and the date, "July of 1932 F.K."

Self Portrait on the Borderline Between Mexico and the United States is a painting on metal plate, a visual joke that is both humorous and melancholy, depicting Frida dressed in a pink western confection with flounces and white gloves. She stands between depictions of the western industrial world and an ancient agrarian landscape steeped in ritual and tradition. Above the Mexican pyramids, the ancient Aztec sun and moon fight their never-ending cosmic battle. In one hand she holds a small Mexican flag as though waiting for a parade to pass. Her right hand holds an "inappropriate" cigarette. Flowers and plants grow from roots that dig deep into the soil of Mexico while industrial dirt offers a crop consisting of an electrical generator, a light bulb and a radiant heater. An American flag rises from Ford's smokestacks as a chorus line of cyclopean roof-top ventilators marches past. Her conflicts are obvious in this work that owes much to Diego's crowded muralist style, but she speaks with her own unique voice.

A store window on a Detroit street, discovered by Frida and Lucienne on a shopping trip for sheet metal, becomes a curious slice of life as *Window Display in a Street in Detroit.* This funky collection of unrelated objects captured her interest as an assemblage more "real" than much of the artfully manipulated work she had seen in galleries. When she described it to him with such excitement, Diego suggested she paint it. The result is a blend of painterly technique and naïve folk art. George Washington peers at us from his picture frame festooned in red, white and blue and resting on a red, white and blue bit of carpet. He's joined by a ceramic eagle plaque and a fuzzy lion growling at the window pane. Behind them a plaster horse is frozen *en passant* in mid stride. In the rear, we see the store is abandoned, ready for redecoration with paint pots, a stepladder and the painter's gloves. The work is a captured moment of juxtaposed objects in the fashion of Edward Weston's photographic images, a complex composition that would be damaged if one element was removed. Frida's

Page 79

Diego Rivera, *Vendedora de alcatraces* (*Calla lily vendor*), 1943.

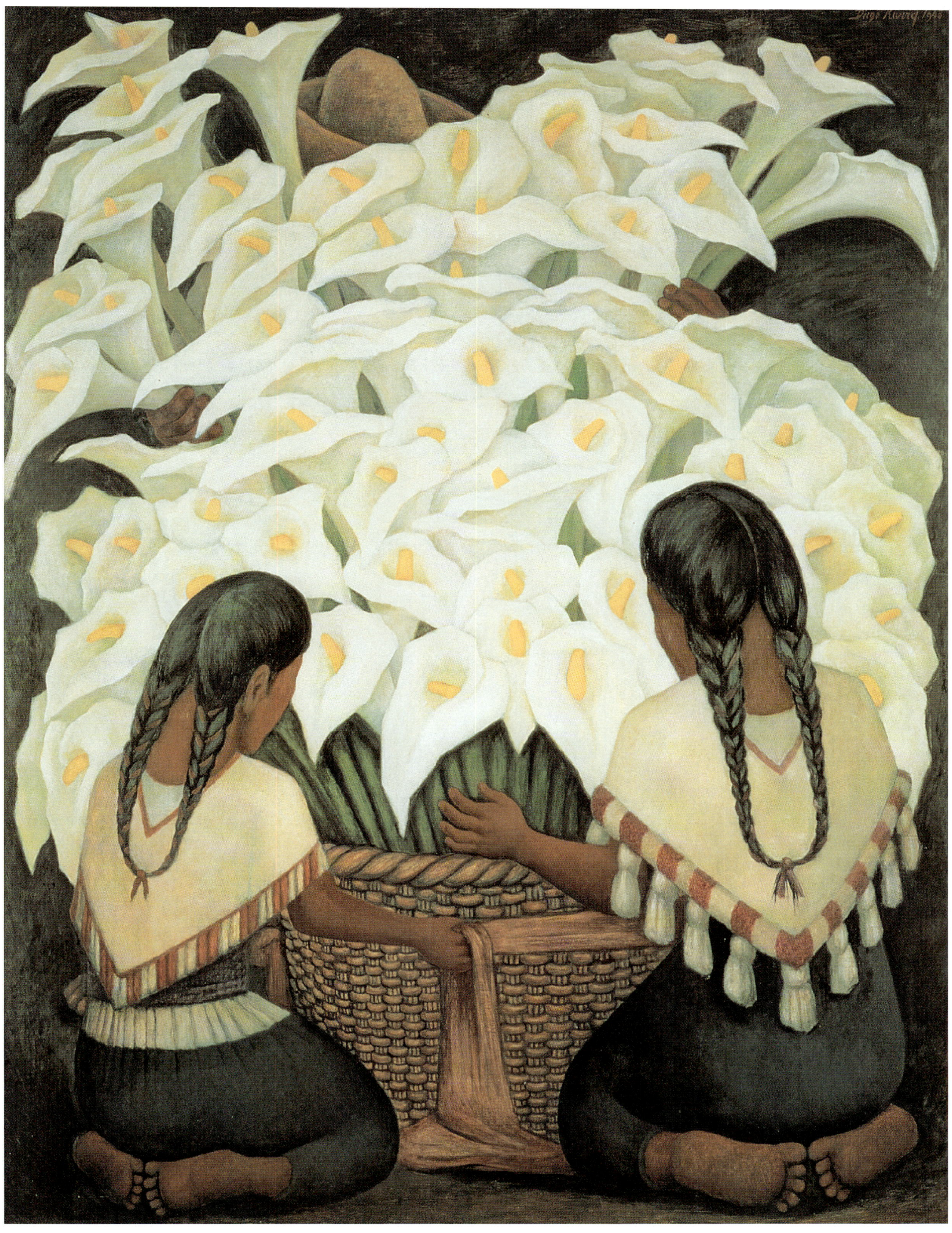

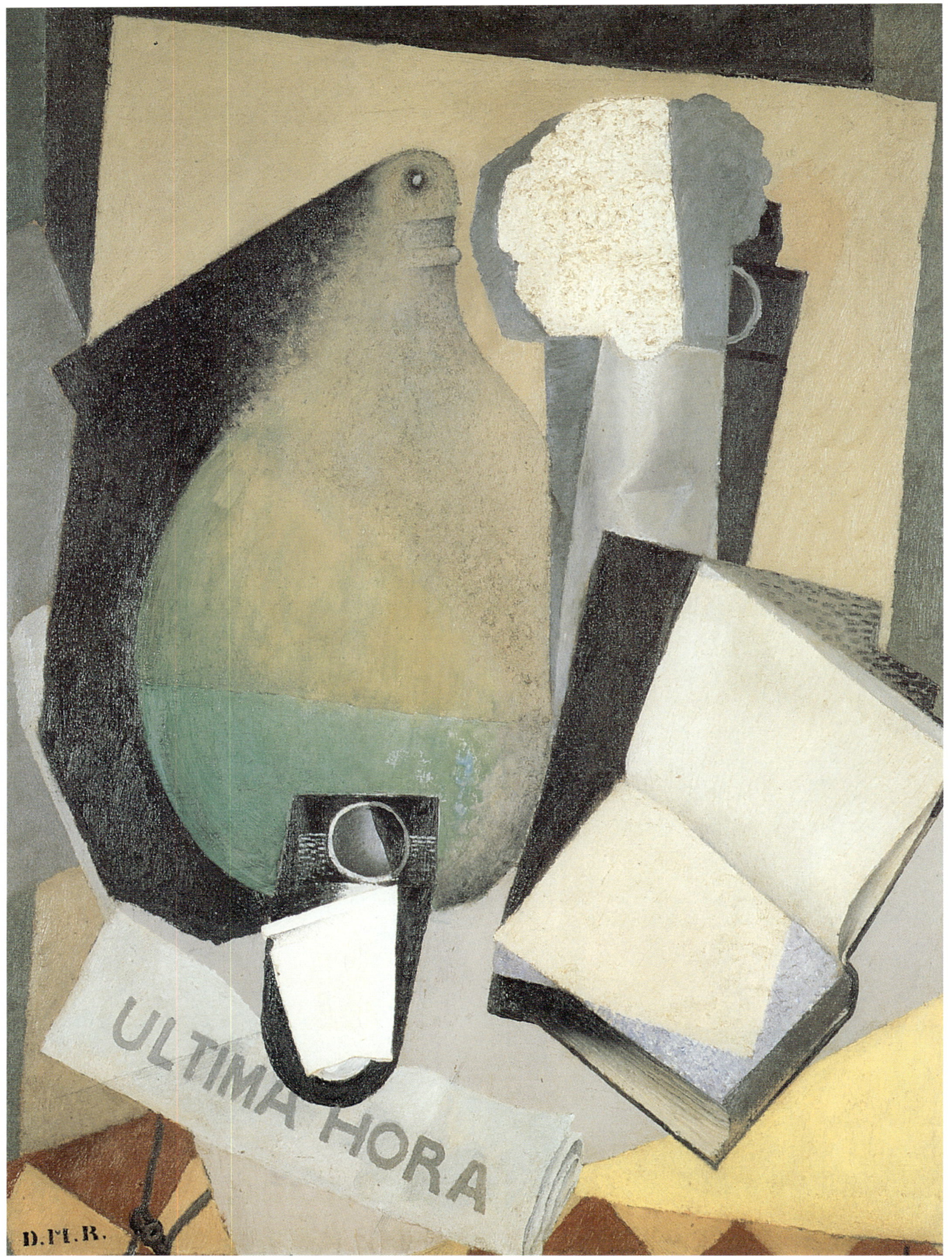
ULTIMA HORA
D.M.R.

eye for found compositions was as keen as her wanderings through the halls of her own fertile imagination. Her bags were packed by the time Diego finished the Detroit mural commission. To his delight, no sooner had the murals been unveiled than the good burghers of the Motor City let fly their outrage in the local press.

"Communistic!"

"A heartless hoax!"

"A travesty on the spirit of Detroit!"

"Hose it off the walls!"

While the protectors of American morality and "right thinking" formed up committees, groups of workers from the auto plants detailed shifts of volunteer guards to protect the murals. Debate caromed back and forth in the press. Exhausted but happy, Diego Rivera, his "dabbler" wife, and their assistants were gone within a week. The final payment check warmed *Panzon's* pocket as the Pullman cars rattled behind their locomotive speeding east toward New York City.

---

[1] Alcantara and Egnolff *Frida Kahlo and Diego Rivera*, Prestel Press, NY, 1999, p. 30

[2] Ibid., Alcantara and Egnolff, p. 35

[3] Weston, Edward, *Daybooks, "California,"* vol. 2. pp 198-199

[4] Ibid., Rummel, p.84

[5] Ibid., Tibol, Raquel pp. 62-63

[6] Ibid., Aleantara and Egnolff, p. 40

[7] Ibid., Rummel, pp. 91-92

[8] Kahlo, Frida, Letters of Frida Kahlo, compiled by Martha Zamora, San Francisco, Chronicle Books, 1995

[9] Ibid., Alcantara and Egnolff, p. 41

[10] Ibid., Rummel, p. 93

[11] Ibid., Herrera, Hayden, p. 159

[12] Ibid., Herrera, Hayden, p. 226

Page 80

Diego Rivera, *Ultima hora (The last hour)*, 1915.

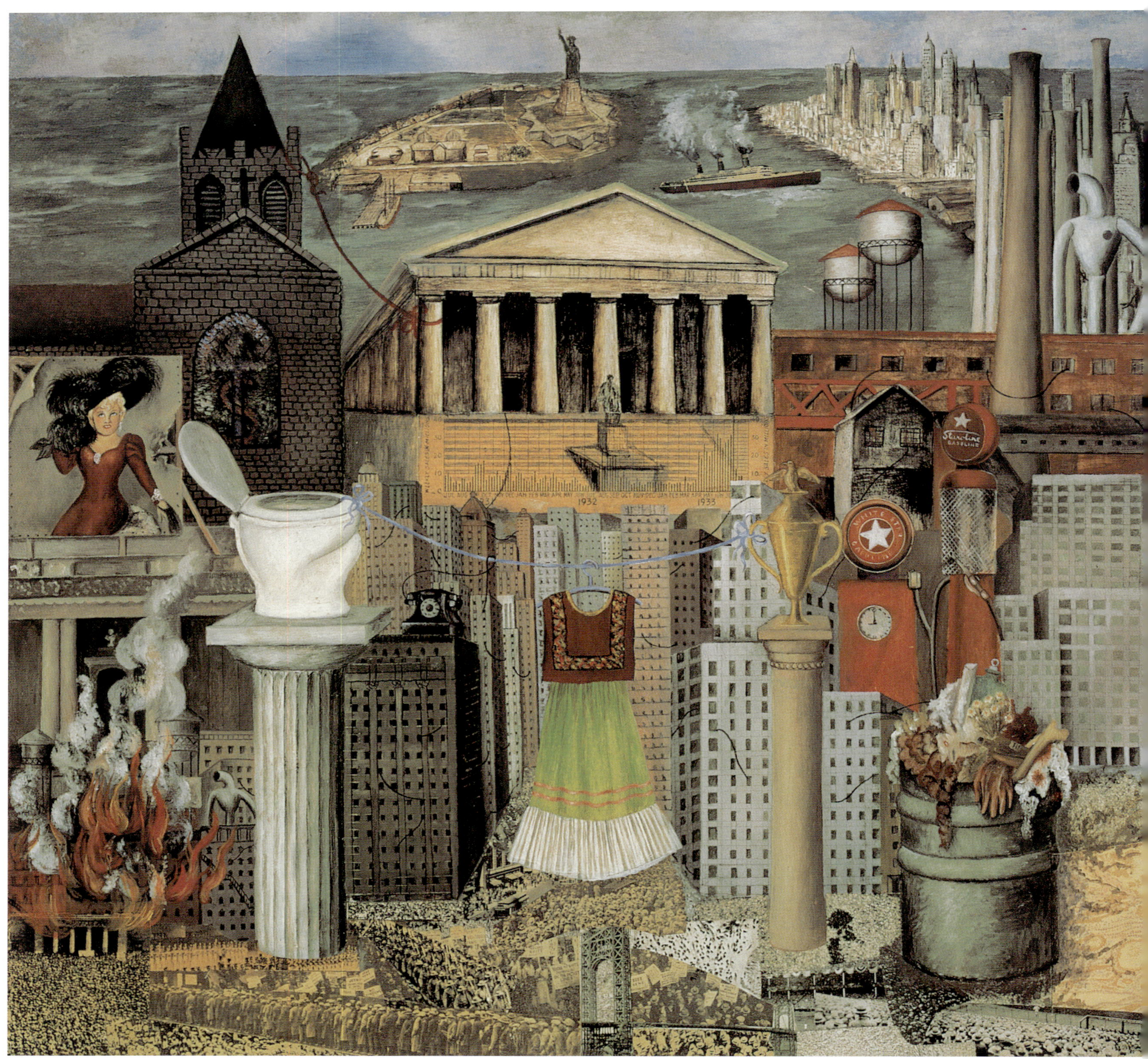
1932
1933

Affair of the Art

New York was in the freezing grip of winter when the Riveras finally unpacked their bags in a suite high above downtown Manhattan in the Barbizon-Plaza Hotel. There was no time to waste setting up scaffolding in the RCA Building lobby and getting his assistants started with preparation of the wall for Nelson Rockefeller's paean to *Man at the Crossroads*. Chicago was waiting for the start of their World's Fair mural all about "man and machinery" titled *Forge and Foundry*. Frida set up camp in a section of the lobby cordoned off for workers and assistants while the public paid money for tickets to come and watch Diego at work. She began bringing lunches as usual, but Diego had no appetite while he labored. An annoying aspect of his work was the constant harping of the Communist Party that he was selling out himself and the Communist cause to these rich capitalists. And yet, Karl Marx and his demagogue inheritors had no more ardent spokesman than Diego Rivera - except maybe his equally impassioned wife, Frida Kahlo.

However much she shook her fist, or sang verses of *The Internationale*, Frida did like the fruits of capitalism and while Diego dragged himself back to the hotel at the end of each session, Frida shopped and hung out with friends from their last visit. She rarely painted, but did dab away at one work that remained unfinished when they left New York for Mexico in December, 1933. The oil and collage is titled, *My Dress Hangs There* (p. 82).

Like her *Self-Portrait on the Borderline between Mexico and the United States,* this tightly packed composition is an example of her dark humor, only this time, it is *sans* Frida. She appears *in absentia*, represented by one of her *Tehuana* dresses suspended on a hanger that dangles from a blue ribbon tied between a gilded loving cup and a flush toilet with the seat up balancing atop a Greek column. From gasoline pumps to Wall Street to a church spire complete with dollar-sign stained glass window, this work chides everything American. A photo of marching military men heads toward a line of unemployed,

Page 82
My Dress Hangs There or *New York*, 1933.
Oil and collage on board, 46 x 50 cm,
Hoover Gallery San Francisco, Bequest of Dr. Leo Eloesser.

shuffling toward a soup kitchen somewhere in the concrete canyons that stare back with their rows and rows of dead-eye windows. Manhattan curves away in the distance, Lady Liberty waves her torch at a departing cruise liner and a giant telephone sits atop a skyscraper. It is a masterful hodge-podge that sums up Frida's deep set prejudices against her "Gringolandia" host. Only her dress remains as if it was left in the hotel room closet when the Riveras checked out.

As the RCA Building mural proceeded along and Frida amused herself enjoying Tarzan movies, dozing at classical concerts and receiving the press peering from under a bed sheet sucking lasciviously on a long piece of peppermint candy, word began to leak out that Diego's version of *Men at the Crossroads Looking with Hope and High Vision to the Choosing of a New and Better Future* had a Red in it. Though the sketches had been approved, somehow the sponsors and young Nelson Rockefeller had missed a portrait among the pantheon of faces that gradually took on the likeness of every capitalist's nightmare, Vladimir Ilyich Lenin.

As if gazing on that bearded and balding Medusa could cause brain fever, ticket sales were cut off, the mural was screened from public view and Rockefeller insisted that Rivera alter the portrait. Not only did Diego refuse, he declared he wanted to finish the work by May Day, the celebration of the Russian Revolution. In a conciliatory move, however, Diego did offer to balance the head of Lenin with a head of Abraham Lincoln of the same size. Shortly thereafter a squad of security guards and the building's rental manager clattered across the lobby's travertine floor, stopped all work on the mural, handed over the balance of money due for the completed mural and bundled Rivera and his band of revolutionaries from the sanctity of Rockefeller Center. A hew and cry went up to save the mural. Picketing and counter-picketing stopped traffic outside the RCA Building. Artists, intellectuals, political gadflies, pundits, powerful panjandrums, and newspaper editorialists jumped into the war of words. Diego, with the check in his pocket, enjoyed the flap right up until he received a phone call from Chicago canceling the *Forge and Foundry* mural. The Windy City's merchant princes and hog butchers wanted nothing to do with any hint of rabble-rousing or mutterings among the Depression-pinched working class. Diego's grand design for

Page 85

Diego Rivera, *El curandero (The healer)*, 1943.

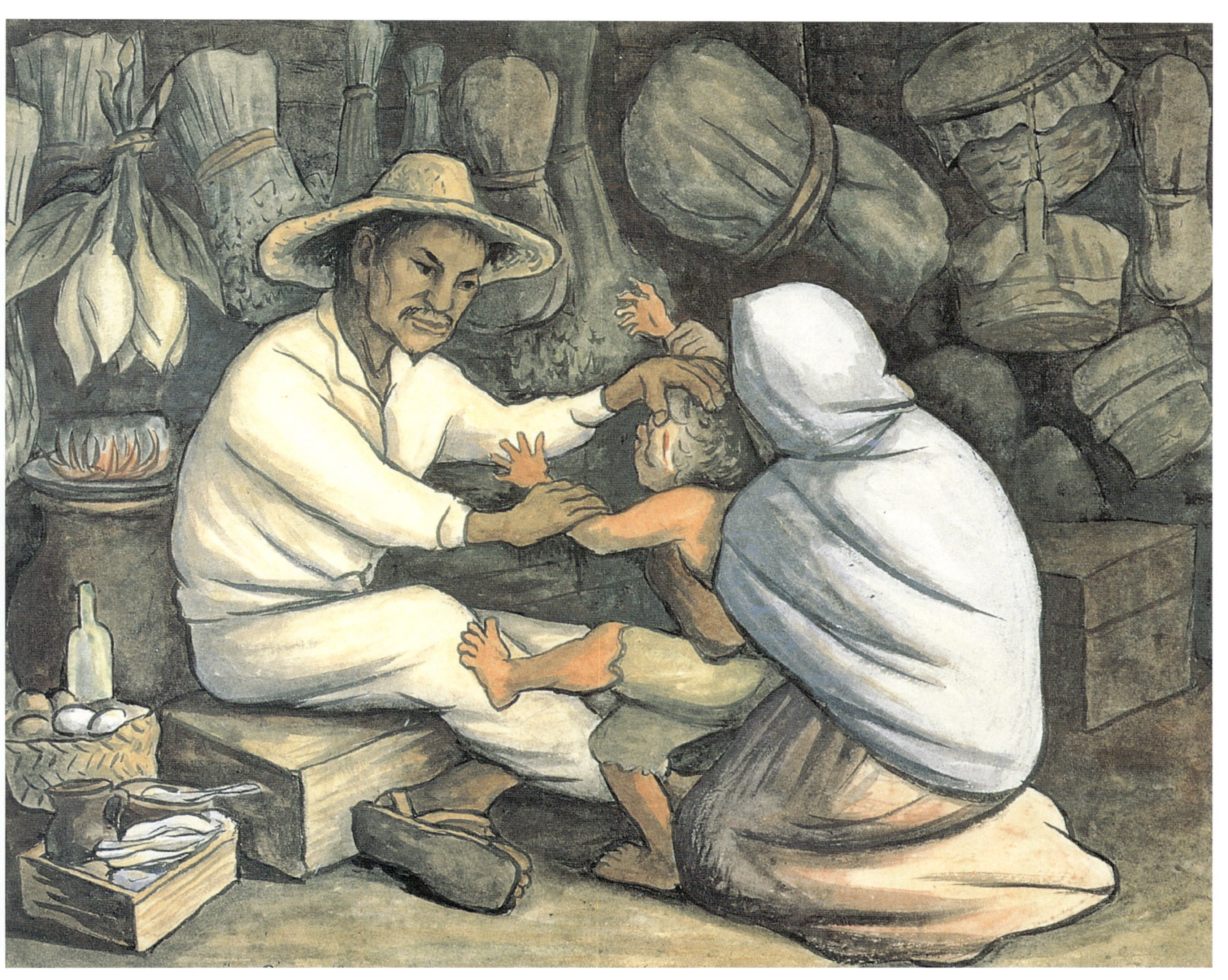

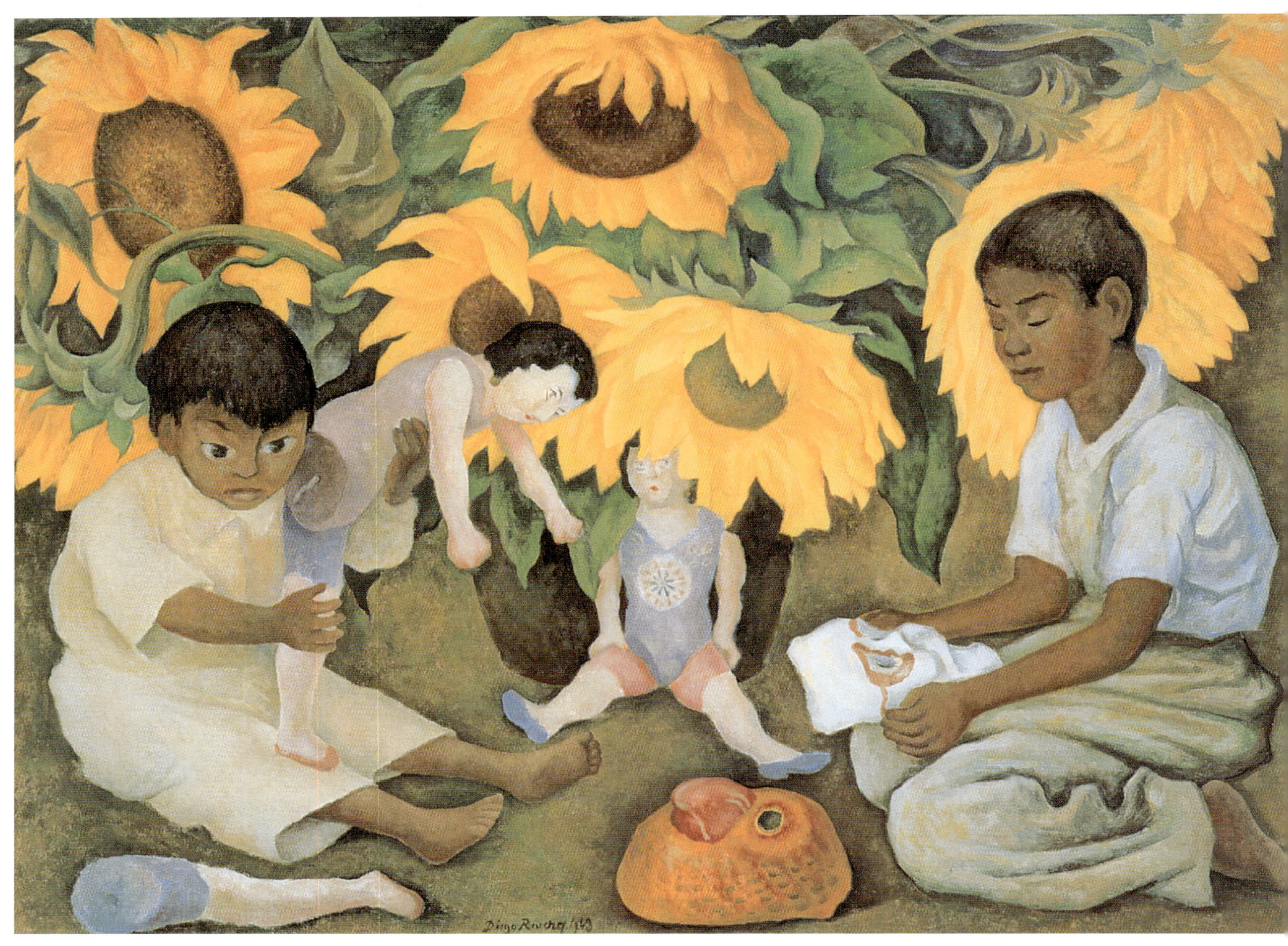
Diego Rivera 1943

establishing the muralist movement in the U.S. as a force for social change began crumbling. Very soon after work stopped on the RCA mural, the wall on which it was painted began crumbling under the bite of jackhammers and chisels, crashing to the lobby floor in jagged chunks and swirls of plaster dust.

Defiant, Rivera determined to spend every cent of Rockefeller's money slapping up free murals on the walls of the Free Worker's School and smaller panels to decorate the Union Square offices of the New York Trotskyites. He managed to blow through the capitalist cash by the end of the year.

In public, Frida spoke to the press,

> *The Rockefellers knew quite well the murals were to depict the revolutionary point of view – that they were going to be revolutionary paintings... They seemed very nice and understanding about it and always very interested, especially Mrs. Rockefeller...*[1]

During the summer of 1933, Frida created *Self-Portrait with Necklace.* This oil on metal head-and-shoulders painting is an assertive self presentation. We are looking at Frida the artist, confident and open to whatever might be in her future. Seventy years later, this picture would grace a United States thirty-seven cent commemorative stamp.

In her private letters and among close friends, she condemned the "sullen" American *cabrones* (bastards) and their hypocritical posturing. But despite the fist-shaking over his work, Diego liked America and the American bohemians and intellectuals who championed his painting and iconoclastic spirit. He also liked what his idolatry purchased in a society that could afford him despite the crushing Depression. He didn't want to go back to Mexico. Frida thought of nothing else. He had gone through their money and they were broke. After many rows and lack of any gainful employment in the U.S., the Riveras accepted boat tickets from their friends and departed with empty pockets on December 20, 1933 on the *Oriente* via Cuba to Vera Cruz.

Page 86

Diego Rivera, *Girasoles (Sunflowers)*, 1943.

Page 88

Self-Portrait, 1948.

Oil on masonite, 50 x 39.5 cm,

Private collection, Mexico City.

Page 89

Self-Portrait with Necklace, 1933.

Oil on metal, 34.5 x 29.5 cm,

Collection Jacques and Natasha Gelman,

Mexico City.

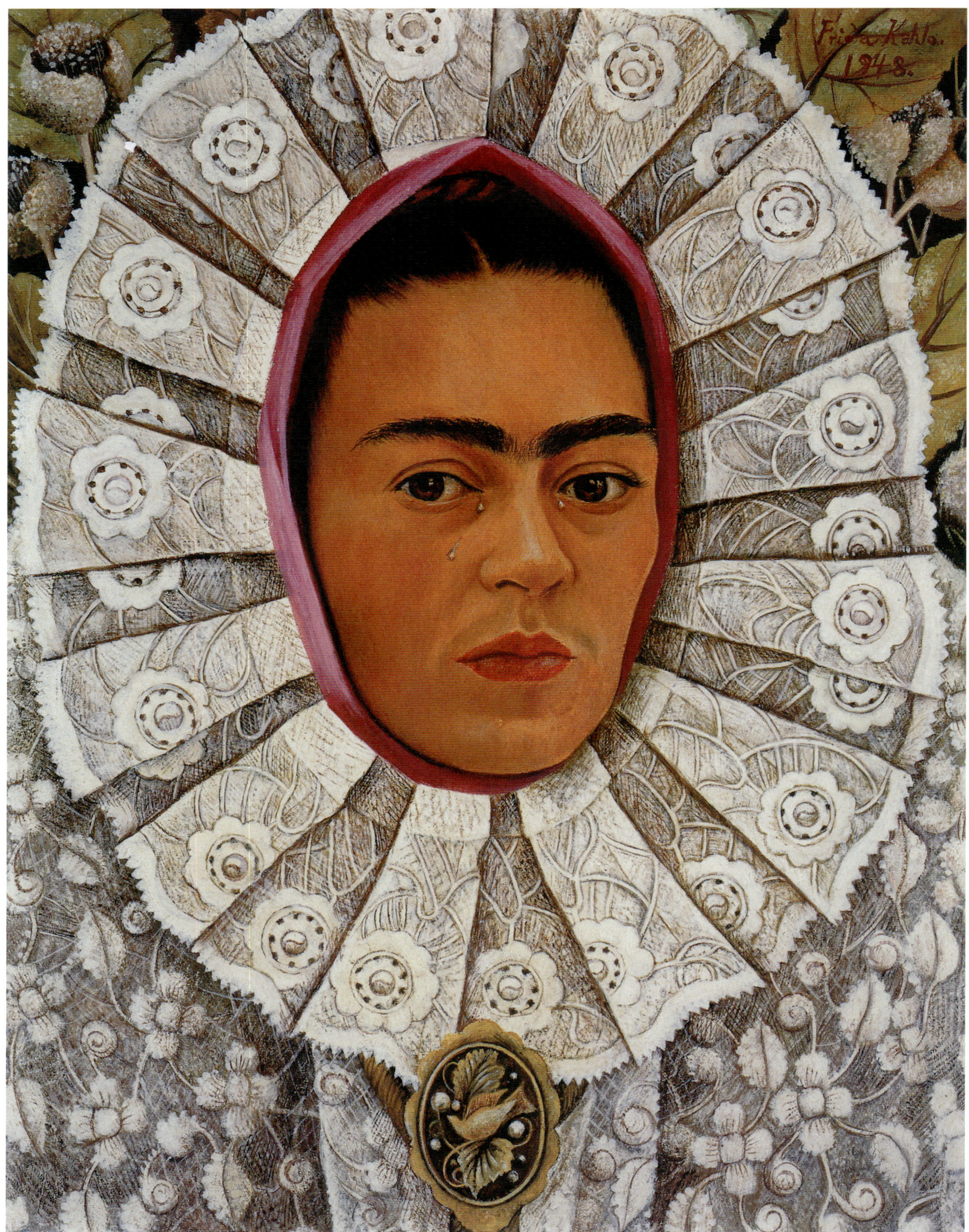
Frida Kahlo.
1948.

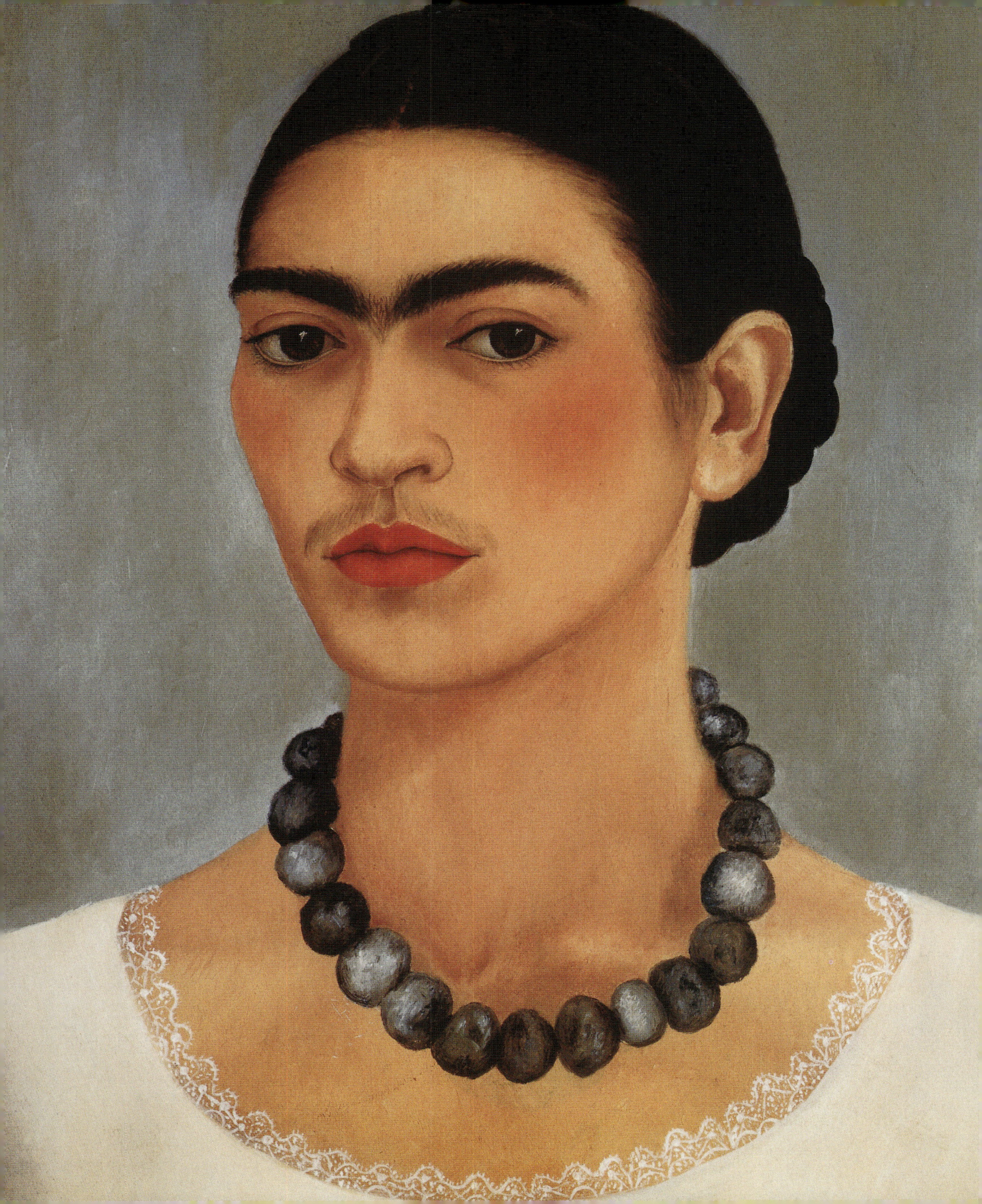

On returning, they moved into the dual house Diego had commissioned at the corner of Palmas and Altavista in the Mexico City suburb of San Angel. The two houses, joined by a footbridge across their second story, became an ironic portrayal of their relationship. The houses were a pair of Bauhaus cubes, his pink and larger, hers smaller and blue. While he saw the design as a bestowed recognition of her independence, she saw it as his backing away from her assertiveness. In either case, considering their relationship was in tatters, they both appreciated having their own spaces. She plunged into a spate of decorating. The ground floor was a garage while the first floor was the living space with a dining room, living room, and kitchen. A spiral staircase led up to her bedroom, bathroom and studio - a curious design choice considering her continued infirmities, often requiring her to employ crutches or a cane to get around. Through 1934, the studio went virtually unused except to finish her painting, *My Dress Hangs There* (p. 82), begun in New York.

In the big pink house, Diego must still have been feeling the disappointment of losing his American mural commissions. Prior to returning to his murals at the National Palace in Mexico City, he began making sketches of Cristina Kahlo, Frida's younger sister by 11 months. The two sisters had always been close, especially during Frida's confinements for months on end. Cristina was as soft, pliable, feminine and delicate as Frida was assertive and aggressive around men and her pals. Cristina had wed, but her husband had abandoned her and their two children. The two women complemented each other, but Cristina became Diego's favorite model, her Rubenesque nude body appearing in the hall of honor in the Secretariat of Health as the figures "Knowledge" and "Life". Not too long after arriving back in Mexico, Rivera began - or possibly intensified - a destructive affair with Cristina.

Frida knew the signs that Diego was once again involved with someone else, but when the "someone" turned out to be Cristina, Frida was at first crushed and then enraged. She had been betrayed by the two people closest to her. She locked the door to her side of the foot bridge. In a fit of anger, she chopped off her long hair and shoved her *Tehuanan* dresses, skirts and blouses into the closet. About this same time, in 1934, her health took a downward spiral. Severe pains sent her into the hospital for an appendectomy, and in the

Page 91

Self-Portrait dedicated to Marte R. Gómez,

1946.

Pencil on paper, 38.5 x 32.5 cm.

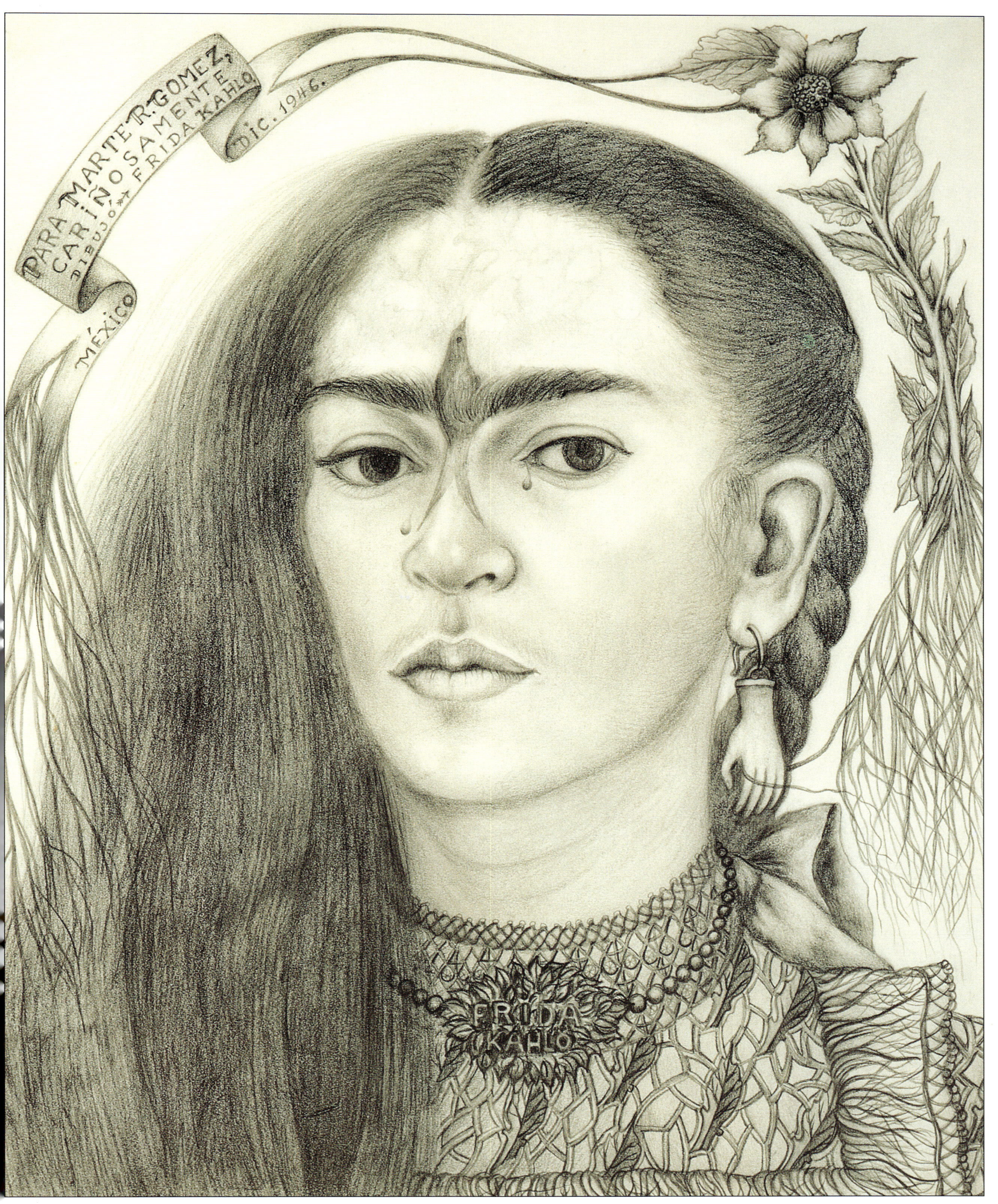
PARA MARTE R. GOMEZ,
CARIÑOSAMENTE
DIBUJO FRIDA KAHLO
Dic. 1946.
MÉXICO
FRIDA
KAHLO

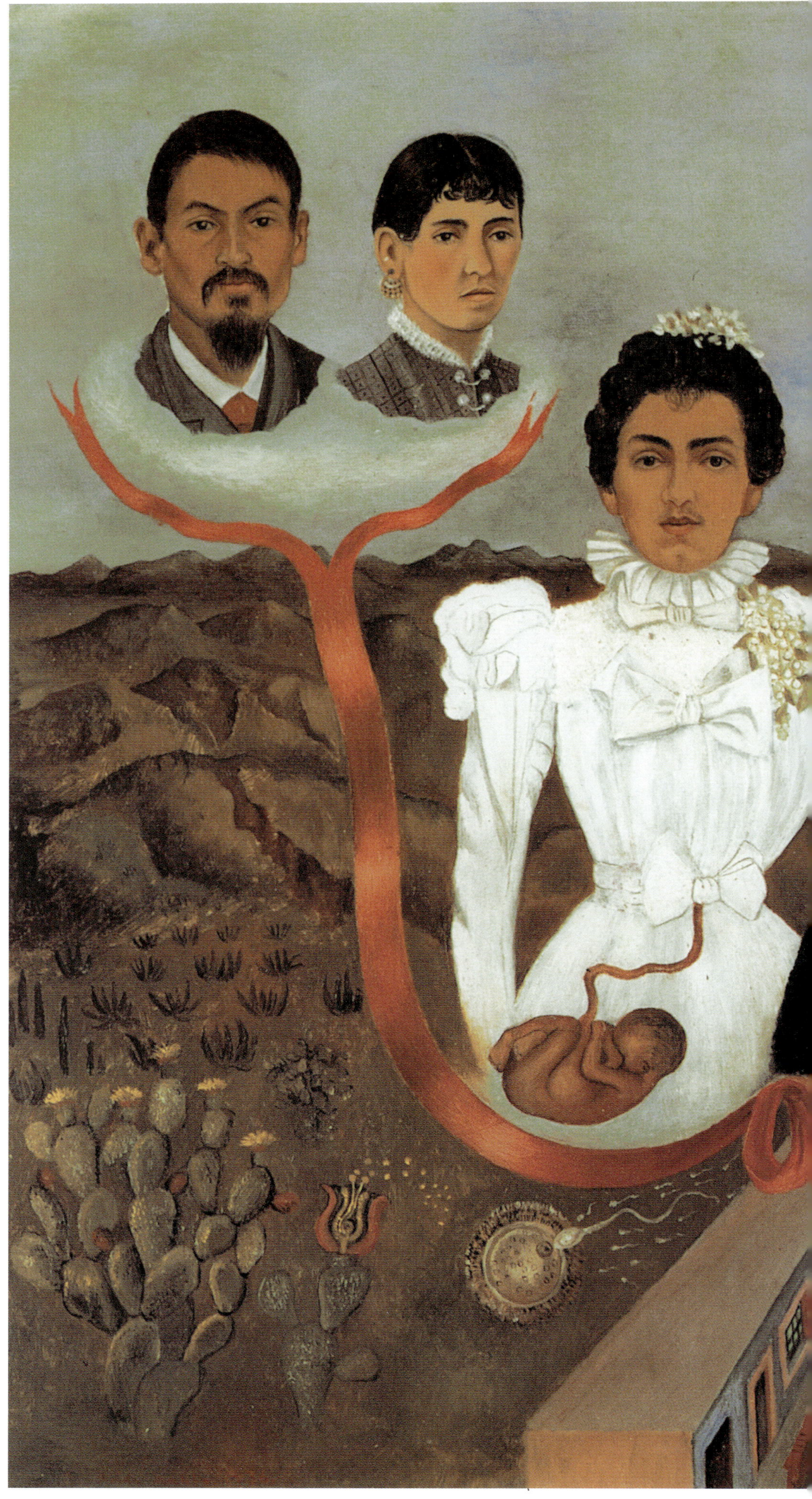

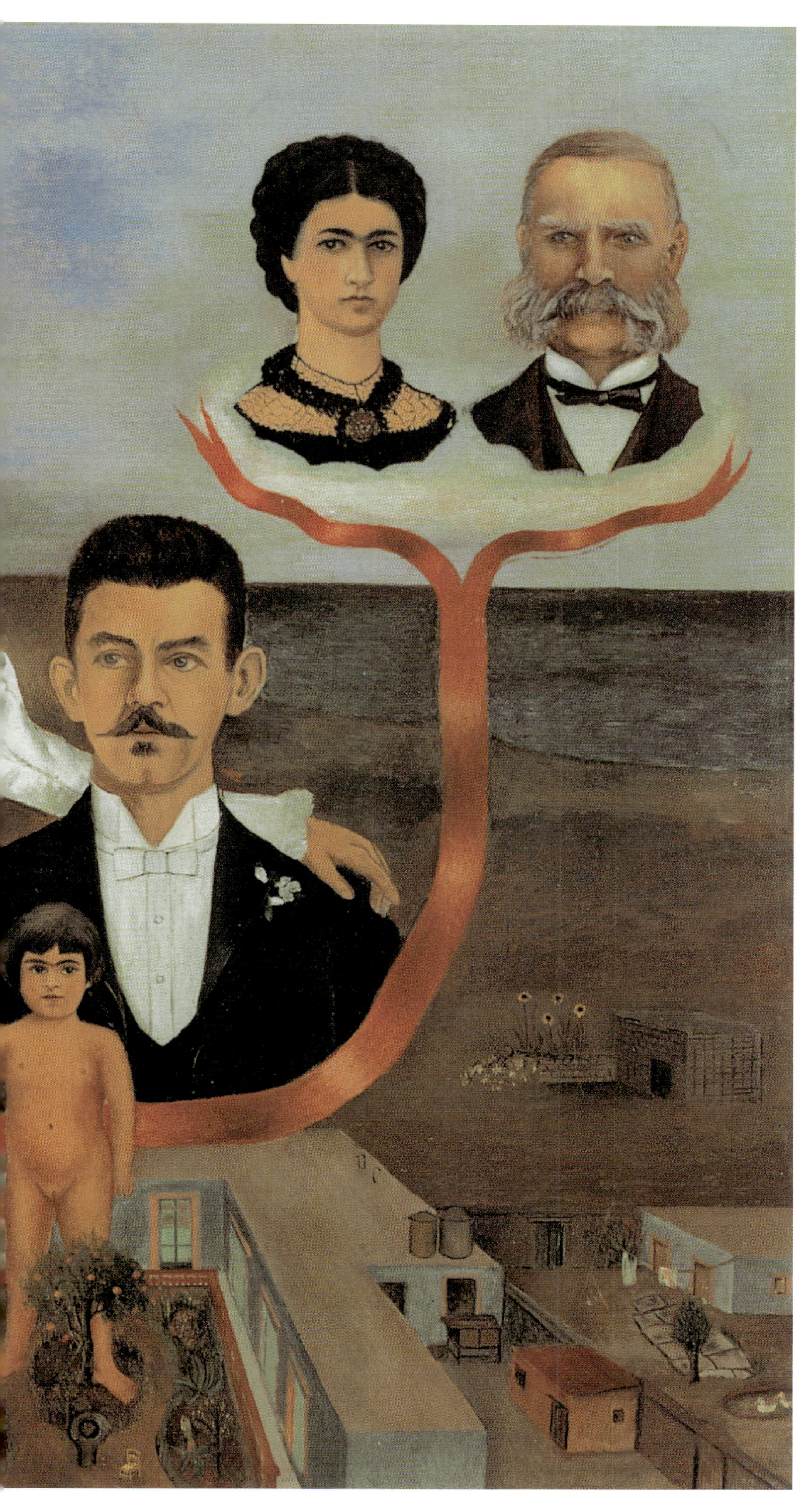

Page 92-93

My Grandparents, My Parents and I, 1936.

Oil and tempera on metal, 30.7 x 34.5 cm,

The Museum of Modern Art, donation by

Allan Roos, M.D. and B. Roos, New York.

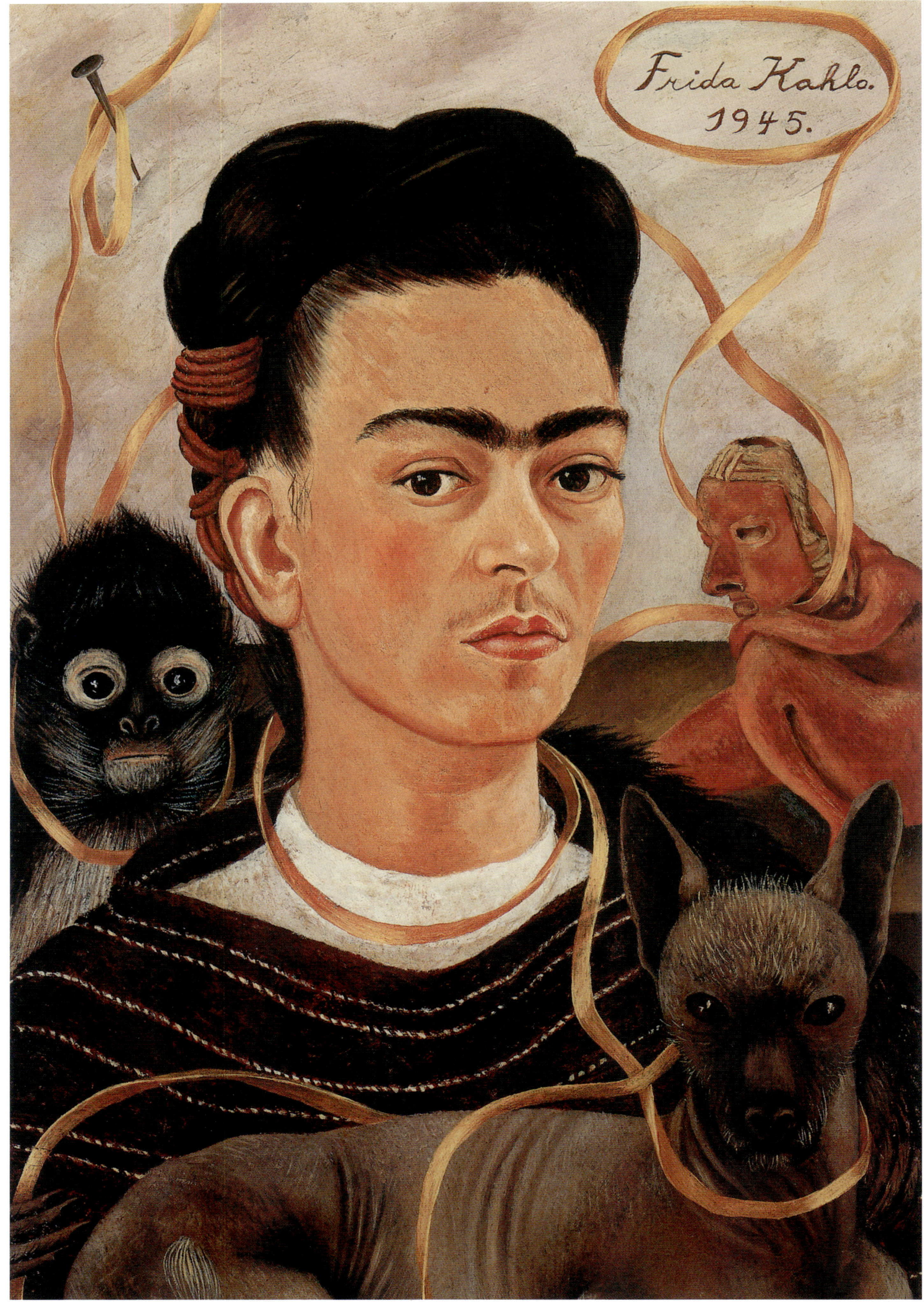
Frida Kahlo.
1945.

third month of yet another unwanted pregnancy, she had an abortion. Lesions opened up in her right foot and became infected.

In the big pink house, Diego's health deteriorated as well. He had dieted in Detroit and the result proved debilitating, leaving him open to a number of disorders, both real and imagined. Frida wrote to a friend,

> *...he thinks that everything that is happening to him is my fault, because I made him come to Mexico... and that this is the cause of his being the way he is...*[2]

Throughout her writings to confidants and in her diary, Frida continually defended Diego's petulant moods, his affairs, his depressions and small cruelties to her. She rationalized them as part of his nature. How often she pictured him as a child in her arms, an infant with his soft baby face needing to be cuddled. A mother always defends her child's shortcomings and Frida accepted her dual role as wife and mother to this man who had never developed his emotions beyond those of a young boy.

To his considerable discredit, the sullen and petulant Diego did not break off the affair with Cristina once Frida discovered them. He went on to paint a rather glamorous portrait of the younger sister with her two children in the National Palace mural, partially obscuring a dowdy image of Frida. All this emotional strife resulted in little creative output from the devastated Frida. But in 1935, the accumulated pain and suffering produced the most horrific of her *retablo*-style paintings on metal. She painted a murder and called it, *A Few Small Nips.*

A slaughtered female corpse lies on a bloody bed. Stab wounds are evident all over her contorted nude body. On one leg she wears a black shoe, a stocking and a colorful garter rucked down to her ankle. Above her stands her smirking murderer, still holding his blood-clotted knife. A banner floats above them, carried by a white and a black dove of good and evil. It reads, "A Few Small Nips". This murder actually took place and was in the newspaper headlines when Frida painted this gore besotted abattoir, letting the blood wash down across

Page 94
Self-Portrait with Monkey, 1945.
Oil on masonite, 60 x 42,5 cm,
Museo Dolores Olmedo Patiño, Mexico City.

the frame. Those were the uncaring words of the murderer, a likely stand-in for Diego Rivera. Once again, she laid bare her emotions with allegory and in doing so helped flush out some of the anguish.

She seemed bent on divesting herself of her previous life, expunging her ties to Rivera, changing her appearance and continuing her painting. She packed up and moved from the Bauhaus blue house to Mexico City, setting up housekeeping at 432 Avenida Insurgentes in a small but well appointed apartment. Diego, always ready with a gesture, promptly bought her and Cristina matching chrome furniture sets trimmed in red leather. The year became devoted to establishing her new persona, hooking up with old friends and shedding all the bad feelings stored up from her long time away from Mexico. Though she spoke out often against the "gringos" and their rich society built on the backs of oppressed workers, she also remembered the artists she had seen in the galleries of major museums and in the halls of these "gringo" collectors. She had seen some of the greatest painters in the world while residing in "Gringolandia," not pictures in a book, but seeing every brush stroke, its pigment-thick track following the artist's direction. As with most of Frida Kahlo's short life, she was at odds and cross-purposes with herself. In her work, she disliked the *Americanos*, but couldn't wait to apply what had been made available to her in their country. In her evolving personal life, for all her posturing about the randy Rivera's duplicity, she saw him almost every day. And he sought her out as well.

Amidst all this catharsis, Frida made an impromptu dash out of town to New York with a packed bag and two friends: Anita Brenner and Mary Shapiro – who had just left her husband. They made the harrowing and exhausting journey aboard a plane, train, and an automobile. Frida took advantage of friends she had made during their previous long stay to unleash all her emotional demons. Lucienne Bloch, and Bertram and Ella Wolfe concluded that Frida still loved Diego and should reconcile with him. On July 23, 1935, following their council, Frida wrote to Diego:

Page 97

Autorretrato con vestido rojo y dorado (Self-portrait with red and gold dress), 1941.

...all these letters, liaisons with petticoats, lady teachers of "English", gypsy models, assistants with "good intentions". Plenipotentiary emissaries from distant places, only

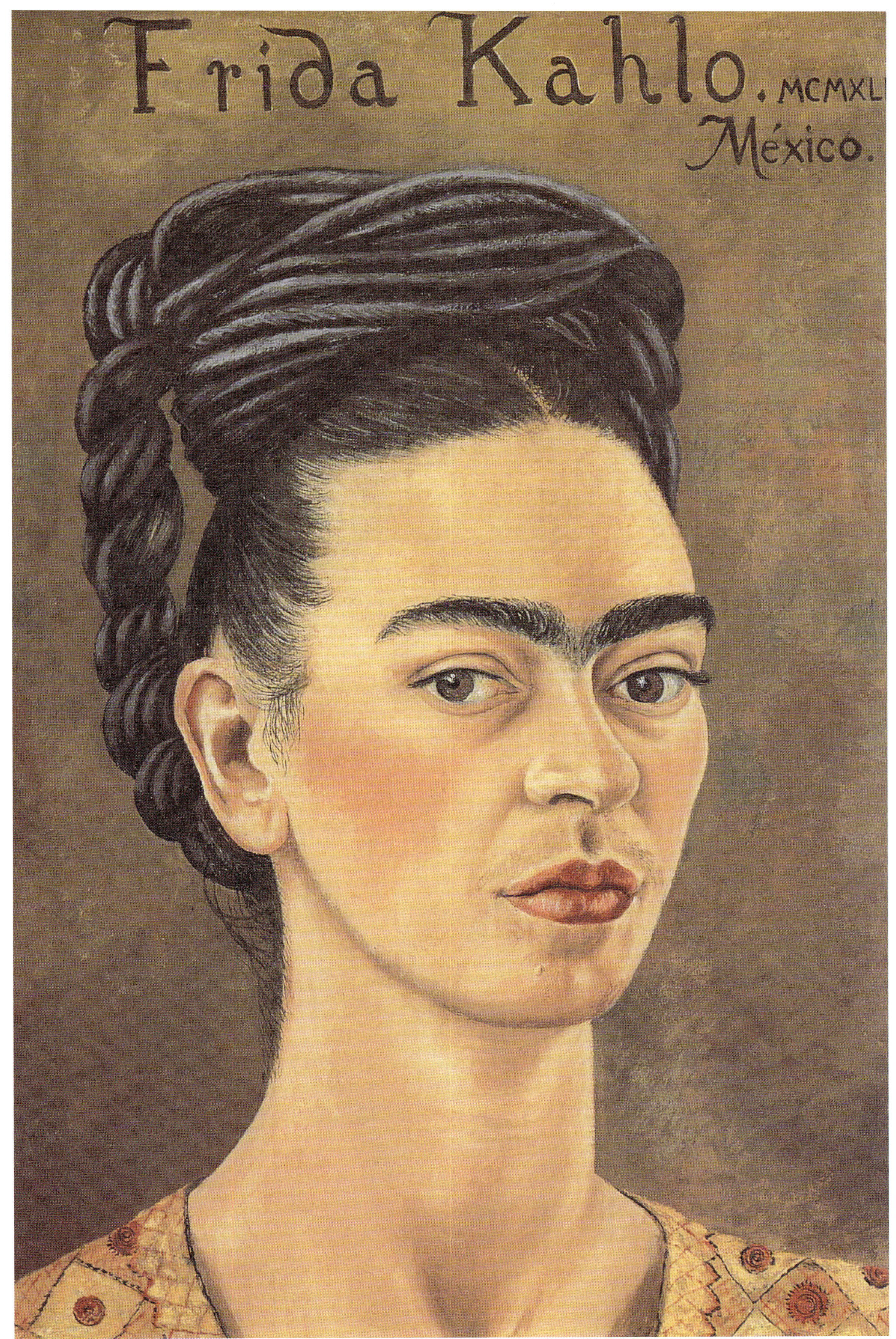
Frida Kahlo. MCMXL
México.

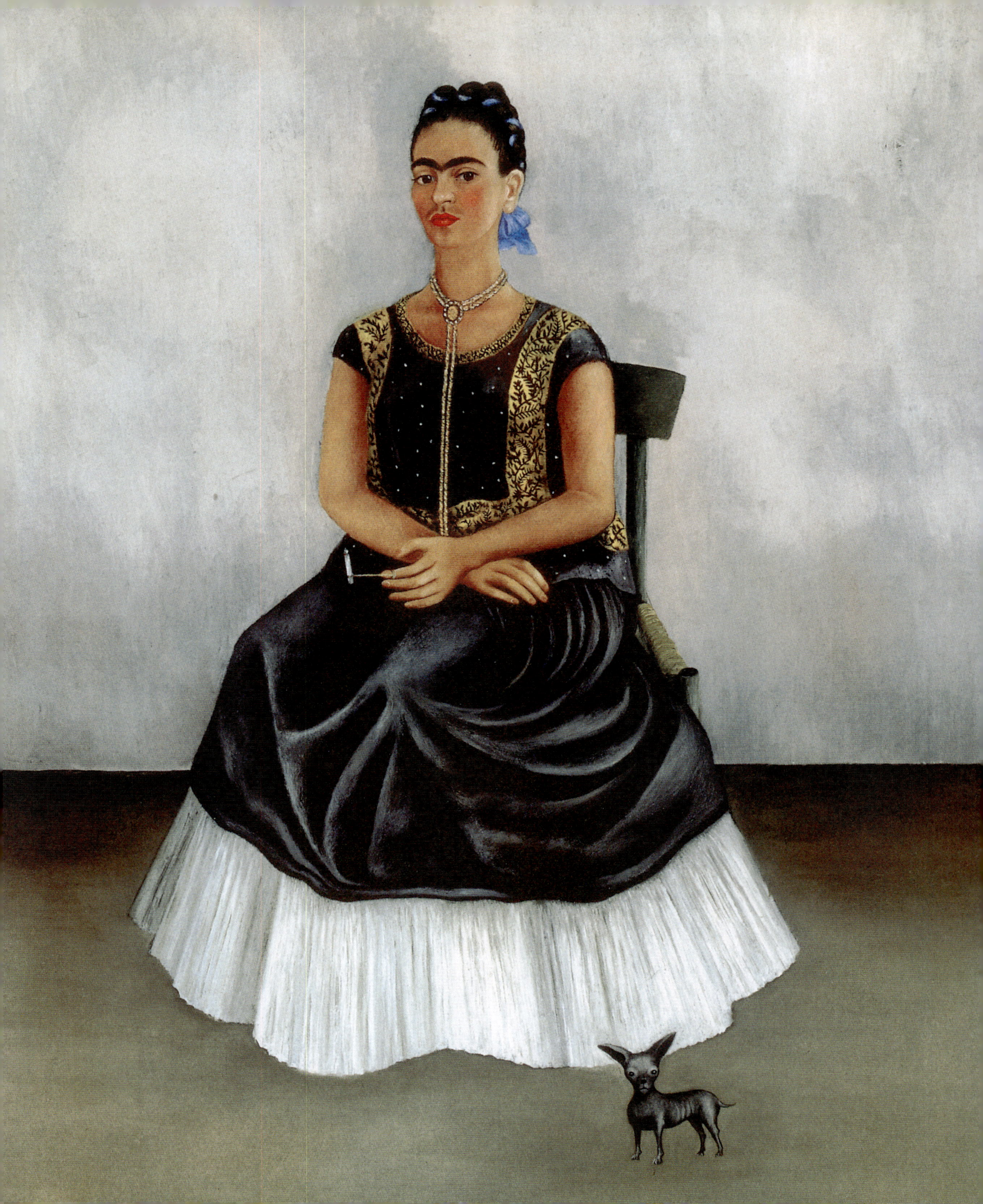

represent flirtations, and that at bottom you and I love each other dearly and thus go through adventures without number, beatings on doors, imprecations, insults, international claims – yet we will always love each other.[3]

It appeared that Frida and Diego had to suffer this nadir of their relationship in order to clear the air once and for all concerning their agreement of "mutual independence". There would be more crises, but with this understanding they could, at least, get on with their work. However, she used up the rest of 1935 exercising that "mutual independence" in a number of lesbian and gentlemen affairs. Diego waved off her affairs with women, but even a "mutually independent" Mexican male drew the line at sharing his wife with paramours.

During the warm days of Mexican summer, Frida slipped out of her apartment for rendezvous with men of her choosing. While her love making with famed Mexican muralist Ignacio Aguirre might have been casual, the American sculptor, Isamu Noguchi, was quite another matter. He fell in love with her. She met him while he worked in Mexico City on a Guggenheim grant. Their assignations were frequent, passionate and carried out with great discretion considering the fact that Noguchi worked alongside Rivera every day.

Noguchi had become obsessed with her and she was besotted with the attentions of the handsome sculptor. She continually shifted their trysting places between Cristina's apartment and *La Casa Azul.* Diego had made it plain that if he ever caught her with another man, he would shoot the *cabrone.* One day, Rivera showed up at the Blue House where Noguchi and Frida were *en flagrante.* Knowing Rivera was usually armed, Noguchi snatched up his clothes and pounded out the French doors into the central courtyard, dashed its length down a corridor of phallic organ pipe cacti and vaulted the wall at its end. Another version has him scrambling up an orange tree and vanishing across the rooftops. In either case, he left behind one sock which Frida's dog kept as a chewy toy.

Some time later, Noguchi visited Frida during one of her hospital stays and Diego entered the room. *Panzon* must have had suspicions about the young sculptor and his wife

Page 98
Self-Portrait with Iztcuintli Dog, c.1939.
Oil on canvas, 71 x 52 cm,
Private collection, USA.

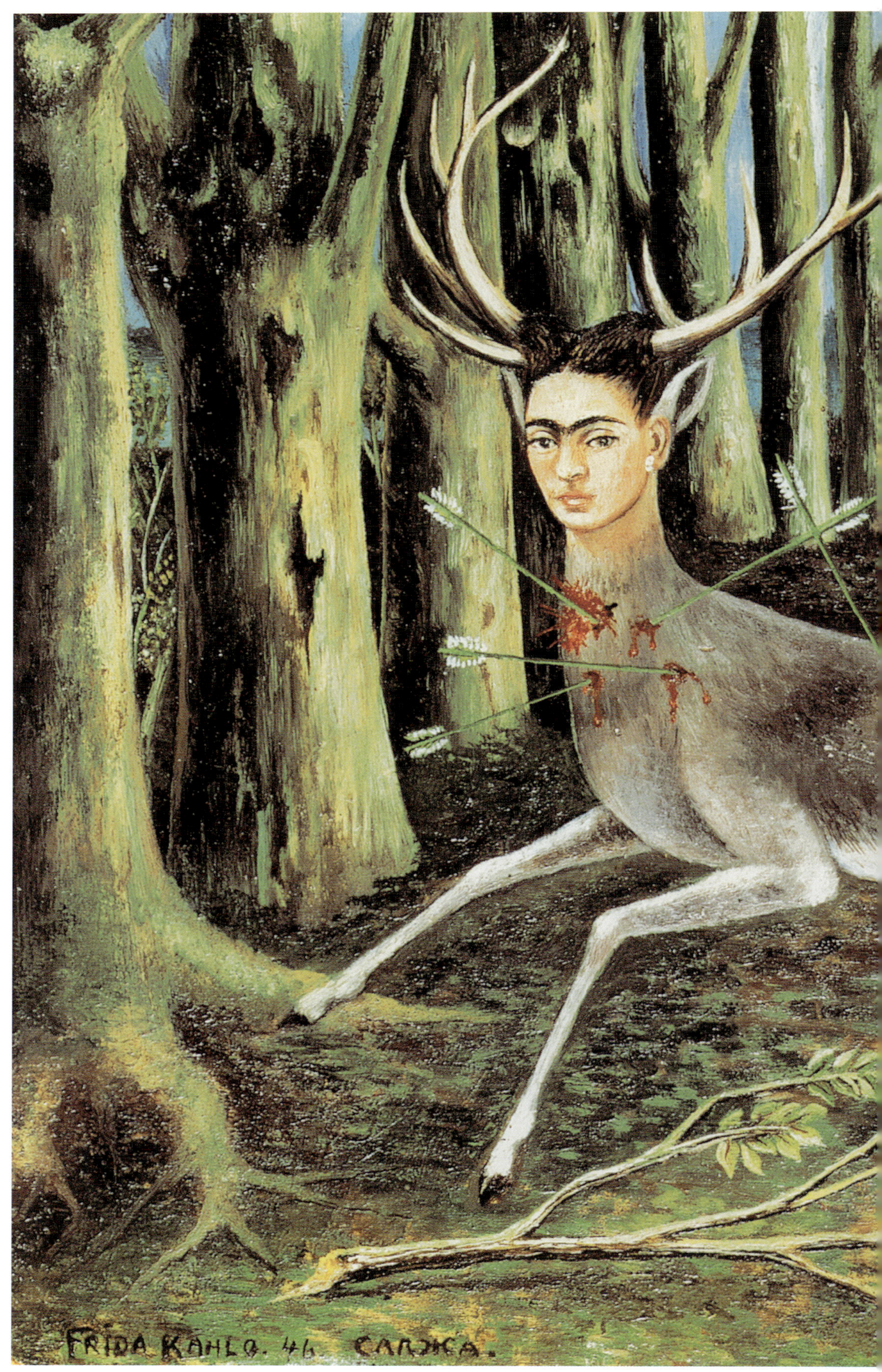
FRIDA KAHLO. 46.

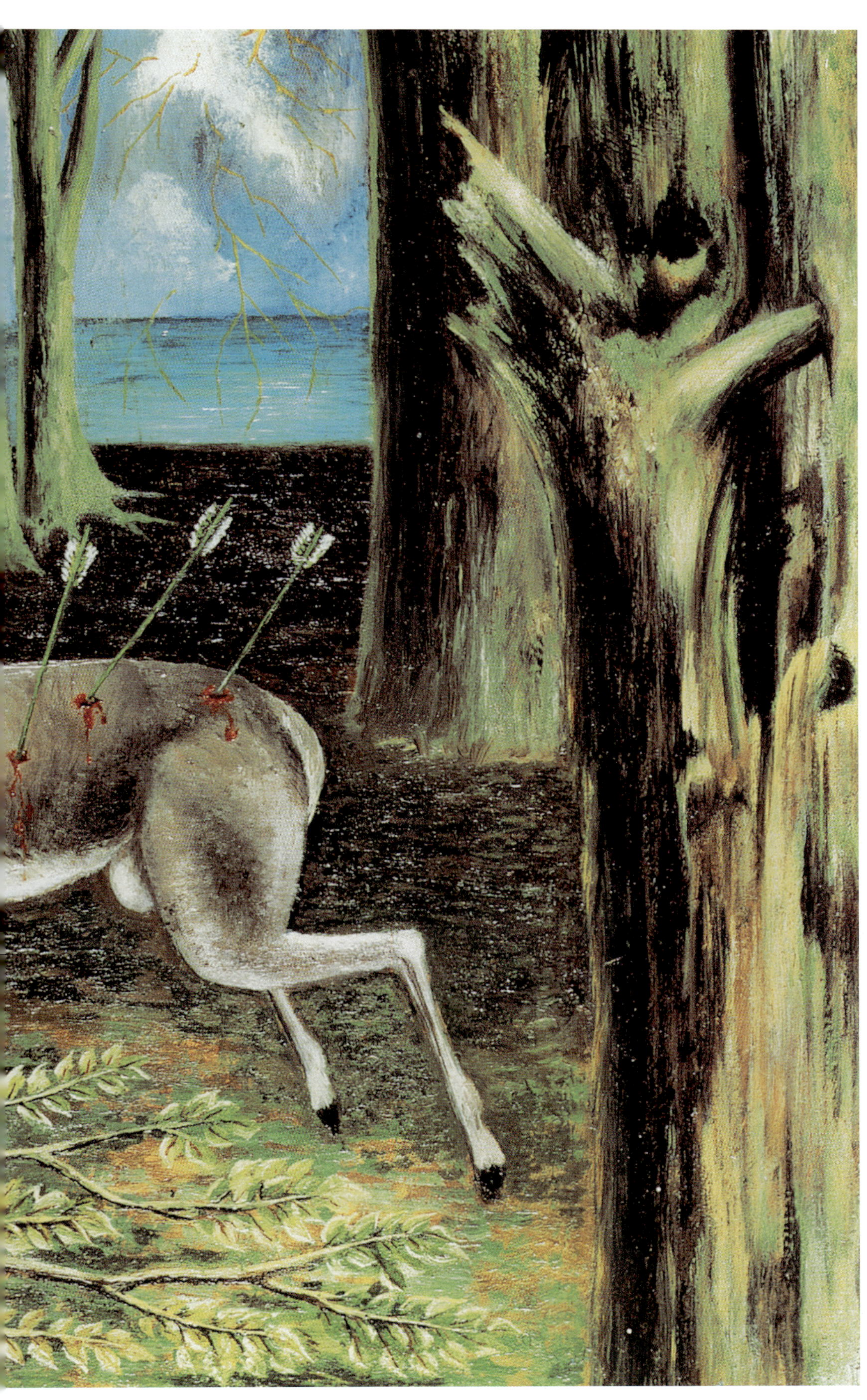

Page 100-101

The Wounded Deer (The Little Deer), 1946.

Oil on masonite, 22.4 x 30 cm,

Private collection, Houston (Texas).

because he drew the big Colt and quietly suggested in effect that one of the bullets in its cylinder had Noguchi's name on it. Isamu's ardor cooled considerably.

The year 1935 ended with very little painting and much soul searching. A single self portrait was produced showing Frida gazing at us from beneath a boyish mop of short curly hair. Her eyes are calm and her mouth gives nothing away. Above her eyes, the trademark eyebrow is more shaggy and exaggerated than usual as is the moustache that darkens her upper lip. It's not difficult to imagine her hands on her hips, ready for whatever came next.

What happened next was alcoholism, still more surgery and Leon Trotsky. Frida had always enjoyed a good party and a few "*cocktailitos*", but during and after *L'affaire Diego*, her consumption rose precipitously. Besides her drinking at social occasions, she began frequenting cantinas in Mexico City and pulquerias in near-by villages. In 1936 she moved her belongings back into her half of the dual house at San Angel. She frequently attended soirées thrown by Diego for visiting artists such as actress Dolores Del Rio, writer John Dos Passos, Mexican photographer Manuel Alvarez Bravo and Mexican president Cardenas.[4]

While her socializing was on the increase, she turned her attention to mending fences with her sister, Cristina. As she didn't want to give up on Diego, her ties to Cristina were also too strong to cut. Frida adored her sister's two children, Isolde and Antonio. Besides her visits to Cristina's apartment, Frida always had time for the children at her studio in San Angel as though they were the children her wounded body denied her.

Her reoccurring bad health forced Frida into the American Cowdray Hospital in Mexico City for another bout of surgery. Though it seems difficult to accept considering her active and strenuous lifestyle, but Frida Kahlo suffered from daily pain and fatigue. Doctors paraded in and out of her life offering various diagnoses and cures directly related to her 1925 accident. Most were wrong, but she listened to them all. As anyone with a chronic bad back, asthma, arthritis, migraines, or any condition that produces lingering or sudden periods of pain understands. Life becomes a distraction, an escape from the pain that is

Page 103
Memory or *The Heart*, 1937.
Oil on metal, 40 x 28 cm,
Private collection, New York.

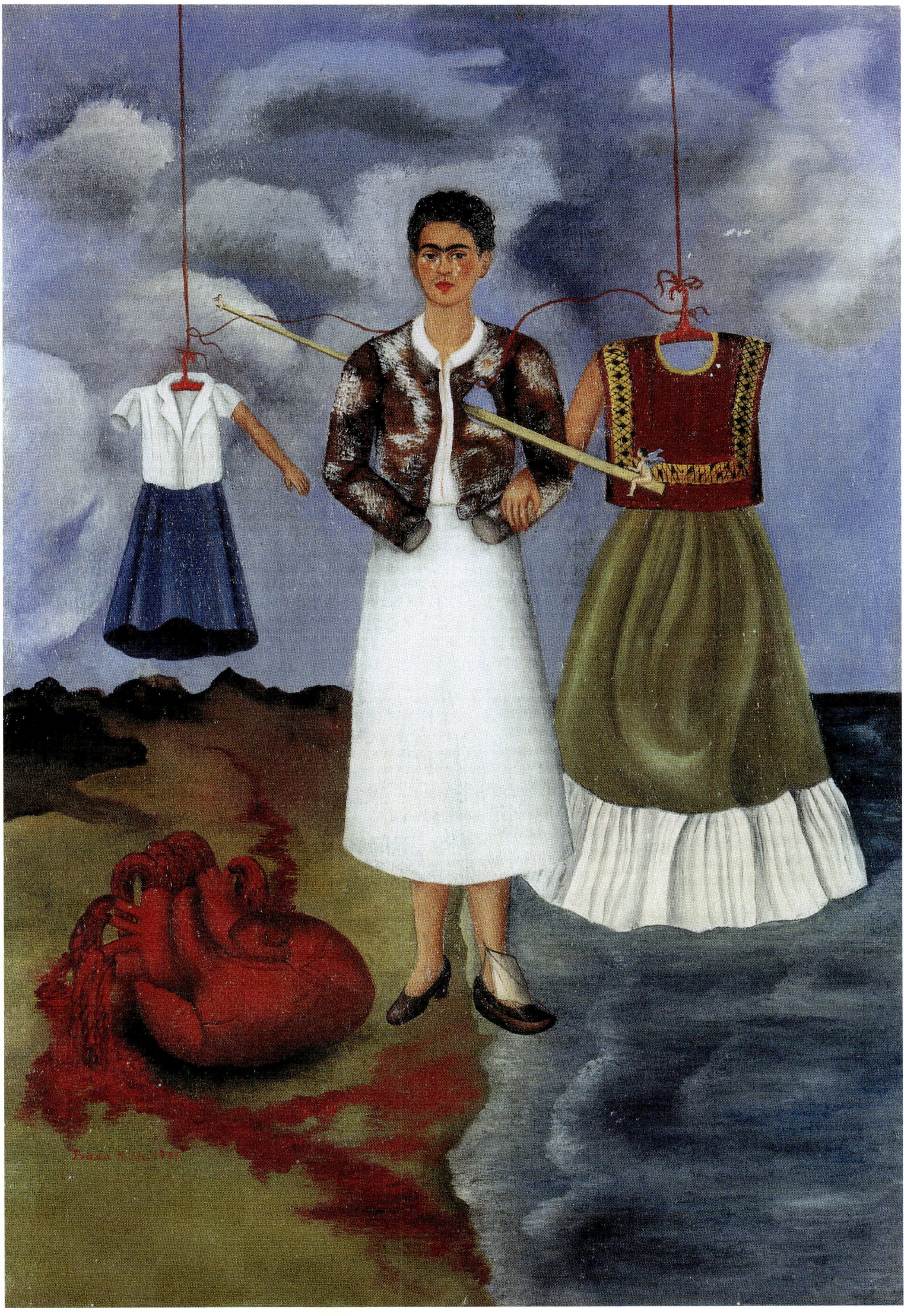

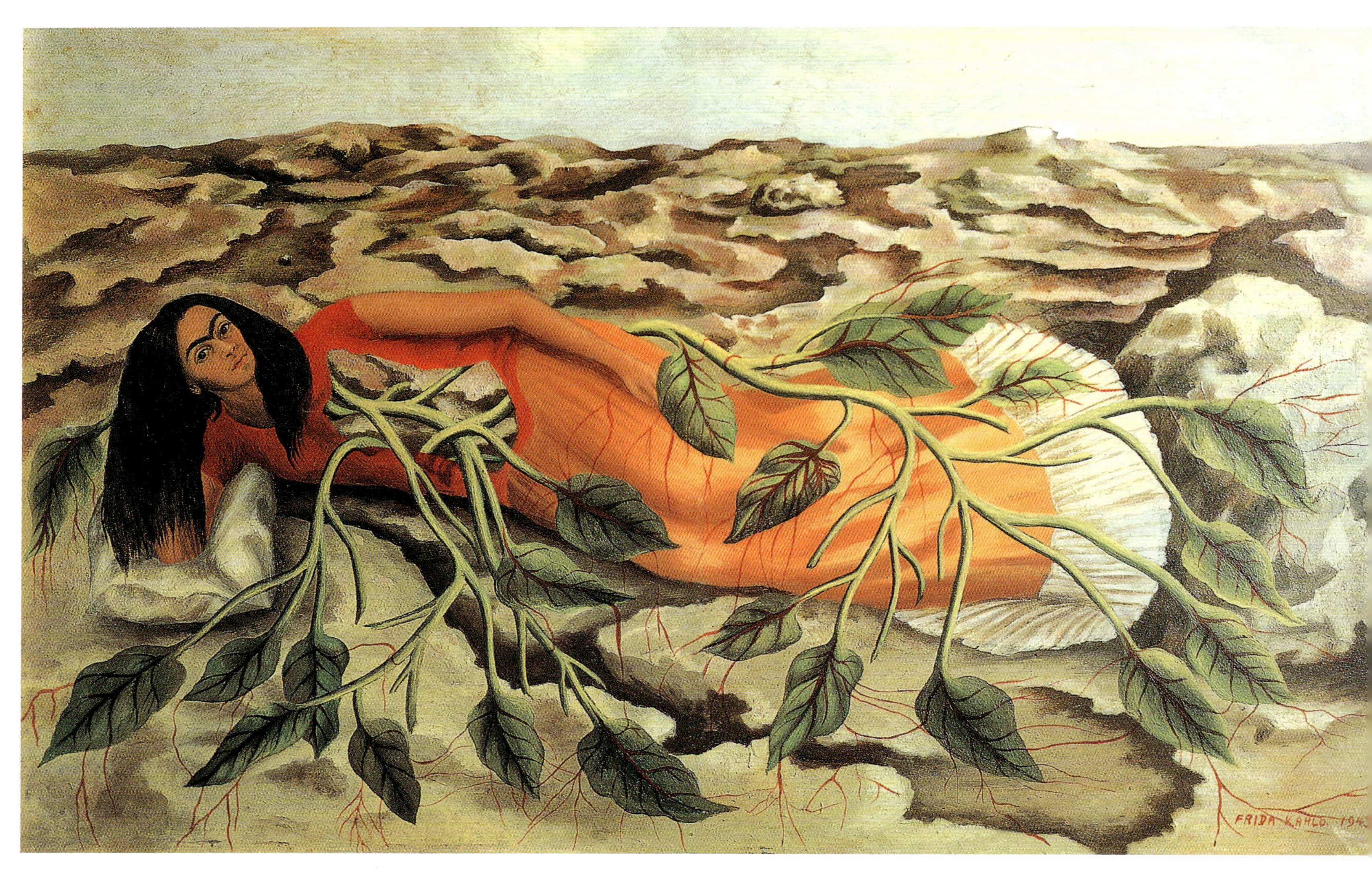
FRIDA KAHLO. 194

always there, an automatic function like breathing and swallowing. Frida pushed her other senses into overload and turned a stoic face to the world.

Today, modern medicine has studied her symptoms, relying on notes from those doctors and in particular, Dr. Leonardio Zamudio who has her complete medical records. The latest diagnosis is she suffered:

> *...posttraumatic fibromyalgia. This prevalent syndrome is characterized by persistent widespread pain, chronic fatigue, sleep disorders, and vegetative symptoms, and by the presence of tender points in well-defined anatomic areas. The concept of fibromyalgia as a clinical entity as we know it today was probably unknown to most physicians of the early twentieth century. This diagnosis explains her chronic, severe, widespread pain accompanied by profound fatigue. It also explains the lack of response to diverse forms of treatment. The onset of fibromyalgia after physical trauma is well-recognized.*[5]

Frida's inward journey to rebuild and reshape her life found expression in her 1936 painting on metal, *My Grandparents, My Parents and I.* A naked five-year-old Frida stands as a giant towering in the courtyard of *La Casa Azul* against a brown and cloudy desert landscape. She clutches a red ribbon that connects portraits of her grandparents joining them to the central wedding portrait of her parents. It's a charming bit of allegorical kitsch, but Frida carries the story further back to her prenatal portrait in the womb connected by the umbilical to her mother. And then further still, as, to the left of the Blue House, a single sperm penetrates an egg, the moment of conception. By acknowledging the ties to her past, this flashback and consolidation of all the genetic elements that sum up her existence - and unfortunately end with her childless state - possibly serves to reinforce the new start to her life, the second birth of Frida Kahlo.

She had begun to paint again, had established some equilibrium in her relationships with Diego and her sister and looked forward to a period of stability in her congenial, Bohemian lifestyle. And then a hunted fugitive, dogged by Stalinist assassins stepped off a rust bucket oil tanker in Tampico and, once more, her life was hurled into emotional chaos.

Page 104
Roots or *The Pedregal*, 1943.
Oil on metal, 30.5 x 49.9 cm,
Private collection, Houston (Texas).

Lev Davidovich Bronstein was born in the Ukraine on Novermber 7, 1879. He was a bright lad and attracted to radical politics during his university years. His activities and oratory in Czarist Russia ended in flight and exile in England where he changed his name to Leon Trotsky. An avowed Marxist, he aligned himself with Vladimir Ilyich Lenin and returned to Russia following the Bolshevik Revolution in 1917. Lenin ("The end justifies the means") and Trotsky, his number two, didn't see eye to eye in their Communist dogma, but both became heroic icons in the Bolshevik movement as the government began to stabilize. Trotsky's high position in the Kremlin halls of power plummeted after Lenin's death and the Marxist ideologue became an obstacle to Josef Stalin's brutish power grab. After being battered about by trumped-up charges of counter-revolutionary activities, Trotsky was kicked out of Russia in 1929. Shortly thereafter, Stalin realized he had made a mistake allowing Trotsky to remain alive and keep up a steady stream of anti-Stalin books and articles. The GPU – Russia's Secret Police – was dispatched to silence Trotsky once and for all. With these killers hot on his trail, Leon and his wife, Natalia, began a long odyssey of globe hopping, relying on friends for their safety.

Diego Rivera was a committed Trotskyite. Though he had been kicked out of the party, he joined Trotsky's *Fourth International*, lending his prestige to this Trotsky organization that stated in their 1936 Olso Convention:

> *The working class of the U.S.S.R. has been robbed of the last possibility of a legal reformation of the state. The struggle against the bureaucracy necessarily becomes a revolutionary struggle. True to the traditions of Marxism, the Fourth International decisively rejects individual terror, as it does all other means of political adventurism. The bureaucracy can be smashed only by means of the goal-conscious movement of the masses against the usurpers, parasites and oppressors.*

Page 107
Self-Portrait dedicated to Dr. Eloesser, 1940.
Oil on masonite, 59.5 x 40 cm,
Private collection, USA.

Aware of Trotsky's nine years of peripatetic wanderings in search of safe haven, Diego petitioned Mexico's President Cardenas to give sanctuary to the revolutionary on the run. Cardenas granted permission providing Trotsky didn't interfere with the Mexican government's internal affairs. On January 9, 1937, Trotsky watched the wooden gangplank

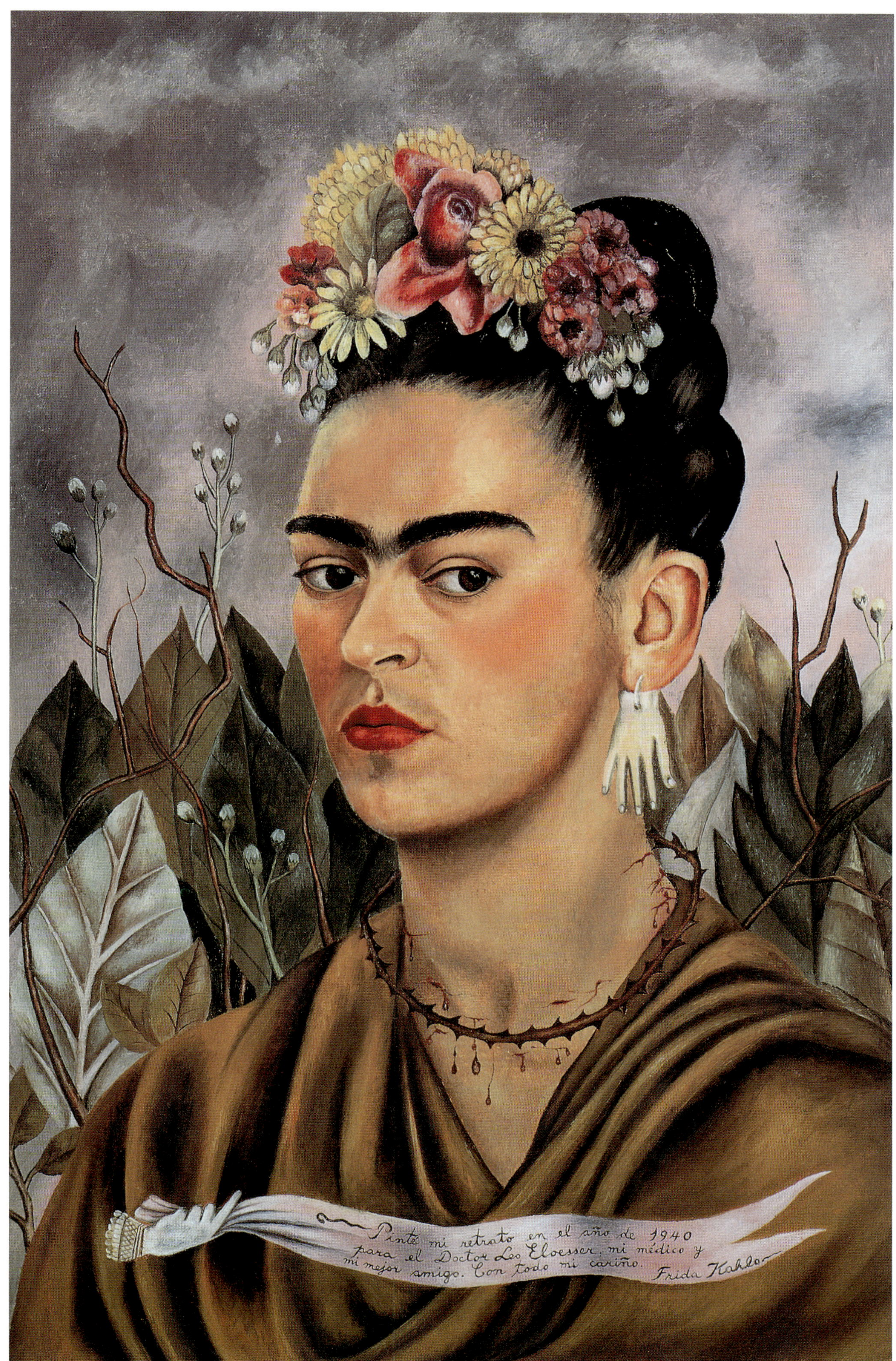
Pinté mi retrato en el año de 1940
para el Doctor Leo Eloesser, mi médico y
mi mejor amigo. Con todo mi cariño.
Frida Kahlo

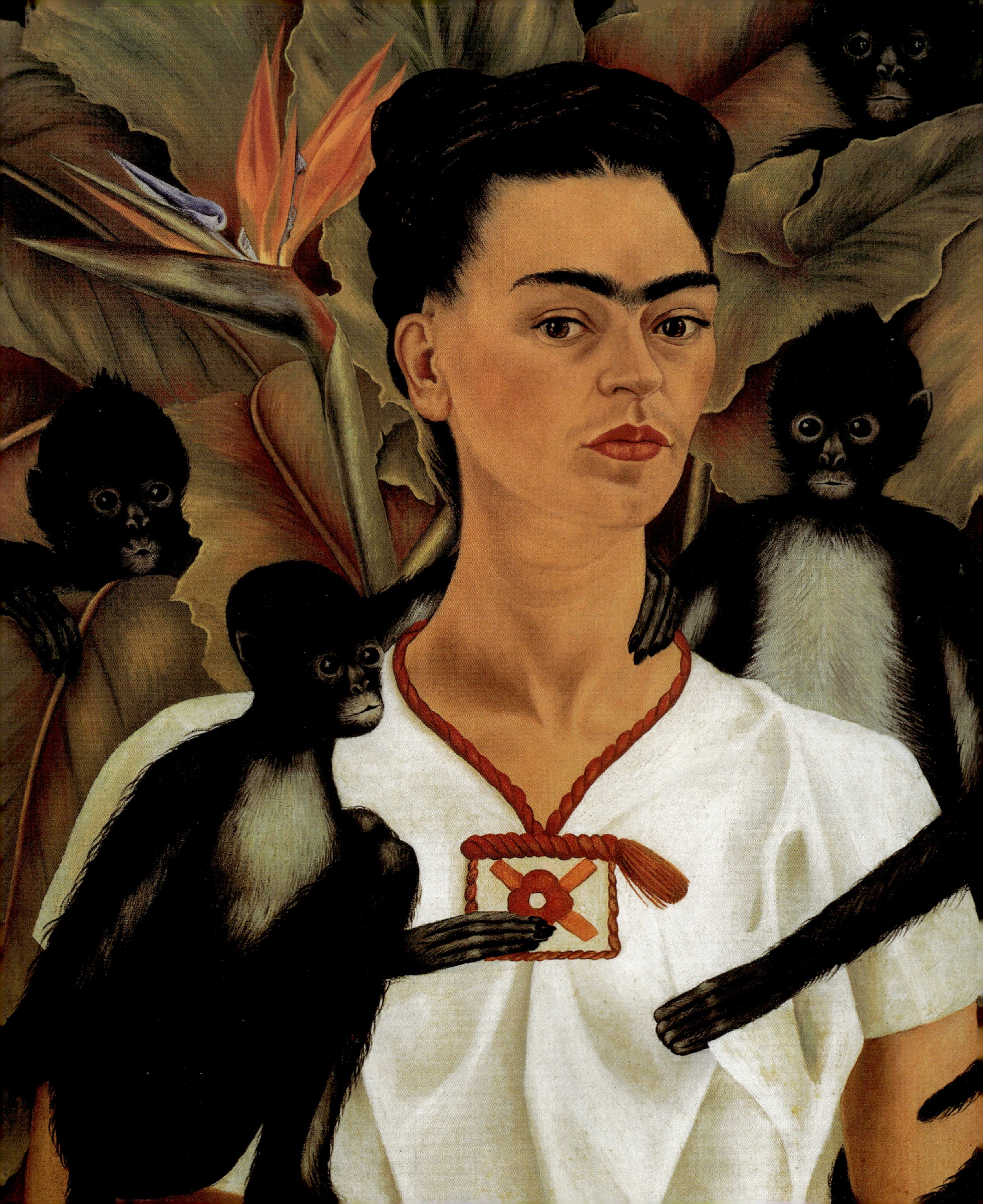

lower onto the dock at Tampico, Mexico. At his elbow, Natalia scanned the greeting party for friendly faces. She'd grown tired of skulking around Europe just ahead of hard-eyed men with guns, knives and bombs. On the dock, looking back at her and Leon, were smiling Trotsky supporters, party functionaries - and Frida Kahlo.

An eye problem coupled with Diego's bad kidneys had kept him in the hospital and Frida represented him at the welcome. The party was quickly bundled into automobiles and then onto a train for the ride to Mexico City. To confuse possible assassins lying in wait, false welcoming parties were established while the train stopped at a small station outside the city. Eventually, the party reached Frida's parents' home, *La Casa Azul* in Coyoacan. On arrival, a makeshift group of bodyguards took up posts outside watching the rooftops and street as the Trotskys hurried inside. Guillermo Kahlo smiled politely and shook hands, not having a clue to the identity of the gray-bearded man with the dowdy wife.

Trotsky and his wife lived off and on at *La Casa Azul* for two years as the aging revolutionary wrote a continuing stream of anti-Stalinist tracts for publication around the world. His age - a hard-lived 58 - did not interfere with his libido, nor did it keep Frida from finding his military posture, piercing eyes and dazzling intellect very attractive. His old-world manners, admonitions against her smoking and excess drink plus Diego's unswerring.

Diego's unswerving devotion to the man made him a perfect target for Frida's considerable powers of seduction and continuing need to give Diego a few more "nips" for his affair with Cristina. She turned up the heat, speaking to Trotsky in English, a language unfamiliar to Trotsky's wife. And if she made no secret of her desires in person, Frida's paintings in 1937 reflected her new confidence and purpose.

The volume of her work increased as did the variety of her subject matter. Continuing the examination of her childhood, she painted *My Nanny and I,* this time adding her roots to ancient Mexico. She was turned over to an Indian wet nurse when she was a baby. Having

Page 108
Self-Portrait with Monkeys, 1943.
Oil on canvas, 81.5 x 63 cm,
Collection Jacques and Natasha Gelman,
Mexico City.

Page 110
My Nanny and I, 1937.
Oil on metal, 30.5 x 34.7 cm,
Museo Dolores Olmedo Patiño, Mexico City.

Page 111
Two Nudes in the Wood or *The Earth* or
My Nanny and I, 1939. Oil on metal,
25 x 30.5 cm, Private collection.

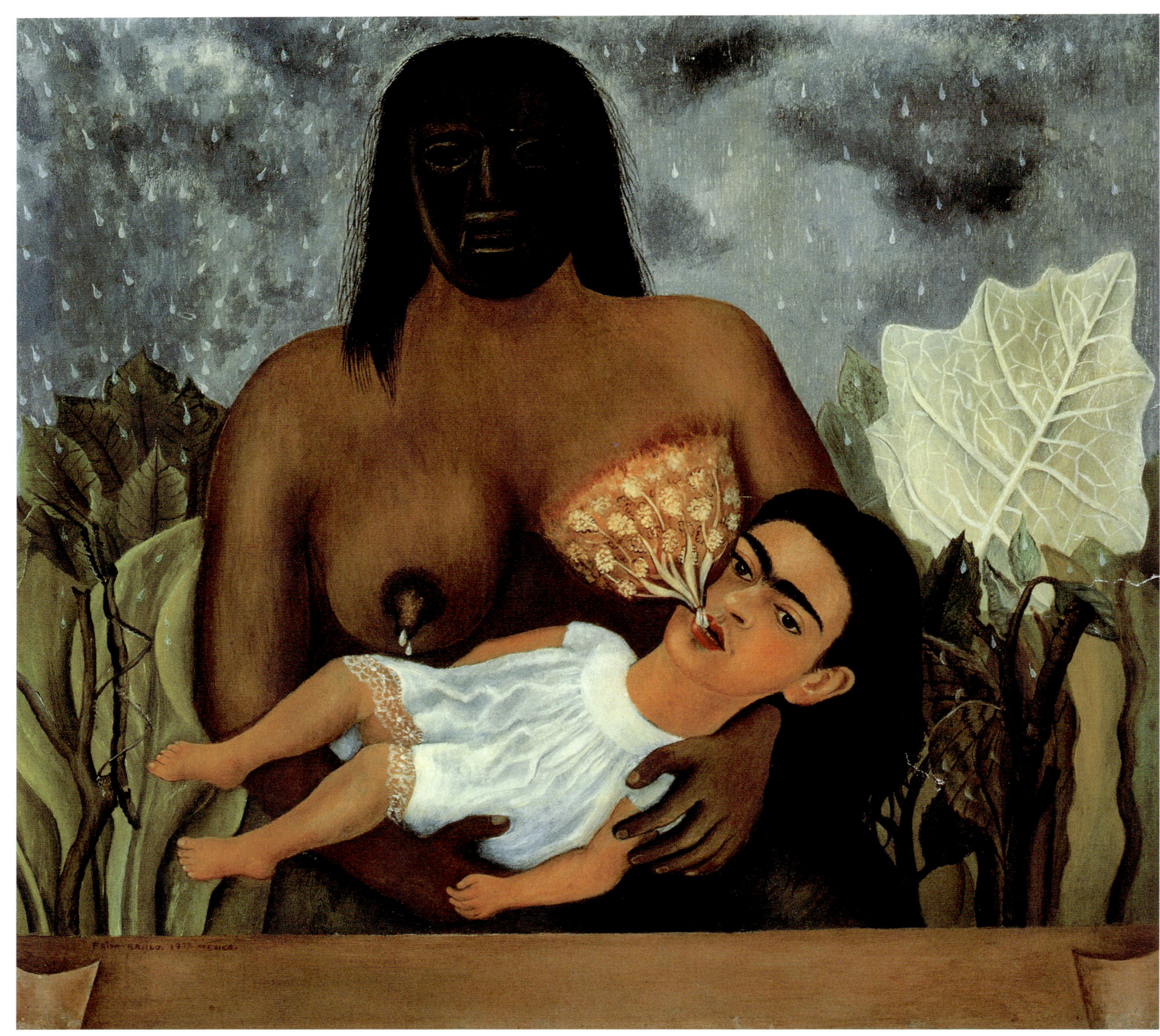

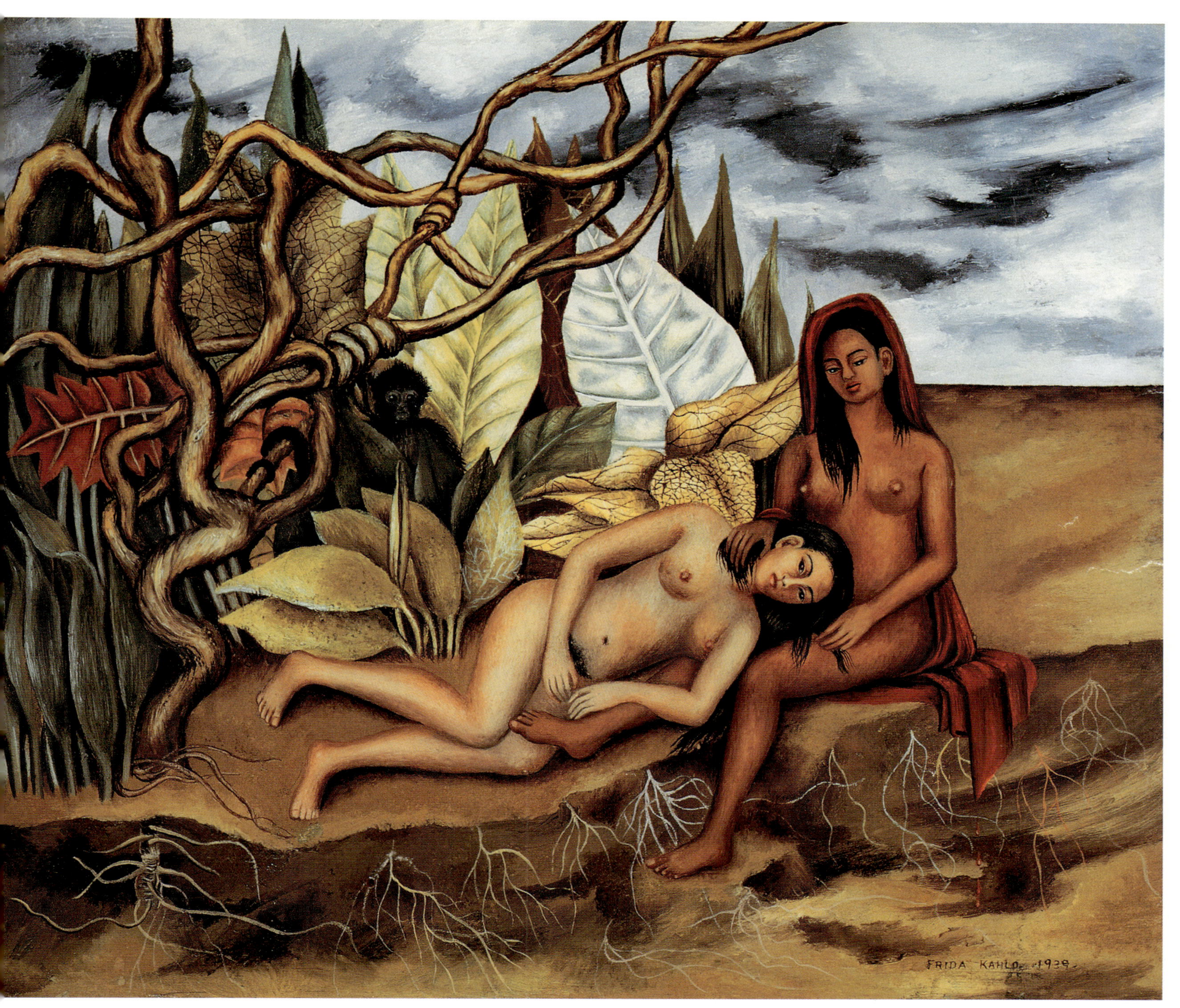
FRIDA KAHLO 1939

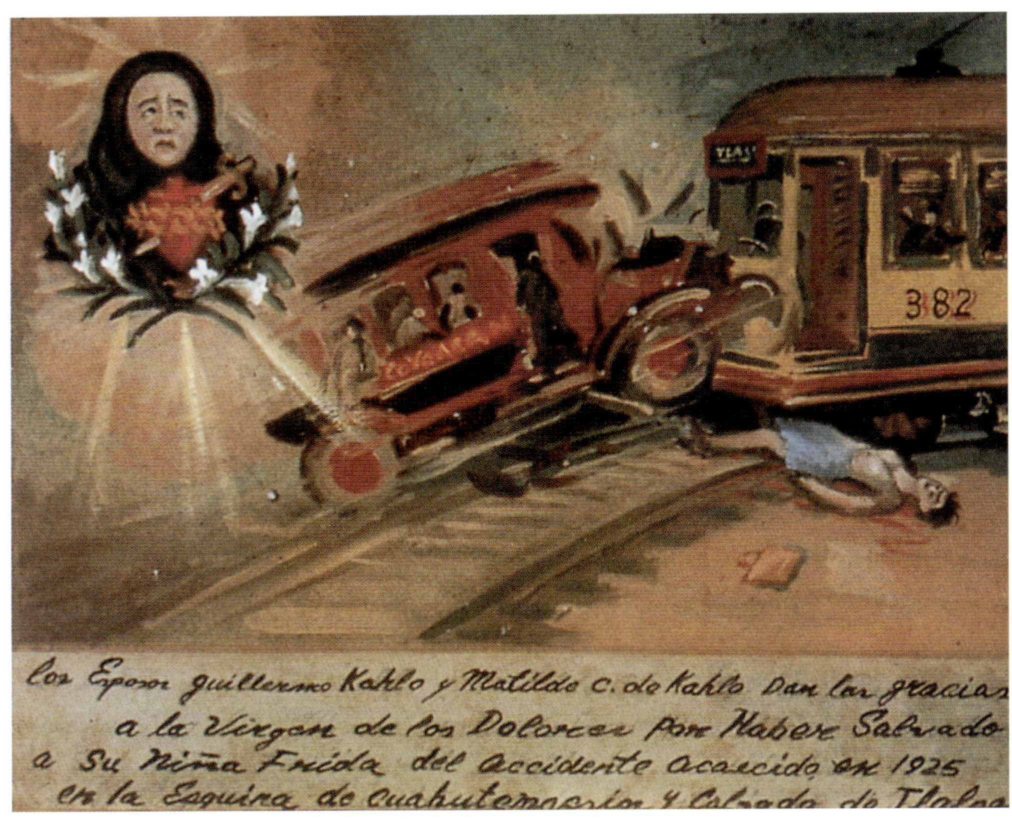

Page 112
Ex voto, c.1943.
Oil on metal, 19.1 x 24.1 cm,
Private collection.

Page 113
Self-Portrait dedicated to Leon Trotsky or *Between the Curtains*, 1937.
Oil on canvas, 87 x 70 cm,
National Museum of Women in the Arts,
donation by Clare Boothe Luce,
Washington D.C.

no recollection of the nurse's actual features, she commemorates that event by depicting the substitute with the face of a carved Indian mask. From the nurse's breast flows the fruit of the soil, nurtured by rain drops pelting down from a cloud-roiled sky – "milk of the Virgin" according to Frida's mother. Frida's adult head grows from the child's body as in *My Birth* (p. 66-77). But here, she's relaxed and accepting in her virtually luminescent white gown trimmed in lace. Curiously, in the arms of the stone-faced, *golem*-like surrogate, the girl seems as much a sacrifice as something cherished. At the bottom of the painting is a *retablo* banner, but it is blank.

Of this painting, Diego Rivera wrote in 1943:

And Frida is the only example in the history of art of someone who tore out her breast and heart to tell the biological truth of what she feels in them. of reason/imagination that is faster than light, she painted her mother and wetnurse, knowing that she really does not know their faces. The nourishing "nana's" face is only the Indian mask of hard

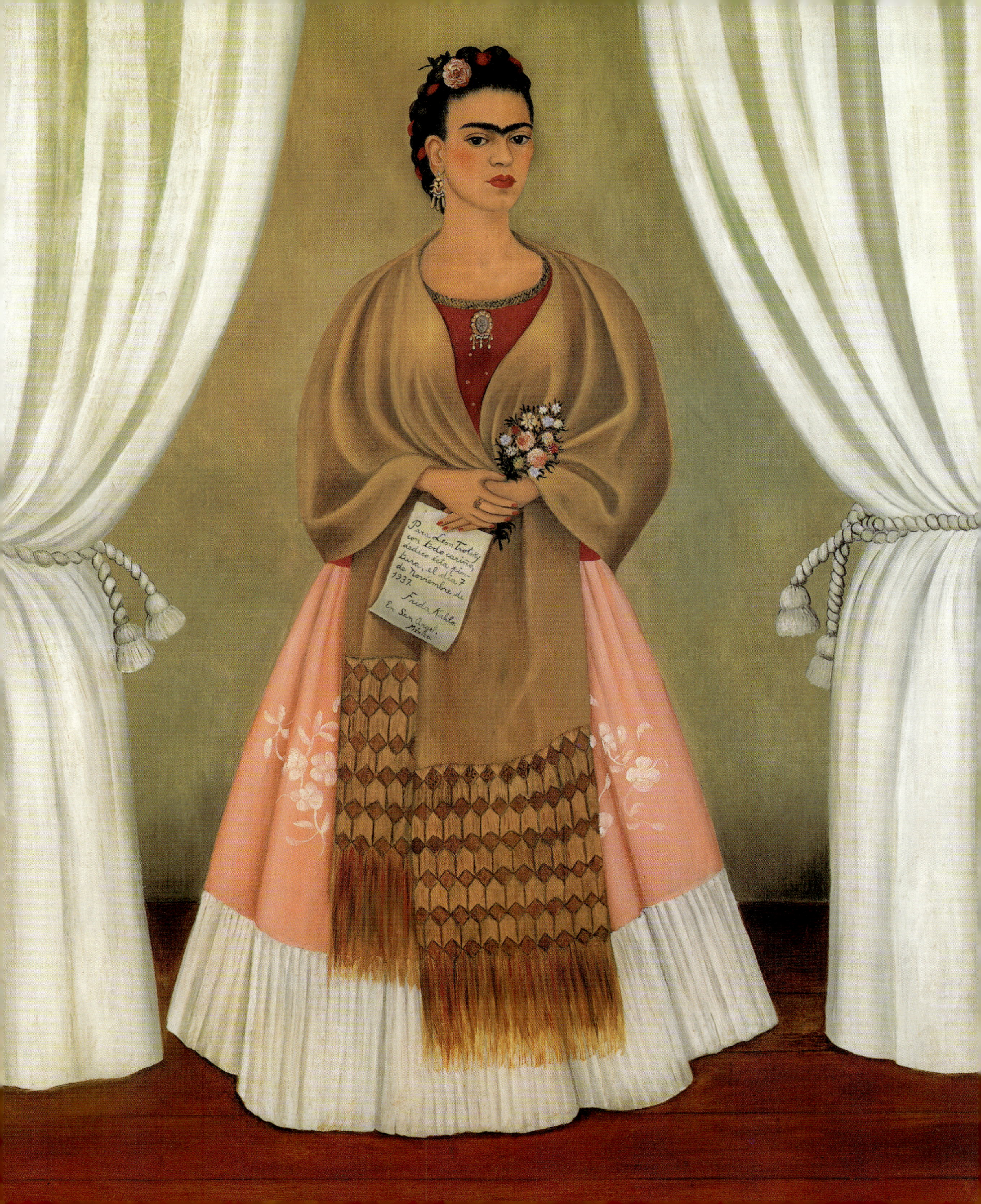
Para Leon Trotsky
con todo cariño,
dedico ésta pin-
tura, el día 7
de Noviembre de
1937.
Frida Kahlo
En San Angel.
México.

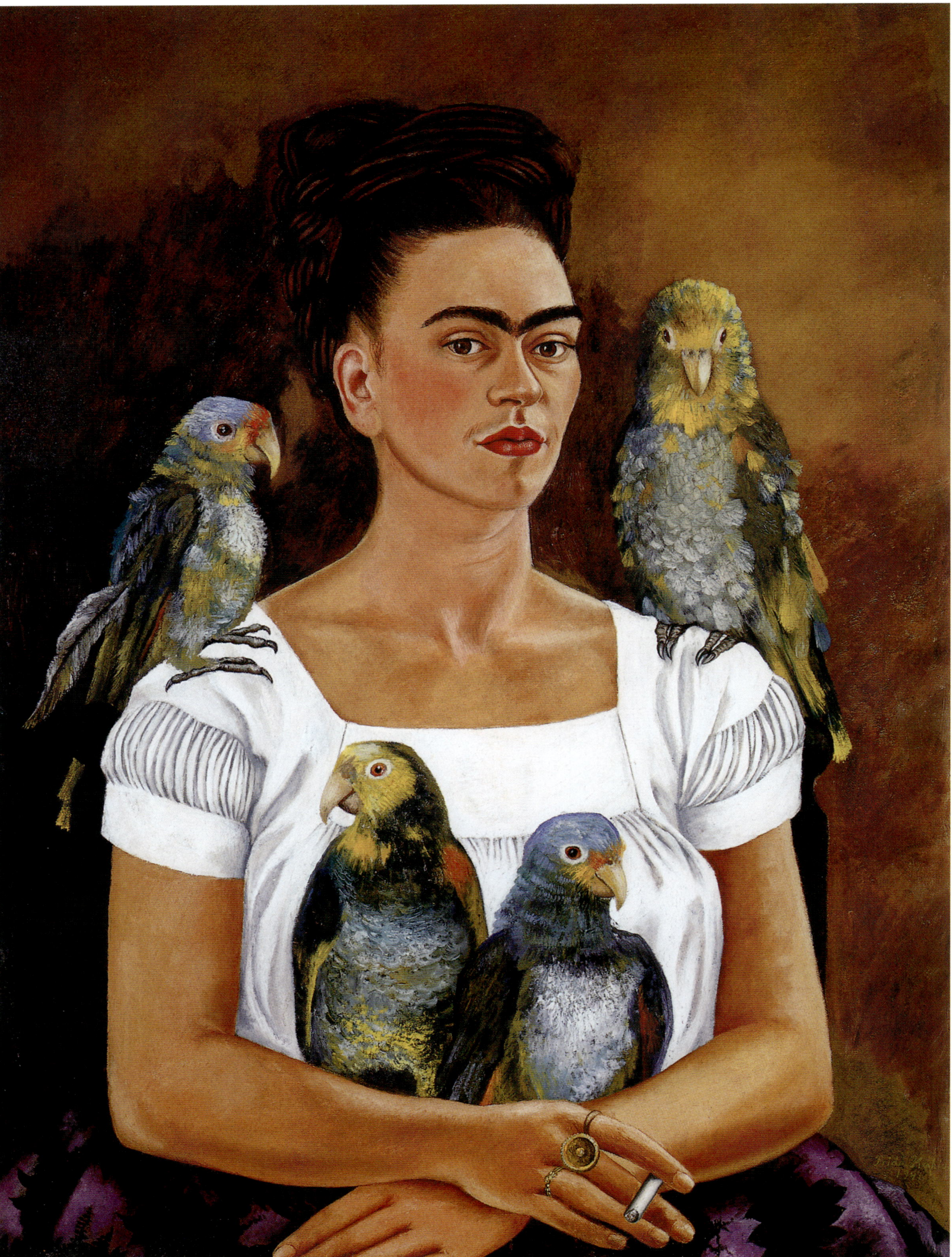

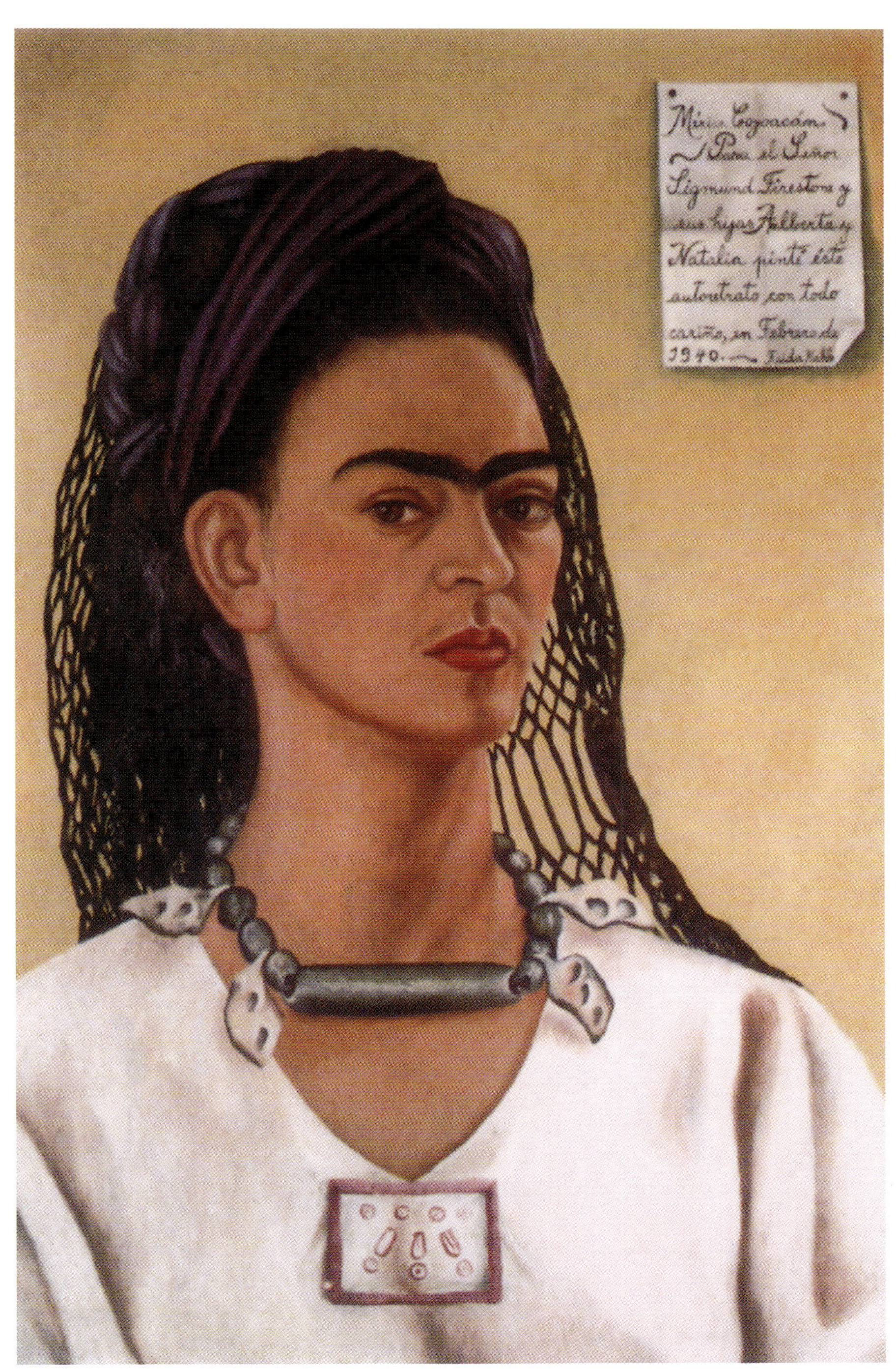

Page 114

Me and My Parrots, 1941.

Oil on canvas, 82 x 62.8 cm,

Private collection.

Page 115

Self-Portrait dedicated to Sigmand Firestone,

1940. Oil on masonite, 61 x 43 cm,

Private collection, USA.

> *rock, and her glands are clusters that drip milk like the rain fertilizes the earth, or like the tear that fertilizes pleasure. The mother is the grieving mater with seven daggers of pain that makes possible the torn opening through which emerges the Child Frida, the only human force that, from the portentious Aztec master who sculpted it in black basalt, has created birth by means of its own action in reality.*[6]

She also painted her only formal portrait of Diego Rivera. The year had not been good for Diego's mural commissions. He looks tired and undernourished, His illnesses and eye problems have taken their toll. Though his own work volume had slipped, he tirelessly devoted much of his time to propping up Frida's confidence in her capabilities. Her rendition of his diminished presence is tender and sympathetic.

On the other hand, his act of callous infidelity with her sister would never be far from Frida's palette and brushes. She created *Memory* in 1937, an enigmatic trio of three Fridas: as a suspended schoolgirl costume at the time of her accident, but with only one arm, and as Frida dressed in white with her cropped hair and wearing a bolero jacket made of cowhide. A wooden lance pierces a heart-shaped, see-through hole in the jacket. No hands extend from the jacket's cuffs, but the third Frida – a *Tehuana* costume on a hanger – extends an arm to the wounded and helpless Frida. As though wrenched from her chest by an ancient Aztec priest, her huge heart lies abandoned on a desert landscape pumping vast quantities of blood into the soil and the sea. Red blood vessels tie the three Frida images together – each of them incomplete and all tied to the pain of a broken heart.

Page 117
The Love Embrace of the Universe, The Earth (Mexico), I, Diego and Señor Xólotl, 1949.
Oil on canvas, 70 x 60.5 cm,
Private collection, Mexico City.

My doll and I, painted in oil on metal, speaks to her childless state, not with pathos, or longing, but rather with an aloof acceptance. She wears a *Tehuana* skirt and blouse and sits next to a naked boy doll. But she's smoking as though waiting for a bus. All her life she loved and collected dolls and yet this one seems abandoned and ignored seated an arm's length away on the bare cane bed.

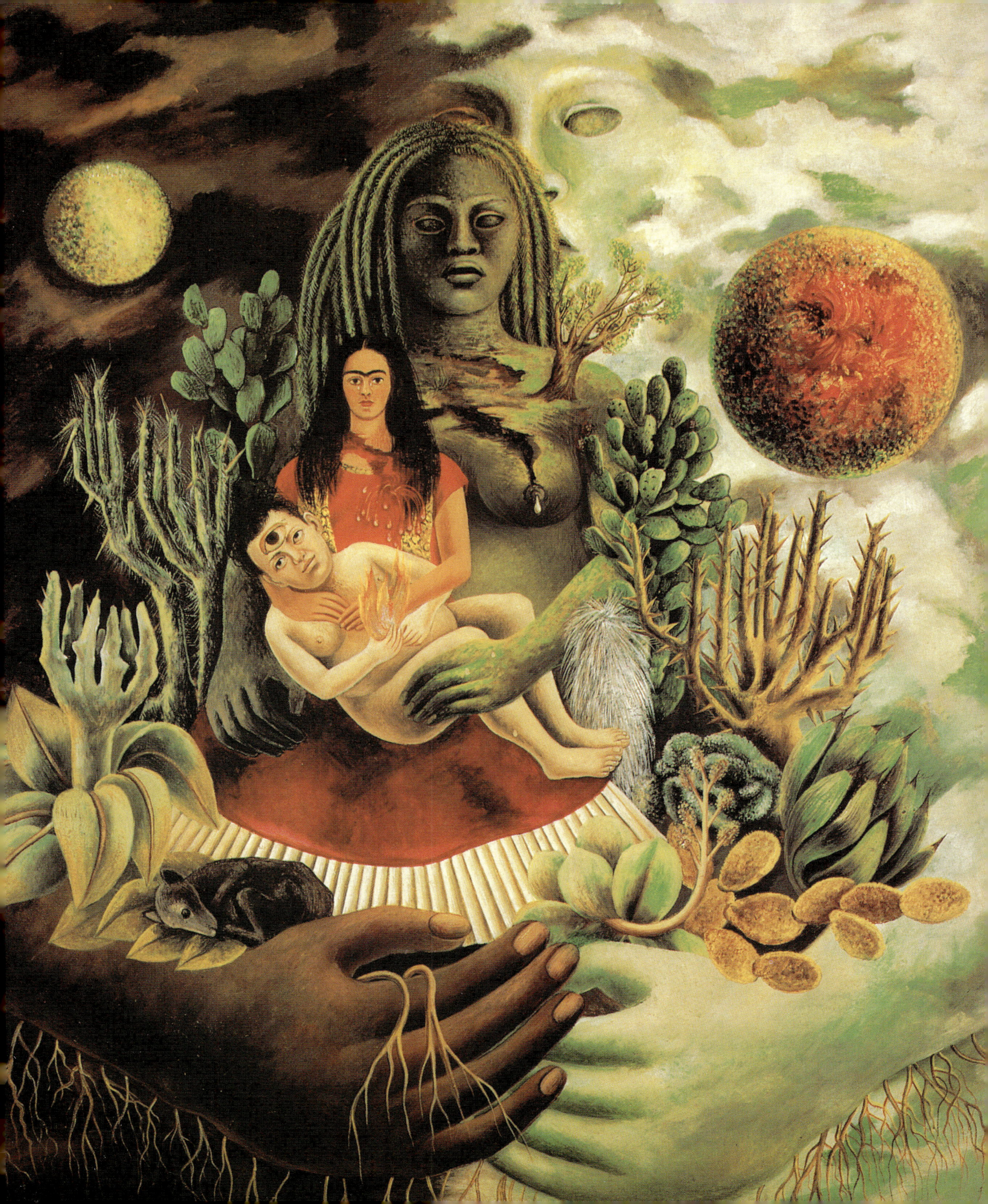

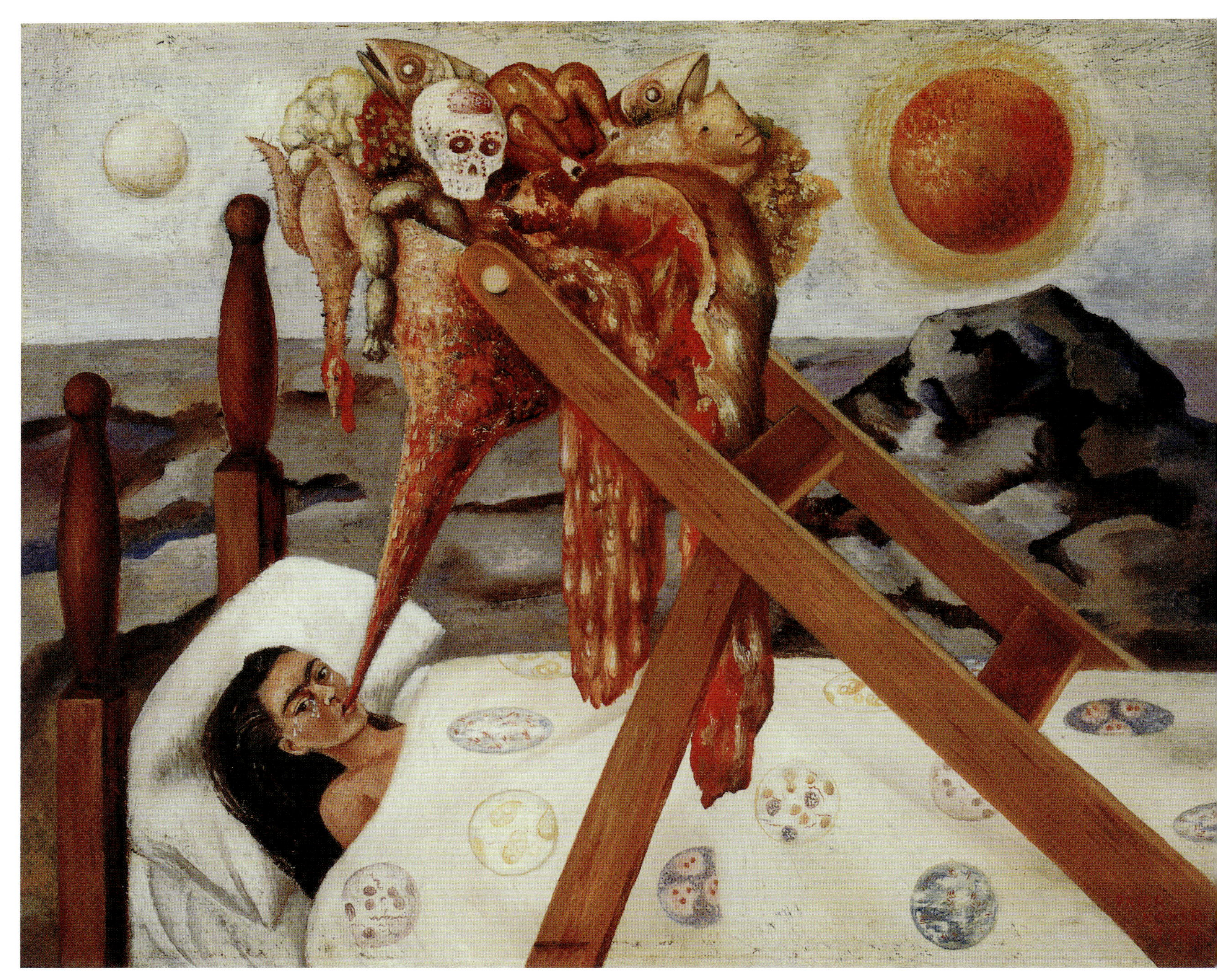

Page 118

Without Hope, 1945.

Oil on canvas, mounted on masonite,

28 x 36 cm, Museo Dolores Olmedo Patiño,

Mexico City.

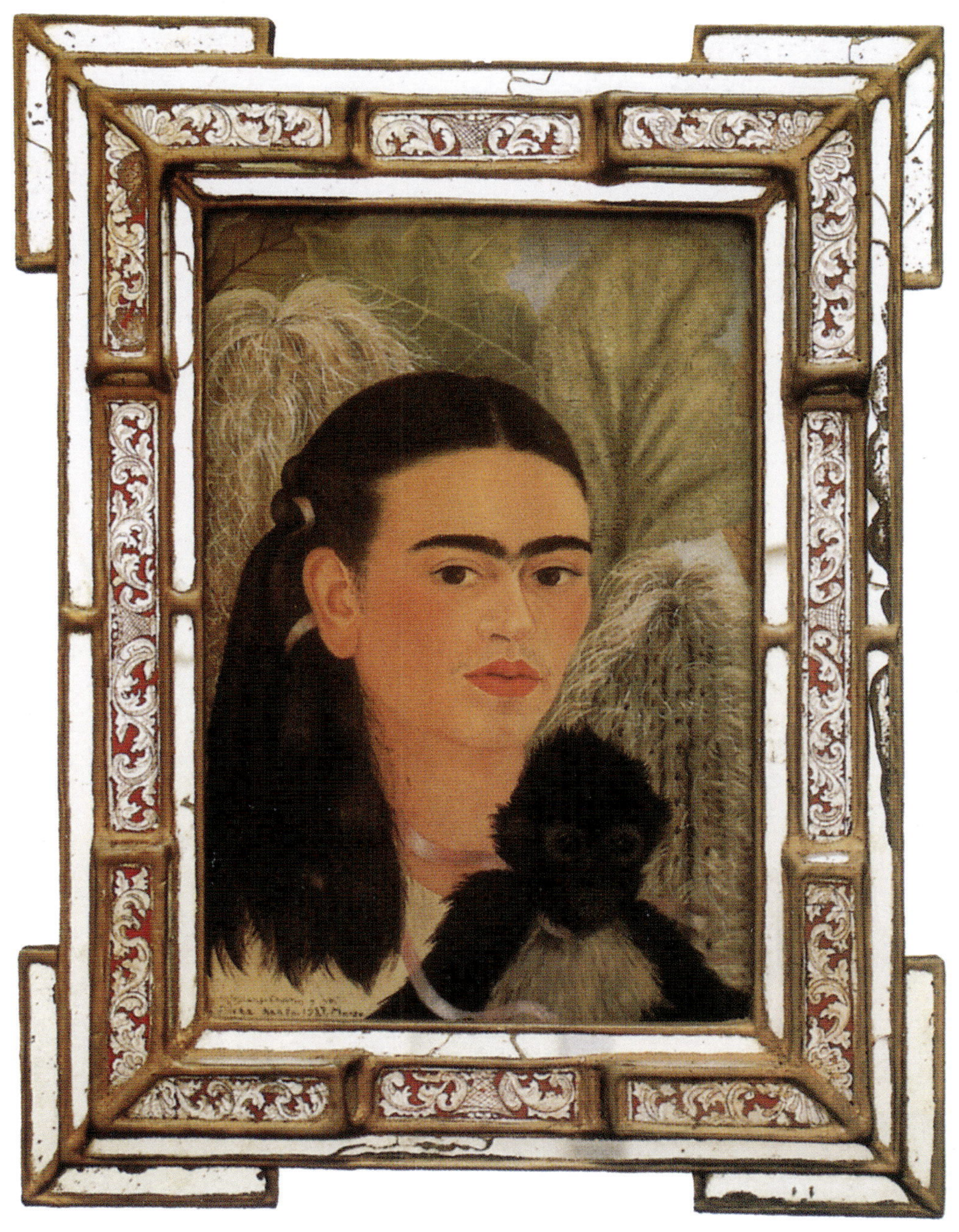

Page 119

Fulang Chang and I, 1937.

Oil on masonite, 40 x 28 cm,

The Museum of Modern Art, New York.

The opposite to this abandonment is *The Deceased Dimas Rosas at the Age of Three* (p. 66-67), a painting on Masonite of a small dead child, swathed in elegant robes of Saint Joseph and crowned in gold-gilded cardboard. This image is part of a tradition of painting or photographing postmortem children dating back to the Sixteenth century. The child is dressed in honor of the Patron Saint of New Spain and holds a scepter of gladiolus. Lying on a woven palm mat amid a scattering of *Cempasuchil* flowers, this "dead angel" is rendered with a delicate, but realistic touch and must have given Frida some hard moments during the painting's execution. She had lost her children before she had a chance to know them.

Page 121

Self-Portrait with Thorny Necklace, 1940.

Oil on canvas, 63.5 x 49.5 cm,

Humanities Reasearch Center, University of Austin (Texas).

Page 122

Diego and I, 1949.

Oil on canvas, mounted on masonite,

29.5 x 22.4 cm,

Private collection, New York.

Page 123

Self-Portrait with Hair down, 1947.

Oil on hard fibre, 61 x 45 cm,

Private collection.

To vent some of her maternal instincts, Frida kept a variety of small animals, mostly little hairless dogs, talking birds and monkeys. One of her favorite critters was *Fulang Chang* which means "Any Old Monkey". In the oil on board painting, *Fulang Chang and I* (p. 119), she surrounds herself with a world of softness: her silky hair, Chang's fur, plant tendrils cascading down in the background. This is a seductive portrait showing the artist at her most feminine.

Amidst this explosion of art, being feminine was important to Frida as she swept into her affair with Leon Trotsky. The old revolutionary succumbed to her charms as she did to his courtly attentions. They were more like giggling students, passing notes hidden in books, covertly seeking opportunities to be alone. Keeping Diego and Natalia in the dark was paramount as the two played their games. Diego never did tumble to the affair as it continued, but Natalia knew the promiscuous appetites of her husband of 35 years and didn't have to understand English to catch on to Frida's not so subtle mooning about.

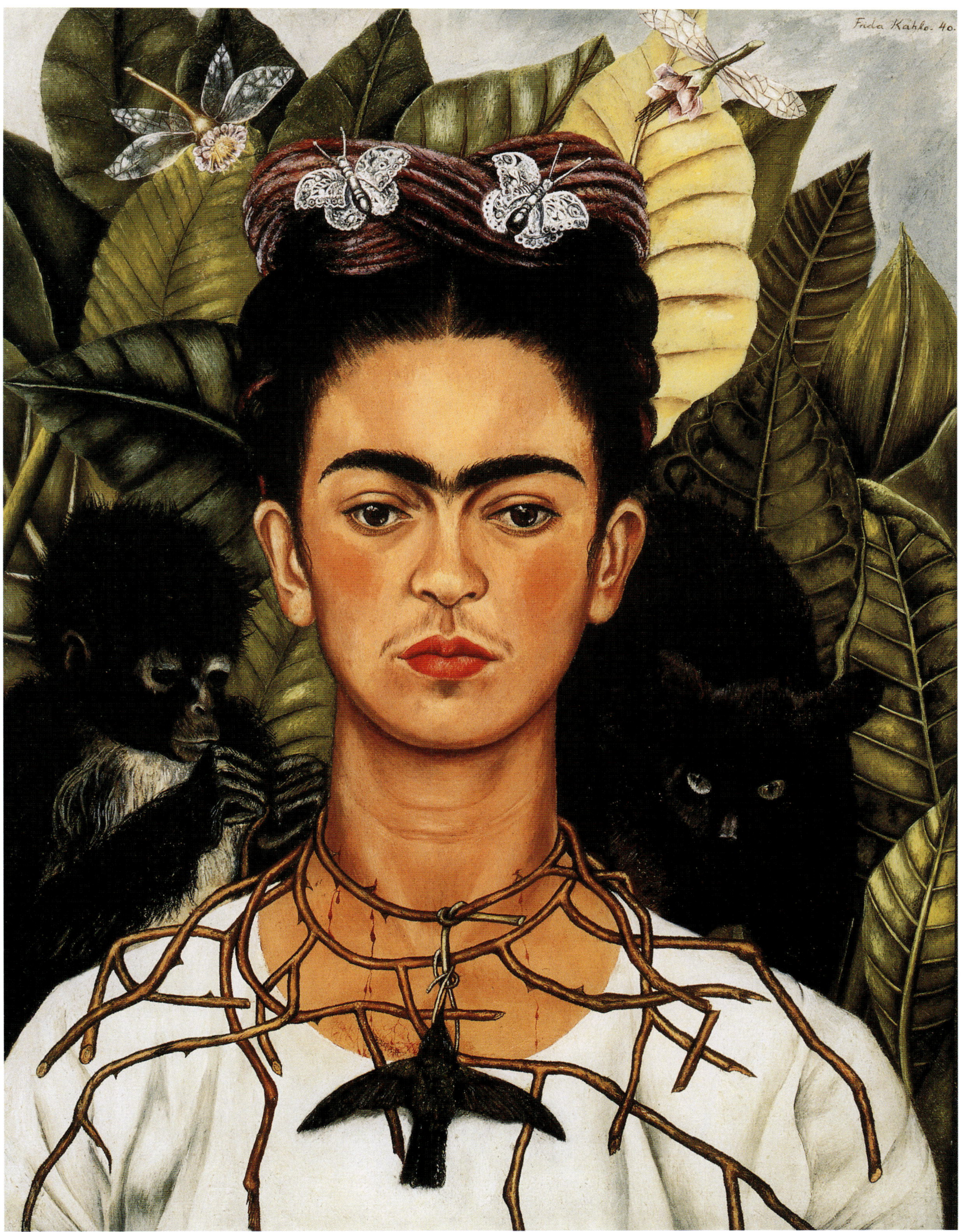
Frida Kahlo. 40.

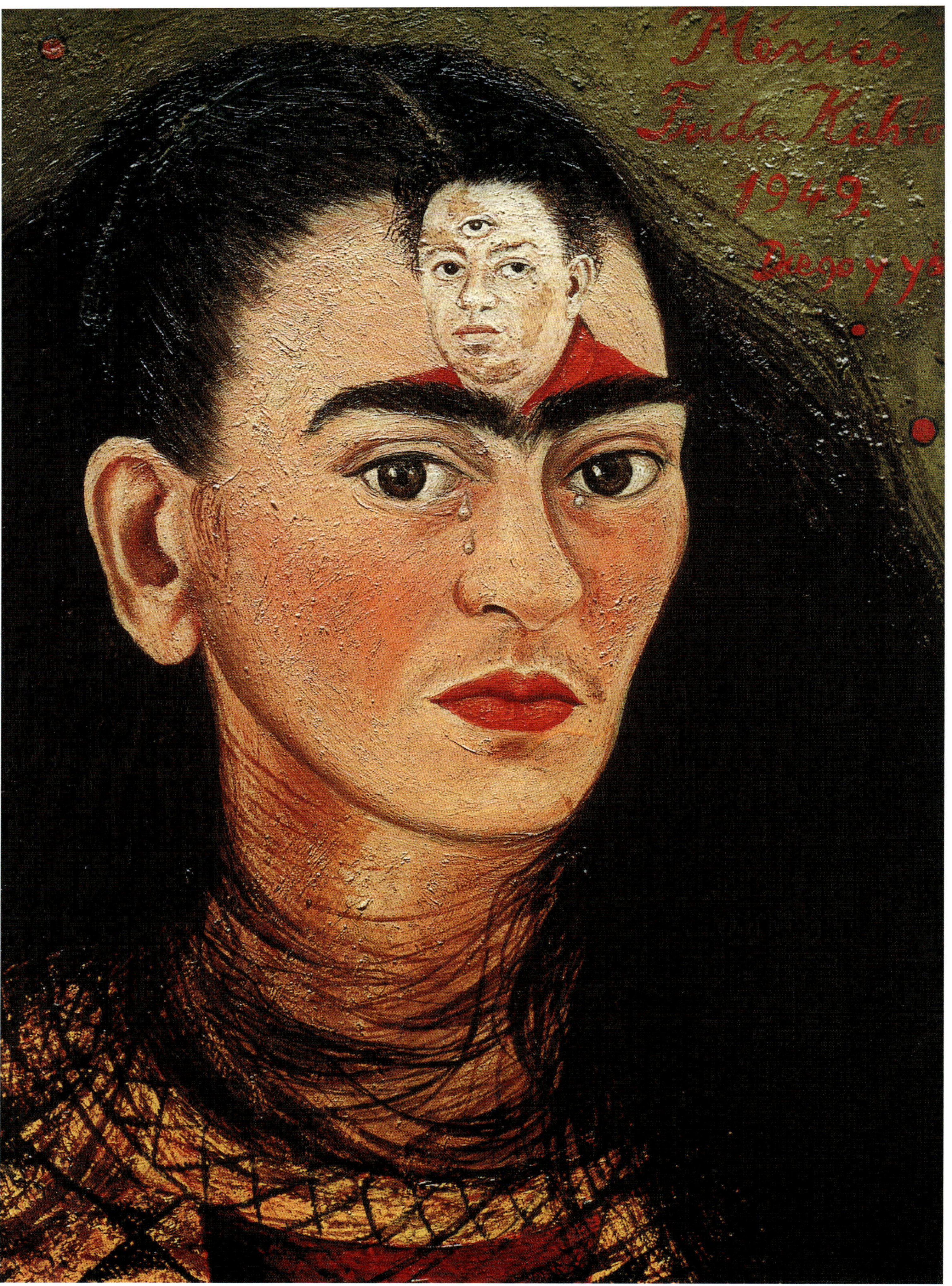
México
Frida Kahlo
1949.
Diego y yo

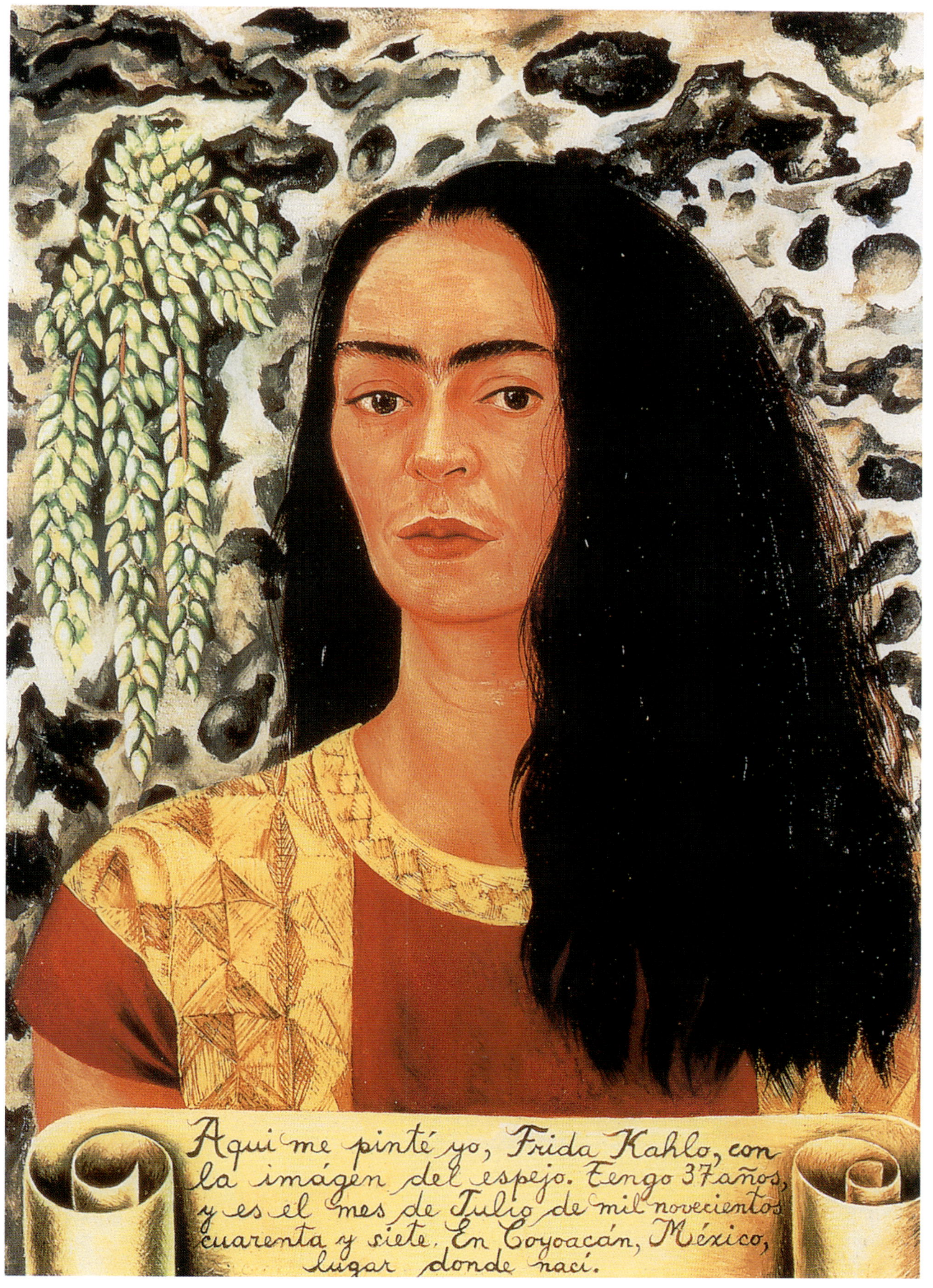
Aqui me pinté yo, Frida Kahlo, con
la imágen del espejo. Tengo 37 años,
y es el mes de Julio de mil novecientos
cuarenta y siete. En Coyoacán, México,
lugar donde nací.

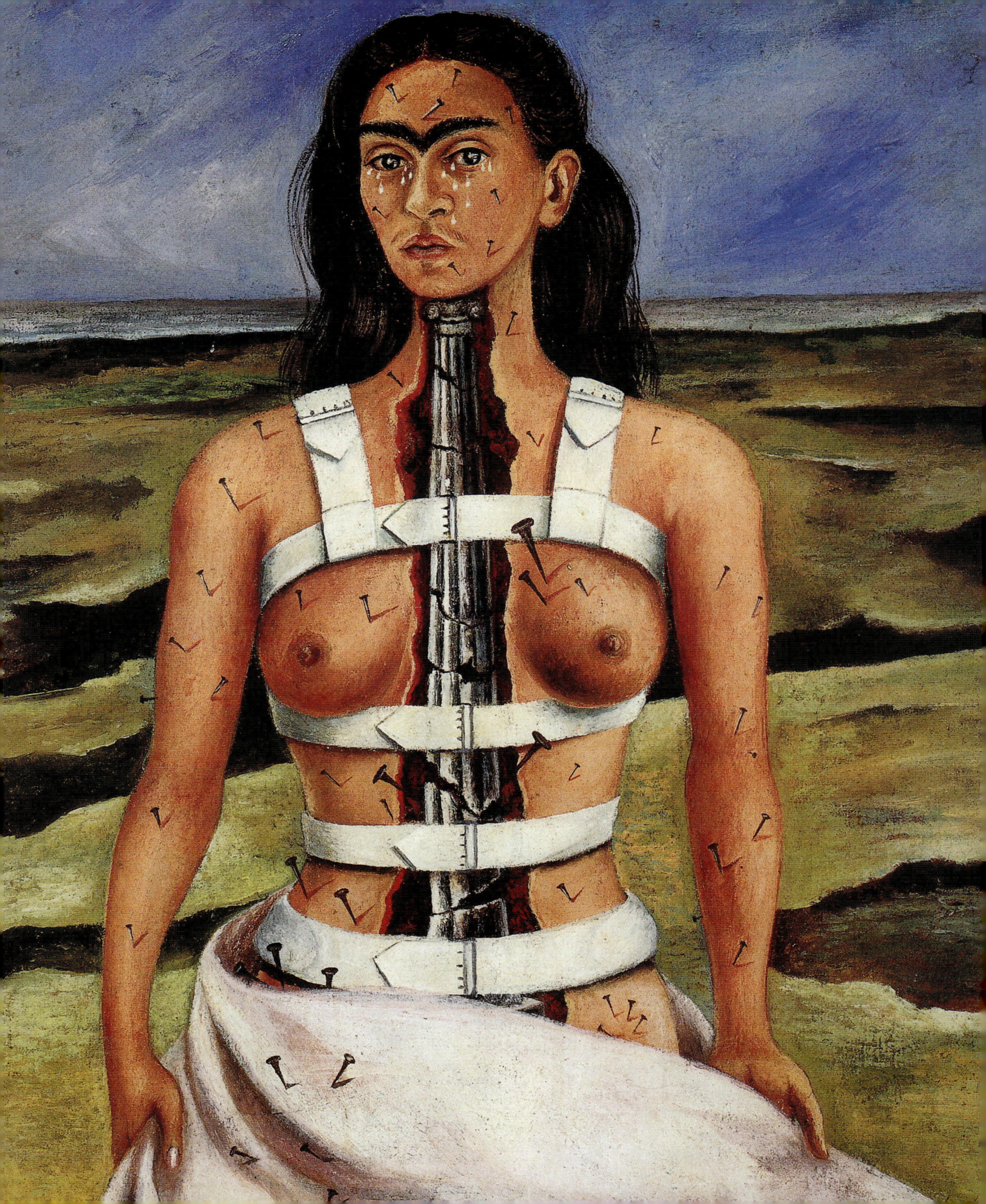

Frida's full length portrait, *Between the Curtains*, that she dedicated in writing to Trotsky - *For Leon Trotsky with all love I dedicate this painting on the 7th of November, 1937* - leaves no doubt about her feelings. The fact that she is dressed in her finest *Tehuana* gown with an intricately woven salmon-colored *reboso* across her shoulders, gives additional weight to the importance of this gift.

At the insistence of his entourage who feared security breeches and also that the affair that might cause a scandal, Trotsky and his party left *La Casa Azul* on July 7, moving to a hacienda 80 miles away from Mexico City. Natalia also added to the pressure and delivered an ultimatum to her infatuated *roué*. The separation and all the other obstacles cooled the affair and soon it ended. Though Trotsky returned to the Blue House 20 days later, the spark was gone. The self portrait, *Between the Curtains*, was given to Trotsky at the end of the affair. He had her again and would have her until the end of his life.

In 1940 a GPU assassin, planted in the household of Trotsky's final bunker-like home in Mexico, killed the "father of the revolution" with an ice axe.

---

[1] Herrera, Hayden, p. 167

[2] Ibid., Herrera, Hayden, p. 181

[3] Ibid., Herrera, Hayden, p. 186

[4] Ibid., Rummel, p.112

[5] Fibromyalgia in Frida Kahlo's life and art, Arthritis Rheum. 2000 Mar;43(3):708-9

Martinez-Lavin, Manuel MD; Amigo, Mary-Carmen MD; Coindreau, Javier MD; Canoso, Juan MD

[6] Rivera, Diego, *Frida Kahlo and Mexican Art*, Buletin del Seminario de Cultura Mexicana, Vol. 1, No. 2 October, 1943

Page 124

The Broken Column, 1944.

Oil on canvas, mounted on masonite, 40 x 30.7 cm, Museo Dolores Olmedo Patiño, Mexico City.

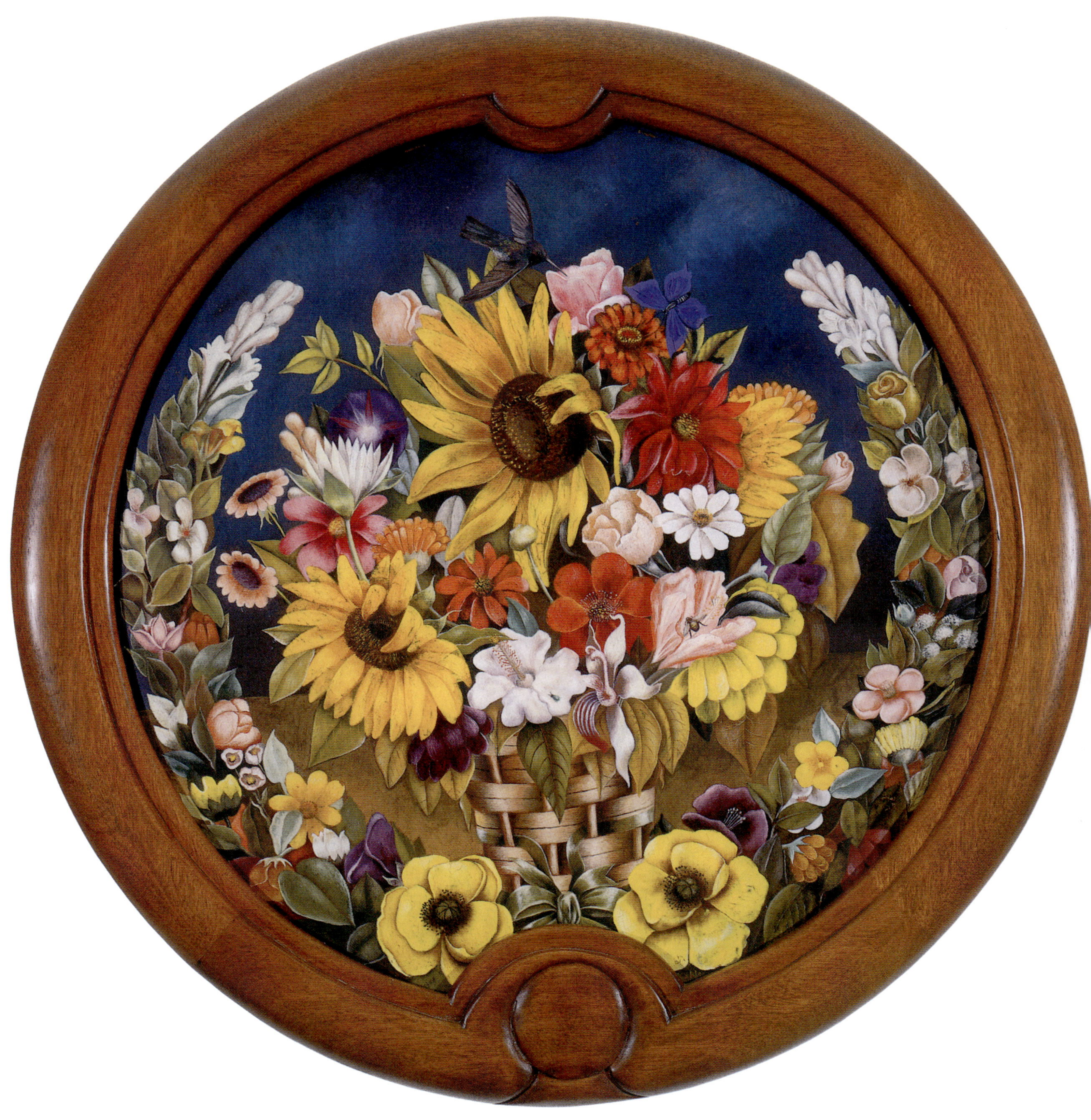

"I urgently need the dough!"

If her search for expression as an artist traveled along many paths in 1937, Frida Kahlo's perception of the economic value of her work began to stir over the next three years. If the truth be told, she never became a self-sustaining artist. Diego Rivera paid her medical bills and kept the refrigerators stocked. Their actual needs were minor, but their whimsical purchases, collections of artifacts and crafts, and other non-essential expenses tallied up huge sums. Though Diego's commissions - and they were sparse from 1937 to 1940 - kept them in funds, Frida handled most of his money. He often left large checks uncashed and buried beneath piles of litter for months. He hated going to the bank. It was "...too much trouble." Since her childhood, Frida had never worried about money. Her father often scrambled for jobs between government changeovers by vote or by bullet, but his reputation as a photographer always kept tortillas on the table. Even before Diego came along, Guillermo managed to pay for Frida's surgeries, treatments and hospital stays. With her considerable medical bills, love of shopping for jewelry, knick-knacks, dolls, her elaborate costumes, and art supplies, plus her growing alcoholism, Frida would be judged "high maintenance" today.

The volume of work begun in 1938 and continued through the 1940s reveals her changed thinking about the paintings from "... not worth offering for sale," to this excerpt from a letter to Emmy Lou Packard dated December 15, 1941 from a charmingly aware saleswoman:

> *...You already know which one it is, right? (My Nurse and I) The one where I am with my nurse suckling puitita leche* (pure milk). *Do you remember? I hope you will encourage them to buy it from me, since you cannot imagine how much I need the bucks now. (Tell them it is worth $250) – I'll send you a photo so you will tell them lots of nice things and you will promote their interest in that "work of art." OK kid! Also tell them about the one with "the bed" (The Dream) that is in New York, it could be they are interested in that one – it is the one with the skeleton on top, do you remember?*

Page 126

Basket of Flowers, 1941.

Oil on copper, 64.5 cm in diameter,

Private collection.

> *That one is worth $300 bucks. Let's see if you can give me a little push, sweetie, for I tell you truly I urgently need the dough.*[1]

But as the calendar ticked over into 1938, Frida still saw herself as a "talented amateur". She had used her work as payment for medical costs to her sympathetic doctor and lifelong friend, Dr. Leo Eloesser. Many friends had her paintings, given to them as keepsakes, but the rest were still stored in her studio or hung on her walls.

Frida Kahlo was no dilettante. She was extensively well read in art history and had personally examined works of great artists during her time in the United States. She had to know her work stood on its own merit and was unique in its themes and execution. But old insecurities die hard. With all the masks peeled away, she was still 13-year-old Frida, "*pata de palo*" (peg leg) to her peers. She was the crippled provincial girl left behind by Alejandro Gomez Arias. She was always cast as the outsider, stared at by the gringos in her Mexican costumes, patronized and condescended to by the press. In person, her shield and armor was the witty, sensuous, mildly vulgar, bisexual party girl she had created and inhabited with apparent relish. Her stoic gazes from photos and her paintings translucently concealed the many psychological hurts and slights she had endured.

But if she wanted to have the last laugh, there was nothing for it but to place her inner secrets, her scars and personal mythology in front of the public inquisition and await the reading of the verdict. At a group exhibition of Mexican art held in the Social Action Department Gallery of the University of Mexico, she sent *My Grandparents, My Parents and I* (p. 92-95) and three other "personal" works to the "...small and rotten place." She confessed to Lucienne Bloch, "...I send them there without any enthusiasm, four or five people said they were swell..."[2]

She was completely unprepared for the letter that arrived a short time after the show closed. Manhattan gallery owner Julien Levy had been approached by someone who had seen the University exhibition. Levy asked if she would consent to an exhibit of her paintings in his gallery on East 55th Street. It's not difficult for anyone who has tentatively pushed one

Page 129
Still Life, 1942.
Oil on copper, c.63 cm in diameter,
Museo Frida Kahlo, Mexico City.

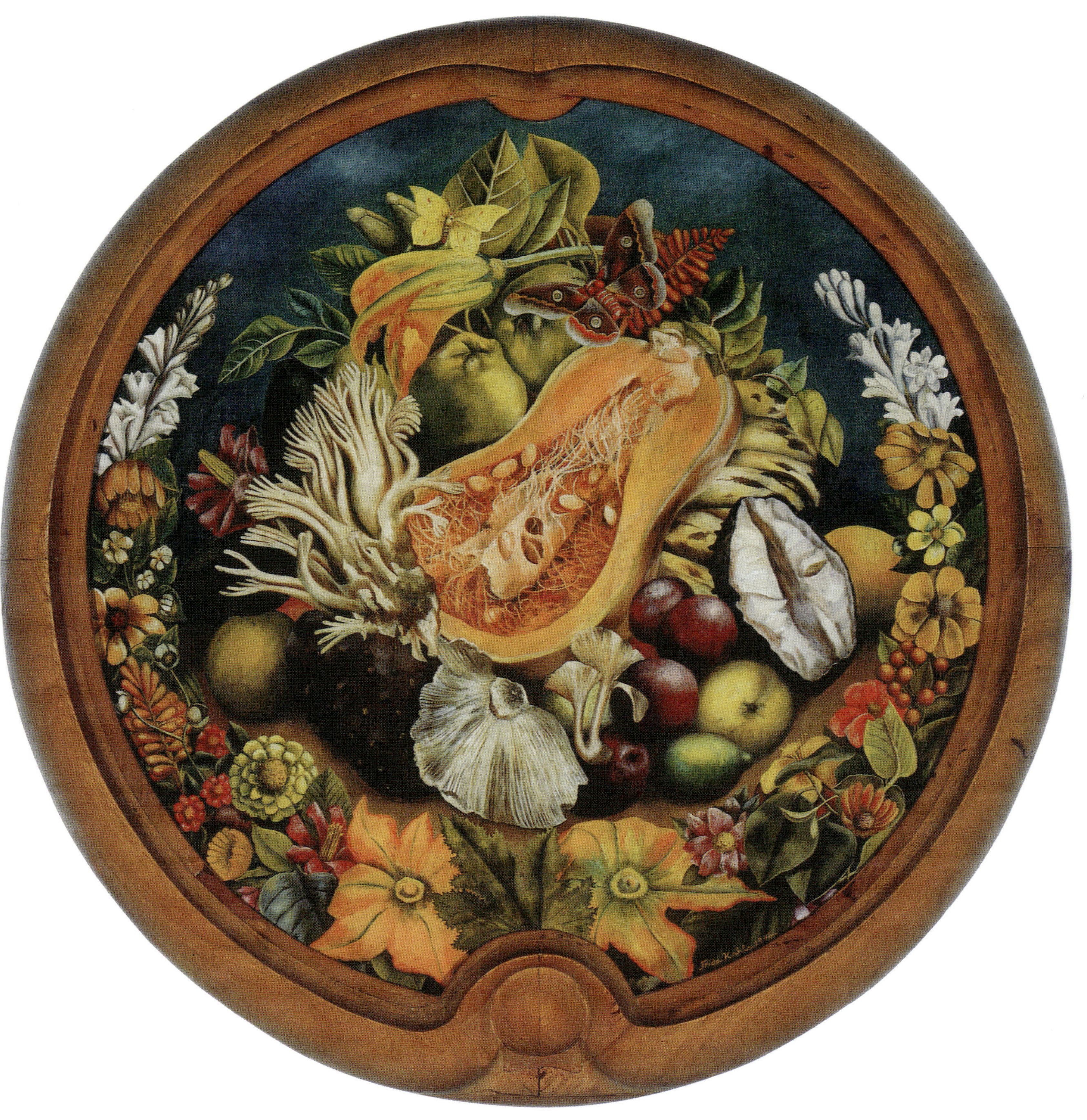

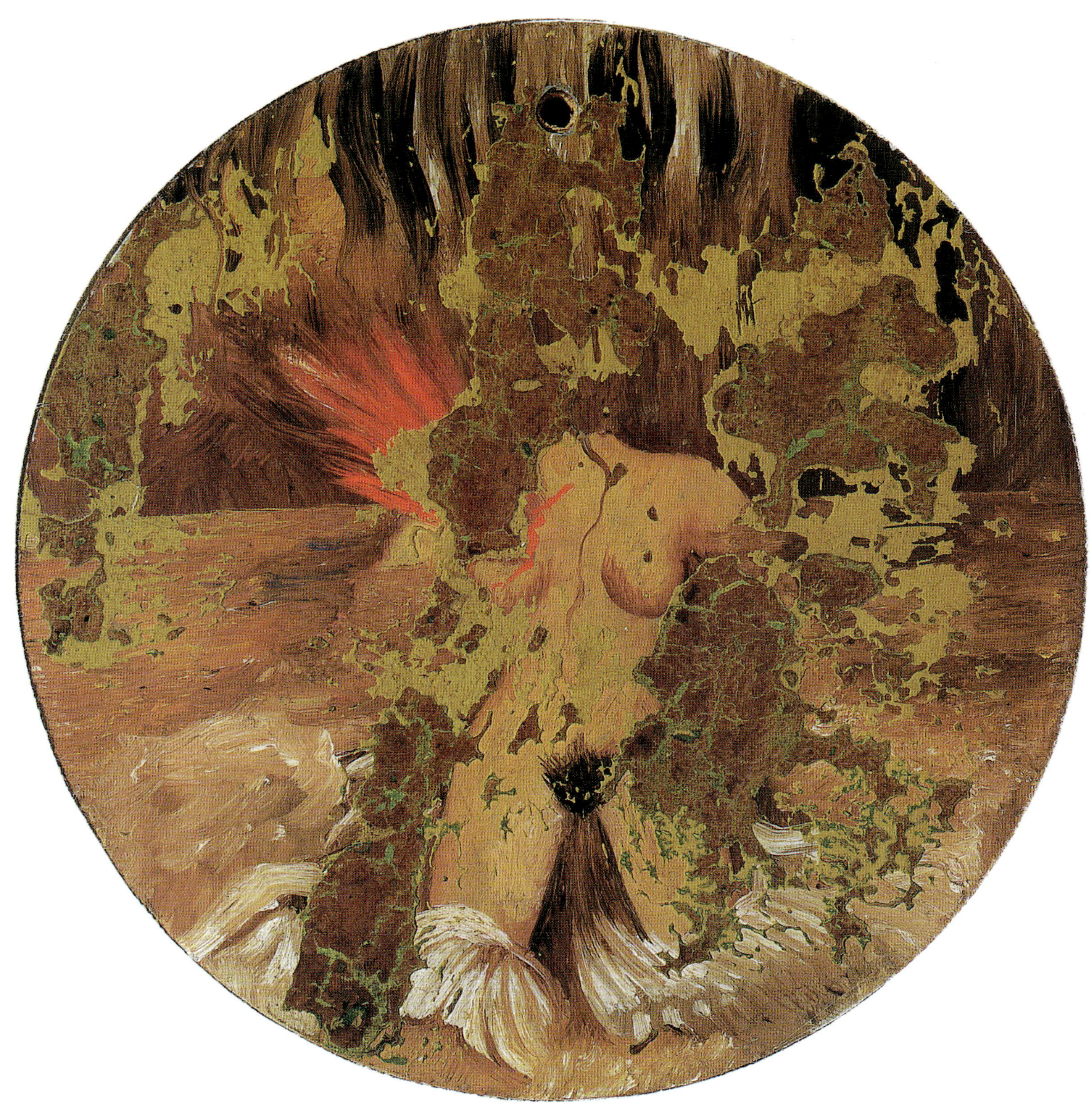

of their darlings out into public for judgment - whether it is a painting, a poem, or a jar of fruit jam - to appreciate the ripple of excitement that must have raced through the hand that held that letter. And yet how many good things had been snatched away? She sent him a few photos of her paintings. Levy answered with another, even more enthusiastic letter. Could she send 30 works by October? Yes, she could and began looking at her works in a new way, as her personal creations hanging on walls in a gallery in New York City.

As preparations moved ahead, another force for change moved into her life. The self-styled "pope" of Surrealism, Andre Breton sailed into Mexico, sent by the French Ministry of Foreign Affairs on a lecture tour. With his beautiful wife, Jaqueline, he hooked up with the Riveras and sought out Trotsky. With Natalia in tow to look after Leon, the three couples set out to view Mexico and hold a series of great discussions on Surrealism, Communism and Mexico's ties with its ancient past as championed by Rivera. Frida and Jaqueline fled Trotski's windy socio-political rants and Andre's determination to see Surrealism behind every bush. The two women struck up a friendship of convenience to entertain each other.

Breton eventually saw Frida's paintings and immediately proclaimed her a *Surrealist.* He became so enamored with her and her work - and her value as a recruit to the Surrealist movement - he gave the imprimatur of his prestige to her paintings with a flowery, rambling essay to be attached to her New York show brochure. For example:

> *This art even contains that drop of cruelty and humor uniquely capable of blending the rare effective powers that compound together to form the philtre which is Mexico's secret. The power of inspiration here is nourished by the strange ecstasies of puberty and the mysteries of generation, and, far from considering these to be the mind's private preserves, as in some colder climates, then displays them proudly with a mixture of candor and insolence...*

His summation of her work, her blending of feminism, exploration of her psyche, and the visceral realities of sensuality and physical pain were comparable to "...a ribbon about a bomb." Along with his grandiloquent text went an offer of a show in Paris following her New York triumph.

Page 130
The Circle, 1951.
Oil on aluminium monted on panel,
15 cm in diameter,
frame in wood: 32 x 31 cm,
no signature and undated
Museo Dolores Olmedo Patiño, Mexico City.

Besides Breton's huffing and puffing, Diego had also been busy on her behalf. The film star, Edward G. Robinson, a well-known art connoisseur and collector visited Rivera's studio. While Frida entertained Mrs. Robinson on the roof of the twin house, Diego hustled Mr. Robinson into Frida's studio. On seeing a line-up of her work, Edward G. Robinson purchased four paintings for a total of $800. On hearing this, Frida's vision of economic independence loomed large. Despite the fact that Diego was her biggest booster, she seemed excited about cutting all ties to him.

Spurred on by the New York show's promise, Frida's output soared. In 1938, she painted *What the Water Gave Me, Four Inhabitants of Mexico City, Girl with Death Mask* and a series of still lifes. Self portraits for that period included the wildly colorful *Framed Self-Portrait* (*The Frame*) and an almost monochromatic *Escuincle Dog with Me.*

This series of paintings demonstrates the wide range of her selected subject matter, palettes, and the storehouse of internal imagery she could call upon. *What the Water Gave Me* is a veritable and literal stew of symbolic images floating, or lying submerged in her bath water. Her feet appear reflected in the water's surface, looking like two disembodied crab-objects. From a New York skyscraper thrusting its way up from the caldera of an ancient Mexican volcano to portraits of her parents among the fertile plants and roots of her upbringing, she creates a panoply of life moments and impressions. Sex, love and death are all part of this composite like many exposures on a single piece of imaginary film.

When Breton saw *What the Water Gave Me* and *Four Inhabitants of Mexico City*, in his mind Frida's place in the pantheon of Surrealists was secure. In the latter work, the four characters standing before the buildings of Mexico City's landscape have an odd Oz-like quality of whimsy: the Judas character, a little girl, the Pre-Colombian idol and a watchful skeleton. Observing them from behind is a woven straw *piñata.* They are a blend of old and new Mexico, of figments of the imagination and reality. Even the little girl seems puzzled by it all.

Page 133
What the Water Gave Me, 1938.
Oil on canvas, 91 x 70.5 cm,
Collection Isidore Ducasse, France.

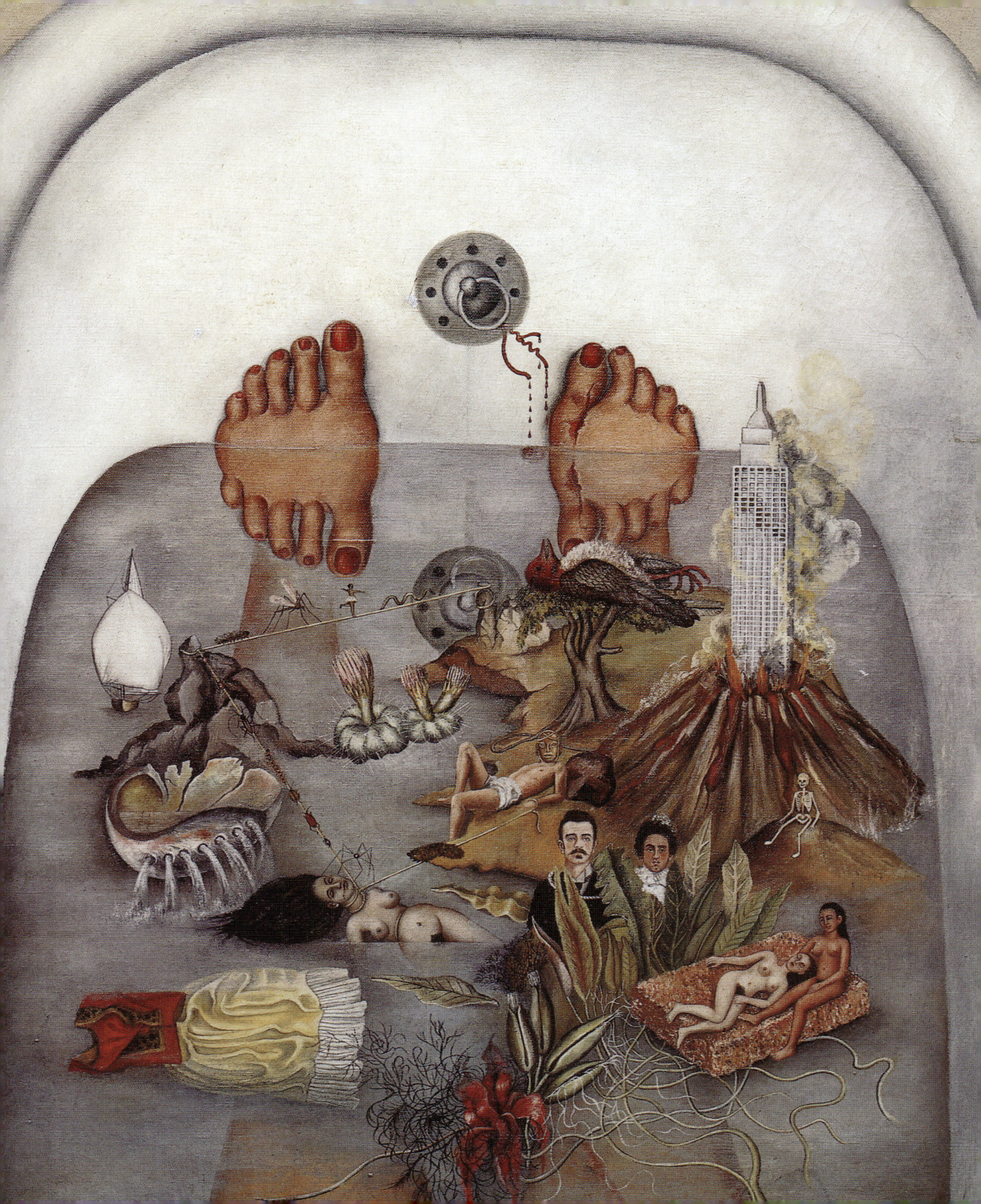

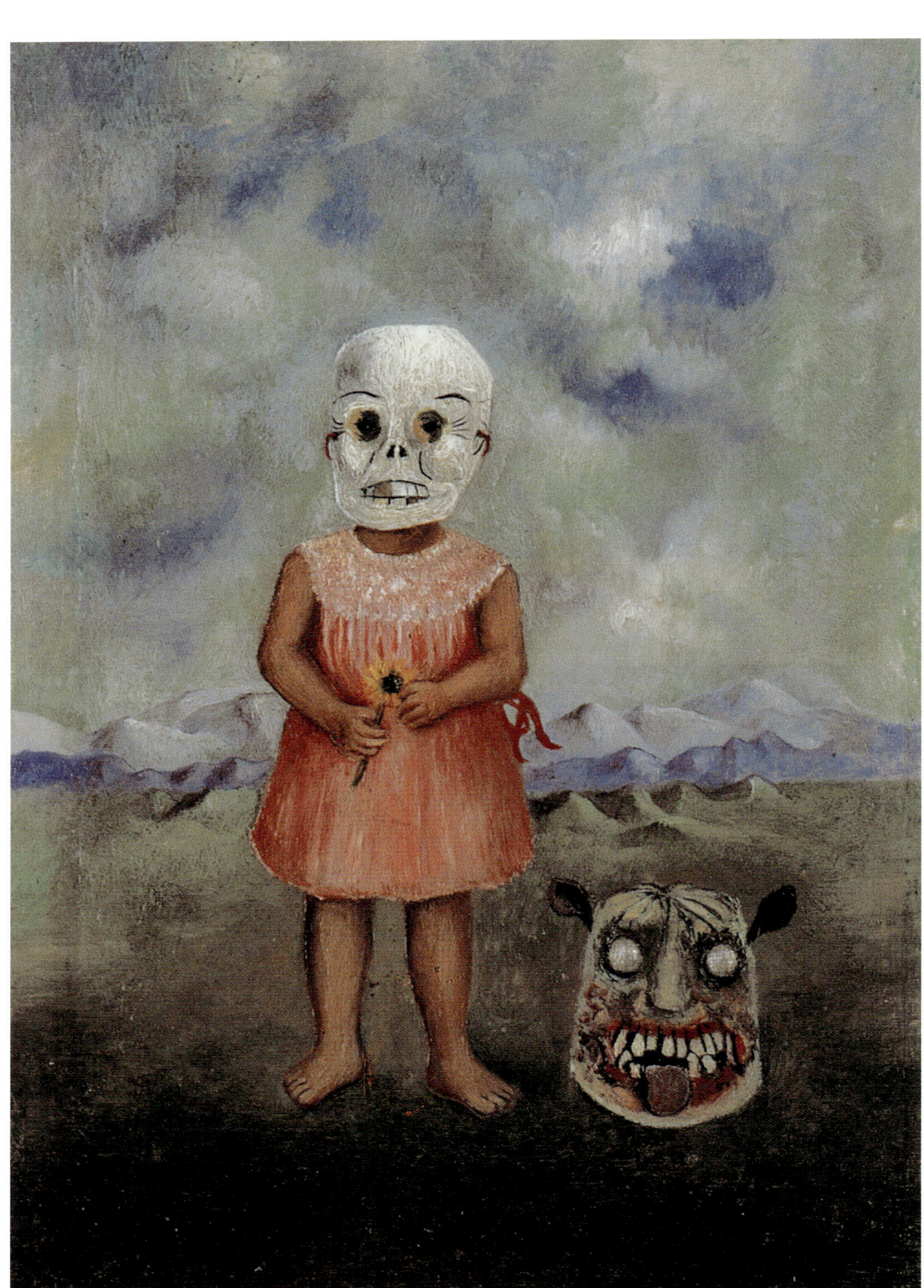

Page 134

Girl with Death-Mask, 1938.

Oil on metal, 20 x 14.9 cm,

Private collection.

Page 135

Marxism Will Give Health to the Sick,

c.1954.

Oil on hard fibre, 76 x 61 cm,

Museo Frida Kahlo, Mexico City.

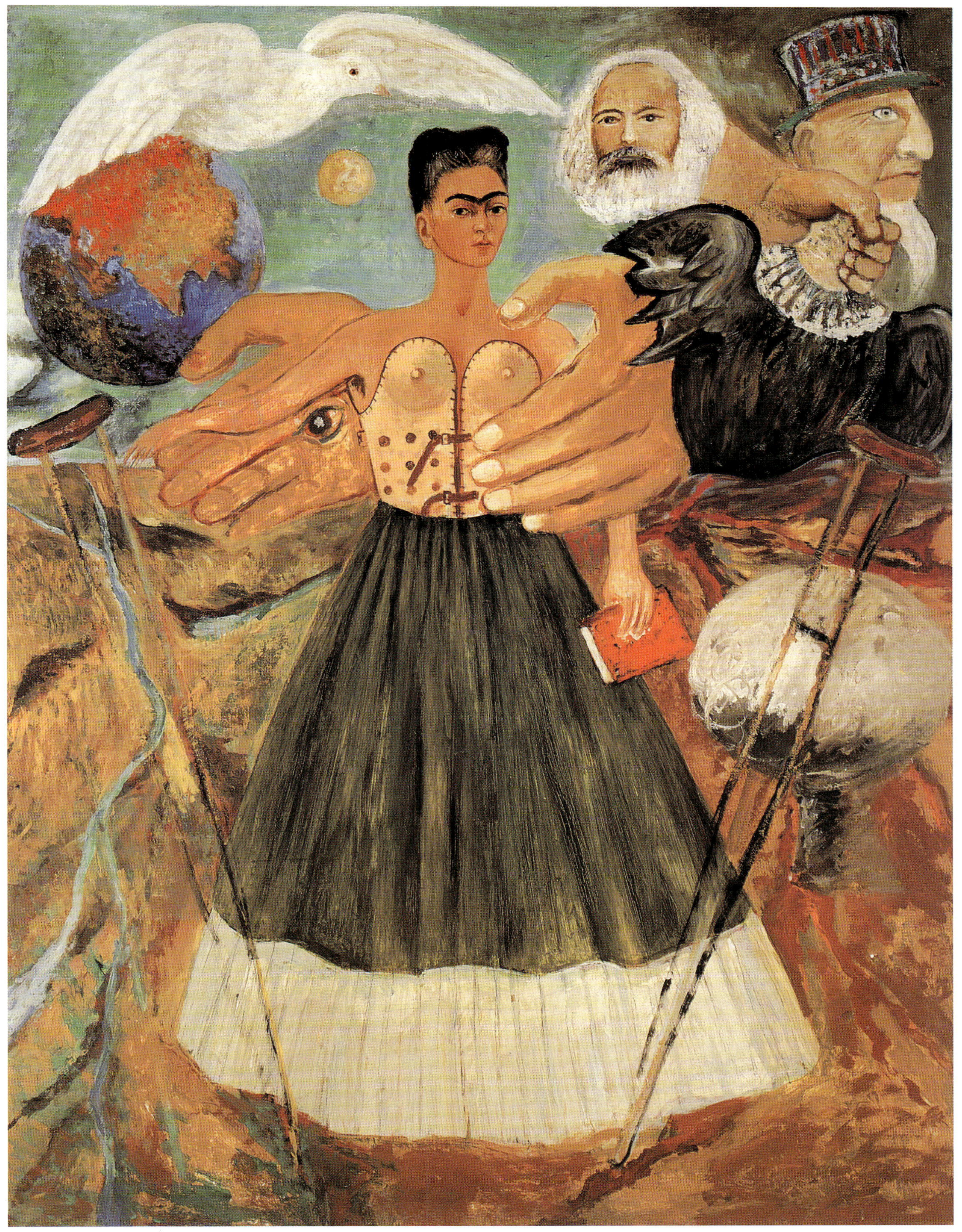

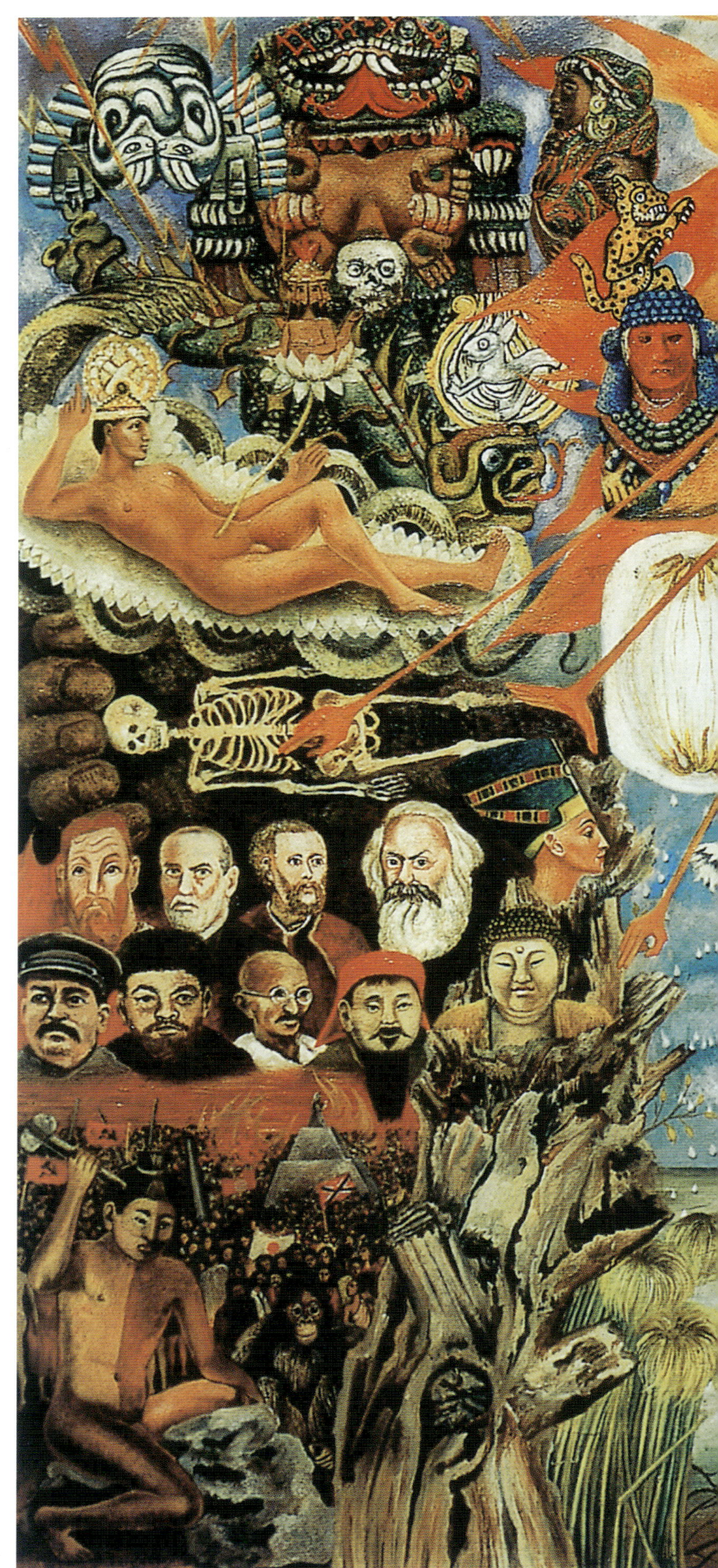

Page 136-137

Moses or *Nucleus of Creation*, 1945.

Oil on hard fibre, 61 x 75.6 cm,

Private collection.

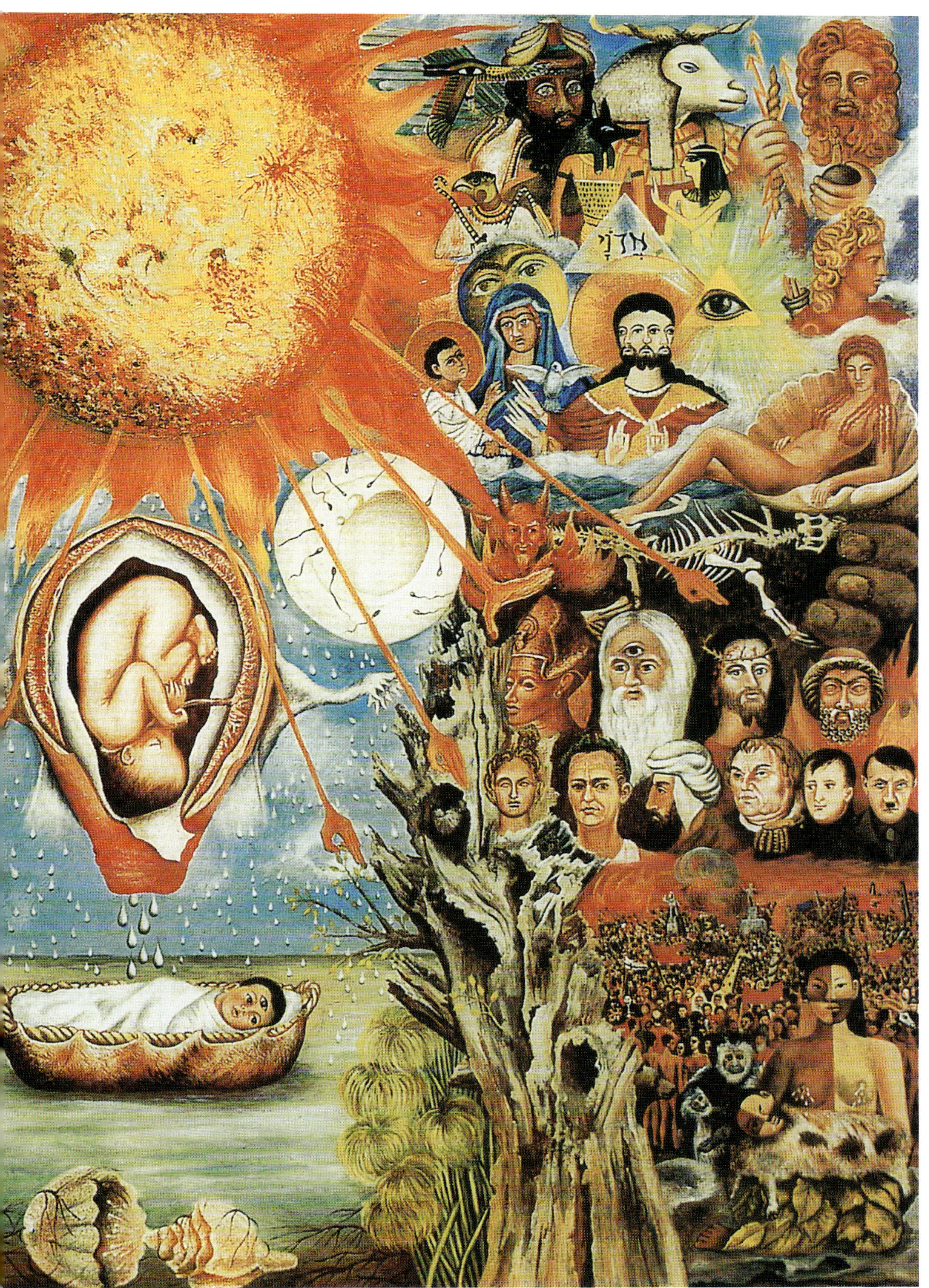

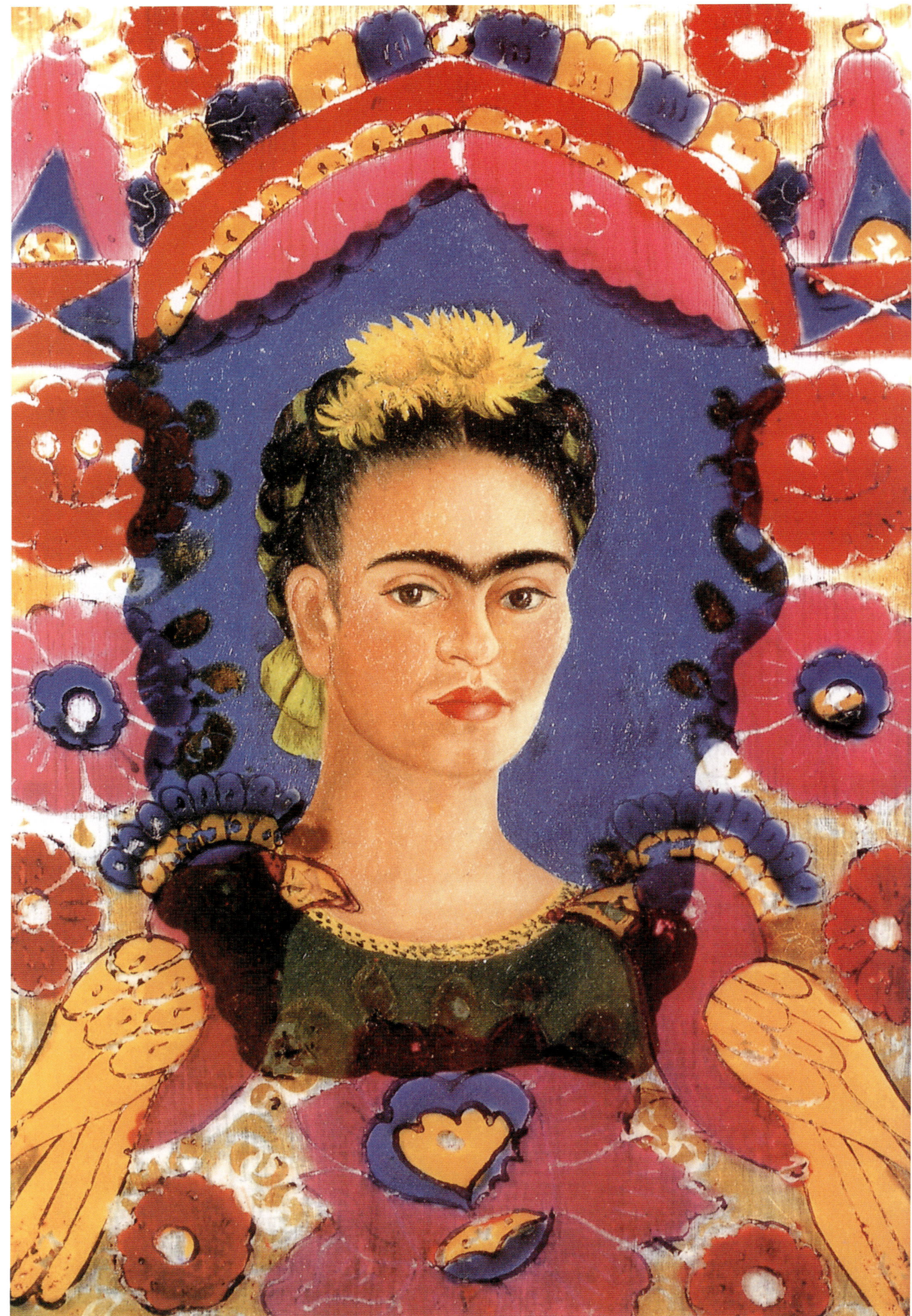

A little girl figures more directly in Kahlo's hand-size painting, *Girl with Death Mask.* Here, all dressed up in a pink party frock, a small and barefoot girl wears a skull mask as if waiting for a Day of the Dead celebration to begin. Next to her, against the roiled stormy sky and desert, rests a horrific ritual mask of a Pre-Columbian monster, its lips besmirched with blood and its tongue protruding between jagged teeth. The yellow flower in her hand is the *zempazuchil,* a traditional decoration for graves during Day of the Dead festivities. Dolores del Rio, the film actress and friend of Frida and Diego, received this painting as a gift. She said it represented the baby Frida never had.[3]

The two self-portraits: *The Frame* and *Escuincle Dog with Me,* demonstrate two radically different views of the artist. In Elizabethan times, the multiple portraits painted of Queen Elizabeth I near the end of her reign used the same face template that was simply applied with different costumes in order to hide her aging. Frida's apparently consistent stoic gaze changes in subtle ways according to her internal and external environment.

In *The Frame* there is a water-color-like transparency to the oils applied to metal, a liquidity on which floats her portrait against a sea-blue background. She is flanked by two tropical birds. On her head is a tiara of flowers that compliments her flushed cheeks and the jade green of her dress. The effect is that of a symmetrical postage stamp featuring a fresh, young Mexican girl. The dark portrait, *Escuincle Dog with Me,* is a polar opposite. Here, she and one of her many lap dogs share a regal sitting on a bare stage. The texture of Frida's *Tehuana* skirt matches the sheen of the dog's coat while her costume is set off by gold brocade and a matching rope necklace. A blue ribbon at the back of her neck is the sole jarring note of color in this rich harmony of earth tones while her omnipresent cigarette is gripped in a goldantique holder looped around her index finger. This is a command performance in her best clothes of the *Señora de la Casa.*

Adding to this collection is the series of still life paintings. Frida frequently referred to the fruits of Mexico's rich soil in her allegory paintings, but here she concentrates on these organic shapes. In her hands, the fruits of the soil take on a somewhat sinister appearance of reaching tendrils and prickly textures, of gashed and hacked surfaces showing blood-red

Page 138

Self-Portrait "The Frame", c.1938.

Oil on aluminium and glass, 29 x 22 cm,

National Museum of Modern Art, Centre

Georges Pompidou, Paris.

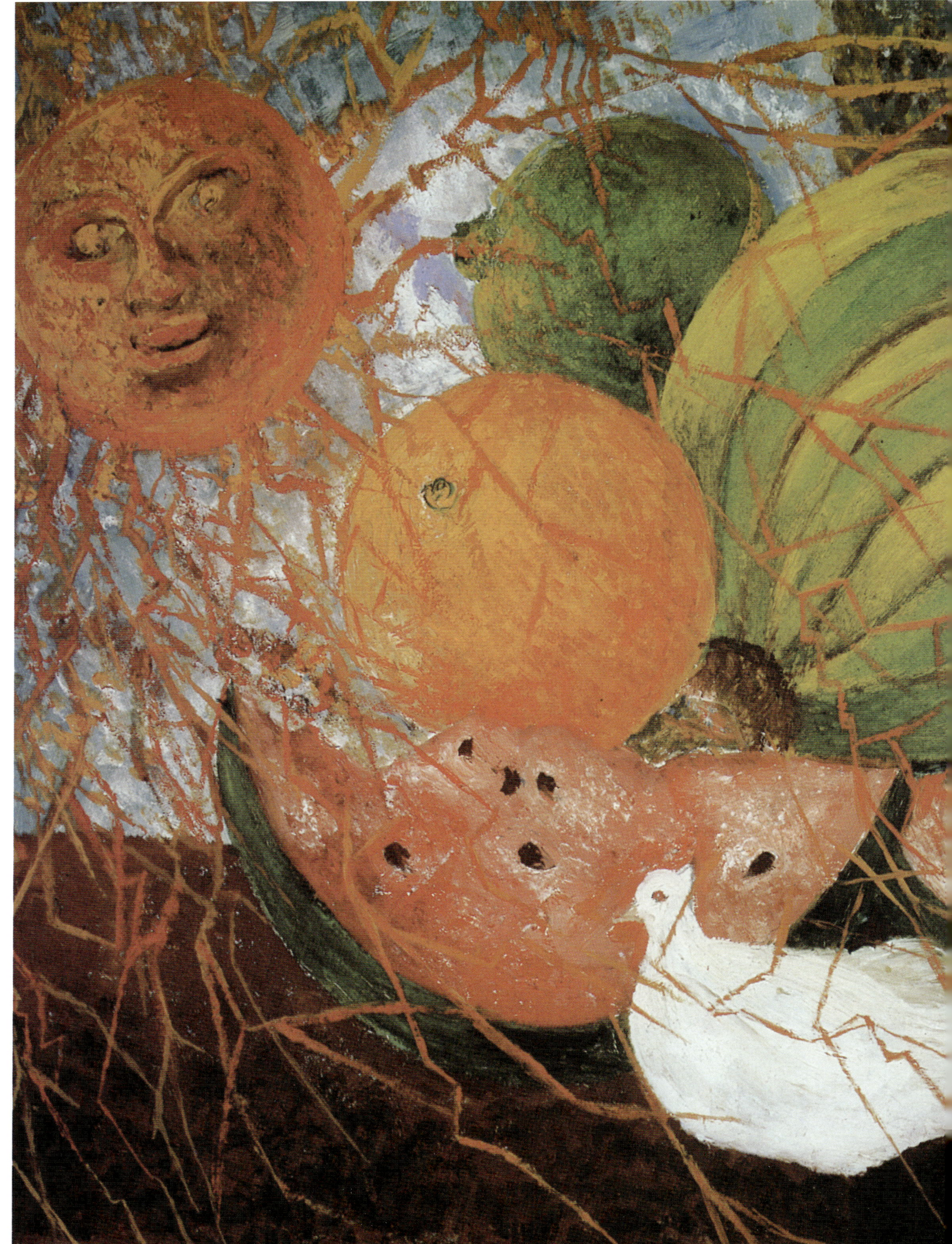

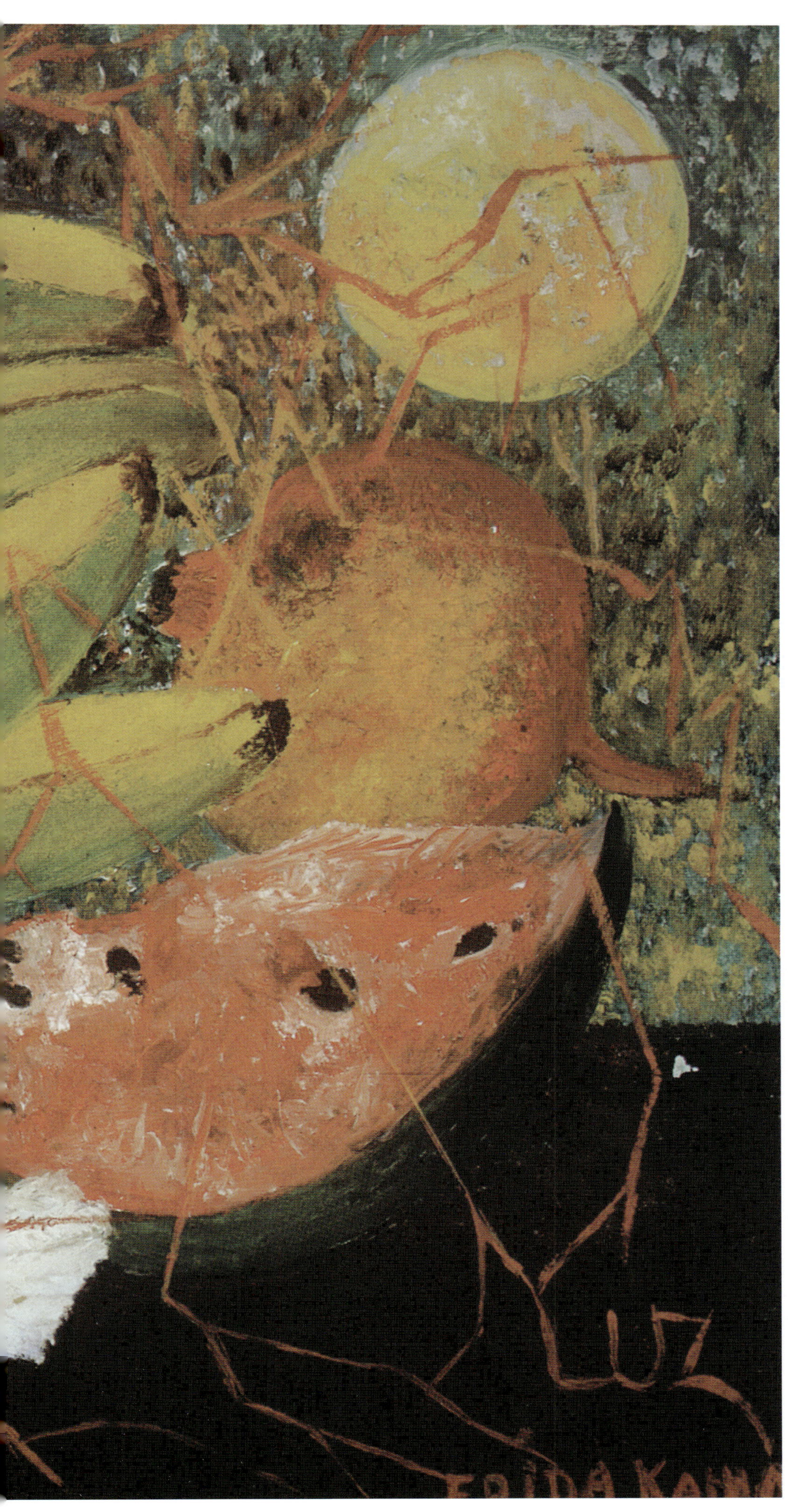

Page 140-141

Fruits of Life, 1953.

Oil on hard fibre, 47 x 62 cm,

Collection Raquel M. de Espinosa Ulloa,

Mexico City.

pulp beneath. Mushrooms and plants become sexual organs and flower petals age and curl inward. There is an over-sweet corruption suggested, a return to the earth with the functions of life having been fulfilled.

One charmingly erotic example of this 1938 collection is *Flower of Life* featuring a male phallus plunging into a female vagina while the act is portrayed as a fuzzy red blossom ejaculated from a matured plant pod. This painting was submitted along with some other floral paintings to the annual Mexico City flower show, *Salon de la Flor.* Imagine show attendees discovering this gem among the petunias and sun flowers.

Fortified with letters of introduction from Diego to the high and mighty of New York's art world and an invitation list representing a powerful cross-section of the social set they had cultivated back in 1933, Frida plunged into the scene. She was an immediate sensation. Critics loaded and cocked their pens, but came away charmed and impressed. Even the Rockefellers and their kin had been included, apparently with the idea that the possibilities of commerce held sway over old grudges.

Though she moved through the opening night crowd as the star of the show, it was obvious that the ghost of Diego Rivera was both a drawing card and a *raison* for New York to pay homage to his third wife. Regardless, she relished the attention. In particular, she enjoyed her distance from Diego and the unfettered freedom to flirt with men and women of her choice. Her exotic presence, her costumes, and even her bold, scrappy, almost mannish aggression drew companions to her. She reunited with her old flame, Isamu Noguchi and hooked up with handsome fashion photographer Nickolas Muray. In hot pursuit, however, was her sponsor, Julien Levy. He fluttered around her, ever the handsome attentive butterfly. At one point, she accompanied him for an overnight visit to one of his clients, millionaire Edgar Kaufmann, at Kaufmann's famous Frank Lloyd Wright designed home, Fallingwater. On arrival, Levy was prepared for a night of incredible passion with his hot-blooded Mexican protégé. Instead, Frida's charms had also ignited Kaufmann's libido and the two men spent part of the night trying to outmaneuver each other in a French farce of tip-toeing up and down staircases and slamming doors. In the end, Levy got his wish when Frida sneaked into his bedroom.

Page 143

Portrait of Doña Rosita Morillo, 1944.
Oil on canvas, mounted on masonite,
76 x 60.5 cm,
Museo Dolores Olmedo Patiño, Mexico City.

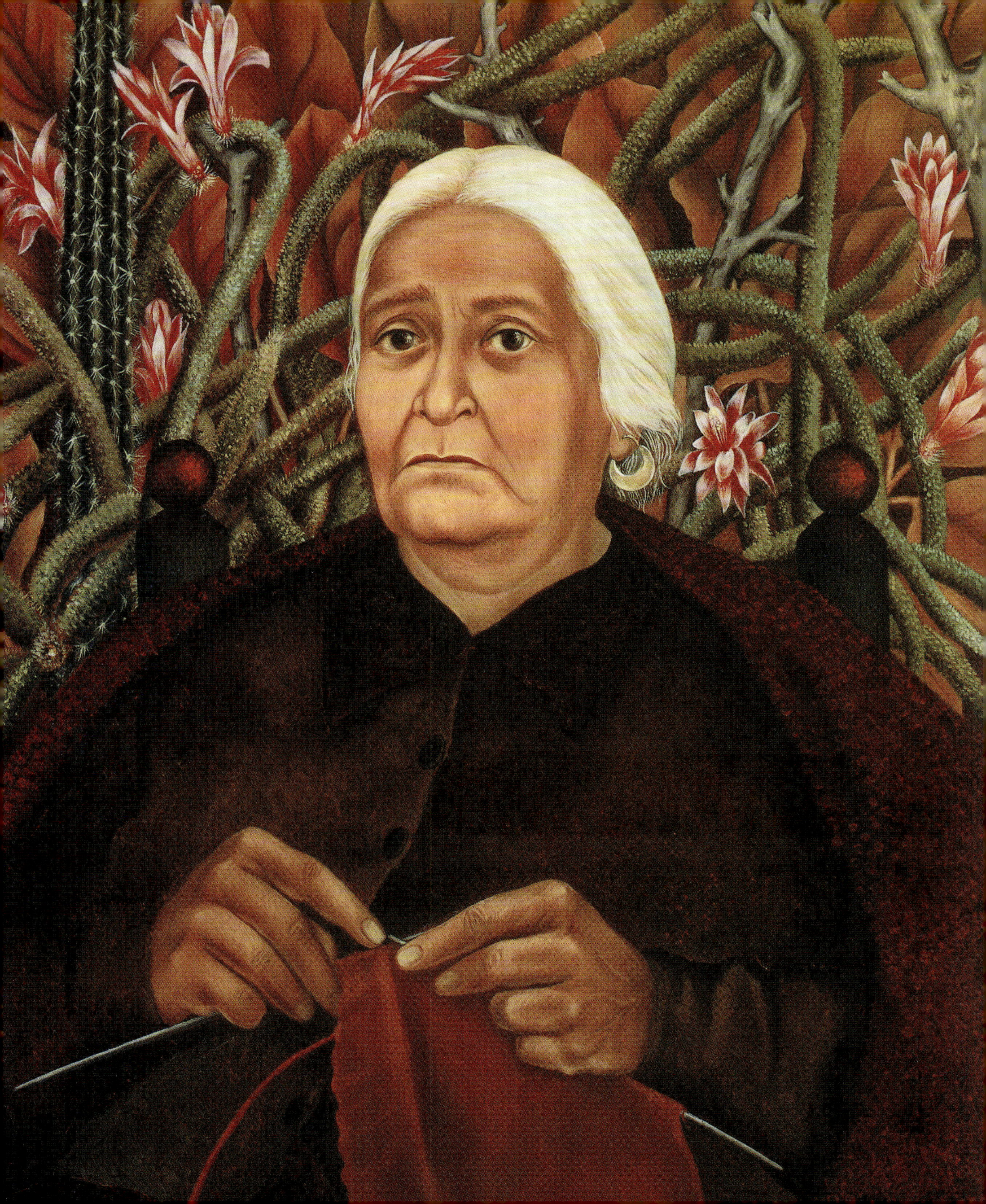

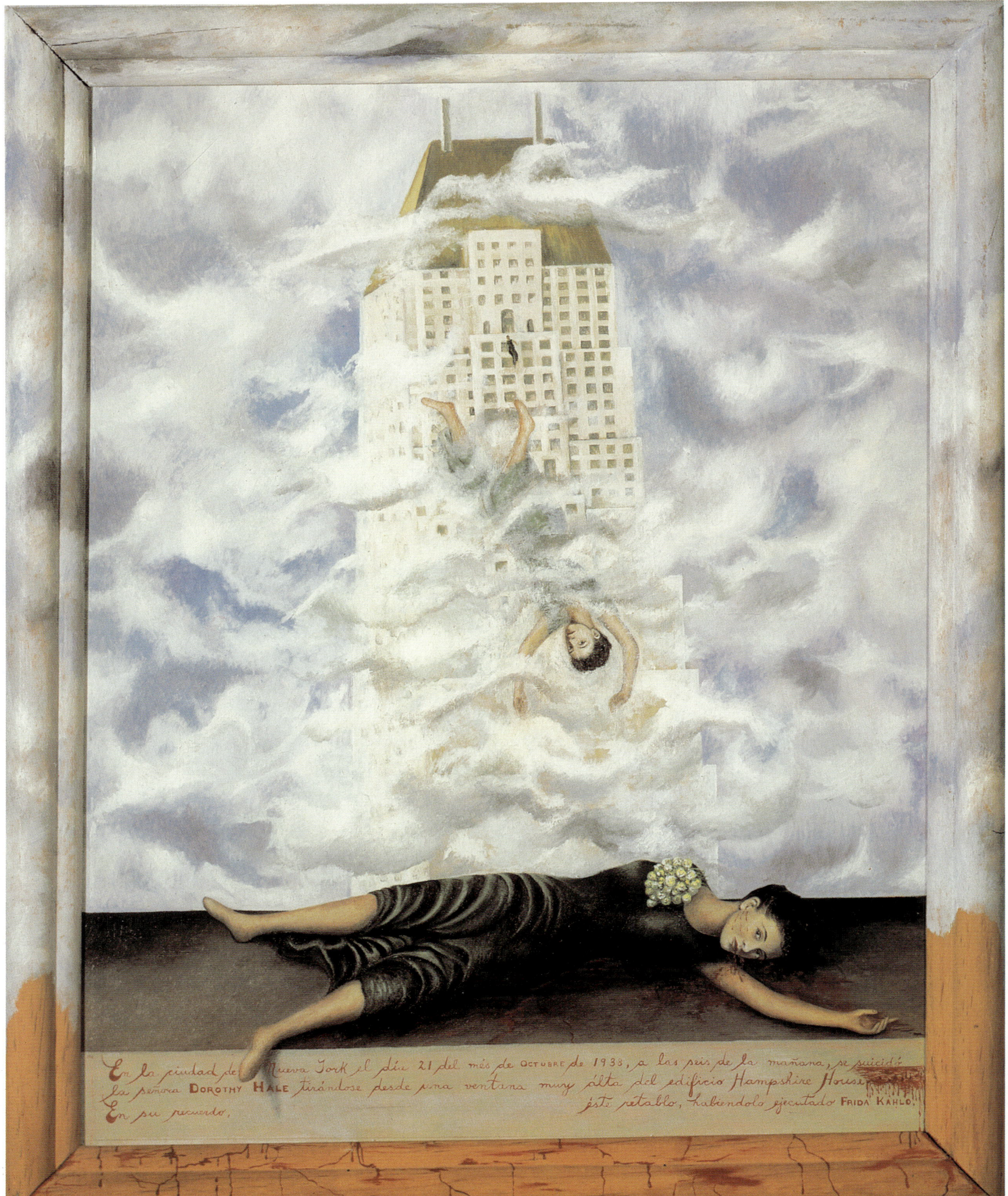
En la ciudad de Nueva York el día 21 del més de OCTUBRE de 1938, a las seis de la mañana, se suicidó
la señora DOROTHY HALE tirándose desde una ventana muy álta del edificio Hampshire House.
éste retablo, habiendolo ejecutado FRIDA KAHLO.
En su recuerdo,

Muray had better luck. He had met Frida in Mexico and helped her with the catalog for her show. The socially prominent photographer was handsome and self-confidant. Their affair began in Mexico City, but without gun-toting Diego lumbering about, they caught fire in New York and she fell hard for him. In a letter to her "...adorable Nick" from Mexico on February 27, 1939, she wrote concerning $400 he had sent her from a "Mr. Smith...":

> *I have enough to stay here a month or more. I have my return ticket. Everything is under control so realy (sic), my love, it is not fair that you should spend anything extra... Any way, you can not imagine how much I appreciated your desire of helping me. I have not words to tell you what joy it gives me to think that you were willing to make me happy and to know how good-hearted and adorable you are – My lover, my sweetest mi Nick – mi vida – mi nino, te adoro.*[4]

Art lovers purchased about half the paintings that were offered for sale - which is a good first outing - and Frida managed to snag a few commissions. Clare Booth Luce ordered a portrait of her friend Dorothy Hale who had recently committed suicide by jumping off a skyscraper. Unfortunately, Frida misunderstood the request and painted a two-part re-enactment of the death, *The Suicide of Dorothy Hale* (p. 144) shows Hale in mid-flight through swirling clouds down the side of the building and also sprawled on the blood-soaked ground. Blood also spatters the base of the frame and the *retablo* banner across the bottom of the work that describes the scene is written in red. All Luce wanted was a memorial portrait to present to her friend's mother. After her first viewing, Luce never laid eyes on the painting again and it was given to her friend Frank Crowninshield for safe keeping.[5]

The painting, *Fulang Chang and I* (p. 119), was so popular that when Conger Goodyear found the work had been given to Frida's friend Dorothy Shapiro (now Sklar), he commissioned another painting of Frida and her monkey. Frida worked in her room at the Barbizon-Plaza Hotel for a week to complete *Self-Portrait with Monkey.*

Page 144

The Suicide of Dorothy Hale, 1938-1939. Oil on masonite with decorated wooden frame, 60.4 x 48.6 cm, Phoenix Art Museum, Phoenix (Arizona).

By the time the show closed, Frida was exhausted. Her health had failed near the end of their stay and she spent considerable time visiting doctors to deal with her back, spine, foot, and leg problems. But she returned to Mexico looking forward to her next sortie, this time into the bastion of the Europeans, a show of her work by Andre Breton in Paris, France.

In 1939, Paris life had a nervous edge to it. Hitler's Germany had spent almost four years testing new military hardware in Spain and was rattling its blooded saber at Poland. The French army was confident that its Maginot Line of fixed fortifications would defeat any attacks. French politicians were confident that Hitler was a blow-hard and would never challenge the Republic. The French people waved the tricolor, sang the *Marseillaise* and updated their passports.

The *Avante Garde* was no longer *avante* as the absurdities of the world stage replaced the fantasies of aging artists, writers, and poets of the 1920s. But Paris still retained much of its allure and cultural *cachet* as it struggled to maintain *sang-froid* in the face of news bulletins. Andre Breton's "Mexique" exhibition of Mexican art arrived at the Colle Gallery in time to provide a distraction.

As a show organizer, Breton turned out to be a disaster. Frida found her paintings still held unclaimed in customs and no gallery had been selected for the show. She was furious. Marcel Duchamps (*Nude Descending a Staircase*) stepped in, rescued her paintings and eventually helped the hapless Breton book the gallery of Pierre Colle.

Frida lodged with the Bretons for a while, but found it impossible to stay as problems with the show deepened. She fumed in her letters about the "...coo-coo sons of bitches of the surrealists." Even after the show found walls, its composition further inflamed her. In a letter to Nickolas Muray, she wrote,

> *Now Breton wants to exhibit together with my paintings, 14 portraits of the XIX Century (Mexican), about 32 photographs of Alvarez Bravo and lots of popular objects which he bought on the markets of Mexico – All this junk, can you beat that? ...the 14*

Page 147

The Chick, 1945.

Oil on masonite, 27 x 22 cm,

Museo Dolores Olmedo Patiño, Mexico City.

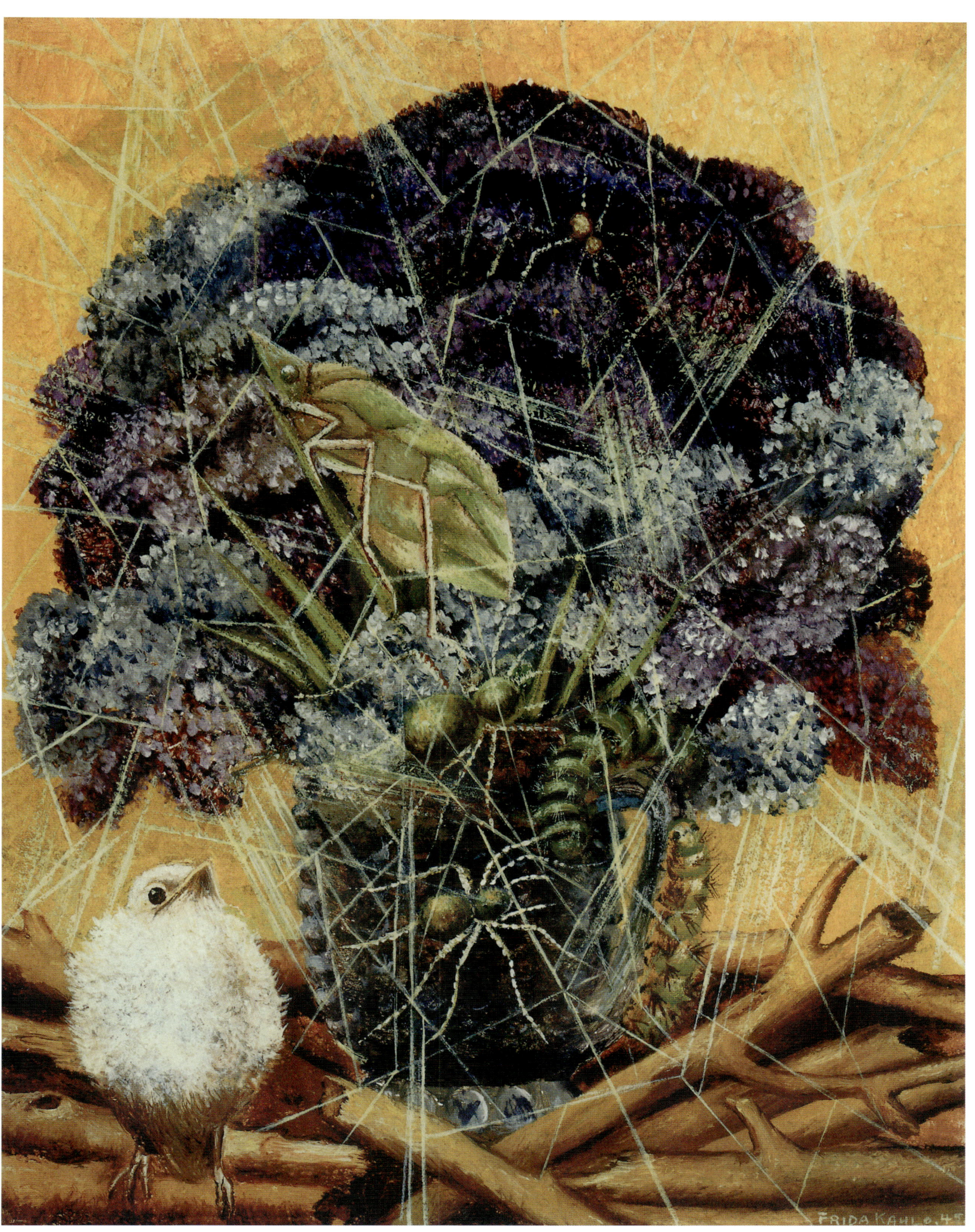
FRIDA KAHLO. 45

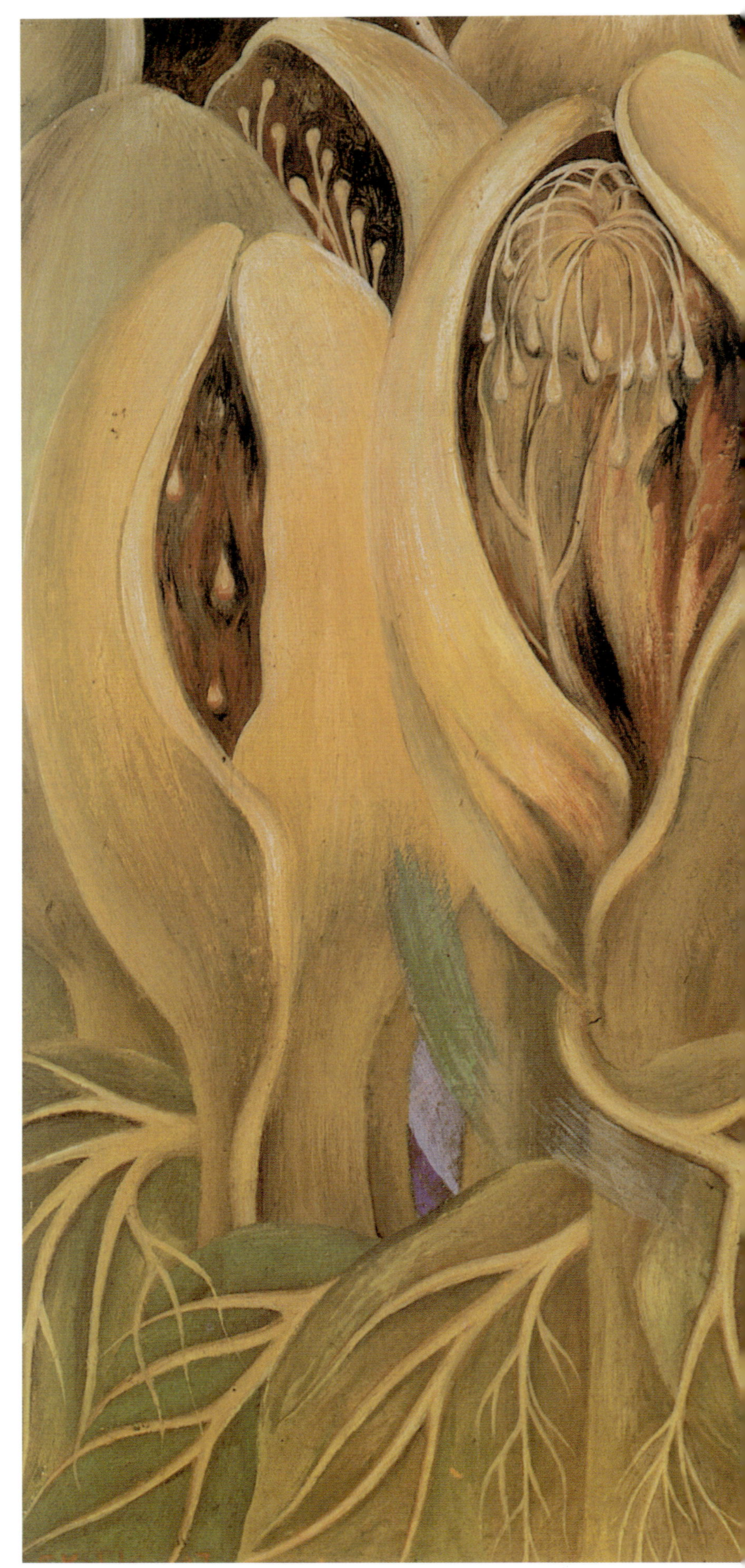

Page 148-149

Sun and Life, 1947.

Oil on hard fibre, 40 x 50 cm,

Galería Arvil, Mexico City.

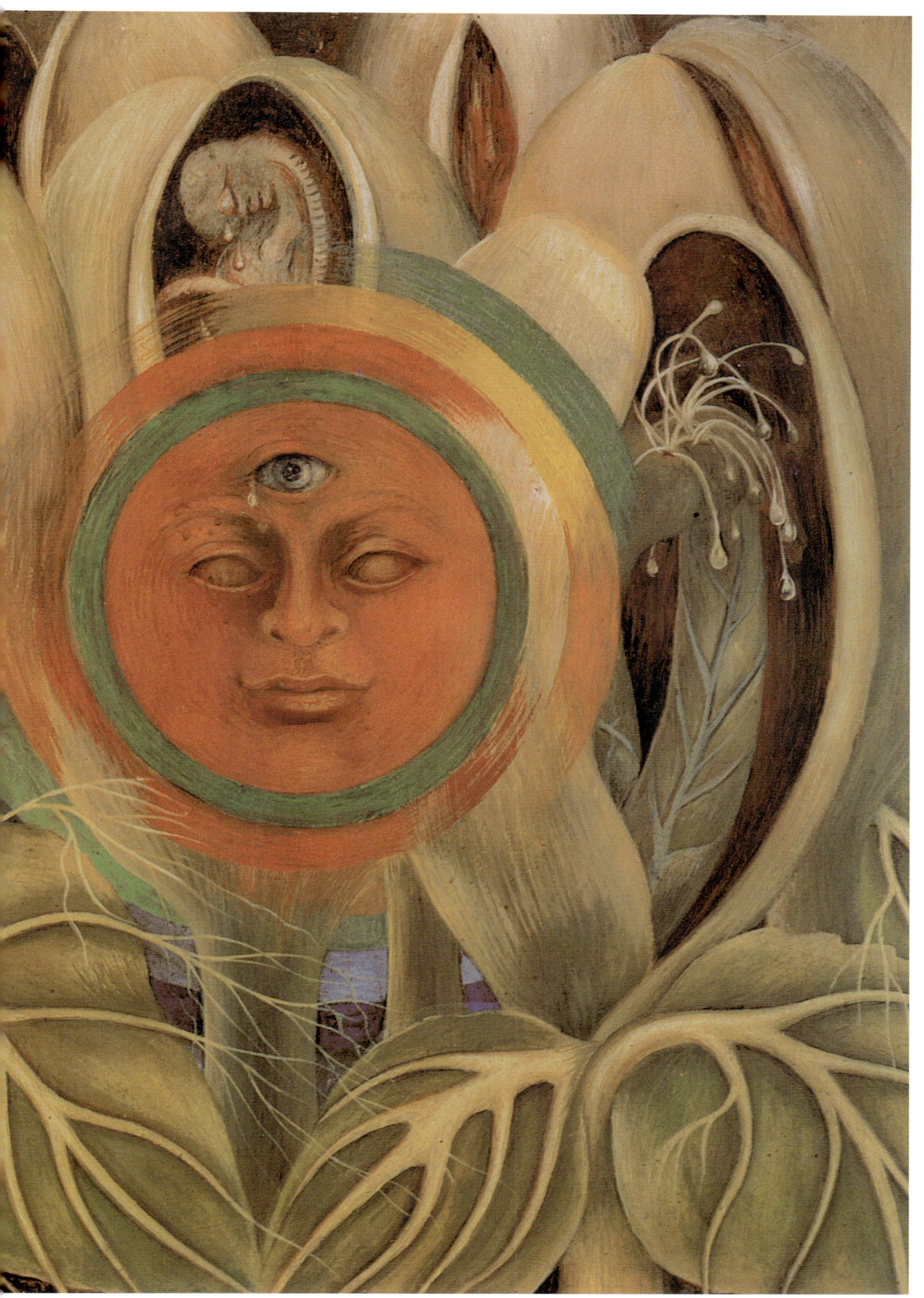

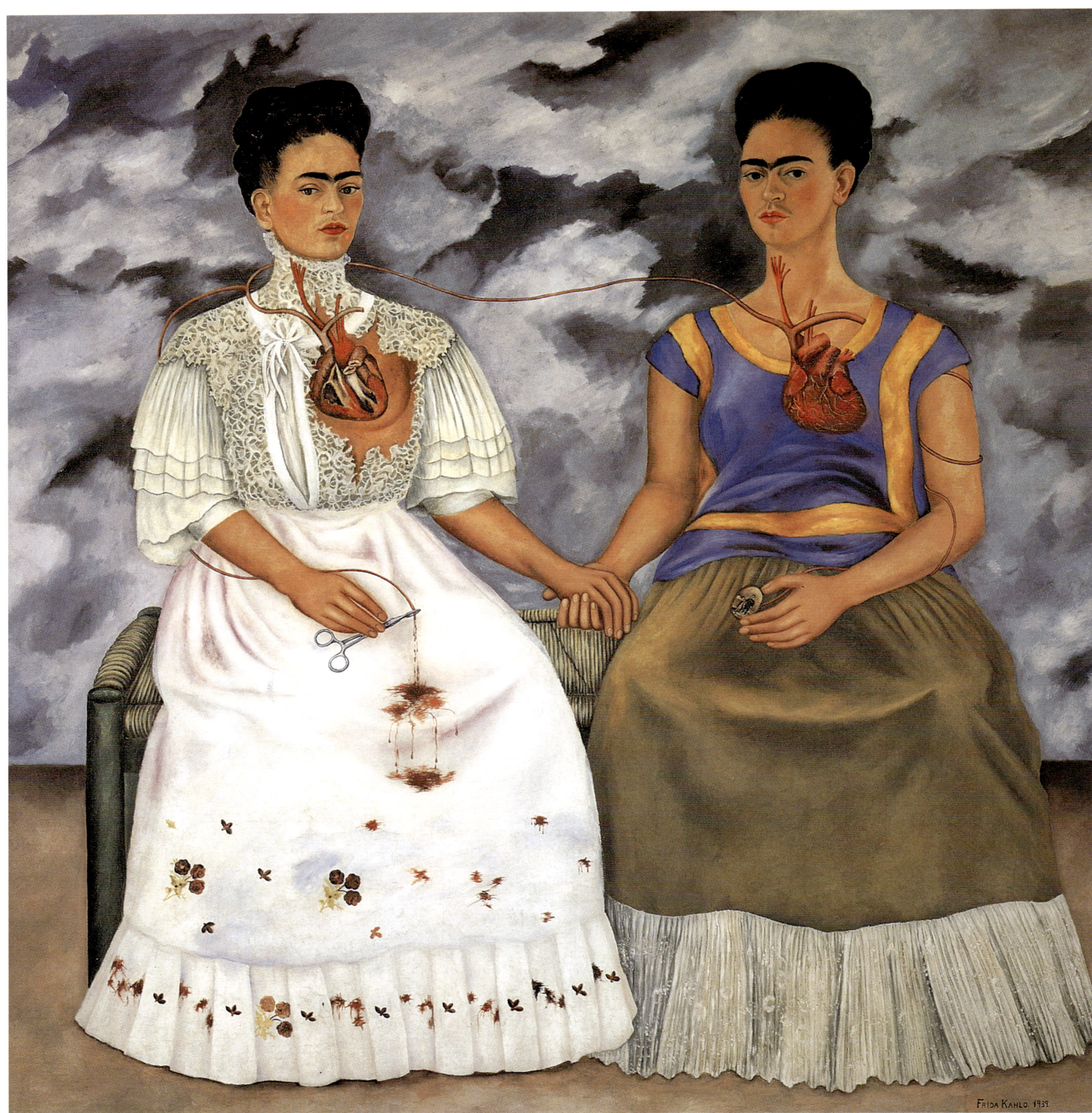
FRIDA KAHLO. 1939.

> *oils of the XIX Century must be restored and the damned restoration takes a whole month. I had to lend Breton 200 bucks (Dlls) for the restoration because he doesn't have a penny. …a few days ago Breton told me that the associates of Pierre Colle, an old bastard and son of a bitch, saw my paintings and found that only two were possible to be shown, because the rest are too "shocking" for the public!! I could kill that guy and eat it afterwards…*[6]

To her benefit, Frida received her closest exposure to the Surrealists since being admitted to their number. Max Ernst, Duchamps, Man Ray and Breton all welcomed her and she did her best to be no less outrageous than they, but she had little sympathy or time for the hangers-on and poseurs.

> *They sit for hours in the "cafes" warming their precious behinds, and talk without stopping about "culture" "art" "revolution" and so on and so forth, thinking themselves the gods of the world, dreaming the most fantastic nonsenses and poisoning the air with theories and theories that never come true.*[7]

Her paintings displayed at "Mexique" received good reviews and her presence was a show in itself. Powerhouses such as Kandinsky and Picasso sang her praises. She also managed a stroke of recognition that had been withheld from her famous husband. The Louvre purchased *The Frame* that today is part of the George Pompidou Centre collection. Unfortunately, *The Frame* was her only sale.

By March, 1939, Frida was sated with Parisian art life and packed up for a trip to New York to spend some time with Nick Muray. As with Noguchi, separation had cooled Muray's love and Frida discovered he was engaged to be married to another woman. The destruction of this romance hurt Frida deeply and pointed out to her how trapped she was in her relationship with Rivera.

Page 150
The Two Fridas, 1939.
Oil on canvas, 173.5 x 173 cm,
Museo de Arte Moderno, Mexico City.

Her life had opened up with many possibilities following her trips abroad and exposure to a new independence, but her identity remained tied to emotionally and professionally. A Noguchi or a Muray might have opened even more doors to her independent life, but she had thrown in her lot with Rivera at such an early age, they were seen as two sides of the same coin, he as "heads" and she as "tails".

She returned to Mexico in May, 1939 and as her relationship with Rivera deteriorated, she poured her emotions and frustration into two paintings. *Two Nudes in the Jungle* transports the pair of women from a floating sponge in *What the Water Gave Me* (p. 133) to a patch of desert land at the edge of a frightening jungle alive with entwined shapes and inhabited by a *voyeur Fulang Chang*. Frida once told a friend that whenever she portrayed her hands over her genitalia, it meant she was masturbating. This pair shares a loving moment, the fair Frida in the lap of the dark Indian girl and yet Frida pleasures herself, still separate from sharing the act with her companion.

The men in her life had done Frida a great disservice from which she would never completely recover. She needed a final act that was both symbolic and real.

Sexual relations had ended. Civility had ended. The gayety and adventures had ended. All that remained were obligations Diego and Frida accepted as parts of an unspoken agreement, the trickle of a relationship that no legality could sever. It is possible that Diego had heard of Frida's affair with Trotsky. Her reasons were obvious and humiliating. He wrote in his autobiography that:

> *The situation between us grew worse and worse… I telephoned her to plead for her consent to a divorce… It worked and Frida declared that she too wanted an immediate divorce… I simply wanted to be free to carry on with any woman who caught my fancy… What she could not understand was my choosing women who were unworthy of me, or inferior to her…*

They were formally divorced on November 6, 1939.

Page 153
Self-Portrait with Cropped Hair, 1940.
Oil on canvas, 40 x 28 cm,
Museum of Modern Art, New York,
donation by Edgar Kaufman Jr.

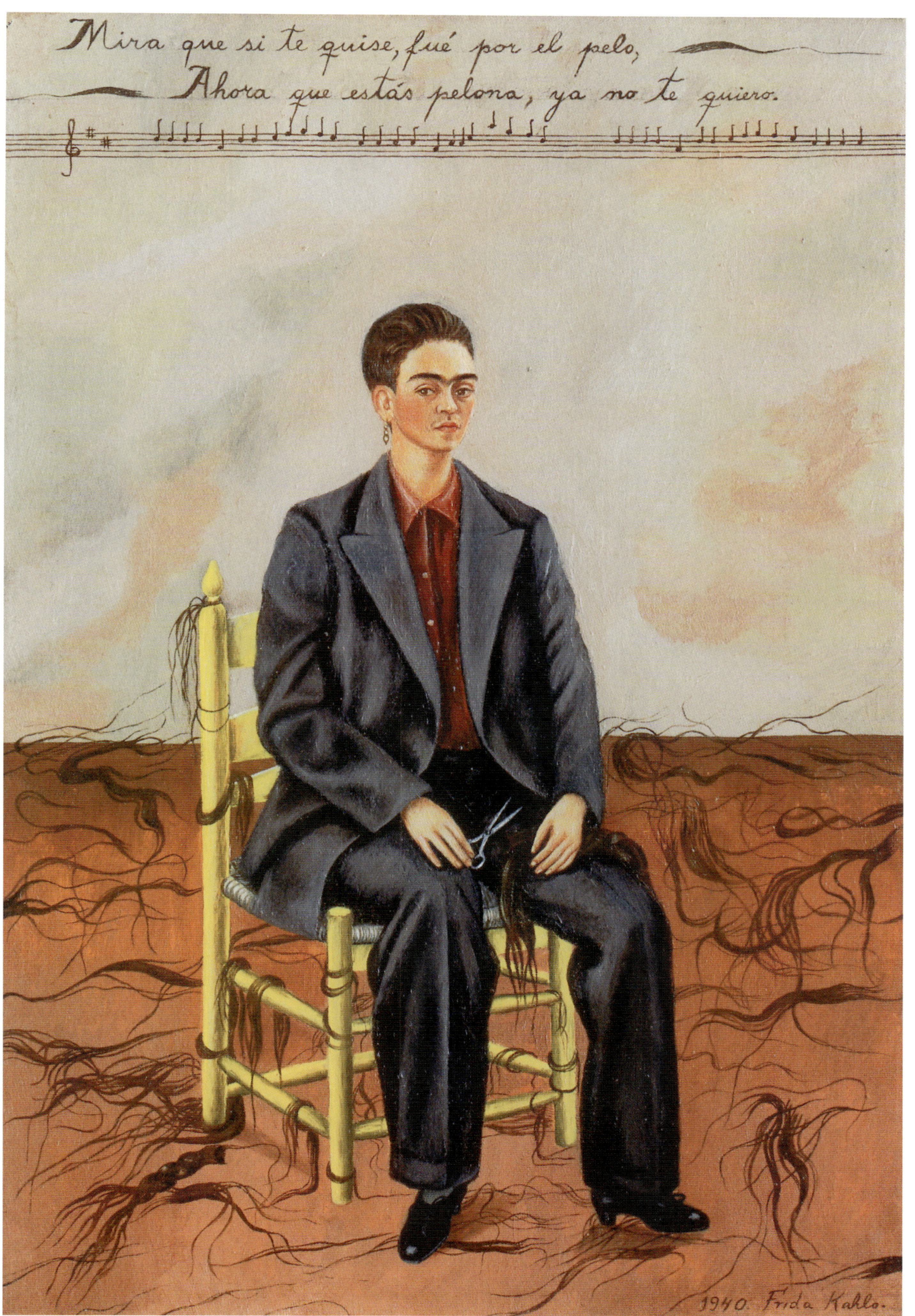
Mira que si te quise, fué por el pelo,
Ahora que estás pelona, ya no te quiero.
1940. Frida Kahlo.

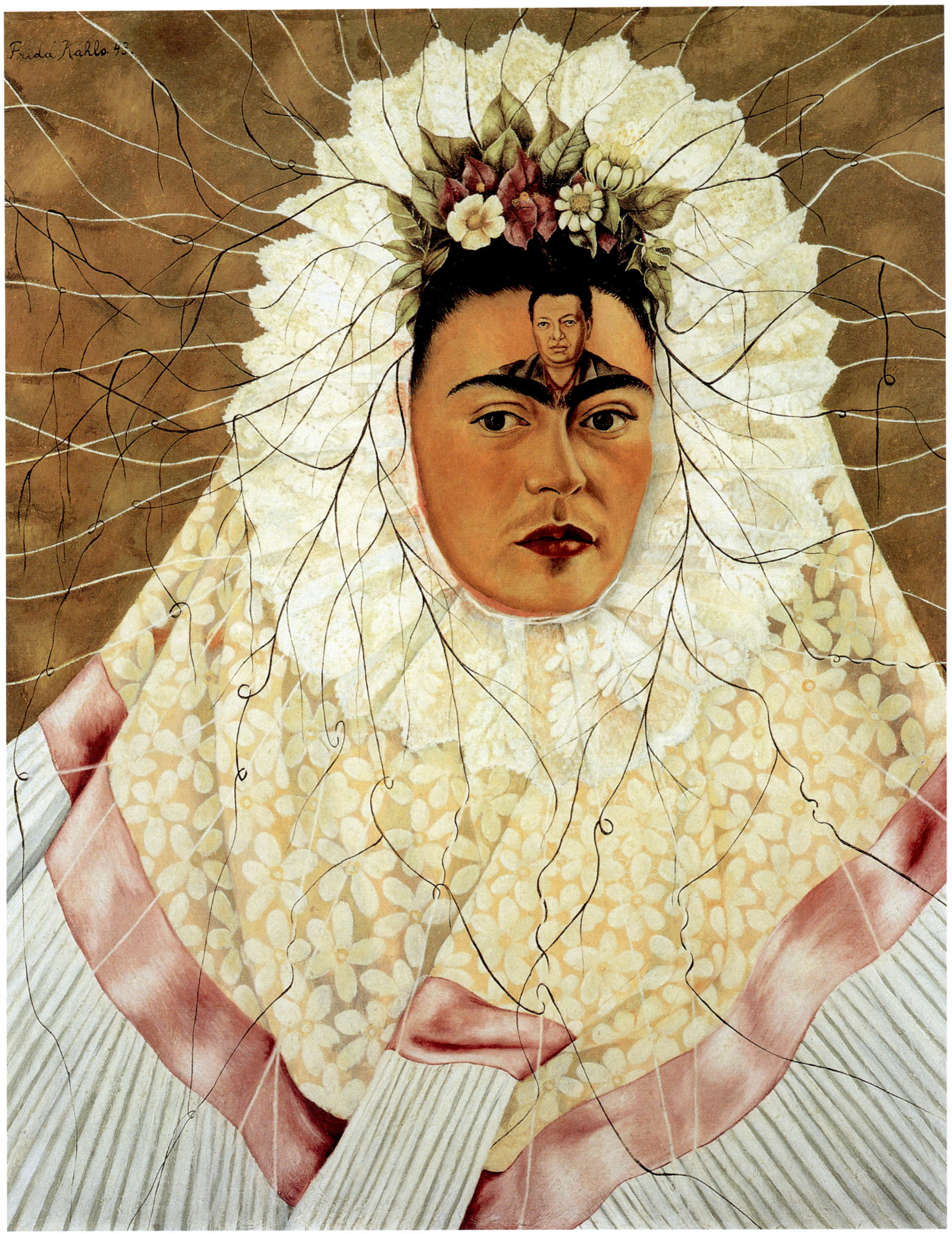
Frida Kahlo 43.

The second painting would become her signature masterpiece, the six-foot square *The Two Fridas* (p. 150). A mirror had long played a central role in her paintings, at first from necessity due to her bed-ridden state. Later, the mirror became a reflection of reality that could be manipulated and translated into a fantasy vision of her very personal *verité*. In *The Two Fridas*, the mirror duality becomes a schizophrenic visualization of Frida's personal dilemma, the European woman (Frida) in white with lace and appliqués befitting a chaste Catholic girl and the *Tehuana* woman of darker skin and colorful costume, the earthy peasant persona encouraged by Diego Rivera. Both hearts are exposed and a vine-like blood vessel connects a small amulet that is a miniature portrait of Diego as a child and the two hearts of the "Fridas". The European "Frida's" heart is ripped and savaged while she grips the end of the shared artery with a surgical clamp. But blood still drips from its end onto her snow white dress.

At this point in her life, she had found a path to her independence, but at a cost she seemed unwilling to pay. The assassination of Leon Trotsky with an Alpine *piolet* (ice ax) on August 20, 1940 by Ramon Mercader - an acquaintance of Frida's who pursued her while she was in Paris - brought everything to a head. Frida and her sister Cristina were hauled away by the police and vigorously interrogated for 12 hours as possible suspects in the assassination conspiracy. Diego fled to San Francisco, leaving her behind. Compared to the humiliations she suffered because of his sexual betrayals, this failure was only a pin-prick, but it capped her resolve that she had done the right thing in divorcing him.

---

[1] Ibid., Herrera, Hayden, p. 442

[2] Ibid., Rummel, p. 119

[3] Ibid., Herrera, Hayden, p. 306

[4] Ibid., Herrera, Hayden, p. 329

[5] Hardin, Terri, *Frida Kahlo A Modern Master*, Smithmark Publishers, New York, 1997, p. 66

[6] Ibid., Herrera, Hayden, p. 334

[7] Ibid., Herrera, Hayden, p. 339

Page 154

Self-Portrait as a Tehuana or *Diego on My Mind*, 1943.

Oil on masonite, 76 x 61 cm,

Collection Jacques and Natasha Gelman,

Mexico City.

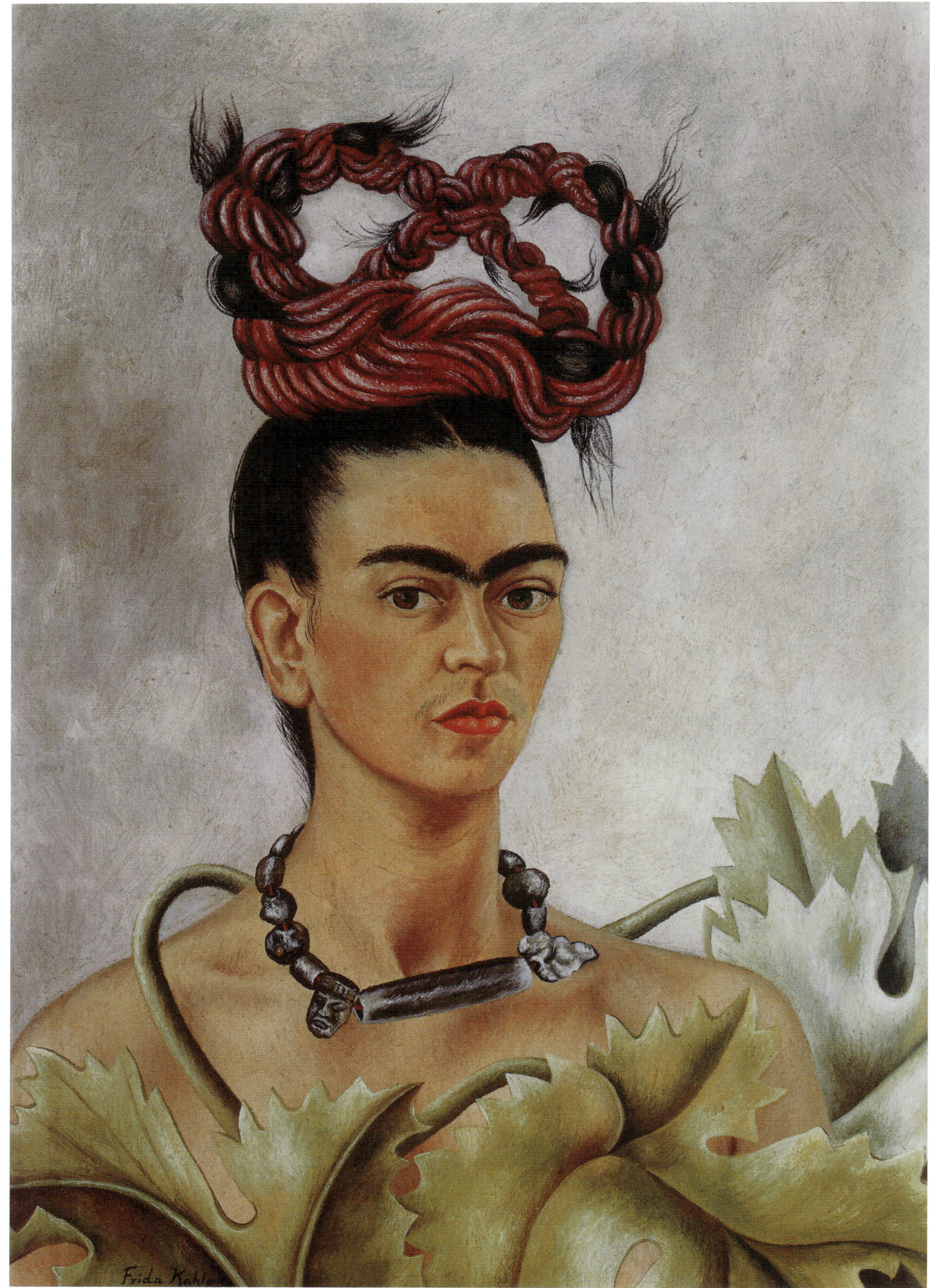
Frida Kahlo

"Long live joy, life, Diego..."

The 1940s came at Frida Kahlo in a rush of contradictions. Legally, she had shed her ties with Diego Rivera, but financially her life was bound to him through a complex banking arrangement where her expenses were paid from sales of his work. She was in complete denial when she wrote to Nickolas Muray:

> *...I don't accept a damned cent from Diego, the reasons you must understand. I will never accept money from any man till I die...*[1]

Her freedom to begin her life anew had been secured – an apparently happy result – and yet her 1940 painting, *Self Portrait with Cropped Hair,* is clearly a regression to her previous "cropped hair" period following Diego's affair with her sister Cristina. Frida sits on a yellow cane chair, her hair cropped like a convict. Scattered on the floor are the cut remnants of her usually abundant coiffure. The hair cuttings don't lie on the ground in realistic perspective, but float dreamlike in suspension like seaweed or the roots of long-dead plants. She wears an outsized man's suit of the kind favored by Diego, giving her the appearance of being undernourished, a refugee or aging petitioner seeking redress. The scissors rest in her lap. Might the pruning process continue?

And, finally, her new reality of independence brought with it the nagging need to back up her financial "revolt" with actual sales. She wrote:

> *I organize things as necessary to live more or less "decently"... I'm always painting pictures, since as soon as I'm done with one, I have to sell it so I have the moola for all the month's expenses.*[2]

As Europe plunged into World War II on the tracks of Hitler's *Panzers,* the world of art seemed oddly remote. Artists' canvasses remained aloof to the calls of patriotism and self-

Page 156
Self-Portrait with Braid, 1941.
Oil on masonite, 51 x 38.5 cm,
Collection Jacques and Natasha Gelman,
Mexico City.

Page 158
Tree of Hope, Keep Strong, 1946.
Oil on masonite, 55.9 x 40.6 cm,
Collection Isidore Ducasse, France.

Page 159
Portrait of Lucha Maria, a girl from Tehuacán, (Sun and moon), 1942.
Oil on masonite, 54.6 x 43.1 cm.

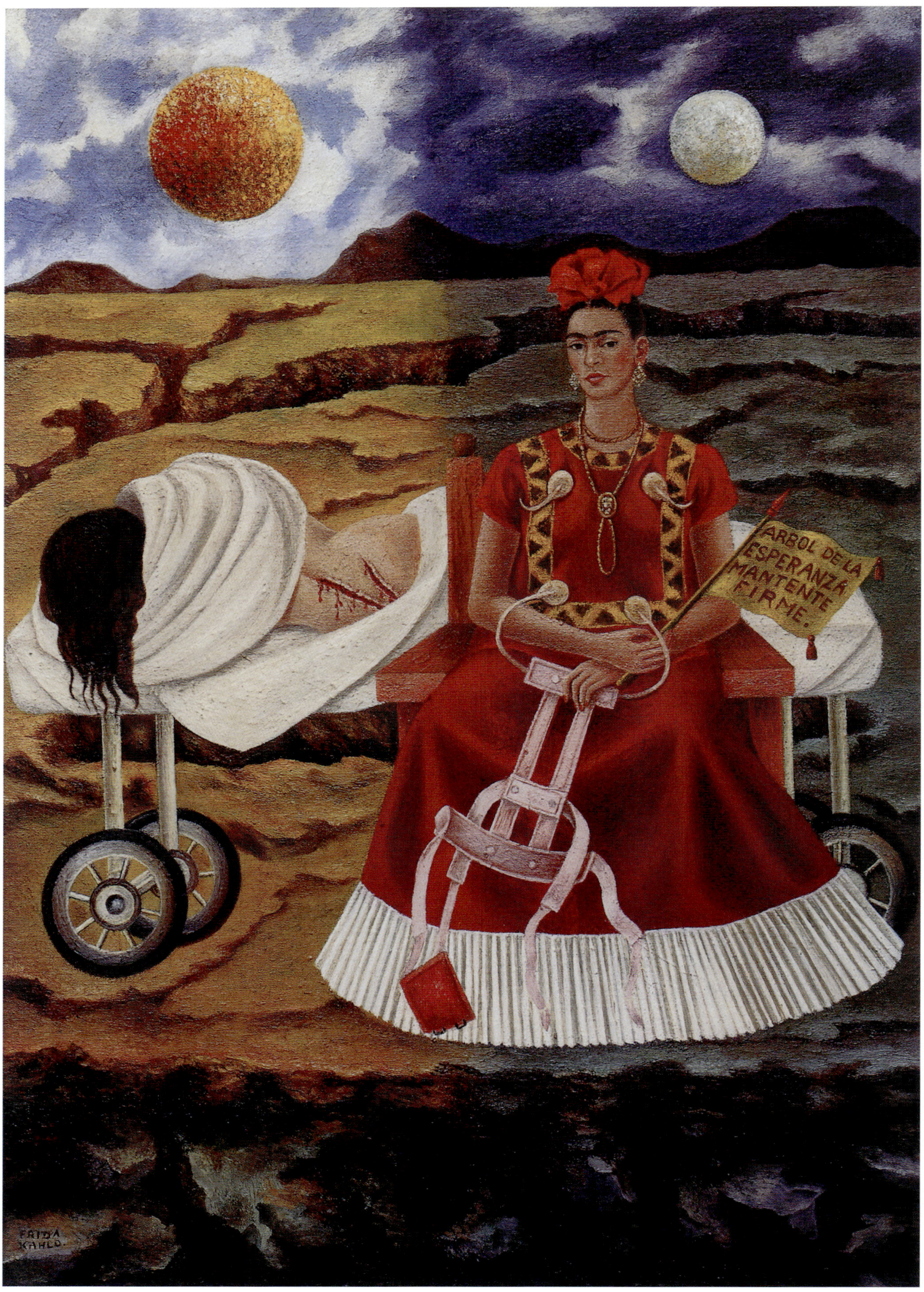
ARBOL DE LA
ESPERANZA
MANTENTE
FIRME.
FRIDA
KAHLO

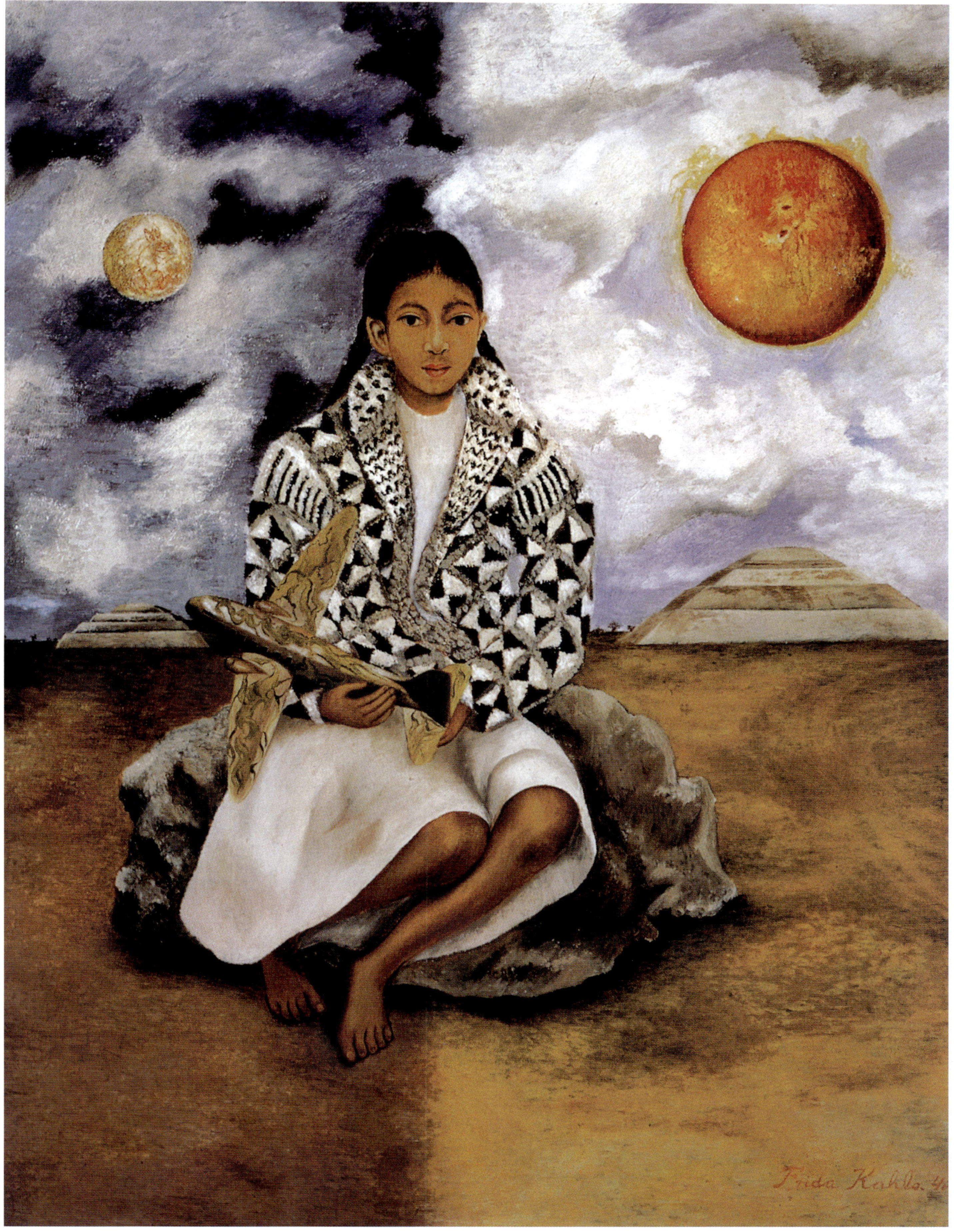
Frida Kahlo. 46

sacrifice. Many artists fled before the insanity of armed conflict engulfed their native countries, or they turned inward and reclusive, doing nothing to earn the wrath of occupying armies. There were few Goyas who documented Napoleon's Peninsular War in Spain, or painters such as John Singer Sargent, Fernand Léger, Oskar Kokoschka, George Grosz, or Marc Chagall who once added their visions to the horrors of World War I, and fewer Picasso's turning out condemnations such as *Guernica,* commissioned by the Spanish Republican government in 1937.

Frida and Diego were both committed to the Communist Party and the anti-fascist cause – even if the Communists had ideological reservations about Diego's commitment to anti-capitalist dogma due to his willingness to accept commissions from anyone who could write a check – and the capitalists had all the money. This Communist thread always seemed to join the two artists regardless of their current conjugal state. They constantly appeared at rallies and fund-raisers, especially after June, 1941 when Hitler invaded Russia.

With her life in this turmoil of contradictions, she doggedly pressed forward with her art. Frida imagined her self esteem could only survive through the success of her paintings in what remained of the art world outside the distraction of world war.

The Wounded Table, painted in 1940, was an explosion of her favorite lexicon of symbolism across a huge horizontal canvas. The old partnership from *Four Inhabitants of Mexico City* returned again: the Judas, the Aztec idol, and the skeleton. Only now, they are the worse for wear, leaking blood into the plank stage behind drawn-back curtains. The little girl from *Inhabitants* has been replaced by the innocents: Isolde and Antonio, her sister Cristina's children, and her pet deer, *El Granizo* complete with camouflage spots. Frida has joined the group as well, but her body is almost lost in the awkward gropings and strokings of her grim companions. The idol's legs are a pair of canes ("*See those canes?*" Lupe Marin had ridiculed at the wedding party when she exposed Frida's withered leg beneath the long skirt. "*That's what Diego must put up with!*")

Page 160-161

Still Life: Viva la Vida (*Long live Life*),

c.1951-1954.

Oil and earth on masonite, 52 x 72 cm,

Museo Frida Kahlo, Mexico City.

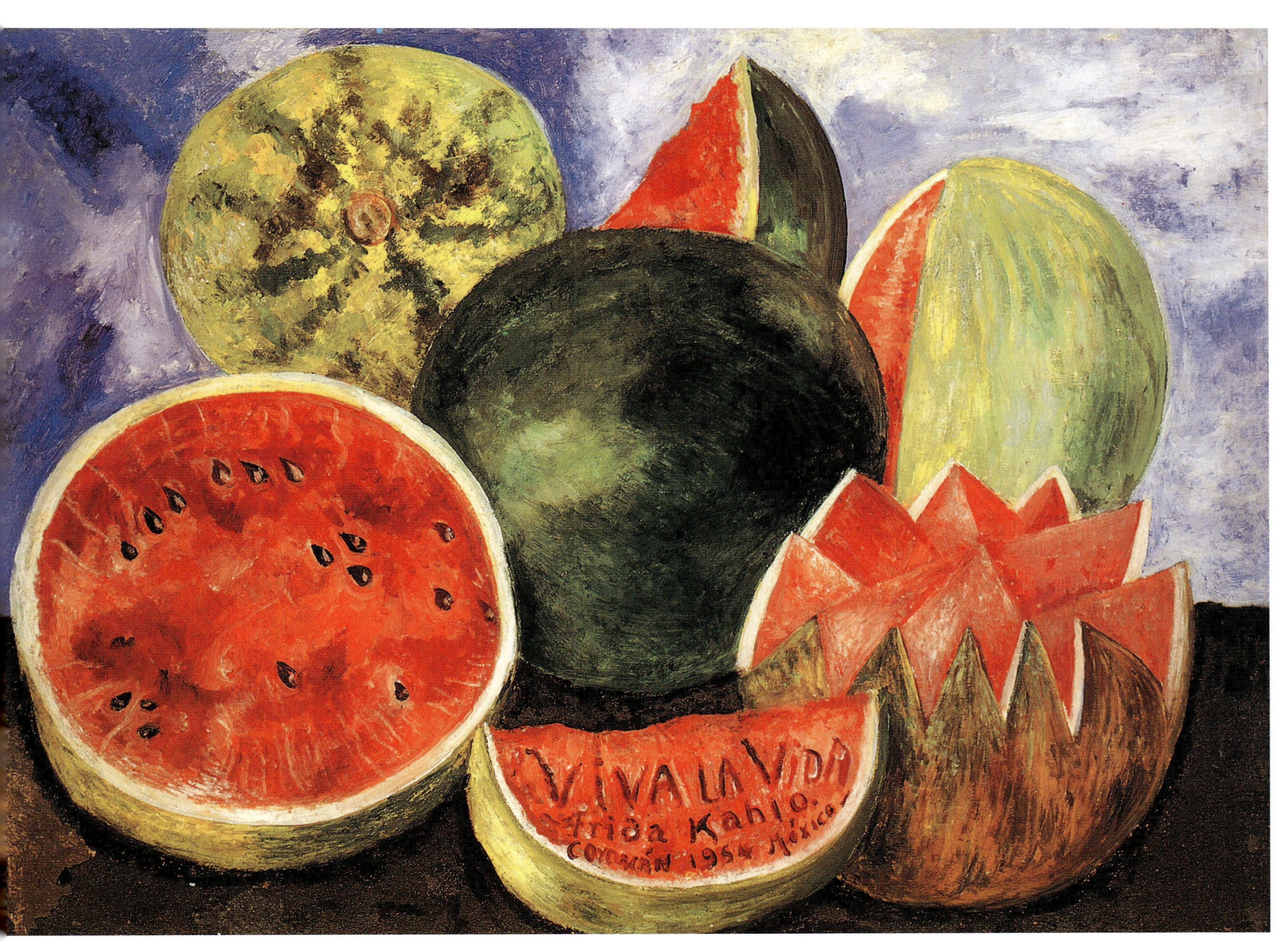
VIVA LA VIDA
Frida Kahlo.
COYOACÁN 1954 México

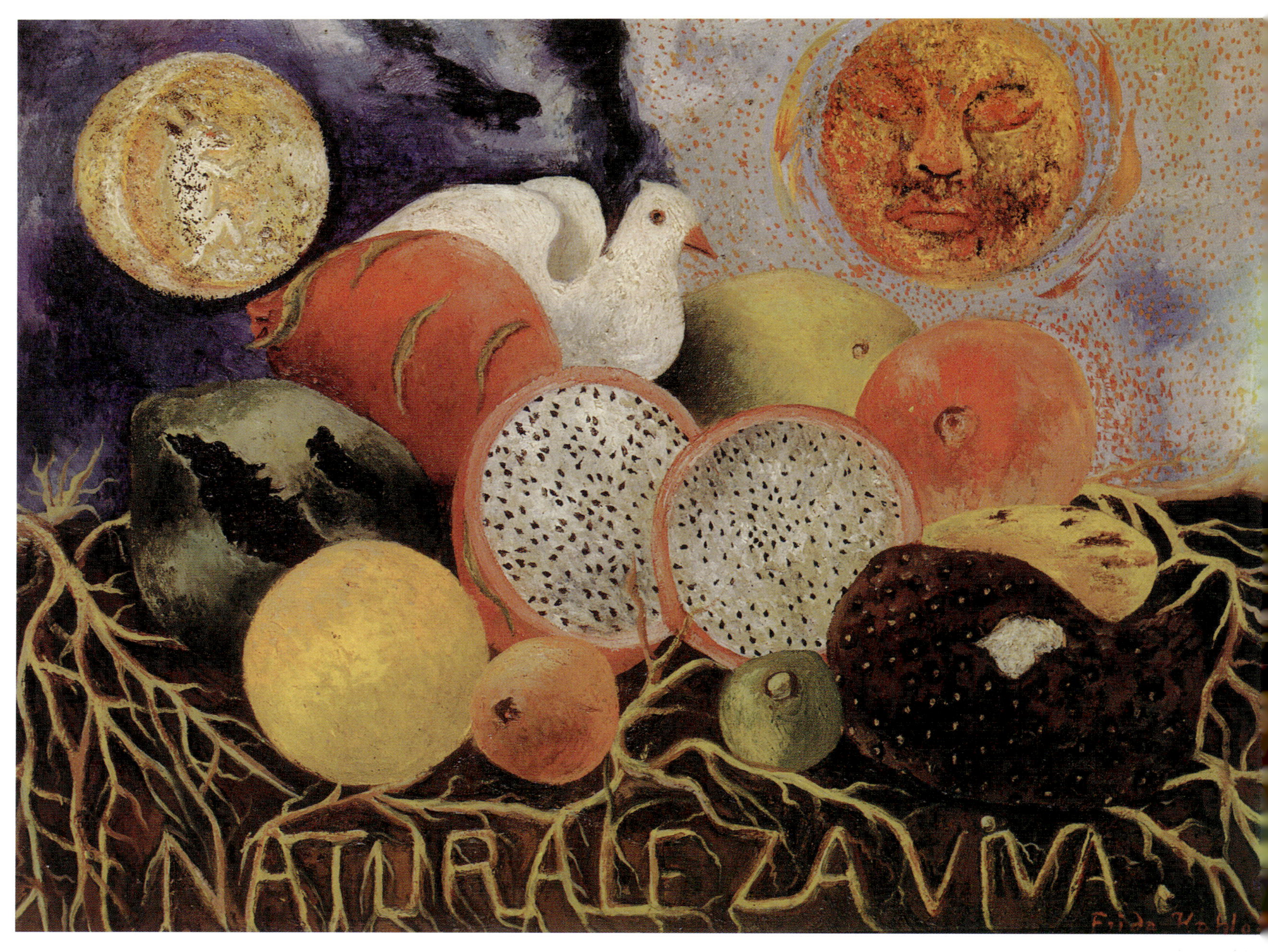

Page 162

Moving Still Life, 1952.

Oil on canvas,

Collection María Félix, Mexico City.

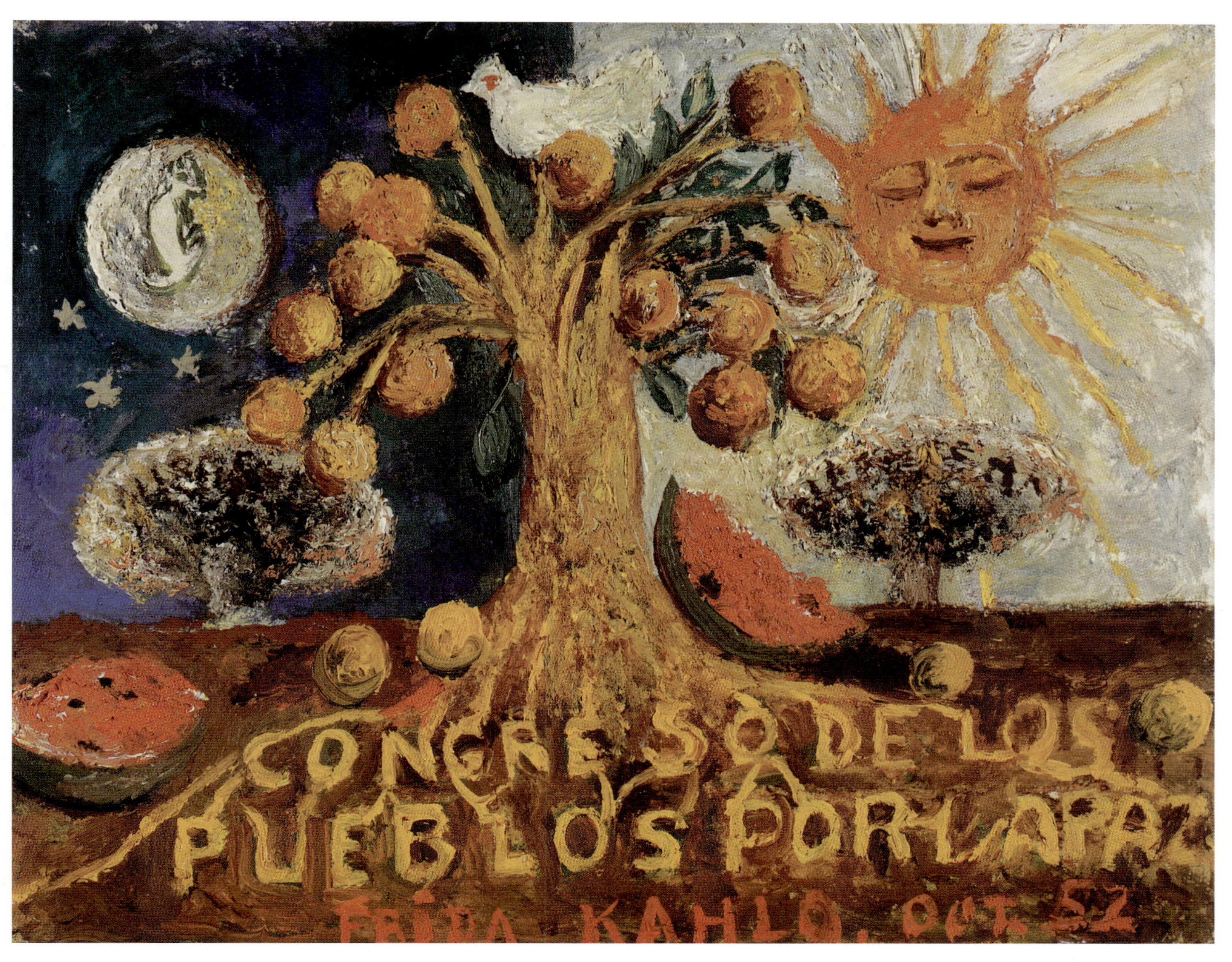

Page 163

Congress of People For Peace, 1952.

Oil and tempera on masonite,

19.1 x 25.1 cm.

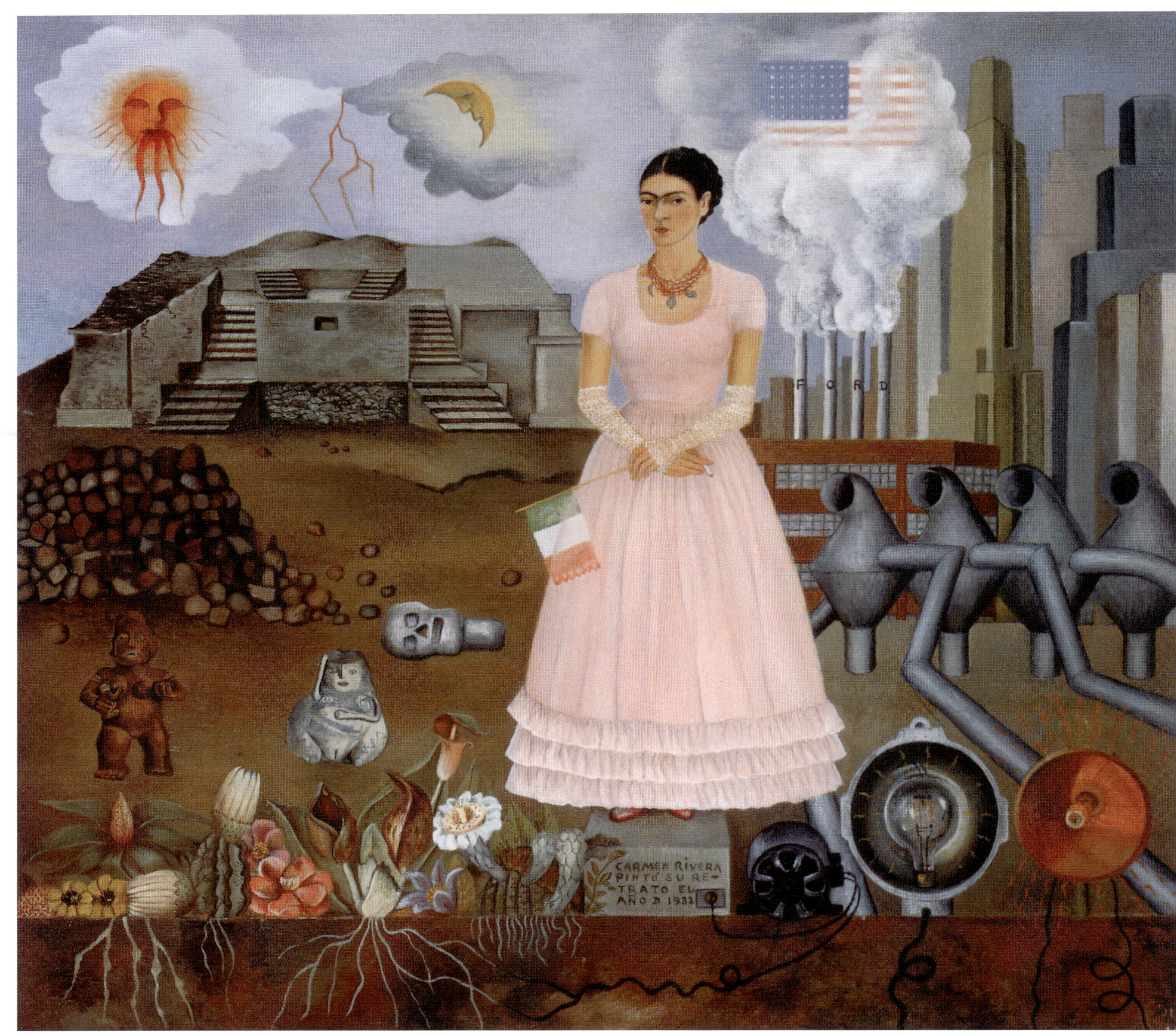
FORD
CARMEN RIVERA
PINTÓ SU RE-
-TRATO EL
AÑO D 1932

The forlorn assembly sits at a table, turning a triage of wounded misfits into a *Punch and Judy* show. Who will speak the first line? The table's legs are flayed human legs. It seems unable to support these broken things that sit awaiting either their cue, or the audience judgment.

Her broken marriage and fragmented life become the focus of her early 1940s work. In *The Dream* (p. 4), the Judas makes an encore appearance, its paper puppet limbs wired as a bomb. He accompanies her four poster bed on its journey floating through a bilious sky. Judas the passenger rests above her on the canopy just where an actual Judas figure reclined in her bedroom in *La Casa Azul.* Her flowered bedspread lives as vines radiate with leaves that reach for and embrace her. *The Dream* is an agitating and uneasy painting to view, complimenting her fragility that is threatened in *The Wounded Table.*

Frida had worked hard on the large *Table* painting for the International Surrealism Convention scheduled to be held in Mexico City. Ultimately, the convention was canceled due to the war. German travel restrictions virtually shut down France and the occupied countries as Hitler's henchmen began spreading their nets to induct labor conscripts and capture Jews.

While she flushed her bad feelings into her paintings, Frida put on a game face and continued her socializing. To break the ice at parties, she had a pair of pink diamond-studded incisors made that she could slip on like caps over her teeth. Her alcohol input increased exponentially and her mood swings from happiness to depression became more frequent. Soon, there was never enough alcohol to escape the depression and uncertainty. Knowing there was a good market for her self-portraits with animals, she poured her state of mind and body into them. Her *Self-portrait with Thorny Necklace* (p. 121) mirrors this period. A dead hummingbird – when portrayed alive it is a symbol worn to bring luck – dangles from a thorny necklace that spreads down across her shoulders as naked vines cover a trellis. The necklace pierces her neck with thorns, drawing blood in a Christ-like martyr's pose. She wears blameless white before a tangle of exquisitely veined jungle leaves. One of her monkeys, *Caimito de Guayabal,* thoughtfully examines the necklace while a black cat crouching behind her left shoulder takes the measure of the viewer. Frida herself seems

Page 164
Self-Portrait (standing) along the Border between Mexico and the United States, 1932.
Oil on metal, 31 x 35 cm,
Collection Manuel and Maria Reyero,
New York.

exhausted in her self-mortification. Her exaggerated eyebrows above drooping eyelids match the arc of the hummingbird's dead wings.

Once again, Diego intervened in her self-destructive lifestyle and consulted their mutual friend, Dr. Eloesser, in San Francisco. The doctor suggested she come to the States. She had spent three months in a traction device connected to her chin and welcomed the invitation from her old friend. Frida arrived in San Francisco in September, 1940. Eloesser immediately committed her to a rest cure and assorted therapies in St. Luke's Hospital for her exhaustion and alcoholism. He also contacted Diego and explained the Mexican doctors' grim diagnoses such as tuberculosis of the bones and a need for spinal surgery were false and what she needed was her *Panzon* at her side during her recovery. While he had her under his cure, the doctor was determined to affect reconciliation between the two artists who were miserable in their self-imposed separation.

During their time together, Diego introduced her to the public relations officer of the Golden Gate Exhibition, a young refugee from Nazi Germany, Heinz Berggruen. She and the young man were immediately attracted to each other and when Frida finished her hospital stay, she made a trip to New York with Berggruen and they spent a tempestuous time together, staying at the familiar Barbizon-Plaza Hotel and touring the Manhattan party circuit. Eventually, Berggruen came to his senses as he accepted Frida's need for someone with the fortitude to support her high maintenance life style and complex emotional needs. Heinz was no Diego Rivera. Even so, their parting was emotional and difficult.

"No sex" and "no cash" were two of Frida's stipulations to make the remarriage work. She had no intention of sharing Diego sexually with any other women and she insisted on making her own way financially and paying half of the household expenses. Diego was pleased with the former and maintained the mutually accepted fiction of the latter. The agony of their separation played itself out on Diego's 54th birthday, December 8, 1940 when they were remarried in a civil ceremony.

Page 167
Self-Portrait "Time Flies", 1929.
Oil on masonite, 86 x 68 cm,
Private collection, USA.

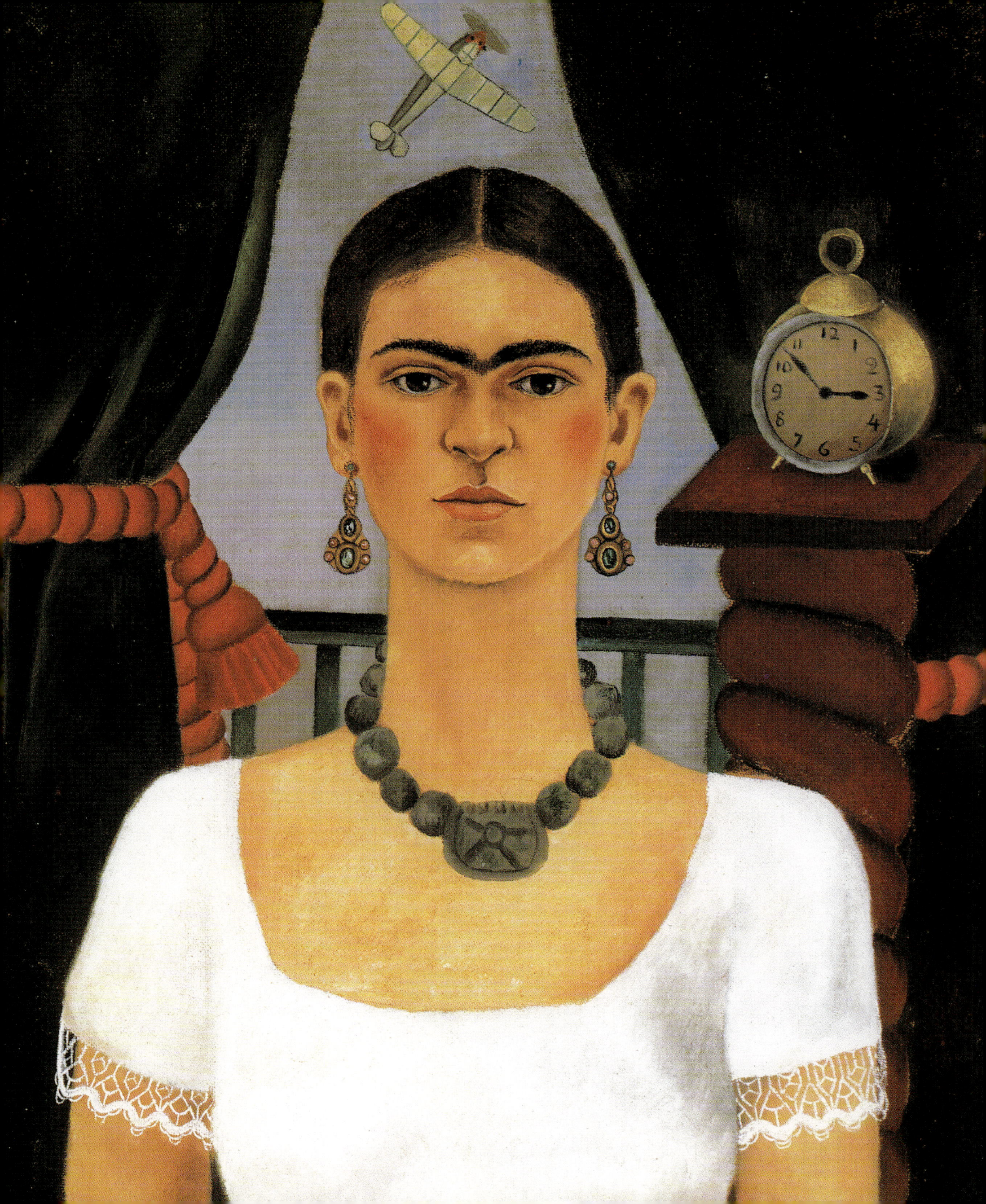

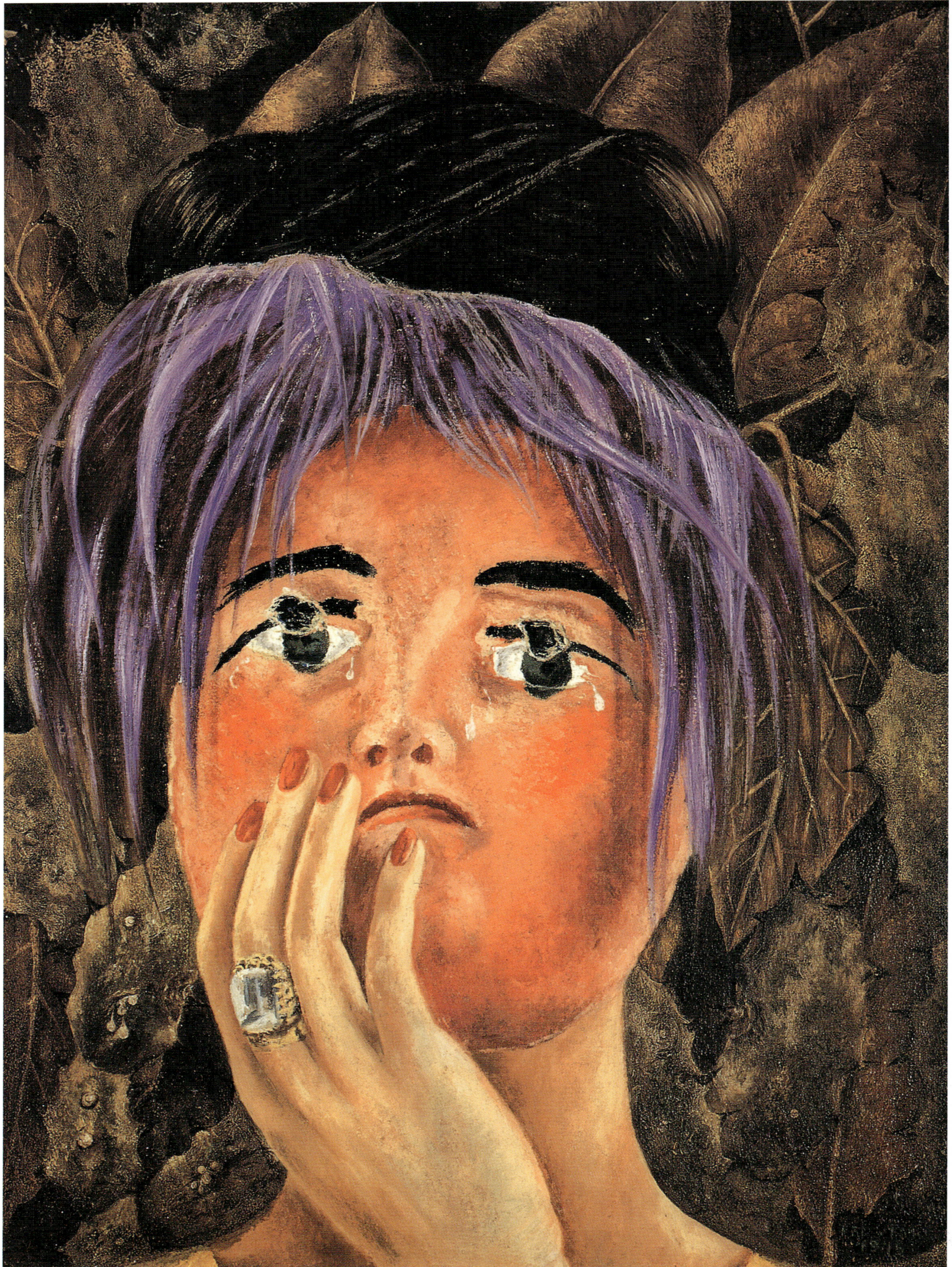

Her fortunes were once again on the rise. She joined Diego in the International Golden Gate Exhibition where he executed a mural on Treasure Island. They spent Christmas in Mexico with Frida's family and then he returned to complete the mural. While he was gone, Frida reveled in a period of relatively good health, shopping in Coyoacon and Mexico City, sunning herself in the garden, or preparing Diego's room for when he returned. *La Casa Azul* had become a repository for their combined collections of Mexican arts and crafts and a zoo for Frida's herd of animals, a mix of species including assorted cats, small deer and parrots who guzzled beer and complained raucously about their hangovers. Besides her big child - Diego - this coterie of critters was indulged as her surrogate children. When her pet osprey, *Gertrude Caca Blanca* (white shit) dropped a load of excrement on a guest's hat, the large bird was laughingly scolded with a waggled finger like a delinquent. Everywhere, Frida's own deep earthy laugh could be heard above the chatter of a never-ending stream of visitors who gathered around the big table, sat in cane chairs at her bedside, or reclined on *petates*, spread on the yellow-painted floor, discussing politics, art, gossip, and drinking from clay mugs.

And still, while caring for Diego's every need and seeing to domestic chores, every day she set aside time to paint through the warm weeks of spring.

Bare shouldered, she peers from her painting, *Self-Portrait with Braid* (p. 156), as if rising from a salad of greens wearing only a heavy jade necklace and a preposterous braid of woven hair on her head. As suggested by some, this crown of hair might represent the cuttings from her "cropped hair" portrait of the year before, a symbol of support for her re-marriage vows to Diego.

She had been encouraged to continue her work by reaction to her paintings when *The Two Fridas* (p. 150), hung at the Museum of Modern Art's show, *Twenty Centuries of Mexican Art*, her participation in the Surrealist show in Mexico City and the *Golden Gate International Exhibition* in San Francisco. She was determined to step from beneath Diego's shadow and avoid such crass comments as Frank Crowninshield offered up in *Vogue Magazine's* coverage of the MOMA show:

Page 168

The Mask, 1945.

Oil on canvas, 40 x 30.5 cm.

> *...the most recent of Rivera's ex-wives* (was) *a painter apparently obsessed by an interest in blood...*[3]

Just as her life had once again settled into a comfortable pattern, the summer heat brought with it a further deterioration in her health, a weakness and loss of weight. In July, her father, Guillermo, died. That blow added to her depression over the war and its horrendous effect on Russia. The June invasion had swept Stalin's rag-tag army before Hitler's mechanized juggernaut. As German troops marched northward, Frida's troop of doctors marched back into her life with brand new plaster corsets for her back, X-rays, hormone injections, cures for the fungus that infected her right hand, pills and injections for angina and *la grippe.* She smoked too much and still drank a few too many *copitas* with meals.

She carefully hoarded her time for painting and maintained the appearance of an income with her self-portraits, still-lifes, portraits of friends and relatives. But her retinue of servants and nurses, shopping sprees, the cost of drugs and horrific doctor bills kept her dependent on Diego. On July 18, she wrote Dr. Eloesser from Coyoacon,

> *My shank is getting better. But my general state is pretty fuc—bulous. I think it's due to the fact that I don't eat enough and that I smoke too much. What is rare is that I am not drinking any small or big aperitifs anymore. I feel pain in my belly and a constant need to burp. (Pardon me, burped!!) My digestion is in a shambles. My mood is really bad; I am becoming more* corajuda *every day... in other words, I am very crabby. If there is a remedy in medicine to control this mood, please give me a prescription so I can take it immediately. We'll see what results I get.*[4]

Besides their painting, Diego and Frida poured considerable time into other pursuits. Diego had begun building a repository for his huge collection of Pre-Hispanic Mexican art, a temple-like museum he called the Anahuacalli, erected on volcanic lava beds outside Coyoacon. Frida had made the initial land purchase, but over the years, Diego had bought up surrounding parcels. She became ensnared in the project, keeping track of the considerable sums he poured into it, his papers, and even filed correspondence with his lady-friends.[5]

Page 171
Self-Portrait with the Portrait of Dr. Farill,
1951. Oil on masonite, 41.5 x 50 cm,
Private collection.

Page 172
Self-Portrait with Stalin or *Frida and Stalin,*
c.1954. Oil on hard fibre, 59 x 39 cm,
Museo Frida Kahlo, Mexico City.

Page 173
Portrait of My Father, 1951.
Oil on masonite, 60.5 x 46.5 cm,
Museo Frida Kahlo, Mexico City.

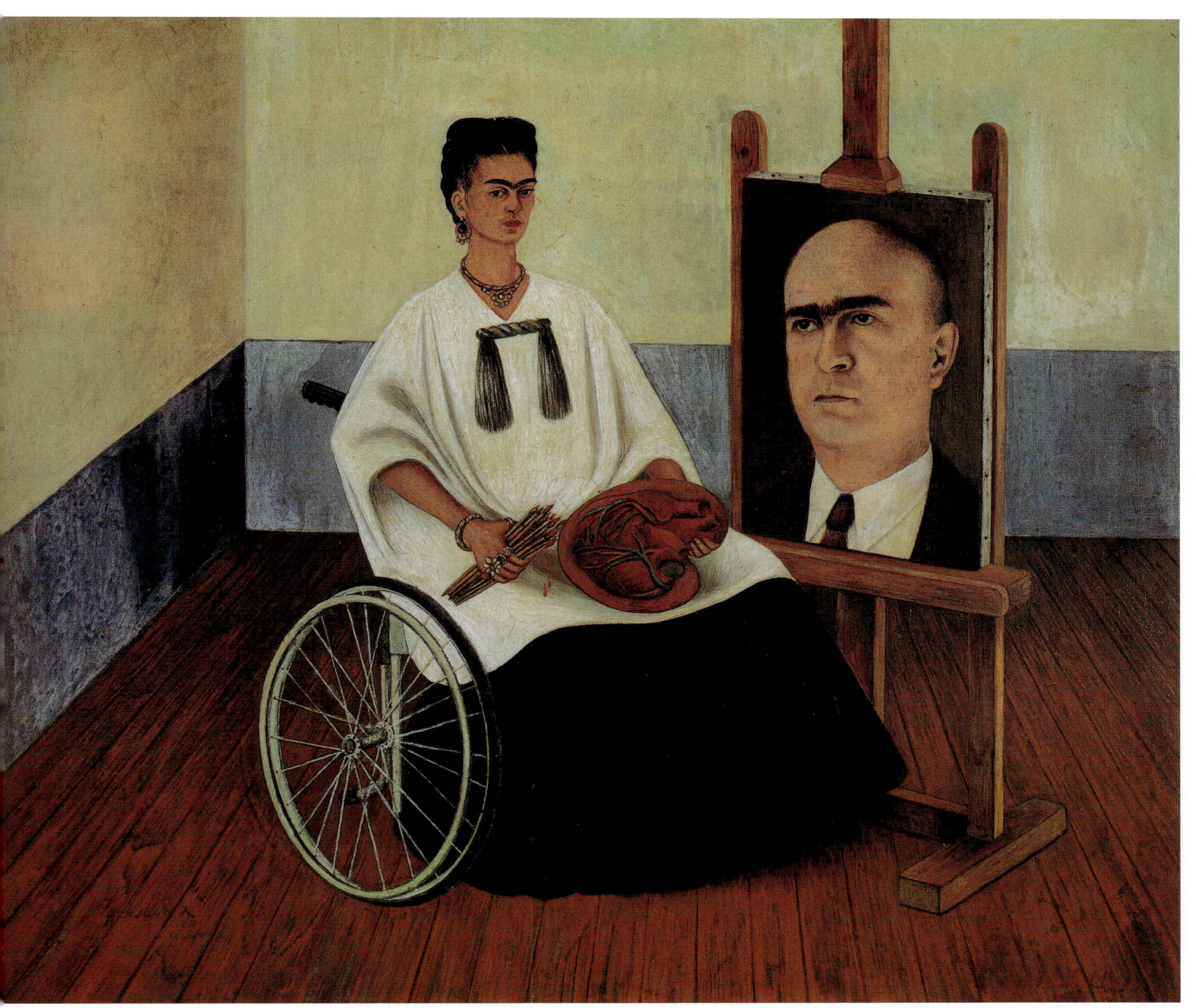

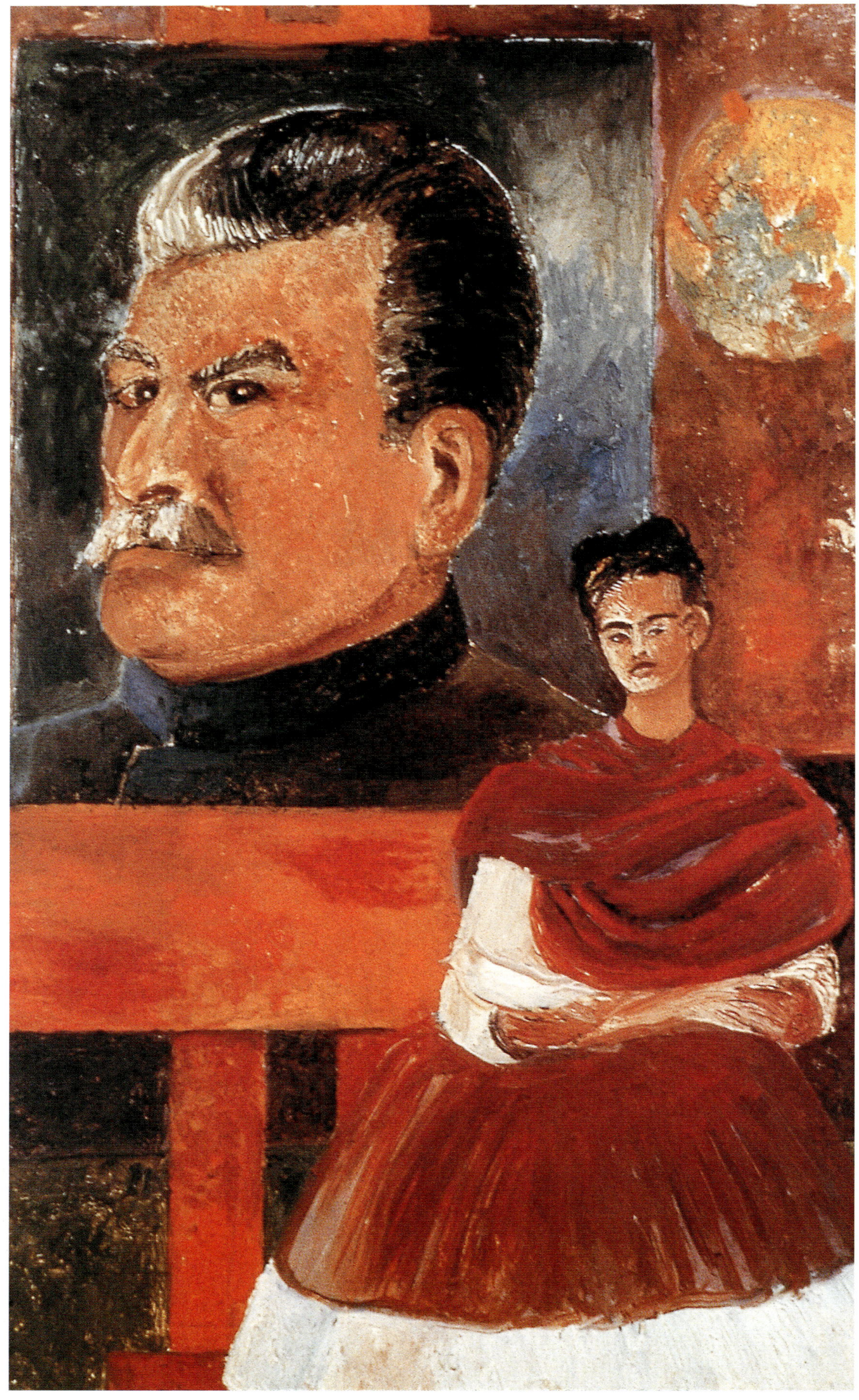

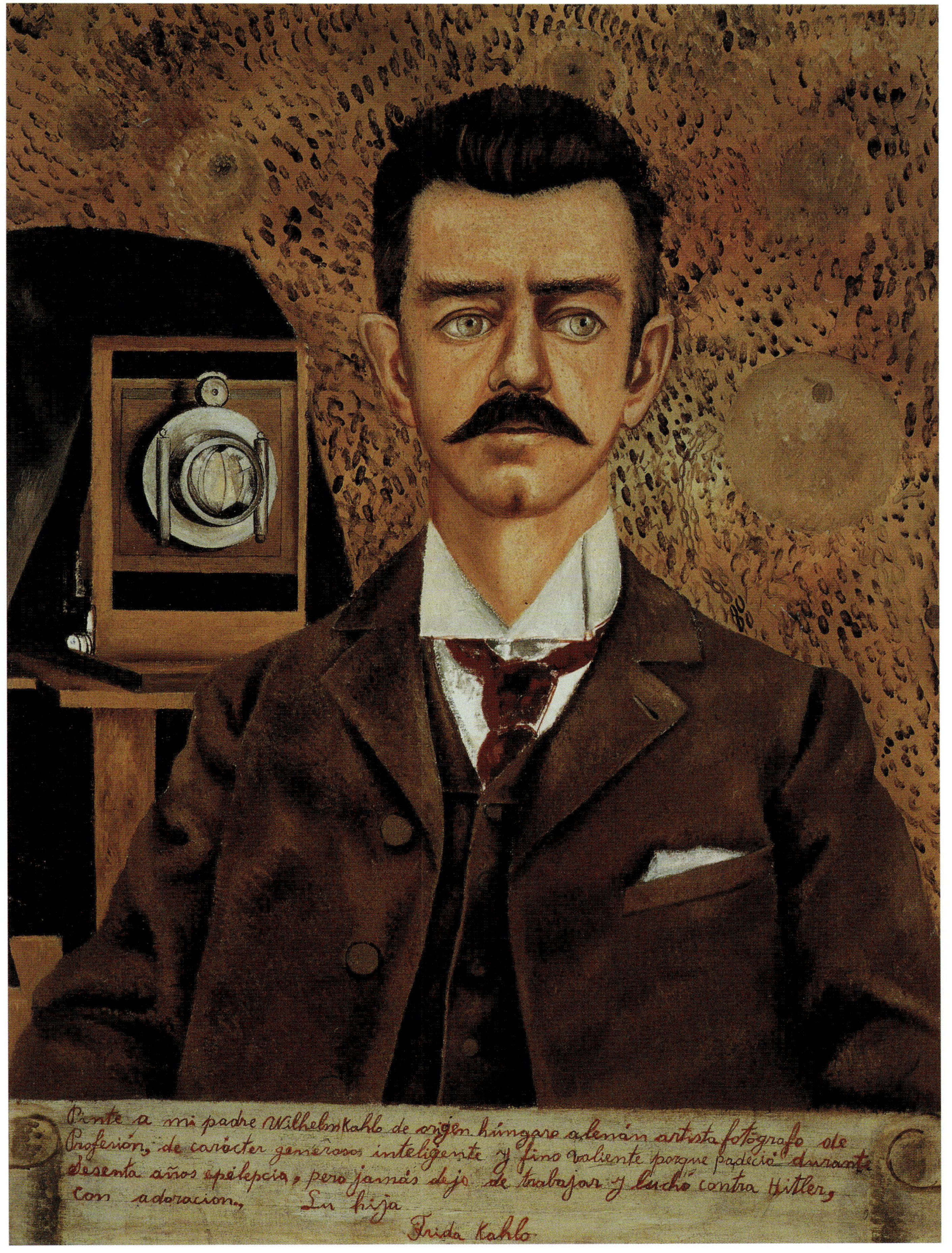
Pinte a mi padre Wilhelm Kahlo de origen húngaro alemán artista fotógrafo de
Profesión, de carácter generoso, inteligente y fino valiente porque padeció durante
sesenta años epilepcia, pero jamás dejó de trabajar y luchó contra Hitler,
Con adoracion, Su hija
Frida Kahlo

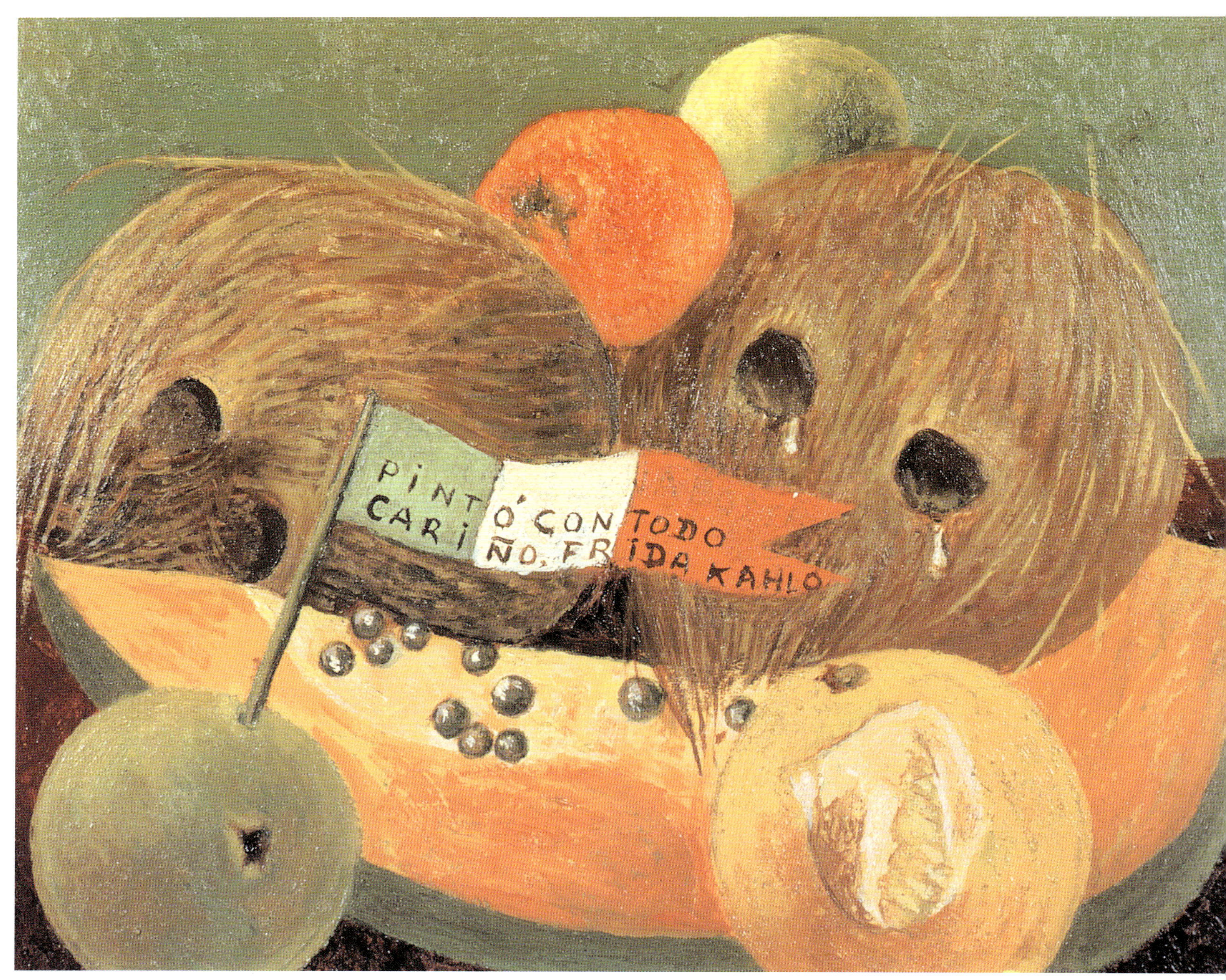
PINTÓ CON TODO
CARIÑO, FRIDA KAHLO

While she toiled as his secretary, archivist, chief cook and bottle washer, when she wasn't painting her own work, she began teaching in 1943 at the experimental School of Painting and Sculpture on Esmeralda Street in the Guerrero District. Like the National Preparatory School she had attended, this *high school secundaria* offered free courses in painting and drawing as well as French, art history, Mexican Art and culture. Like her own self- designed Bohemian education, she took her students beyond the walls of the school and into the streets to observe and experience life for their work. Her health forced the painting and drawing classes - such as they were - to be held in *La Casa Azul.* Often, instead of painting, the instructor and students engaged in long conversations, opening their minds to new ideas - some of which got her into trouble with the politically conservative school administration. She expanded their experience beyond easel painting by procuring commissions for them to paint murals on the walls of a *pulqueria* (street corner saloon), some houses and a laundry building. She loved this work and was, in turn, loved by her students, who came to be called, *Los Fridos.*

To keep generating revenue, Frida accepted portrait commissions from local politicians, friends, and her patrons. After the unfortunate misunderstanding over the *Suicide of Dorothy Hale* for Clare Booth Luce, Frida was careful not to offend her clients with overstating what she saw, or transferring her current personal demons into symbolism that obscured the client's expected result. Even diluting her visual intensity, Frida managed to achieve some remarkably intimate portraits.

A friend and sincere patron of her work, engineer and career diplomat, Eduardo Morillo Safa, ordered Kahlo portraits of himself and his family. Of this series, the most sensitive and beautifully seen example is the 1944 *Portrait of Doña Rosita Morillo Safa* (p. 143), Eduardo's mother.

The family matriarch sits in front of a seething background of flowering vines, cactus and leaves. Her simple brown cloak covers the shoulders of her black dress that is buttoned to the neck. *Doña Rosita's* ample bosom serves to support and isolate her head and frames the large-knuckled working hands that knit with rough brown yarn. Everything is painted in

Page 174

Coconut Tears (*Crying Coconut*), 1951.

Oil on masonite, 23.2 x 30.5 cm.

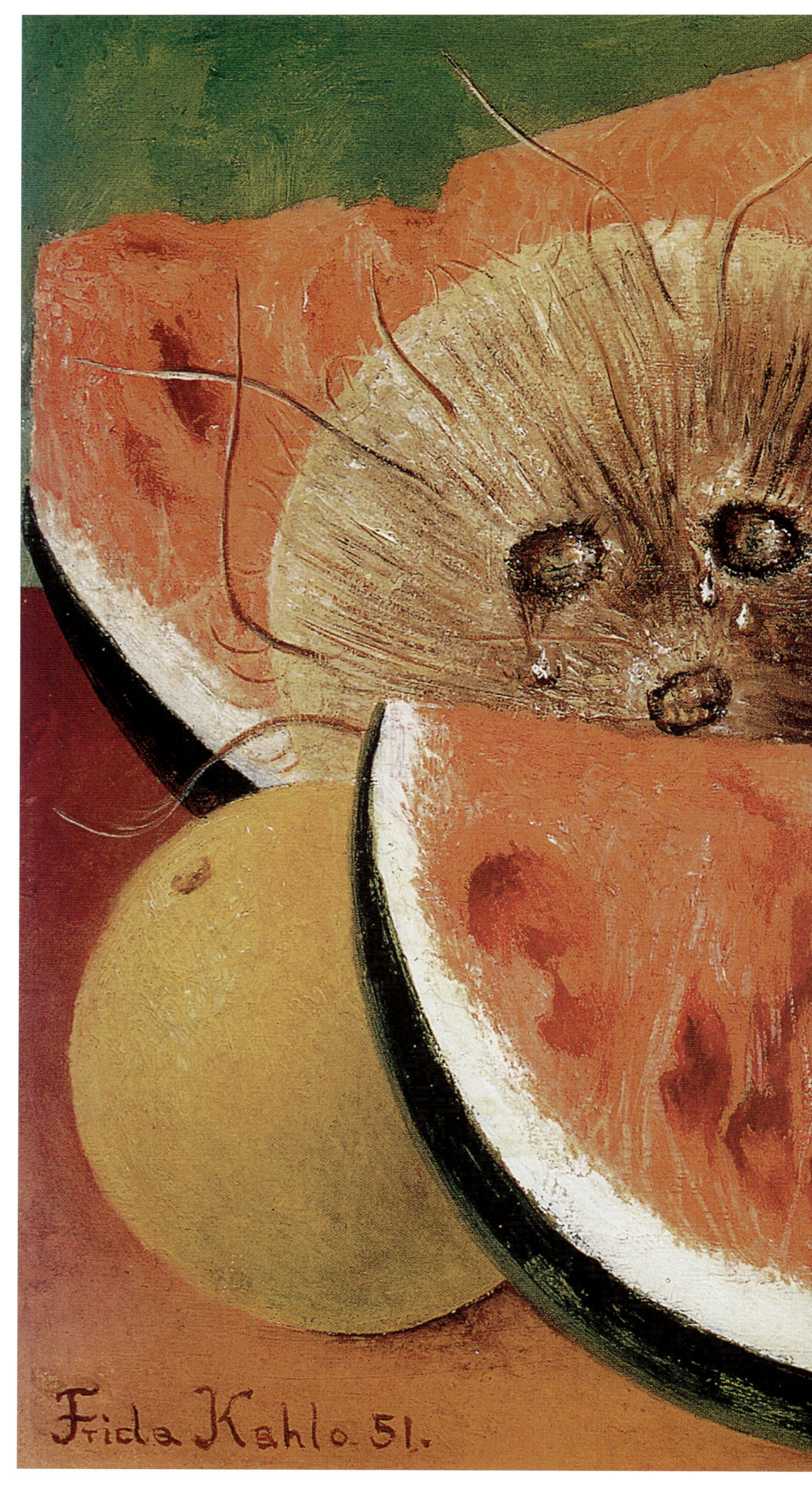

Page 176-177

Coconuts (*Glances*), 1951.

Oil on masonite, 25.4 x 34.6 cm.

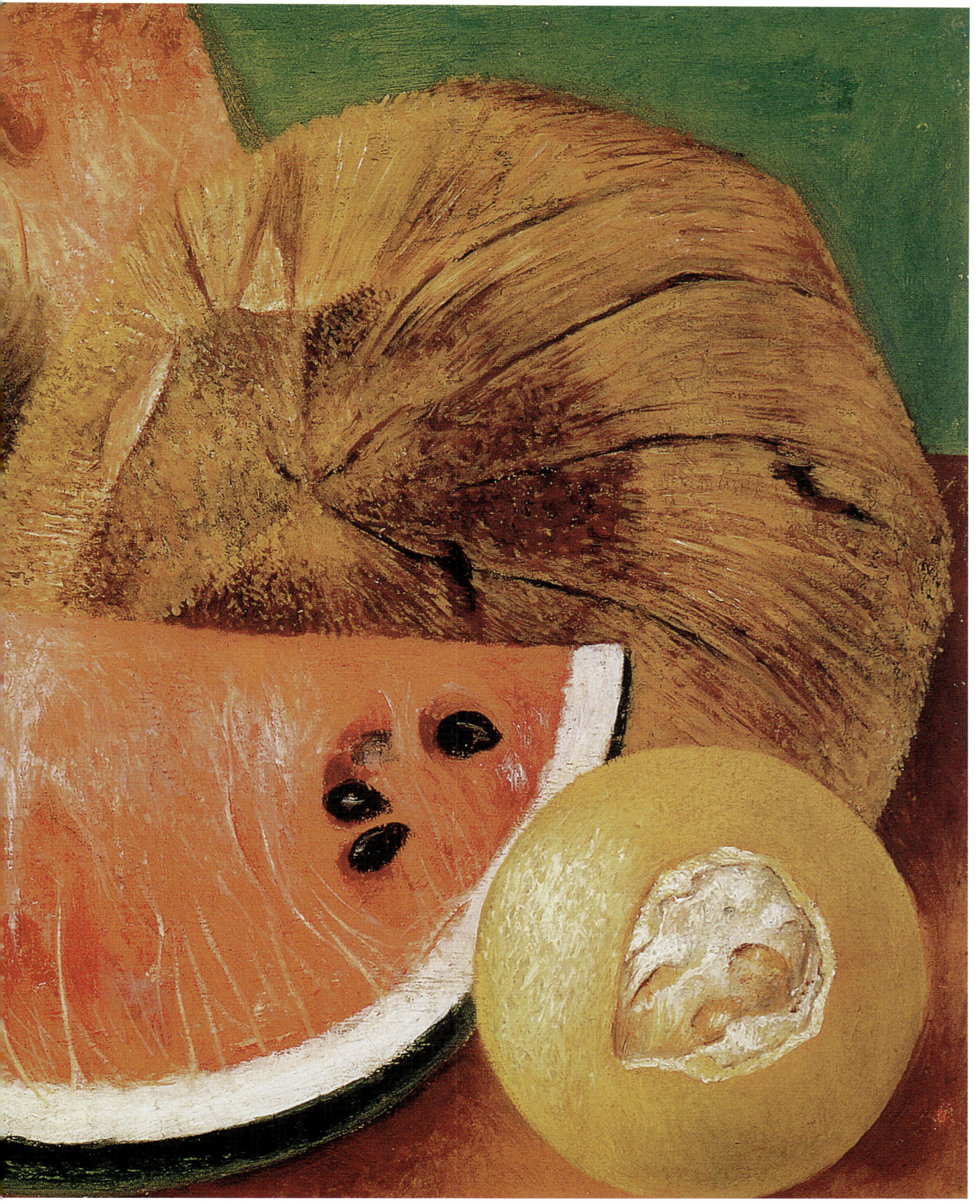

earth colors. Her luminous dark-skinned face capped by a crown of silver white hair looks out from the frame wearing an expression of weariness that must have touched Frida. *Doña Rosita* has fewer days in front of her than have passed. She is alone without her husband and is the guest of her children in her old age. There are more memories than expectations in those inward-focused eyes. The expression is not worn for the benefit of the artist, but has been etched there by life, smoothed and rounded by the erosion of time.

These portraits executed in the 1940s demonstrate how far Frida Kahlo had come from her early groping with technique and struggle to see beneath the skin. These are not primitive copies of the *retablo* style churned out by local religious painters, but truly realized discoveries created by the facility of communication between her hands and fingers and the instinctual vision that drove them.

Her own self-portraits benefited from this visual and mechanical maturity during this rich period in her creative arc. In letters to friends, she begged, "Don't forget me!"[6] She preserved the memory of her presence in a symbolic tapestry of her fears and dreams as well as her stoic public image of the "survivor." Alejandro Gomez Arias offered that these portraits served as,

> *...a recourse, the ultimate means to survive, to endure, to conquer death..."*[7]

The self-portraits persisted as the body cannibalized itself toward eventual destruction and her mind endured the metamorphosis from youthful anticipation to the dawning realization that the fantasy of a life without daily stabs of physical pain was a false hope. In effect, Frida created her own exhibition of self images that, over time, produced a visual documentary displaying the day by day corruption of her physical and mental world from behind a mask that never complained or cried. Every day, she added a brush stroke to her own impassive monument.

Another outlet for Frida's increasing introspection into her own mortality and the fragility of life appeared in her ongoing still life paintings. These works first appeared in

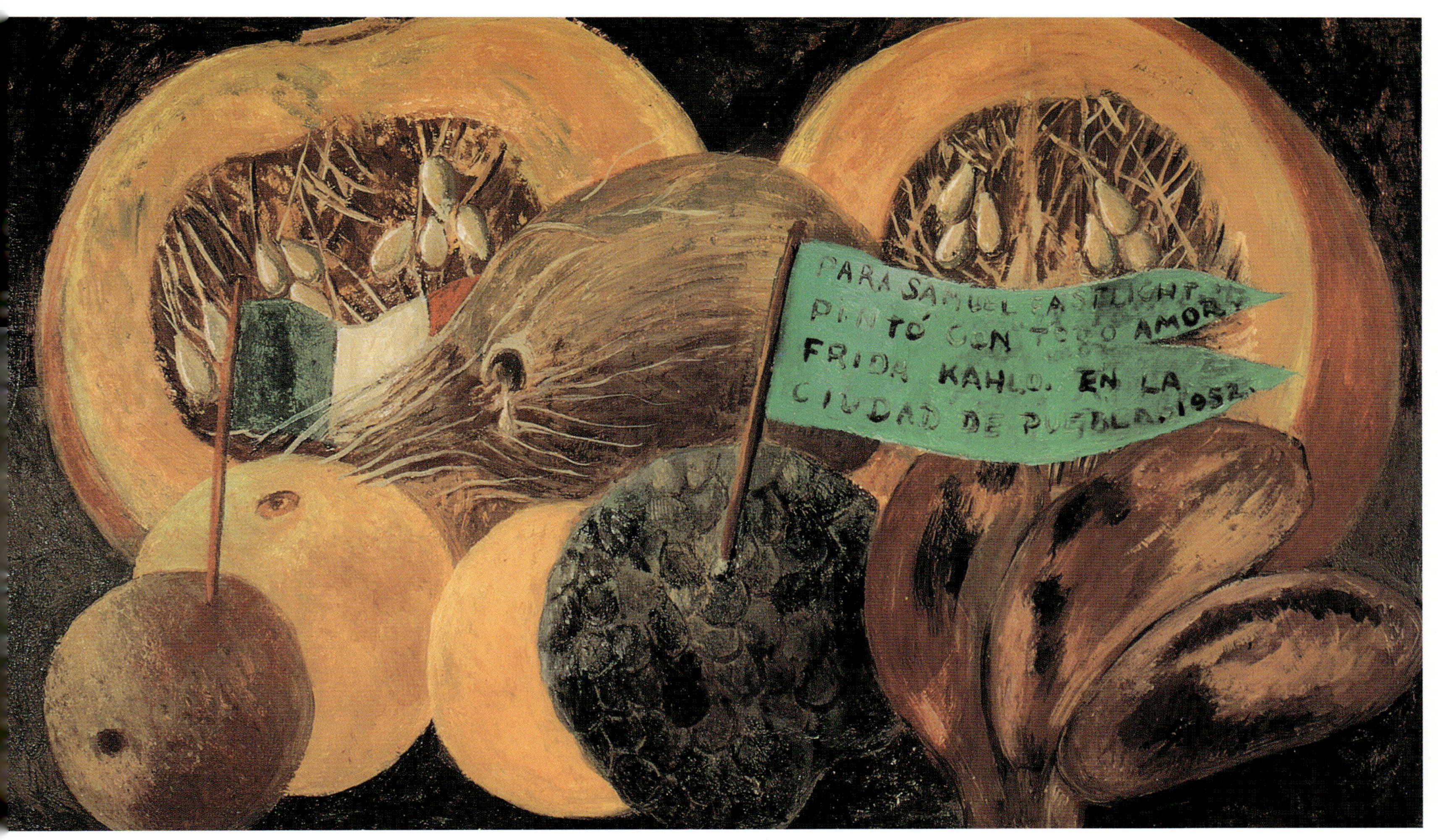

the late 1930s with that erotic gem, *Flower of Life* - also called *The Flame Thrower* – and simple dishes of fruit (*Still Life with Pitahayas*, 1938 and *Still Life with Prickly Pear* (Tunas) *Fruits*, 1938, both painted on metal). They allowed her to explore uncomfortable internal ideas using benign subject matter that didn't immediately scare away potential buyers. One particular example of this genre was the 1943 painting, *The Bride Frightened at Seeing Life Opened*.

The "bride" in this oil is doll-like, wearing a virginal white wedding dress and viewing a prickly landscape of quartered watermelons resembling pointed teeth and open jaws. There are cocoanuts with the "eyes" of one resembling the face of a small furry animal. It huddles next to blemished plantains beneath the stick legs of a striding locust. A sharp-leafed

Page 179

Still Life dedicated to Samuel Fastlicht, "painted with all my love", 1952.

Oil on canvas mounted on wood,

25.8 x 44 cm.

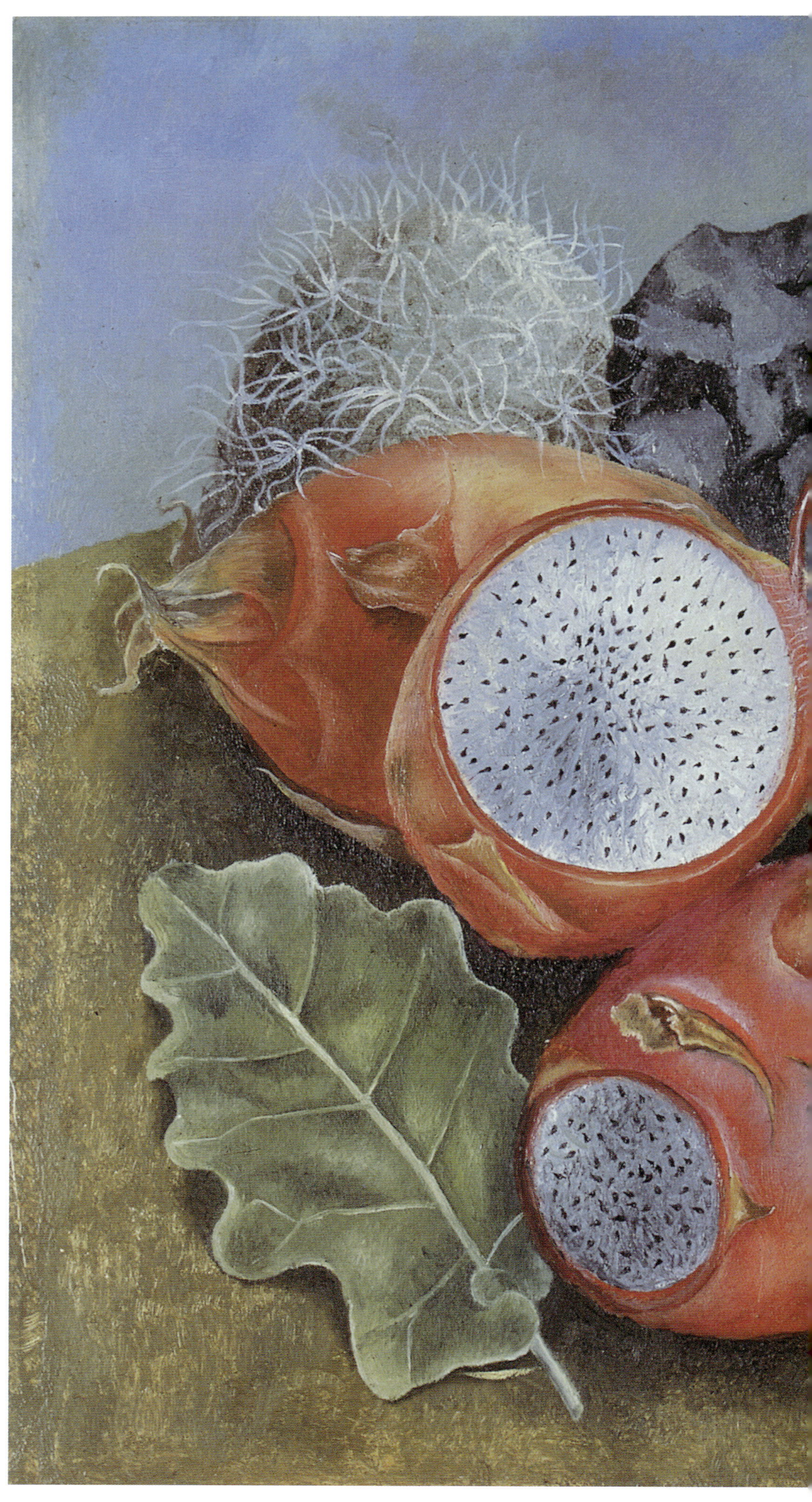

Page 180-181

Still Life with Pitahayas, 1938.

Oil on plate, 25.4 x 35.6 cm.

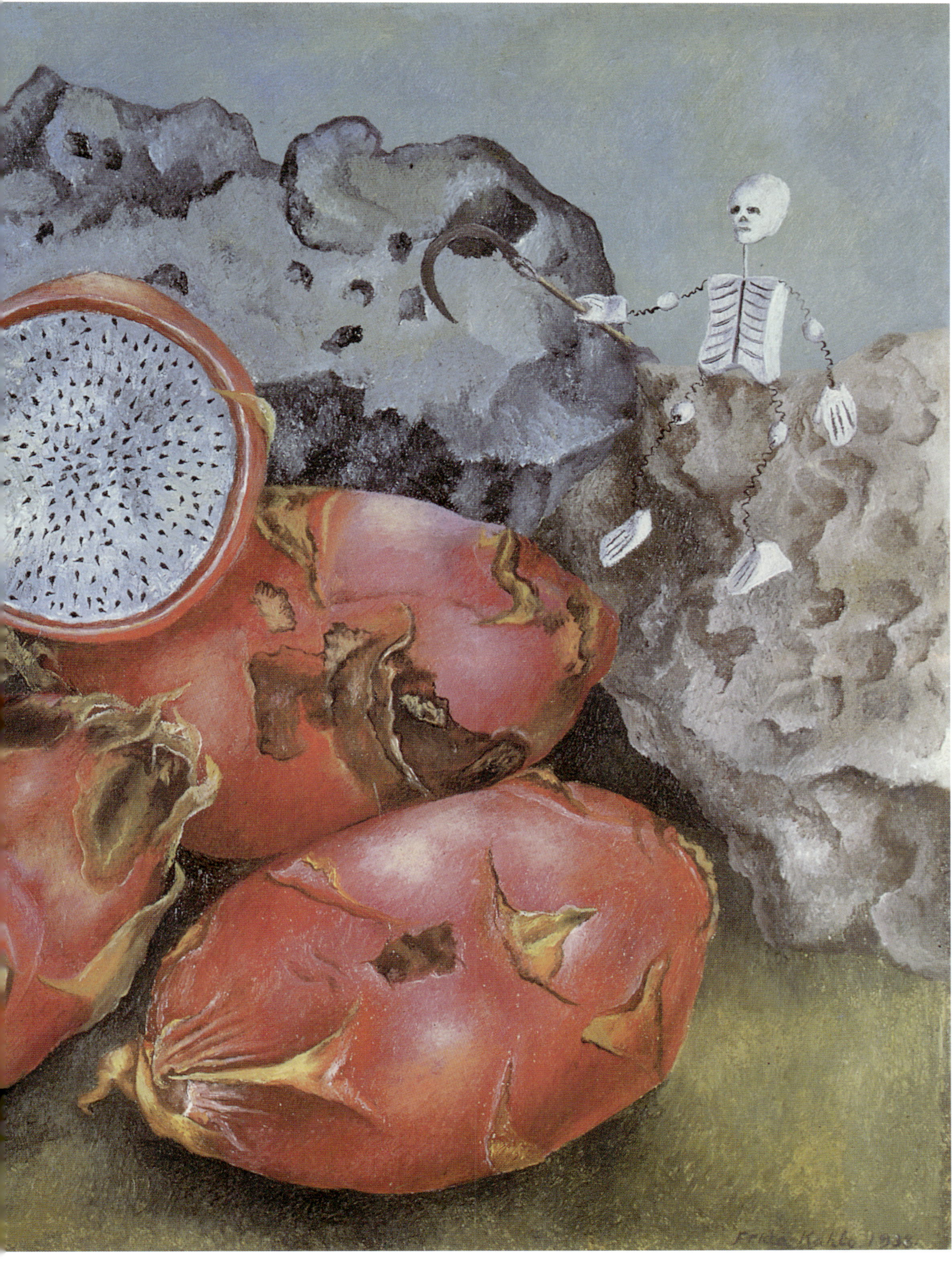

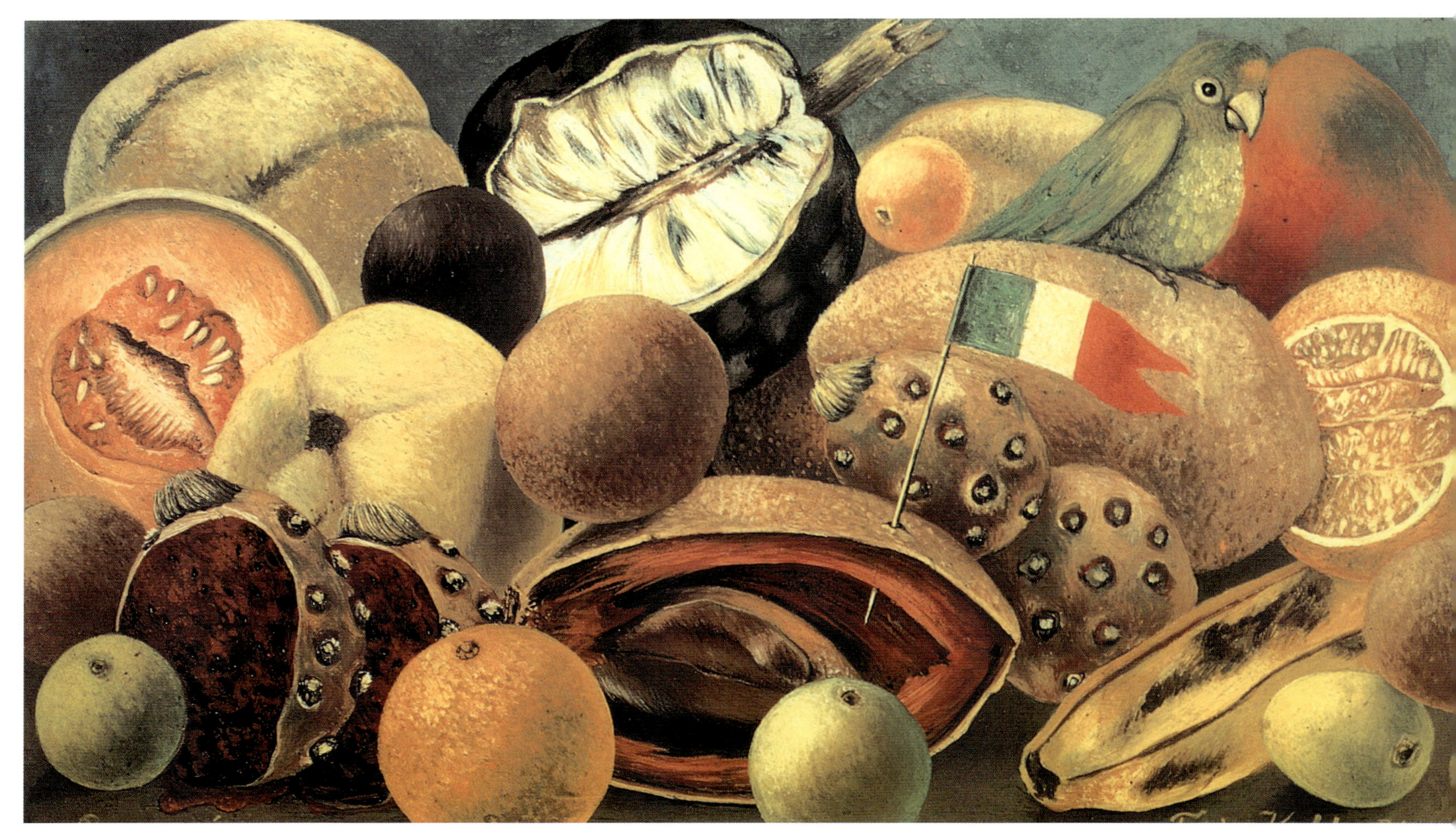

pineapple holds down the right side of the composition, just behind a fierce-eyed parrot. At the top is a cleft melon overripe with black seeds ready to pour out. This table top covered with fruits has been transmogrified into a trap that seems to pulse with life and promise of good things, but is actually a fragile illusion.

Another – this time truly frightening – still life from her mind is *The Chick* (p. 147). On a nest of barren sticks, a chick – you can almost feel it trembling – watches huge spiders continue to engulf a handled vase filled with lilacs, a caterpillar, a grasshopper and fronds with a network of sticky webbing. You want the chick to move away from the death trap, but it seems frozen in place, held in a thrall, vulnerable to the web and the terror of capture. It is a Hieronymus Bosch nightmare with the web slashed on with uncharacteristic palette-knife strokes.

Page 182

Still Life with Parrot and Flag, 1951.

Oil on masonite, 28 x 40 cm.

In 1944, Frida Kahlo created two significant windows into to her persona. She painted *The Broken Column* and began a diary that she continued until her death. If anyone needs to understand her suffering during the last years of her life, viewing the *Column* (p. 124) and reading her diary dispels any questions.

The downward spiral of her health kept a gaggle of doctors busy. The pain in her right foot had become virtually constant and the need for permanent relief, not drugged respite that impaired her ability to paint, became a constant quest.

A Doctor Alejandro Zimbron decided a steel corset would ease the pain and give her back support. With it in place, she began fainting and lost 13 pounds in six months. The pain was still there. Zimbron added spinal injections to the treatment. She experienced excruciating headaches. A year later, in 1945, Doctor Ramirez Moreno diagnosed syphilis and began blood transfusions. The pain continued and syphilis was never proved. Zimbron tried again with a traction device that hung her face-down suspended by her chin from the ceiling to relieve stress on her spine. With sandbags laced to her feet, she hung there for three months, painting for at least an hour every day.

While she dangled, other doctors conceived a variety of corsets made with plaster, steel, plaster and steel, leather, and one applied by an inexperienced doctor that didn't cure properly and almost suffocated her before being frantically cut away. She had 28 corsets lashed or slathered onto her torso during her last ten years. The toes of her right foot contracted gangrene and required amputation. Actually, they dropped off of their own accord. Most of these "cures" only exacerbated the pain and deepened her addiction to narcotics which didn't go well with the bottle of brandy she downed almost every day.

By the late1940s, Frida's physical condition consumed her. Metamorphosed into the shape of a deer pierced by arrows that have drawn blood, she hurries through a wood of barren trees in *The Little Deer* painted in 1946. That same year she traveled to New York for major surgery. Doctor Philip Wilson, a back specialist, had suggested fusing certain of her vertebrae and fixing them in place with a steel rod.

The Broken Column shows Frida against a ripped and rent desert background. She wears her hair long down her back and stands, as if for an examination, stripped to the waist except for the belts of Zimbron's wrap-around corset that hugs her nude torso. Down the center of her body is a jagged autopsy-like slash revealing an Ionic column that is broken in a half-dozen places along its fluted length. Her naked flesh is pierced all over with pointed tacks. Tears pour down her cheeks, the tears that will be increasingly familiar in future compositions.

Frida's diary, also begun in 1944, became a constant companion as she lay in bed, later in a wheelchair, and finally housebound. It seems to be written in a world other than the one she was experiencing. The pages are filled with colorful drawings, doodles, cartoons and no small amount of bawdy humor, long rambling cadences of poetry, gentle insights, and raucous *leperadas* – off-color words. Accidental drools of ink are turned into profiles of heads and fantastic shapes. A reader can almost feel the numbing narcotic course through her veins as her pen moves across the page. Like her paintings, but with greater spontaneity, it maps her state of mind in a chaotic world that becomes less real as the end draws near.

Anguish and pain, pleasure and death, Frida writes, *are no more than a process.*[8]

---

[1] Ibid., Rummel, pg.133

[2] Ibid., Rummel, pg. 133

[3] Ibid., Herrera, Hayden, p. 436

[4] Zamora, Martha, *The Letters of Frida Kahlo*, Chronicle Books, San Francisco, 1995

[5] Zamora, Martha, *The Brush of Anguish*, Chronicle Books, San Francisco, 1990

[6] Ibid., Zamora, Martha, *The Brush of Anguish*, p. 102

[7] Ibid., Zamora, Martha, *The Brush of Anguish*, p. 102

[8] Kahlo, Frida, *The Diary of Frida Kahlo*, Harry N. Abrams, Inc., New York, 1995

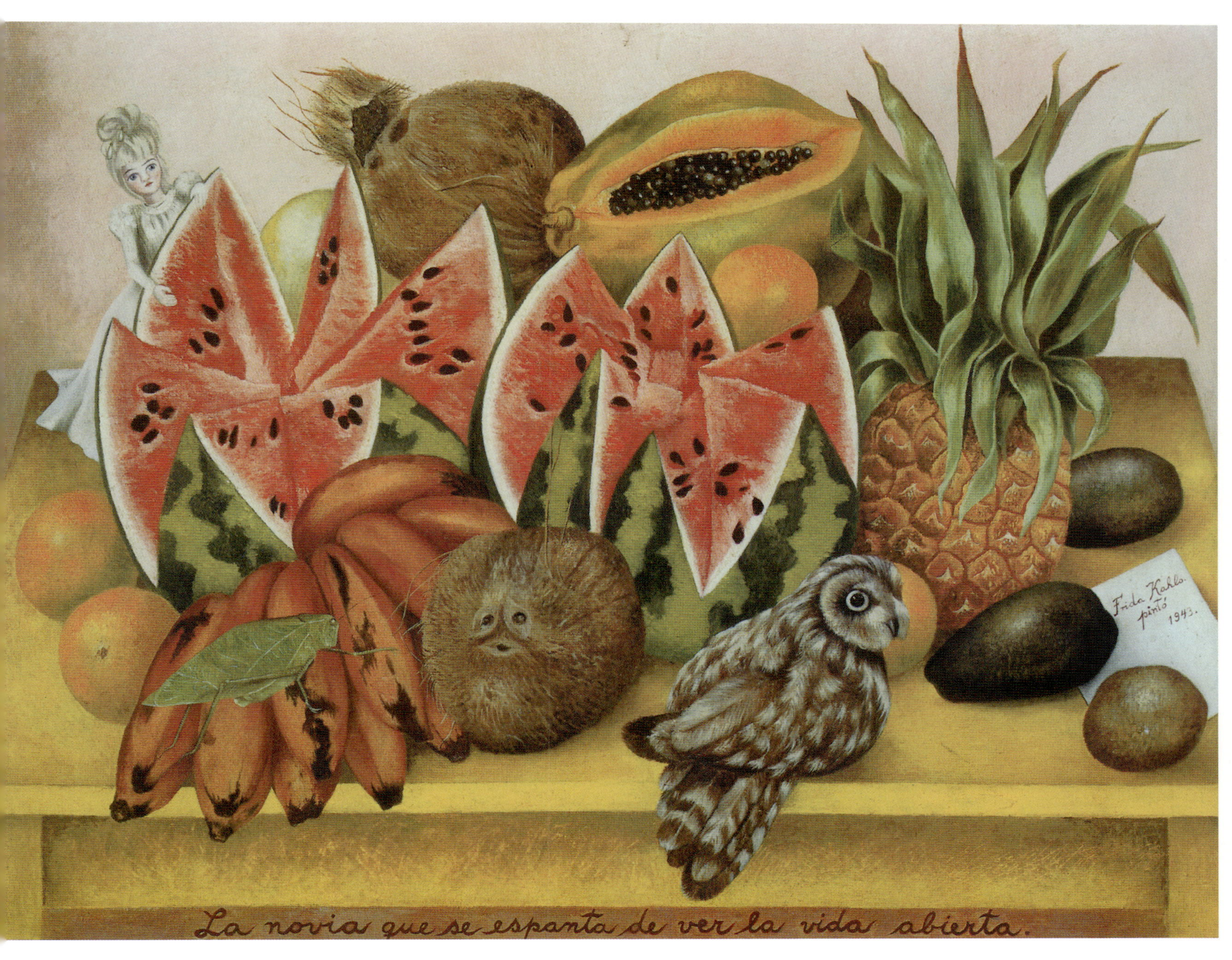

Page 185

The Bride Frightened at Seeing Life Opened, 1943. Oil on canvas, 63 x 81.5 cm, Collection Jacques and Natasha Gelman, Mexico City.

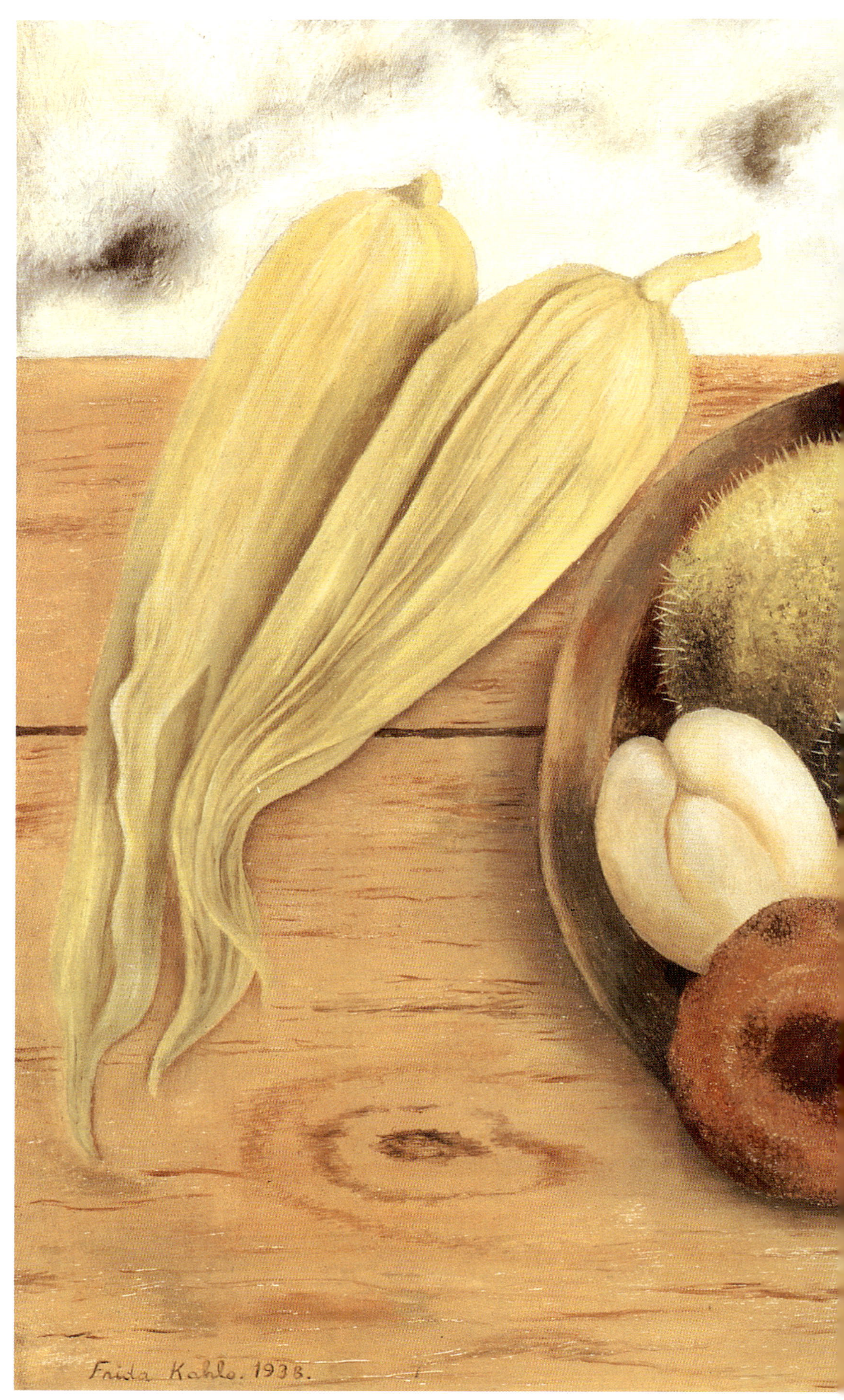

Page 186

Fruits of the Earth, 1938.

Oil on masonite, 40.6 x 60 cm,

Collection Banco Nacional de México,

Fomento Cultural Banamex, Mexico City.

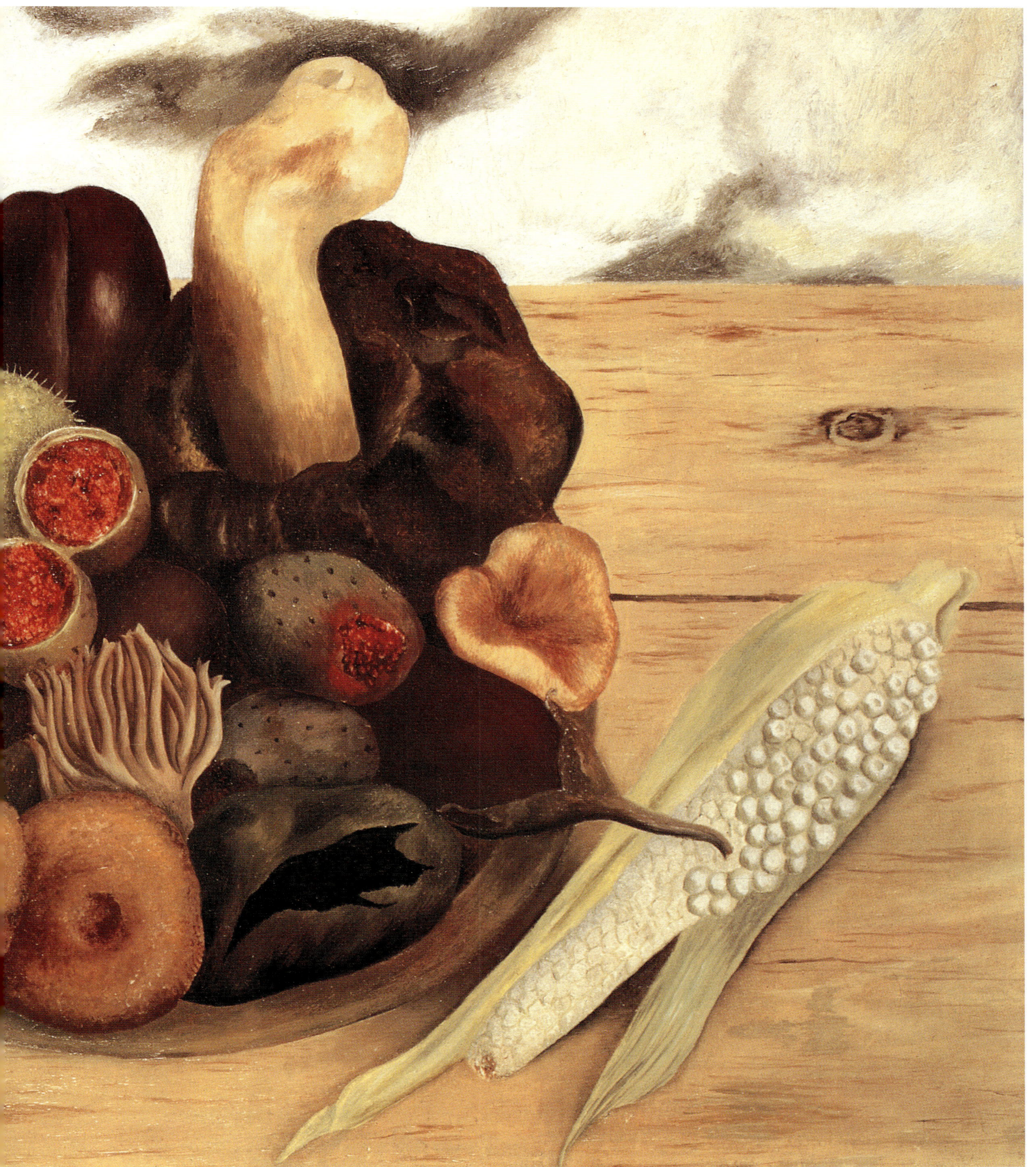

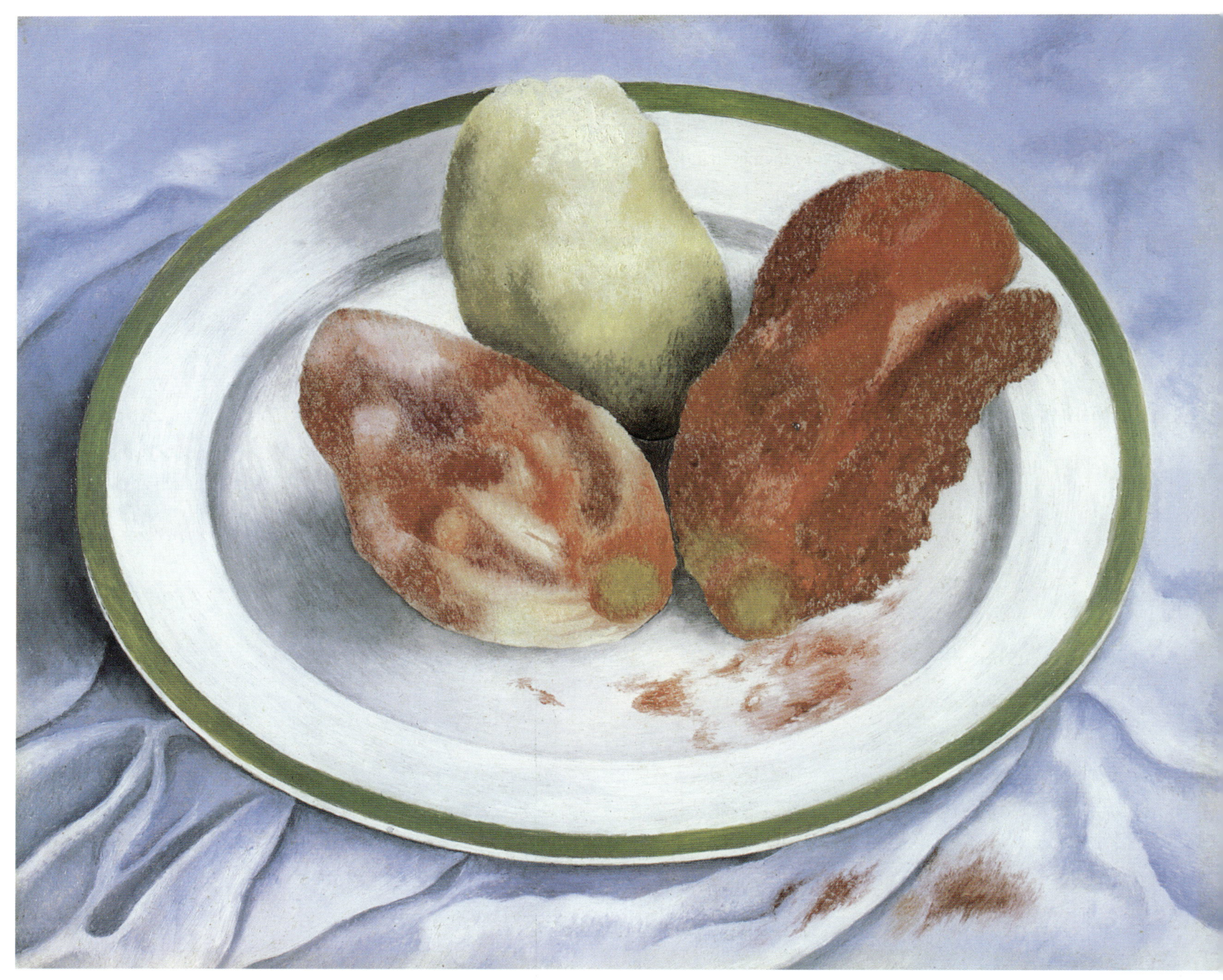

Conclusion

In 1938, Sigmond Freud fled Vienna to live in London and returned to a previous study of the story of Moses. He also returned to themes that constantly resurfaced in his work, the impact of trauma on memory and a people's identification with a leader who has both uplifted and disappointed them. Frida borrowed a copy of *Moses and Monotheism* from one of her patrons, Jose Domingo Lavin. He suggested she take some of Freud's ideas and commit them to a painting. When she had finished the book, she took three months to create one of her more revealing masterpieces, titled simply, *Moses* (p. 136-137). Of all her later work, *Moses* recalls her multi-subject story compositions painted in the mid-1930s, specifically *My Dress Hangs There* (1933) (p. 82) and *What the Water Gave Me* (1938) (p. 133). But in *Moses*, the frame barely contains the mural-like explosion of portraits, birth symbols and historic vignettes. It is a "mural" only in its stylistic tying together of diverse story elements *à la* Diego Rivera, David Alfaro Siqueiros and Jose Clemente Orozco. While she uses the birth of Moses, a heroic character, as the core *raison* for the painting, Frida manages to turn it into a personal pastiche of gods, demigods, philosophers, Judeo-Pharonic symbolization, sociopaths, and mythic heroes stirred together with her own iconic code. At an informal gathering at Lavin's home, she explained some of her personal beliefs and how they are enmeshed in a portion of the work:

> *...Like Moses, there have always been lots of "high-class" reformers of religions and human societies. It could be said that they are a kind of messenger between the people they manipulate and the gods they invent to be able to do it. Many gods of this type still exist, as you know. Naturally, I didn't have enough space for all of them, so I placed on both sides of the sun those, who, like it or not, are directly related to the sun. On the right are the Western (gods) and on the left the Oriental ones ...*[1]

Whatever her mix of verbal and artistic gymnastics, *Moses* captured the attention of the Mexican art establishment. She received the Ministry of Education National Prize of Arts and Sciences and the sum of five thousand pesos. Frida Kahlo's ingenuous use of language

Page 188

Tunas (Still Life with Prickly Pear Fruit), 1938.

Oil on plate, 19.7 x 24.8 cm.

in her diary and here, explaining one of her more densely populated and philosophically impenetrable works, gives away the core of her personality and one reason for her legion of friends and admirers. Each life that touched hers came away with a reflection that matched an expectation. Each took away a piece of the Frida Kahlo puzzle as a revelation, a personal discovery and a gift.

But if *Moses* conveys her ability to control a multi-dimensional philosophical concept, the sheer brutality of her situation comes forward in brush strokes loaded with thick impasto as she is either expecting to be force fed, or has just spewed out a conglomeration of food that hangs draped in a gelatinous mass from her bed easel. This unsettling scene titled *Without Hope* (p. 118) plays out on a devastated landscape beneath a broiling sun. She peers at the viewer through tears from beneath a bedspread decorated with microscopic life, the persistent infections that dogged her.

The following year, 1946, she created *Tree of Hope* (p. 158) where she lives in a divided world. The "two Fridas" in this case represent an incised but as yet unstitched post-operative patient stretched out on a hospital cart behind the seated *Tehuana*-dressed beauty clutching one of her many corsets that has been painted bilious pink and in the other hand a flag that reads, "Tree of Hope, keep firm." Despite this rallying cry and the ministrations of her doctors, the spiral continued downward. Hope, in this case was denied her as Wilson's vertebrae fusing operation failed to ease the pain, possibly because Wilson fused the wrong vertebra. Of course, it didn't help that Frida refused to obey his recommendation for bed rest and a more sedentary lifestyle.

In 1950 a bone graft from a piece of her pelvis followed the failed fusion and was equally unsuccessful. And by now, a previous fungus growth appeared once again on her hand. An abscess was discovered beneath one of her corsets and another surgical wound that had not healed properly stank, "...like a dead dog." She spent that year in bed. For much of her stay, Diego took a room next to hers and did what he could to keep her spirits up.

Frida had symbolically reduced Diego to a benign and helpless infant in her maternal arms as they both face the fates in her 1949 painting, *The Love Embrace of the Universe* (p. 177),

Page 191
Diary page, 1953.
The two tortured feet refer to the pain that the artist suffered in her legs and feet throughout her life. In 1953, she agreed to have her foot amputated.

Page 192
One of the last pages of Frida's diary.

Page 193
The last picture in her diary.

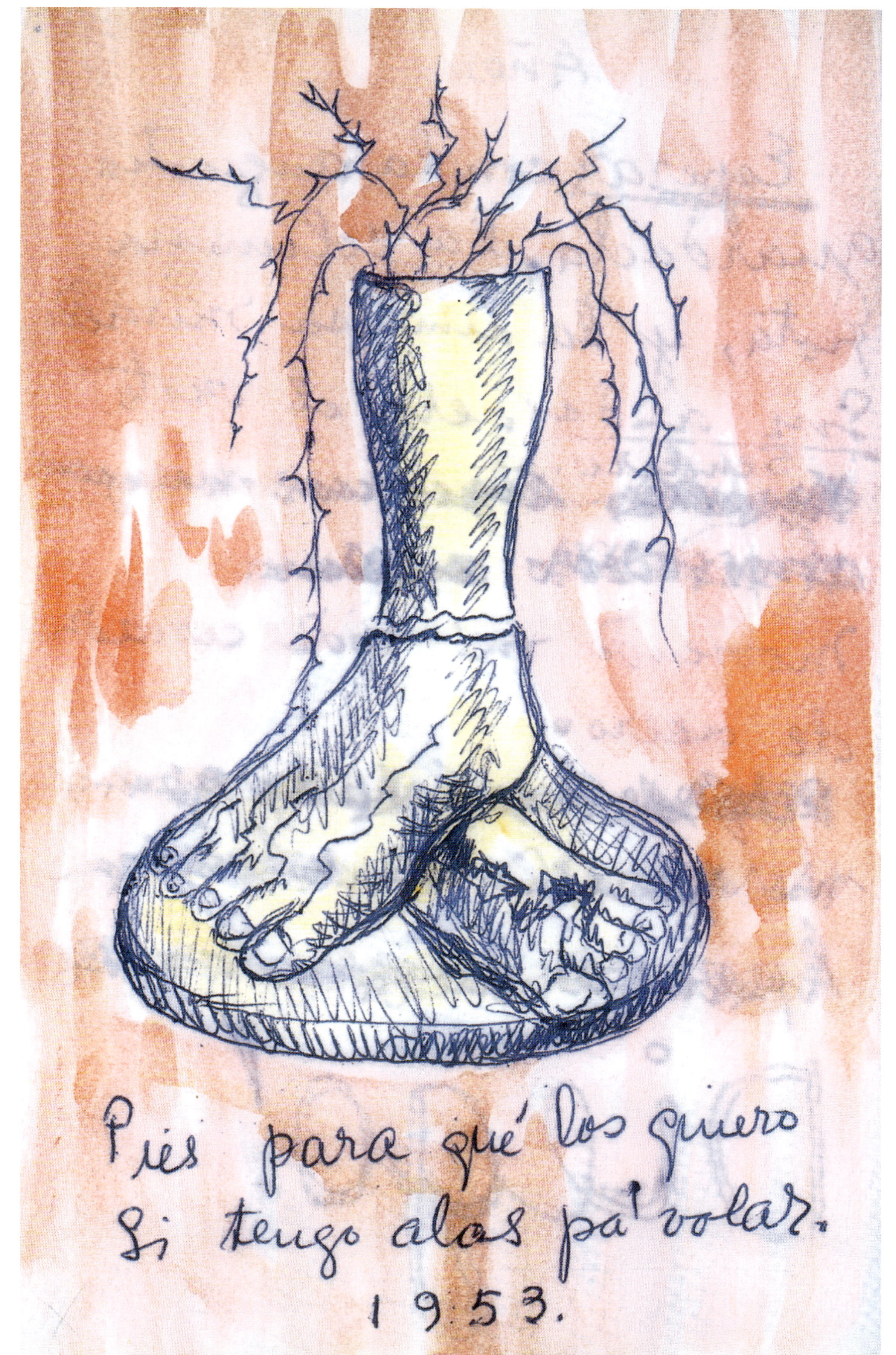
Piés para qué los quiero
Si tengo alas pa' volar.
1953.

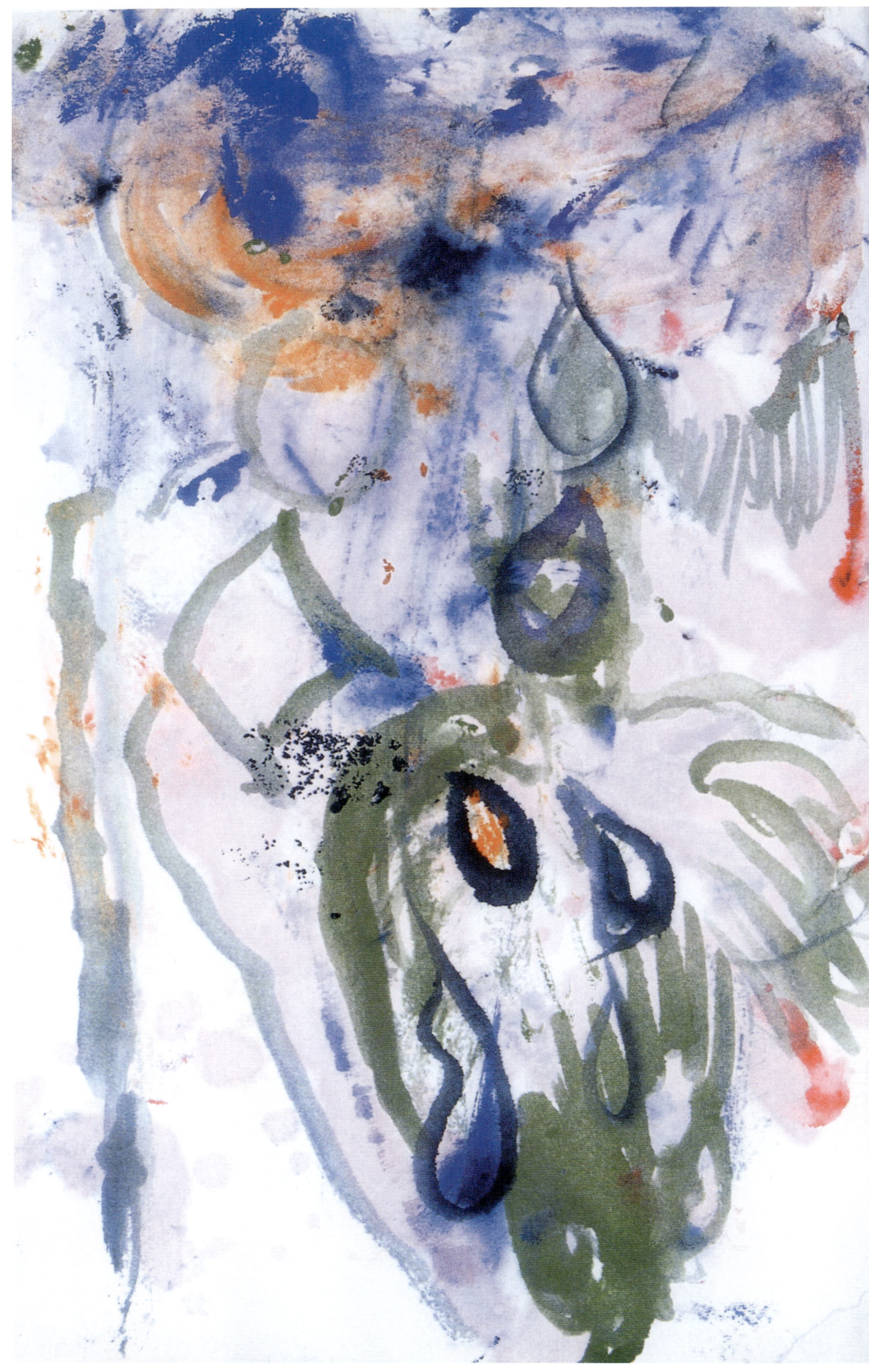

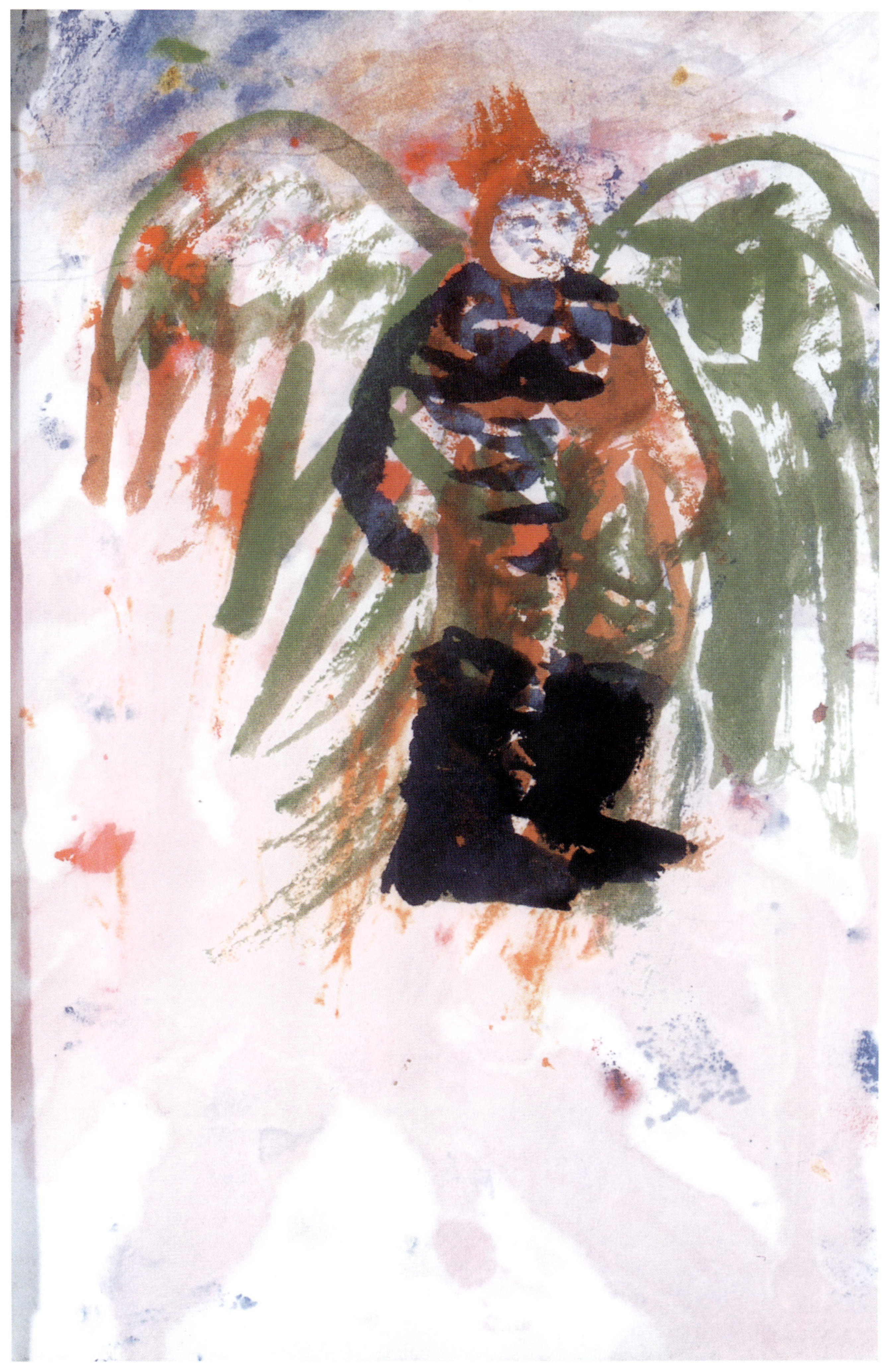

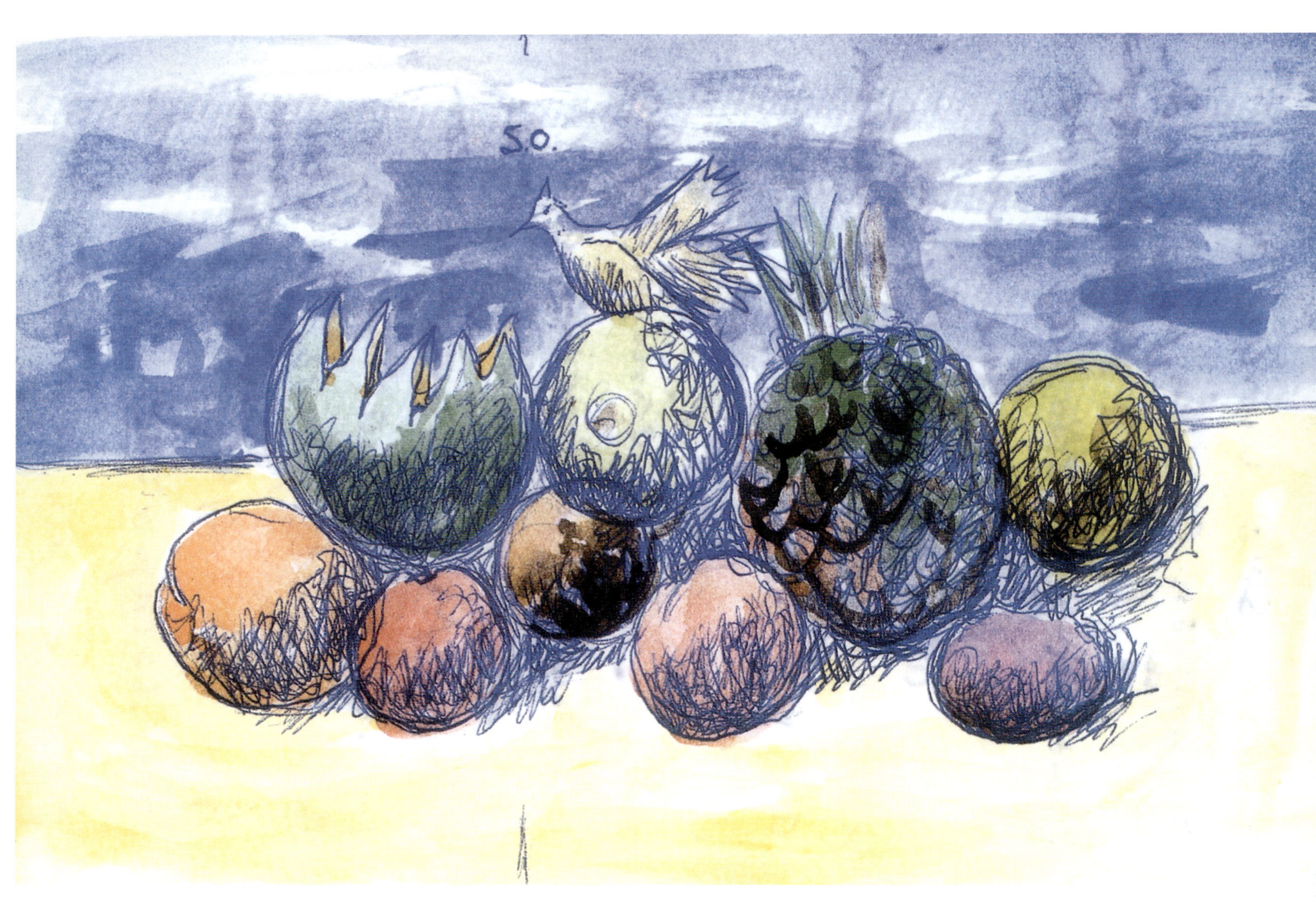
S.O.

The Earth, Diego, I and Señor Xóloth. She also placed in the center of his forehead her single eye of truth and wisdom. He had become the single constant in her life that she trusted - regardless of his infidelities. He began to age visibly as he watched her paint in shades and hues of pain.

By now, Diego Rivera was part of an aging mythos, the Mexican mural movement that began in 1922. Though he remained popular, his legend appeared in the past tense as Frida Kahlo's was in ascendancy. Her work had appeared in a number of group shows around the world and earned decent prices from a growing number of collectors. Diego took great pride in her success and took every opportunity to show her off and praise her talent. That didn't stop him from having affairs, or stop her from abusing doctors' orders as if to hurl more guilt in his face when her body rebelled. But as his trips to the hospital became more frequent with the illnesses of aging, she cheered him and sent him small presents as though he was her ailing child.

By 1951, she emerged from her year of hospitalization to be confined to a wheel chair. But in her *Self-Portrait with Portrait of Dr. Juan Farill,* her outward gaze remains steady while her engorged heart is affixed to her palette suggesting she is painting with her life's blood. Another portrait marked this year, a picture that tied up loose ends and her coming to grips with the death of her father 10 years earlier. *Portrait of Don Guillermo Kahlo* is a sympathetic treatment of the man who urged her to seek her own path in life. He is portrayed with the view camera of his trade and the text in red on *retablo* banner inscrolled beneath the likeness ends, "with adoration, your Frida."

By this time, she must have sensed that there was not much time left to her. As with many who face death, she sought a return to her only religion, the only cause that had sustained her interest and commitment. Frida rejoined the Communist Party. Even in her wheel chair, she could still offer up her rally voice singing the *Internationale* and raise her fist in solidarity with her comrades. Her loyalty to Mexico was finally honored in April, 1953 when Frida's friend, Dolores Alvarez Bravo, devoted her *Galleria de Artes Contemporaneo* to a one-woman show of Frida Kahlo's work. This was the only such show accorded Frida

Page 194

Page from the diary.

Page 196

Page from Frida's diary demonstrating her continued belief in Communism.

Page 197

Page from her diary (1946-1954) showing the artist's personal conflict in *Moon, Sun, I?*

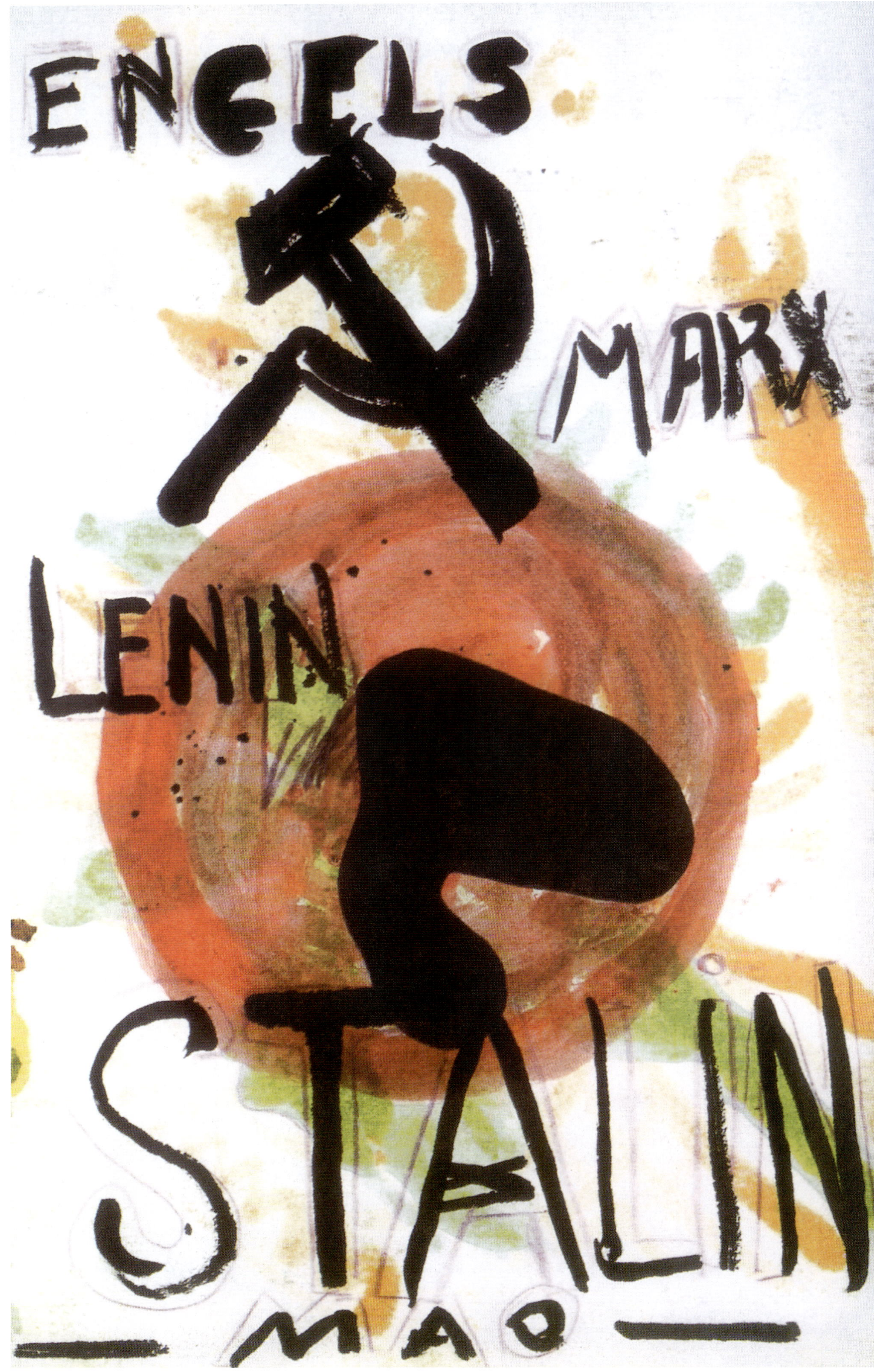
ENGELS
MARX
LENIN
STALIN
MAO

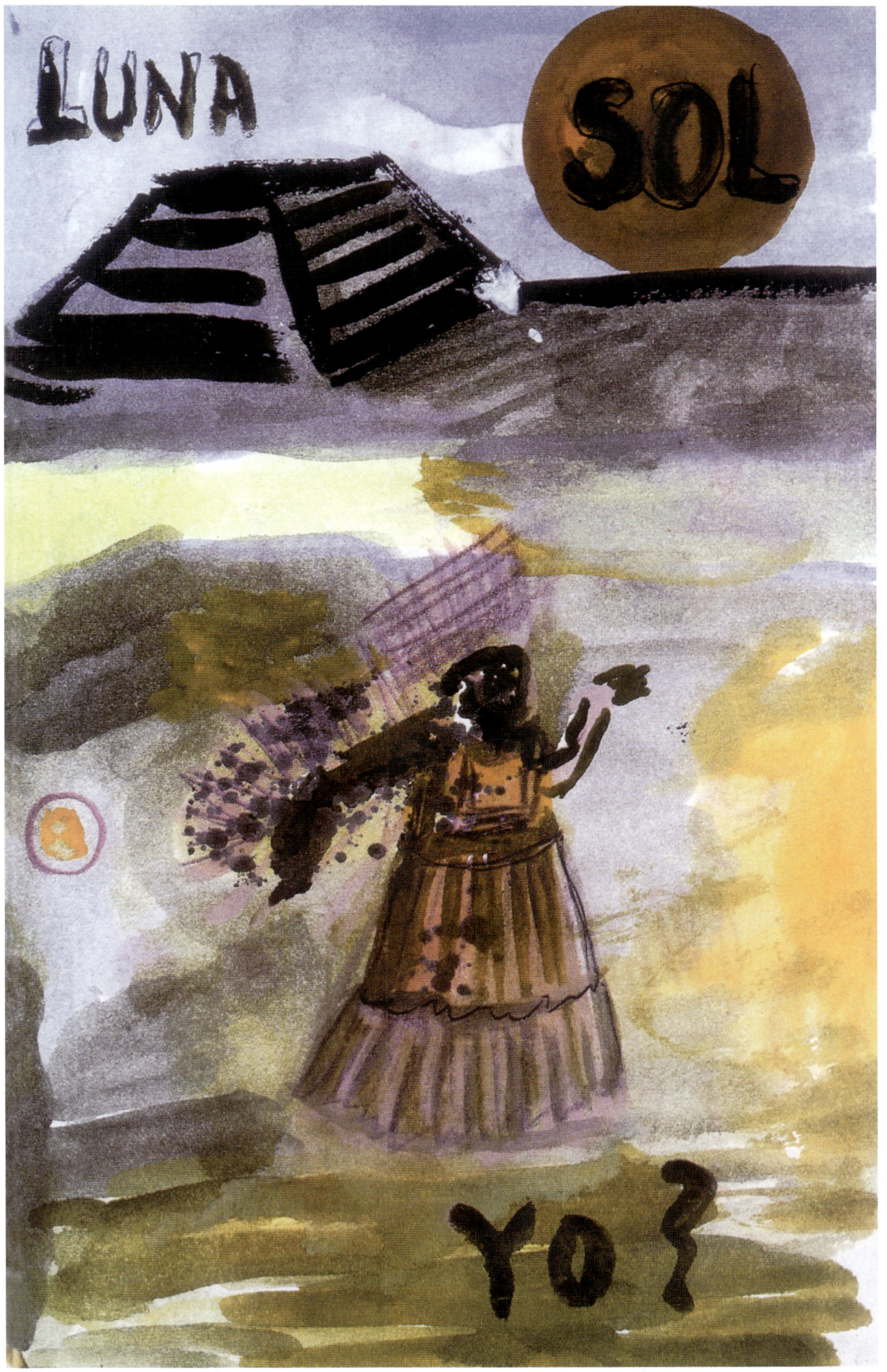
LUNA
SOL
YO?

through a bronchitis attack and she was confined to her bed. She and the bed were delivered to the gallery behind an escort of police sirens and blowing horns. There, heavily sedated, she became part of her exhibit, smiling up from her four-poster resting place at well-wishing faces from her past and those silent familiar witnesses looking down from the walls.

As 1953 drew to a close, her painting continued though its brushwork had reverted to a more primitive style from her learning years in the 1920s. She seemed to collapse into herself following the amputation of her right leg that had become septic with gangrene. She had kept that leg since her brush with polio at age 13 when it was turned into a withered "cane". The bus accident had broken it in 11 places. She had dragged it with her for more than 30 years and in all her paintings of that treacherous limb, she had used a mirror reflection and rendered it as her *left* leg. Now, it had been hacked off below the knee. Frida grudgingly accepted a wooden leg, but she was too frail to get much use from the prosthetic. Her addiction to pain killers and reliance on alcohol also made its conveneince more hazardous than useful.

Despite daily injections that left her back and arms covered with scabs, she managed long periods of lucidity, keeping notes in her diary, and working on an autobiography through 1953. Her final painting titled, *Viva la Vida (Long Live Life)*, depicts a collection of chopped watermelons with those words inscribed into a melon's pulp. She attended a Communist rally on July 2, 1954 shaking her fist and chanting wit the crowd. Ten days later as Diego sat with her holding her hand she gave him a silver ring celebrating their 25th wedding anniversary 17 days distant. When he questioned the timing of her gift, she said, "...because I sense that I'll be leaving you very soon."

On July 13, 1954, Frida Kahlo died at age 47. In a drawer near her bed was a large cache of Demerol vials, but some of her friends claimed she would never have taken her own life. Others disagreed. The official death certificate cites "pulmonary embolism". She had chosen cremation because after spending so many years of her short life stretched out on a bed, she had no wish to spend eternity lying on her back. Meticulously dressed in a *Tehuana* costume and bedecked with her jewelry, Frida's body was driven to the Palace of Fine Arts in Mexico City where more than 600 visitors paid their respects beneath the

Page 199
"Pinté de 1916".
The first illustration in the diary which Frida kept from 1946-1954.
Museo Frida Kahlo, Mexico City.

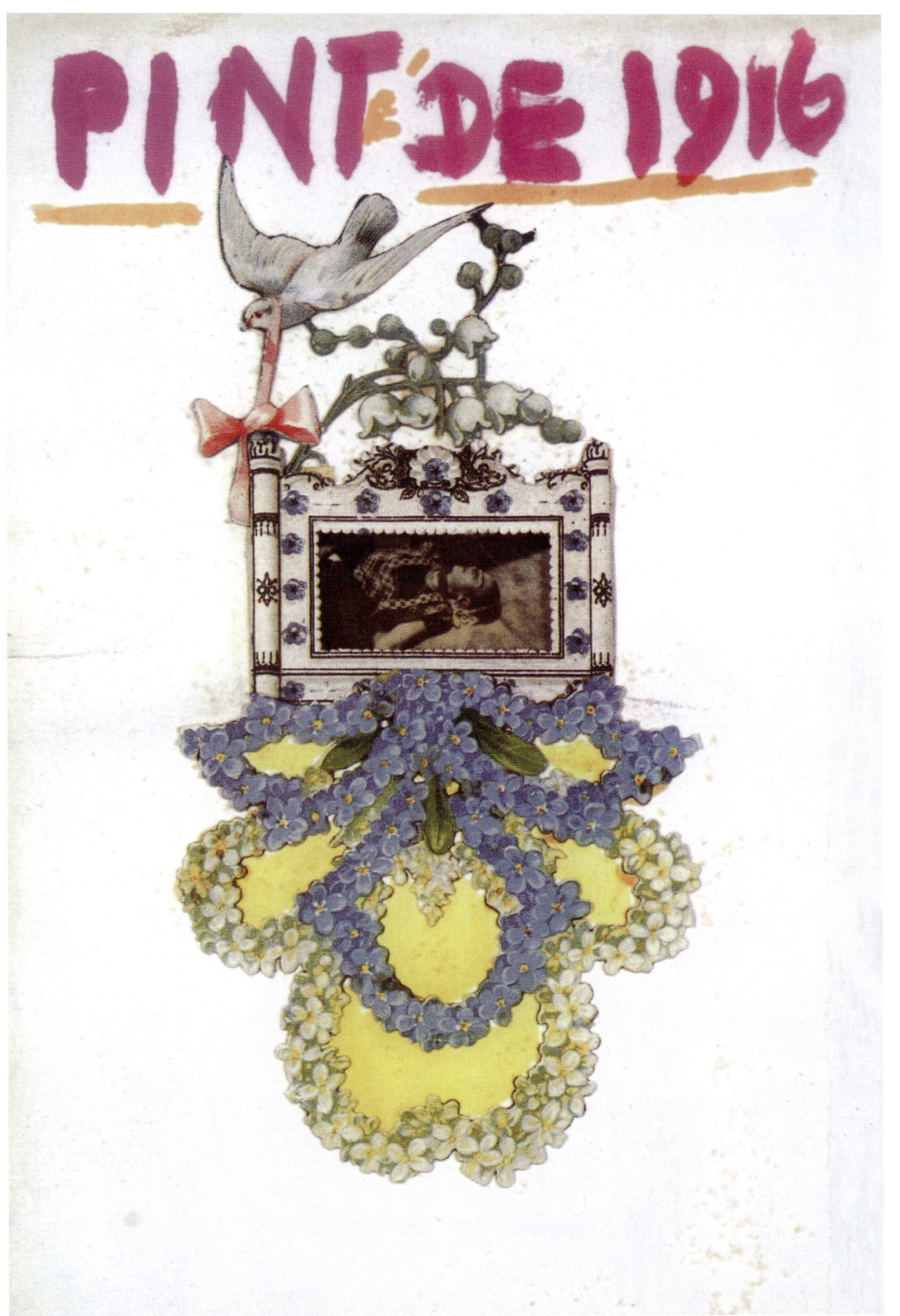
PINT DE 1916

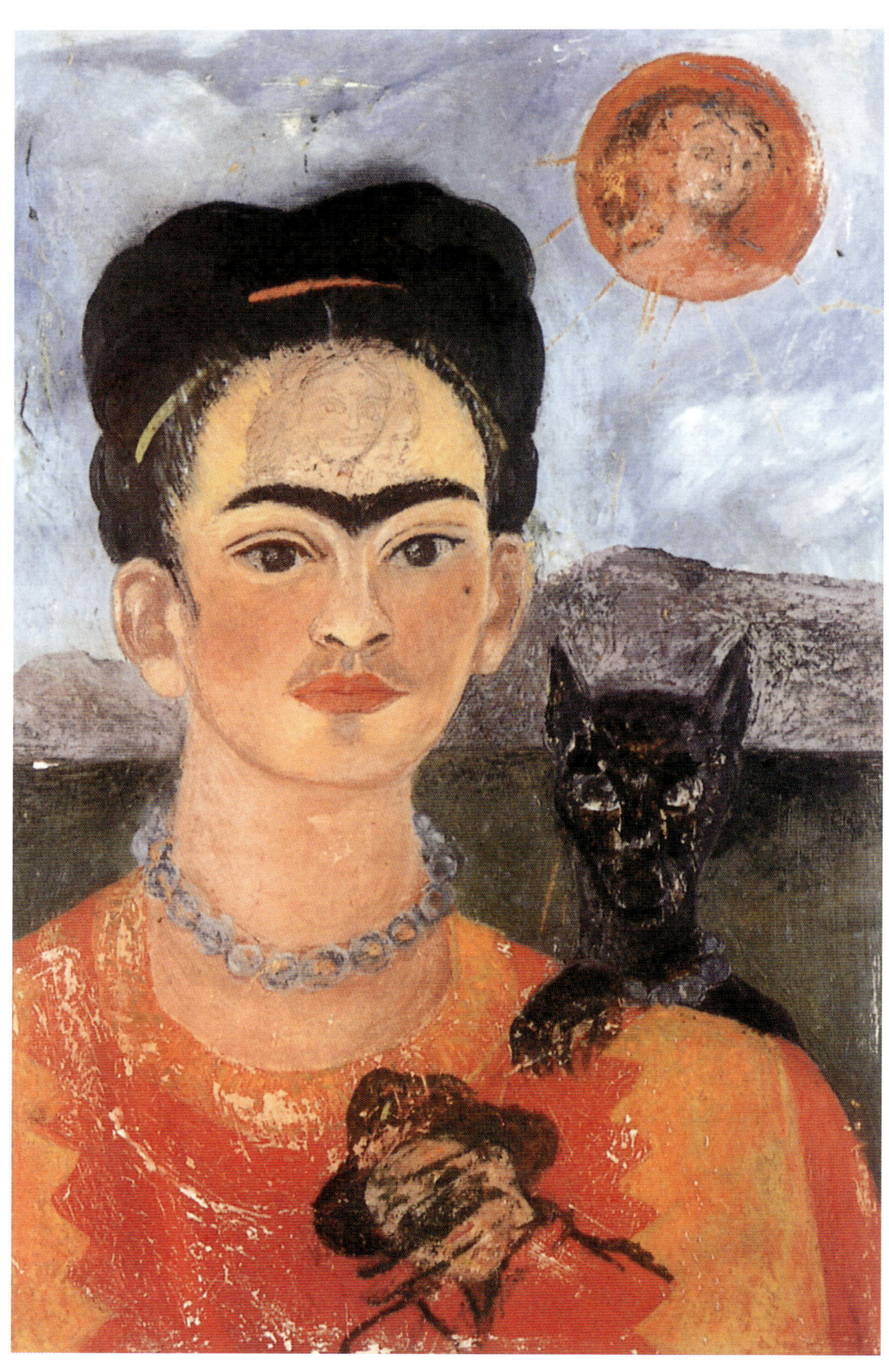

Page 200

Self-Portrait with the Image of Diego on My Breast and Maria on My Brow, 1953-1954.

Oil on hard fibre, 61 x 41 cm,

Locality unknown.

lobby's towering neoclassical ceiling. A distraught and shaken Diego Rivera sat at her side throughout the visitation. Earlier, in his state of weeping denial, he had her veins cut to make sure she was truly dead. The funeral became a politically charged (a red hammer-and-sickle Communist flag had been draped on her coffin), overwrought, emotional event totally in keeping with her chaotic lifestyle.

A light rain fell on the cortege as the mourners walked down the Avenida Juarez behind the hearse to the *Panteon Civil de Dolores*, the civil cemetery. At the center of the front line of walkers was Frida's poor old *Panzon*. Gone was the jaunty Stetson hat, the baggy suit with its pocket sagging from the weight of his Colt pistol. He wore a raincoat and looked like an aging banker. With his last kiss still lingering on her cold forehead, what remained of Frida left him behind at the crematory doors to cope with the final three years of his life.

In his autobiography, he admitted, *"... Too late now, I realized that the most wonderful part of my life had been my love for Frida."*[2] Diego Rivera died in Mexico City in 1957. In her 1953 autobiography, Frida wrote:

> *My paintings are well-painted, not nimbly but patiently. My painting contains in it the message of pain. I think that at least a few people are interested in it. It's not revolutionary. Why keep wishing for it to be belligerent? I can't. Painting completed my life. I lost three children and a series of other things that would have fulfilled my horrible life. My painting took the place of all of this. I think work is the best.*[3]

Gerry Souter
October 29, 2003
Arlington Heights, Illinois

---

[1] Ibid., Zamora, Martha, *The Letters of Frida Kahlo* p. 122

[2] Diego Rivera / Gladys March, *My Art, My Life: An Autobiography*, Citadel, New York, 1960

[3] Ibid., Zamora, Martha, *The Letters of Frida Kahlo*, p. 157

Biography

1907
Magdalena Carmen Frida Kahlo is born July 6, in la Casa Azul in Coyoacán, Mexico, daughter of a German, Wilheim Kahlo, and Mathilde Calderón.

1910
Beginning of the Mexican revolution which overthrows Porfirio Diaz. Kahlo adopted this year as that of her birthday, in line with a new Mexico. Considered an accessory by her father who considered her a substitute for a son, she became his assistant in his photograph studio.

1916
Polio leaves her right leg handicapped.

1921
The Mexican government orders a large mural from Diego Rivera – returned to the country after fourteen years spent in Europe – to be sent to the National Preparatory School.

1923
Frida Kahlo enters the National Preparatory School, reserved for the Mexican elite. She was one of thirty-five girls in an enrollment of two thousand pupils. She secretly admired Diego Rivera's painting *La Création*.

1925
Frida Kahlo suffers a very serious accident. The bus carrying her is involved in a collision with a tramway. She suffers numerous fractures and internal lesions. She must remain confined to her bed, and begins to paint. Through painting, she expresses the struggle of her existence.

1928
Frida becomes a member of the Mexican Communist Party. She meets Diego Rivera.

1929
Frida Kahlo and Diego Rivera marry August 21.

1932
Frida Kahlo has a miscarriage in Detroit where Diego Rivera is making a fresco for the Institute of Art before working at the Rockfeller Center in New York. In September, her mother dies.

1934
The couple returns to Mexico. Diego begins his relationship with Cristina, Frida's sister. Tired of her husband's attitude, Frida Kahlo moves out and takes Isamu Nogushi as a lover.

1937
Trotski and his wife take refuge in Mexico and are welcomed at the Casa Azul. The Russian revolutionary has an affair with Frida Kahlo.

1938
André Breton comes to Mexico. The three couples have long discussions about politics and culture. Frida Kahlo has her first exhibition at the Julien Levy Gallery in New York: she is able to begin to sell her paintings. She enters into an affair with the photographer Nickolas Muray.

1939
The surrealists dedicate an exposition to her. Diego and Frida divorce in November.

1940
Frida undergoes medical treatment in San Francisco with the help of Dr Eloesser. In August, Diego and Frida remarry.

1941
Her father dies. The couple move into Casa Azul.

1943
Frida becomes a professeur at the "Esmeralda" art school. She soon teaches at her home due to health problems.

1946
She receives the national painting prize for her *Moses*.

1950
Her health worsens. She is subjected to nine operations for the spine.

1953
For the first time in Mexico, an exhibition is dedicated to her courtesy of Cola Alvarez Bravo.

1954
She participates for the last time in a demonstration for peace in Guatemala. Frida Kahlo dies July 13.

1959
After the death of Diego Rivera in 1957, and conforming to his wishes, the Frida Kahlo Museum opens in Casa Azul.

Bibliography

Alcantara and Egnolff,
Frida Kahlo and Diego Rivera, Prestel Press, NY, 1999, p. 30

Diego Rivera and Frida Kahlo Museums Trust,
Frida Kahlo, Bulfinch Press/Little, Brown and Company, New York, 2001

Fibromyalgia in Frida Kahlo's Life and Art,
Arthritis Rheum. 2000 Mar; 43 (3): 708-709

Hardin, Terri,
Frida Kahlo A Modern Master, Smithmark Publishers, New York, 1997, p. 66

Kahlo, Frida,
Letters of Frida Kahlo, compiled by Martha Zamora, San Francisco, Chronicle Books, 1995

Kahlo, Frida,
The Diary of Frida Kahlo, Harry N. Abrams, Inc., New York, 1995

Lindauer, Margaret A.,
Devouring Frida, University Press of New England, 1999

Martinez-Lavin, Manuel MD; Amigo, Mary-Carmen MD; Coindreau, Javier MD; Canoso, Juan MD

Maso, Carole,
Beauty is Convulsive – The Passion of Frida Kahlo, Counterpoint, New York, 2002

Rivera, Diego with March, Gladys,
My Art, My Life: An Autobiography, Citadel, New York, 1960

Rivera, Diego,
Frida Kahlo and Mexican Art, Buletin del Seminario de Cultura Mexicana, Vol. 1, No. 2 October, 1943

Rummel, Jack,
Frida Kahlo – A Spiritual Biography, The Crossroad Publishing Company, New York, 2000

Tibol, Raquel,
Frida Kahlo An Open Life, Translated by Elinor Randall, University of New Mexico Press, 1993

Weston, Edward,
Daybooks of Edward Weston, "California," vol. 2., Horizon Press, New York, 1961, pp. 198-199

Zamora, Martha,
The Brush of Anguish, Chronicle Books, San Francisco, 1990

Zamora, Martha,
The Letters of Frida Kahlo, Chronicle Books, San Francisco, 1995

List of Plates

- *One of the last pages of Frida's diary.*
- *Page from Frida's diary demonstrating her continued belief in Communism.*
- *Page from her diary (1946-54) showing the artist's personal conflict in Moon, Sun, I?*
- *Page from the diary.*
- *The last picture in her diary.*

1906
- Diego Rivera, *Self-Portrait.*

1915
- Diego Rivera, *Ultima hora (The last hour).*

1916
- *"Pinté de 1916".*

1926
- *Self-Portrait with Velvet Dress.*

1927
- *Pancho Villa and Adelita.*
- *Portrait of Alicia Galant.*
- *Portrait of Miguel N. Lira.*

1928
- *Portrait of Alejandro Gómez Arias.*
- *Portrait of My Sister Cristina.*

1929
- *Girl in Diaper.*
- *Portrait of a Lady in White.*
- *Portrait of Virginia.*
- *Self-Portrait "Time Flies".*
- *The Bus.*

1930
- Diego Rivera, *Nude of Frida Kahlo.*
- *Self-Portrait.*

1931
- Diego Rivera, *Paisaje con cactus (Landscape with cactus).*
- Diego Rivera, *The Making of a Fresco, Showing the Building of a City.*
- *Frida and Diego Rivera* or *Frida Kahlo and Diego Rivera.*
- *Portrait of Dr. Leo Eloesser.*
- *Portrait of Eva Frederick.*
- *Portrait of Luther Burbank.*
- *Window Display in a Street in Detroit.*

1932
- *Frida and the Cesarean Section.*
- *Henry Ford Hospital* or *The Flying Bed.*
- *My Birth.*
- *Self-Portrait (standing) along the Border between Mexico and the United States.*

1933
- *My Dress Hangs There* or *New York.*
- *Self-Portrait with Necklace.*

1935
- *A Few Small Nips.*

1936
- *My Grandparents, My Parents and I.*

1937
- *Diego Rivera, Modesta (Modest).*
- *Fulang Chang and I.*
- *Memory* or *The Heart.*
- *My Nanny and I.*
- *Portrait of Diego Rivera.*
- *Self-Portrait dedicated to Leon Trotsky* or *Between the Curtains.*
- *Self-Portrait Sitting on the Bed* or *My Doll and I.*
- *The Deceased Dimas Rosas at the Age of Three.*

1938
- *Fruits of the Earth.*
- *Girl with Death-Mask.*
- *Self-Portrait "The Frame".*
- *Self-Portrait with Monkey.*
- *Still Life with Pitahayas.*
- *The Suicide of Dorothy Hale.*
- *Tunas (Still Life with Prickly Pear Fruit).*
- *What the Water Gave Me.*

1939
- *Self-Portrait with Iztcuintli Dog.*
- *The Two Fridas.*
- *Two Nudes in the Wood or The Earth or My Nanny and I.*

1940
- *Self-Portrait dedicated to Dr. Eloesser.*
- *Self-Portrait dedicated to Sigmand Firestone.*
- *Self-Portrait with Cropped Hair.*
- *Self-Portrait with Monkey.*
- *Self-Portrait with Thorny Necklace.*
- *The Dream or The Bed.*

1941
- *Autorretrato con vestido rojo y dorado (Self-Portrait with Red and Gold Dress).*
- *Basket of Flowers.*
- *Me and My Parrots.*
- *Self-Portrait with Braid.*

1942
- *Portrait of Lucha Maria, a Girl from Tehuacán, (Sun and Moon).*
- *Self-Portrait with "Bonito".*
- *Self-Portrait with Monkey and Parrot.*
- *Still Life.*

1943
- *Diego Rivera, El curandero (The Healer).*
- *Diego Rivera, Girasoles (Sunflowers).*
- *Diego Rivera, Retrato de la Señora Natasha Gelman (Portrait of Mrs Natasha Gelman)*
- *Diego Rivera, Vendedora de alcatraces (Calla Lily Vendor).*
- *Ex voto.*
- *Retrato de la Señora Natasha Gelman (Portrait of Mrs Natasha Gelman).*
- *Roots* or *The Pedregal.*
- *Self-Portrait as a Tehuana* or *Diego on My Mind.*
- *Self-Portrait with Monkey.*
- *The Bride Frightened at Seeing Life Opened.*
- *Thinking about Death.*

1944
- *Portrait of Doña Rosita Morillo.*
- *The Broken Column.*

1945
- *Moses* or *Nucleus of Creation.*
- *Self-Portrait with Monkey.*
- *The Chick.*
- *The Mask.*
- *Without Hope.*

1946
- *Self-Portrait (Dedicated to Marte R.Gómez).*
- *The Wounded Deer (The Little Deer).*
- *Tree of Hope, Keep Strong.*
- *Untitled* (Drawing with Cataclysmic Theme).
- *Untitled* (Drawing with Subject inspired by Eastern Philosophy).

1947
- *Self-Portrait with Hair down.*
- *Sun and Life.*

1948
- *Self-Portrait.*

1949
- *Diego and I.*
- Diego Rivera, *Self-Portrait.*
- *The Love Embrace of the Universe, The Earth (Mexico), I, Diego, and Señor Xólotl.*

1951
- *Coconut Tears (Crying Coconut).*
- *Coconuts* (Glances).
- *Portrait of My Father.*
- *Self-Portrait with the Portrait of Dr. Farill.*
- *Still Life with Parrot and Flag.*
- *Still Life: Viva la Vida (Long live Life).*
- *The Circle.*

1952
- *Congress of People For Peace.*
- *Moving Still Life.*
- *Still Life dedicated to Samuel Fastlicht* "painted with all my love".

1953
- Diary page.
- *Fruits of Life.*
- *Self-Portrait with the Image of Diego on My Breast and Maria on My Brow.*

1954
- Diego Rivera, *Artist's Studio.*
- *Marxism Will Give Health to the Sick.*
- *Self-Portrait with Stalin* or *Frida and Stalin.*

1956
- Diego Rivera, *1st May Parade in Moscow.*

Index